Computer Science

Computer Science

**Edited by
Tom Halt**

www.willfordpress.com

Published by Willford Press,
118-35 Queens Blvd., Suite 400,
Forest Hills, NY 11375, USA

ISBN: 978-1-68285-412-9

Cataloging-in-Publication Data

Computer science / edited by Tom Halt.
    p. cm.
Includes bibliographical references and index.
ISBN 978-1-68285-412-9
1. Computer science. I. Halt, Tom.
QA76 .C66 2018
004--dc23

For information on all Willford Press publications
visit our website at www.willfordpress.com

Contents

Preface

This book was inspired by the evolution of our times; to answer the curiosity of inquisitive minds. Many developments have occurred across the globe in the recent past which has transformed the progress in the field.

Computer science studies the theory and engineering of computers as well as computation processes. It is a widely applied field that has many branches such as computer programming, complex systems, artificial intelligence, robotics, etc. Computer graphics, user interaction, computer security, and database management are some of the other concerns of this field. This book is a valuable compilation of topics, ranging from the basic to the most complex advancements in the field of computer science. Coherent flow of topics, student-friendly language and extensive use of examples make this book an invaluable source of knowledge.

This book was developed from a mere concept to drafts to chapters and finally compiled together as a complete text to benefit the readers across all nations. To ensure the quality of the content we instilled two significant steps in our procedure. The first was to appoint an editorial team that would verify the data and statistics provided in the book and also select the most appropriate and valuable contributions from the plentiful contributions we received from authors worldwide. The next step was to appoint an expert of the topic as the Editor-in-Chief, who would head the project and finally make the necessary amendments and modifications to make the text reader-friendly. I was then commissioned to examine all the material to present the topics in the most comprehensible and productive format.

I would like to take this opportunity to thank all the contributing authors who were supportive enough to contribute their time and knowledge to this project. I also wish to convey my regards to my family who have been extremely supportive during the entire project.

Editor

A comparative analysis on artificial neural network-based two-stage clustering

Cheng-Ching Chang[1] and Ssu-Han Chen[2]*

*Corresponding author: Ssu-Han Chen,Department of Industrial Engineering and Management, Ming Chi University of Technology, New Taipei City, Taiwan

E-mail: ssuhanchen@mail.mcut.edu.tw

Reviewing editor: Duc Pham, University of Birmingham, UK

Abstract: The artificial neural network (ANN), which is capable of noise removal and data complexity reduction, has been regarded as one of outstanding intermediaries in the two-stage clustering procedures. Various ANN-based two-stage clustering procedures have been individually proposed; however, the performance among those methods has not been examined yet. In this study, a preliminary comparative analysis is conducted in four benchmark data-sets and a real-world market data-set, which are used to simulate various conditions for evaluation purposes. The experiment results suggest that high-accuracy self-organizing feature map can potentially improve the effectiveness of decision-making.

Subjects: Artificial Intelligence; Neural Networks; Computer Engineering

Keywords: two-stage clustering; k-means algorithm; self-organizing feature map; adaptive resonance theory

1. Introduction

Life is full of data. Every day, people process massive information that may be stored or represented as data for further analysis and management. One of the essential tools in coping with these data is to assign them into two or more unknown groups, rendering certain similar properties to members in the same group. A general inquiry faced by researchers in conducting many applications is how to discover meaningful structures in observed input vectors. That is, how to develop valid taxonomies (Xu & Wunsch, 2005). Cluster analysis encompasses a variety of unsupervised algorithms. Take the artificial neural network (ANN) for example, it is capable of grouping them into easily interpreted distinct clusters if the data-set was well separated (i.e. input vectors with topologically mutually exclusive). Ideal condition, however, is not always the case. Usually, the clustering results of the ANN do not exhibit distinct clusters, but ill-defined boundaries, resulting in undesirable mumbling or ambiguity about the cluster structures and membership. The follow-up in-deep analysis may primarily depend on analyzers' intuition or subjective opinion (Abidi & Ong, 2000). An acceptable way to solve the mentioned

ABOUT THE AUTHOR

Ssu-Han Chen is an assistant professor in the Department of Industrial Engineering and Management in Ming Chi University of Technology, New Taipei City, Taiwan. He received his PhD degree in Industrial Engineering and Management from National Chiao Tung University (NCTU), Taiwan, in 2010. His current research interests include digital image processing, machine vision, pattern recognition, patentometrics, and social network analysis.

PUBLIC INTEREST STATEMENT

In this study, we compare the two-stage clustering procedures which are based on the artificial neural network (ANN). Well-know unsupervised ANN such as self-organizing feature map (SOFM), adaptive resonance theory 2 (ART2), and fuzzy adaptive resonance theory (Fuzzy ART) are evaluated based on four benchmark data-sets and a real-world marketing data-set. The results show that SOFM is relatively better than the other methods.

problems is to draw upon a synergy between the ANN and a partition-based technique such as k-means algorithm. In the first stage, to yield prototypes without any information about clustering numbers, the unsupervised neural model was used to map the input vector. However, it is a universal truth that the number of generated prototypes of ANN is always too huge for quantitative or qualitative interpretation. In the second stage, to facilitate cluster identification and interpretation, further grouping of similar prototypes together can delimit cluster numbers and prototype boundaries.

The two-stage clustering procedure has been found excelling in setting boundaries, compared to direct clustering, in many previous studies. Among them, the hybrid of self-organizing feature map (SOFM) and k-means, or SOFM + k-means, is the most well-known procedures. Vesanto and Alhoniemi (2000) and Abidi and Ong (2000) are the forerunners of clustering prototypes obtained by pre-treating input vectors with SOFM. Hereafter, numerous studies applied similar idea on distinct applications. Sugiyama and Kotani (2002) analyzed and categorized the gene expression data. Canetta, Cheikhrouhou, and Glardon (2005) concerned problems on group technology and purchased components in industrial company. Godin, Huguet, and Gaertner (2005) discriminated acoustic emission signals to monitor the chronology of the damaging process. Chaimeun and Srivihok (2005) clustered handicraft customers to understand the customer background and behaviors for the purposes of enhancing the marketing strategy and planning. Khedairia and Khadir (2008) identified the meteorological day types of the Annaba region. Wu, Xia, Chen, and Cui (2011) researched on classifying moving objects into pedestrians, bicycles, and vehicles in traffic video. Chen, Pan, and Jiang (2013) applied rolling SOFM + k-means clustering for fault diagnosis. Hayfron-Acquah and Gyimah (2014) matched fingercodes using SOFM and then classified fingerprints with the help of k-means. In addition, adaptive resonance theory (ART) neural network was recently excavated to be another intermediate step for clustering analysis. Ding, Shi, Shi, and Jiang (2008) combined ART2 and k-means to detect anomaly (named ART2 + k-means). Park, Suresh, and Jeong (2008) integrated fuzzy ART with k-means to develop a sequence-based clustering for Web usage mining (named Fuzzy ART + k-means). Hung, Chen, Yang, and Deng (2013) used ART2 + k-means to mine the elder self-care cluster patterns. The prior arts agreed with the fact that the two-stage clustering procedure considerably removes potential outliers and noise, as well as reduces data complexity. Since a prototype is the local average of a set of nearby input vectors, the clustering is less sensitive to outliers and noise. These advantages implicitly prompt the two-stage clustering procedures to yield a satisfied quality and efficiency of clustering assignment.

The above two-stage clustering procedures are proposed separately, and performance comparison among them has not yet been examined. Consequently, we conducted a comparative study on these methods. These comparisons are primarily based on the analysis of four benchmark data-sets: iris, wine, image segmentation, and handwritten digit. Comparing clustering results of using ANN as an intermediate with those obtained from direct method, we can, therefore, demonstrate how the use of ANN improves clustering quality. In order to further evaluate these two-stage clustering procedures, the comparison is extended to a real-world market segmental application.

The rest of this paper is organized as follows. In Section 2, related methodologies are surveyed. In Section 3, the clustering procedures are described and the experimental results are presented. The concluding remarks are discussed in Section 4.

2. Literature review
In view of the ability to compress information, the ANN is an ideal tool for analyzing large data-sets (Juntunen, Liukkonen, Lehtola, & Hiltunen, 2014). In this section, the unsupervised ANN techniques under consideration are sketched. For simplification, we describe the various ANN methods using pseudo-algorithms. Please refer to the original works if interested.

2.1. Introduction of SOFM network
The SOFM network, proposed by Kohonen (1990), converts a higher dimensional input space into a lower dimensional map space and preserves the topological properties of the input vectors by means of a neighborhood concept. SOFM network consists of neurons that associated with weight vectors

in input space and a position in the map space. The arrangement of neurons, so called as SOFM lattice, is presented in a triangular, rectangular, or hexagonal grid. The steps of the SOFM algorithm can be summarized as follows:

Step 1: Initialization. Initialize learning rate (α) and synaptic weights ($\mathbf{w}$).

Step 2: Sampling. Sample a training input vector ($\mathbf{x}$) from input space.

Step 3: Matching. Calculate $y = \|\mathbf{x} - \mathbf{w}\|$ and find the best matching unit (BMU) with $\mathbf{w}_j$ closest to $\mathbf{x}$.

Step 4: Updating. Apply the weight update equation

$$\Delta\mathbf{w}_i = h_J \times (\mathbf{x} - w_i) \tag{1}$$

where $h_{ic} = \alpha \times \exp(\|r_i - r_c\|^2/2 \times \sigma^2)$ is a neighborhood function around the BMU. The weight vectors of the BMU and it neighborhood in the SOFM lattice are updated together toward this input vector.

Step 5: Iteration. Keep returning to Step 2 until the map stops to change.

2.2. Introduction of ART2 network

The ART2 network, proposed by Carpenter and Grossberg (1987), solves the stability and plasticity dilemma in clustering problem. It swiftly updates its model to the new input vector without specifying the number of clusters. The main advantages of ART2 are: learning and adapting to a non-stable environment rapidly, stability and plasticity, unsupervised learning of preferences behavior, as well as deciding the number of groups automatically. The steps of the ART2 algorithm can be summarized as follows:

Step 1: Initialization. Initialize the nameless parameters (a, b, c, d, and e), learning rate (α), vigilance value (ρ), synaptic weights of bottom-to-top ($\mathbf{b}_j$) and top-to-bottom ($\mathbf{t}_j$), and neurons at F1 layer ($\mathbf{w}, \mathbf{s}, \mathbf{u}, \mathbf{v}, \mathbf{p}, \mathbf{q}$).

Step 2: Activation of short-term memory (STM) in F1 layer. Randomly chosen input vector activates six neurons in F1 layer by calculating the following equations and proceeds along the bottom-to-top weight vector ($\mathbf{b}_{ij}$) to F2 layer.

$$\mathbf{w} = \mathbf{x} + a \times \mathbf{u} \tag{2}$$

$$\mathbf{s} = \mathbf{w} / (e + \|\mathbf{w}\|) \tag{3}$$

$$\mathbf{u} = \mathbf{v} / (e + \|\mathbf{v}\|) \tag{4}$$

$$\mathbf{v} = f(\mathbf{s}) + b \times f(q) \tag{5}$$

$$\mathbf{p} = \mathbf{u} + d \times t_J \tag{6}$$

$$\mathbf{q} = \mathbf{p} / (e + \|\mathbf{p}\|) \tag{7}$$

where $f(x) = x$ if $x \geq 0$, otherwise $f(x) = 0$.

Step 3: Activation in F2 layer. The $\mathbf{p}$ is sent to F2 layer for calculating $\mathbf{y} = \Sigma(\mathbf{p} \times \mathbf{b}_j)$ and finds the maximum activation unit J in the F2 layer.

Step 4: Pattern Matching. Update $\mathbf{p}$ and $\mathbf{u}$ and then calculate match value ($\mathbf{r}$)

$$\mathbf{r} = (\mathbf{u} + c \times \mathbf{p}) / (e + \|\mathbf{u}\| + \|c \times \mathbf{p}\|) \tag{8}$$

Step 5: Reset or resonant. If $\|r\| + e < \rho$, then $\mathbf{y}_J = -1$ and inhibit the unit J (go back to Step 3). Otherwise, it represents that STM has gone into resonant state, such that long-term memory (LTM) start to learn. If all of the neurons in F2 layer are inhibited, a brand-new neuron is generated and is initialized in terms of the novelty.

Step 6: Learning process of LTM. The slow-learning rule updates the synaptic weights of unit J is:

$$\mathbf{b}_J = \alpha \times d \times \mathbf{u} + [1 + \alpha \times d \times (1-d)] \times \mathbf{b}_J \tag{9}$$

$$\mathbf{t}_J = \alpha \times d \times \mathbf{u} + [1 + \alpha \times d \times (1-d)] \times \mathbf{t}_J \tag{10}$$

Step 7: Iteration. Keep returning to Step 2 until the number of epochs is reached.

2.3. Introduction of fuzzy ART network

The fuzzy ART network, proposed by Carpenter, Grossberg, and Rosen (1991), possesses similar advantages of ART2. It benefits the incorporation of fuzzy set theory and ART principle, thus enhancing generalizability. Another distinct characteristic of fuzzy ART is the complement coding, a mean of normalization process that rescales and doubles the dimension of input vector, which helps avoid the problem of category proliferation but still preserves most information of input vectors. The steps of the Fuzzy ART algorithm can be summarized as follows:

Step 1: Initialization. Set parameters of learning rate (α), constant (β) and vigilance value (ρ) and initialize synaptic weights (**w**).

Step 2: Complement coding. Input vector (**x**) is augmented by complement coding ($\bar{x}$) in F1 layer.

Step 3: Activation in F2 layer. Calculate the net to each template: $\mathbf{y}_j = \|\bar{\mathbf{x}} \wedge \mathbf{w}\| / (\beta + \|\mathbf{w}\|)$, where $\wedge$ is the fuzzy min operator. The largest net of unit J is the winner.

Step 4: Pattern Matching. Calculate match value (**r**)

$$\mathbf{r} = \|\bar{\mathbf{x}} \wedge \mathbf{w}_J\| / \|\bar{\mathbf{x}}\| \tag{11}$$

Step 5: Reset or resonant. If $\|r\| < \rho$, then $\mathbf{y}_j = -1$ and inhibit the unit J (go back to Step 3). Otherwise, network starts to learn. If all neurons are inhibited, a new neuron is generated.

Step 6: Learning process of weight. The learning rule updates the synaptic weights of unit J is:

$$\mathbf{w}_J = (1-\alpha) \times \mathbf{w}_J + \alpha \times (\bar{\mathbf{x}} \wedge \mathbf{w}_J) \tag{12}$$

Step 7: Iteration. Keep returning to Step 2 until the number of epochs is reached.

3. Experiments and results

The flowchart of implemented work is shown in Figure 1. Benchmark and real-world data-sets are used for evaluating both the direct clustering method and the ANN-based two-stage clustering procedures. The clustering results are then evaluated by several cluster validations if there is no class label information in advance; otherwise, not only validations, but also accuracy rate comparisons will be conducted. Using a self-programming toolkit, the analysis was conducted under the "MATLAB R2007a" environment.

3.1. Clustering analysis

3.1.1. Direct clustering method

Before applying the routine of k-means algorithm on a given data-set, some tricks should be noted. First, the unit and range of the variables may discrepant. It is meaningless if the segment results are

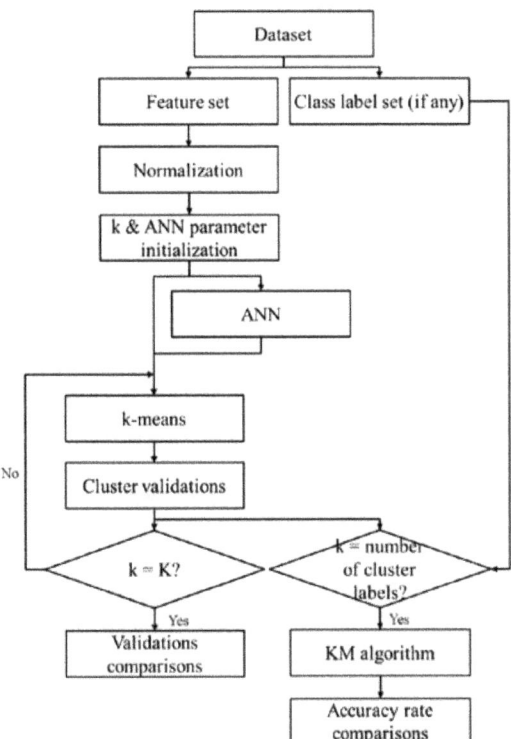

Figure 1. Flow chart of the implemented work.

obviously dominated by certain variables. Since normalization equalizes the scale for computing distance, the data prepared for feeding for k-means algorithm must be normalized. A normalization equation suggested by Weiss and Indurkhya (1998) is given as follows:

$$\mathbf{z} = (0.9 - 0.1) \times (\mathbf{x} - \min) / (\max - \min) \tag{13}$$

Second, the clustering results of k-means algorithm depend on what initial centers were selected. Accordingly, we duplicated each experiment 100 times, each with a new set of initialization, and selected the best results to reduce the effect of local minimum in initialization.

3.1.2. ANN-based two-stage clustering procedures

First of all, the input vectors are preprocessed by means of Equation 13. The parameters and synaptic weights of each network are basically initialized in terms of the recommendation setting of original authors (Carpenter & Grossberg, 1987; Carpenter et al., 1991; Kohonen, 1990), except for the number of topological nodes of SOFM and the vigilance value of ART2 or fuzzy ART. In this study, the number of topological nodes is set to $M = 5 \times N^{1/2}$, where N is the number of input vectors (Vesanto & Alhoniemi, 2000) and the vigilance value is assigned a high value, e.g. $\rho = 0.99$. In addition, we re-feed the random arranged input vectors into the learned network for 100 times. Such a design

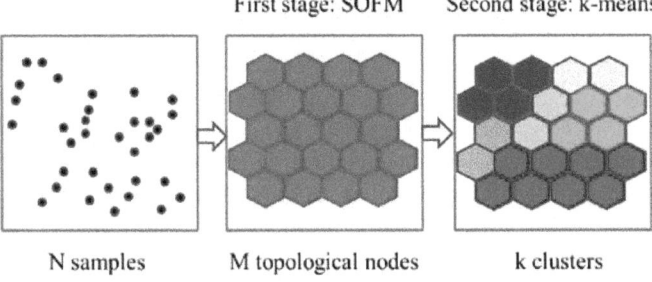

Figure 2. Concept of SOFM + k-means algorithm.

First stage: ART   Second stage: k-means

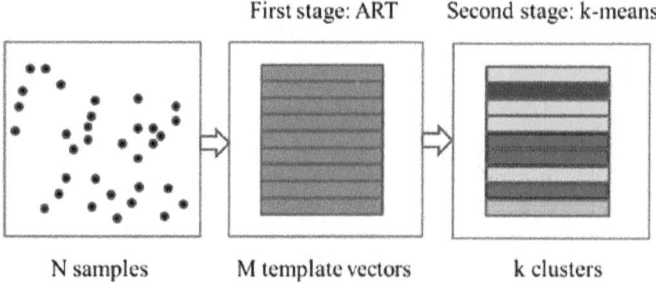

N samples   M template vectors   k clusters

Figure 3. Concept of ART + k-means algorithm.

may enable neural networks to learn much sufficiently. After the learning process of each neural network, each input vector is allocated to a most similar synaptic weight/template. For each fired synaptic weight/template, the average of its input vectors is calculated to generate a set of proto-type vectors. Finally, the prototype vectors are conveyed into k-means algorithm for second-stage clustering. Figures 2 and 3 are the flow charts of the two-stage clustering procedures.

3.1.3. Clustering validation

Several clustering validation indexes are used to determine well-defined partitions, which exhibit both strong external isolation and tight internal cohesion. Since no consistent conclusions were drawn to a close in literatures, with respect to clustering validation indexes, Davies–Bouldin Index (DBI) (Davies & Bouldin, 1979), Calinski–Harabasz Index (CHI) (Calinski & Harabasz, 1974), Ray–Turi Index (RTI) (Ray & Turi, 1999) and Dunn Index (DI) (Dunn, 1974), are all included. These validation indexes are adopted since are practically proved to be excellent indexes for evaluating clustering results (Bezdek & Pal, 1998; Bandyopadhyay & Maulik, 2001; Chen & Dai, 2004; Charrad, Lechevallier, Ahmed, & Saporta, 2010; Vesanto & Alhoniemi, 2000). Among those indexes, DBI is a function of the ratio of sum of within-cluster scatter to between-cluster separation (Davies & Bouldin, 1979). The ideal DBI presents minimal ratio of within-cluster scatter and between-cluster separation; therefore, minimizing within-cluster scatter and maximizing between-cluster separation are desired. CHI is a function of the ratio of sum of squares among the clusters to sum of squares within the clusters. A better clustering result is indicated by a higher CH value. RTI is a function of the ratio of the intra-cluster distance to minimal of inter-cluster distance. It took only the minimum of inter-cluster distance because they need the smallest of this distance to be maximized, and the other larger ones will be bigger than this value automatically (Ray & Turi, 1999). The clustering result which gives a minimum RTI will tell us what the ideal number of clusters is since minimizing inter-cluster distance and maximizing inter-cluster one are presented. DI is a function which takes the minimal ratio of inter-cluster distance to maximal intra-cluster distance. The main goal of DI is to maximize inter-cluster distances and minimize intra-cluster distances. Therefore, the number of clusters that maximizes DI is taken as the ideal clustering result.

3.2. Comparison analysis

3.2.1. Comparison bases on benchmark data-sets

The simulating experiments use four benchmark data-sets obtained from distinct domains and sources. First, the iris data-set contains three classes and each class consists of 50 instances, where each class refers to a type of iris plant and each instance is represented by four features (Fisher, 1936). Second, the wine data-set describes three wines derived from different cultivars in terms of 13 chemical constituents (Forina, Lanteri, Armanino, & Lauter, 1991). Third, the image segmentation data-set records seven kinds of outdoor images, which are quantized by 19 continuous geometric attributes. Only 210 samples of train set are adopted from the UCI machine-learning repository (http://archive.ics.uci.edu/ml/datasets.html). Finally, the optical recognition of handwritten digits' data-set includes digits of 0–9 that are scanned as 32×32 bitmaps and then characterized by num-ber of pixels of 4×4 non-overlapping blocks. Only 1797 samples of test set are adopted from the UCI machine-learning repository. Table 1 summarizes the main characteristics of these data-sets. The

Table 1. Summary of the benchmark datasets

Information	Datasets			
	Iris	Wine	Image segmentation	Handwritten digits
Number of instances	150	178	210	1797
Number of dimensions	4	13	19	64
Number of classes	3	3	7	10

sizes of these data-sets range from hundreds to thousands, and the dimensions, from 4 to 64. In this experiment, the clustering result is evaluated by comparing the cluster label (CL_i) of each input vector with its true label (L_i) provided by the data-set. The accuracy is defined as follows:

$$accuracy = \Sigma \delta \left(L_i, \text{map} \left(CL_i\right)\right)/n \qquad (14)$$

where n is number of input vector. The response of the delta function, $\delta(x, y)$, equals to one, if $x = y$; equals to zero, otherwise. The best mapping function, map(x), matches true label and obtained cluster label in which the best mapping can be found automatically by Kuhn–Munkres algorithm.

During clustering procedure, the number of clusters of k-means algorithm is equal to the number of classes of each data-set as shown in the fourth row of Table 1. It should be noted that all of these data-sets are labeled, whereas the labels are omitted during clustering and only used for evaluation. As we can observe in Figure 4, the clustering accuracy of data-sets, iris and wine, is quite satisfied. The majority of these two data-sets reaches 90%. While the other two data-sets only express relatively low accuracy, around 80%. Among them, the accuracies of k-means algorithm are worst; follow by ART2 + k-means. The accuracies of SOFM + k-means and fuzzy ART + k-means are nearly equal in the first two data-sets, whereas the accuracies of SOFM + k-means surpass in the last two data-sets.

Another part of this sub-section is to compare the various methods using four benchmark databases, without imposing the number of clusters in advance. The purpose is to prove the fact that the number of clusters is one the most difficult hurdles in clustering analysis. In this experiment, the setting of clustering number of each clustering algorithm segments benchmark data-sets which are initialized from two, and are then added regularly until an empty cluster signal responds. At the same time, piecewise DBI, CHI, IIVI, and DI against number of clusters are recorded. Generally, well-separated clusters are expected to decrease or increase monotonically as increases until the ideal number of clusters is achieved (Bezdek & Pal, 1998). However, finding the minimum or maximum values is less reliable than finding a knee or a sharp change of slope in the plot. In this study, we determine the number of clusters by finding a knee in DBI and CHI, and by finding a sharp change of

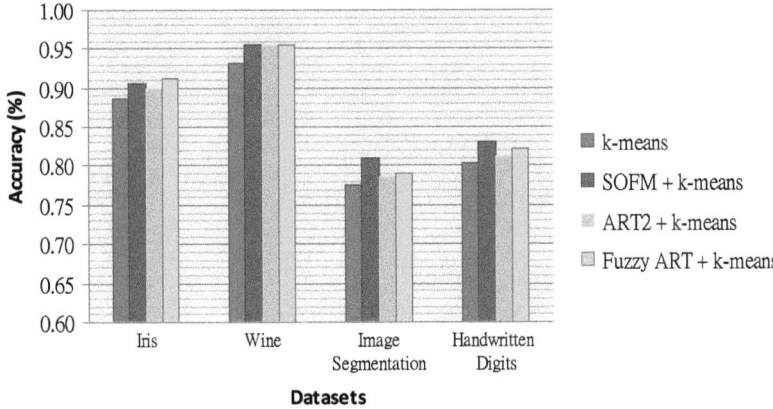

Figure 4. Clustering accuracy of benchmarks in different methods.

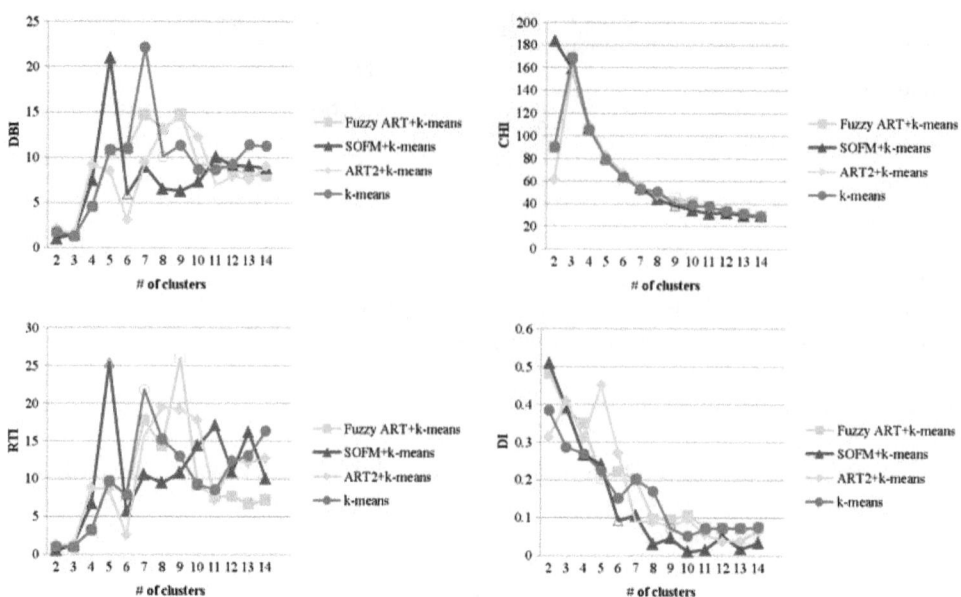

Figure 5. Cluster validations against number of clusters in different methods for wine data-set.

slope in RTI and DI. Take the data-set of wine as an example, the corresponding plots of different cluster validations against number of clusters, ranging from 2 to 14, are given in Figure 5(a–d). Following the above rule of thumb, the recommended number of clusters is marked by hollow symbol. The results are shown in Table 2 where the correct number is marked in bold italics. According to the obtained results, we proved the fact that specifying correct number of clusters is difficult in clustering analysis. None of indexes under different methods finds out the ideal number of clusters, three, for iris and wine data-sets. As for image segmentation and handwritten digits data-sets, parts of indexes under different methods get the work done properly, especially the SOFM + k-means procedure.

Table 2. Number of clusters specified by different indexes and methods

Methods		Datasets			
	Indexes	Iris	Wine	Image segmentation	Handwritten digits
k-means	DBI	6	8	4	*10*
	CHI	5	9	6	9
	RTI	5	7	*7*	*10*
	DI	7	9	5	11
SOFM + k-means	DBI	6	6	*7*	*10*
	CHI	5	9	*7*	*10*
	RTI	5	5	8	*10*
	DI	7	6	*7*	*10*
ART2 + k-means	DBI	7	11	*7*	*10*
	CHI	5	9	*7*	*10*
	RTI	7	7	8	13
	DI	4	7	6	13
Fuzzy ART + k-means	DBI	6	10	6	*10*
	CHI	5	9	*7*	*10*
	RTI	5	9	6	*10*
	DI	6	5	*7*	*10*

3.2.2. Comparison bases on a real-world marketing data-set

Recency, frequency, and monetary (RFM) analysis, introduced by Hughes (1994), is a marketing technique used to quantitate the activity of customers by examining customers' recent purchased, purchasing frequency, and each transaction amount. With customers' purchasing behavior data, RFM variables can be derived from historical transaction records. After mapping the each customer's records into one of the several clusters, each cluster, then, represents a market segment, to which distinct marketing strategy shall apply, helping companies offer each consumer the right promotions and save either propaganda time or miscellaneous costs.

Our experimental data are adopted from a online tea shop in Taiwan, whose members are about 150,000, and 90% of members are over aged 40. Whenever a member logs in the web, the system records the date, time, and goods selected by customers. The online shop has 4,867 members as effective customers. Each of them has their own three-dimensional RFM values. The unit and range of RFM variables are discrepant; therefore, certain specified variables may dominate clustering results. In order to eliminate scale effects, the data prepared as input of cluster algorithms are normalized by Equation 13. The clustering procedure is similar to what we had done in Section 3.2.1 except the clustering performance evaluation method. In this database, there are no predefined classes, and we do not have a clue about how many clusters exist in the data-set. Accordingly, clustering validation indexes are employed to determine well-defined partitions. DBI, CHI, RTI, and DI are used for evaluation purpose, as in Section 3.2.1.

In this experiment, k-means algorithm directly segmented the customer with setting of number of clusters from three to ten, which yielded the corresponding values of validation indexes. The upper limit of cluster number was set mainly because routine always responds to empty cluster once it was larger than 10. On the other hand, during the first stage of two-stage clustering algorithms, 12 of 361 SOFM synaptic weights, five of 210 ART2 templates, and one of 950 fuzzy ART templates were eliminated because there are no customers involved. Then k-means algorithm was applied on the prototypes of individual network with similar setting of the direct method which yielded the corresponding DBI, CHI, RTI, and DI. The plots of different cluster validations against number of clusters for marketing data-set are given in Figure 6(a–d). We observed that the broken line of different validations of k-means algorithm is uniformly higher or lower than those of two-stage clustering procedures, implying that the two-stage clustering procedures generate better

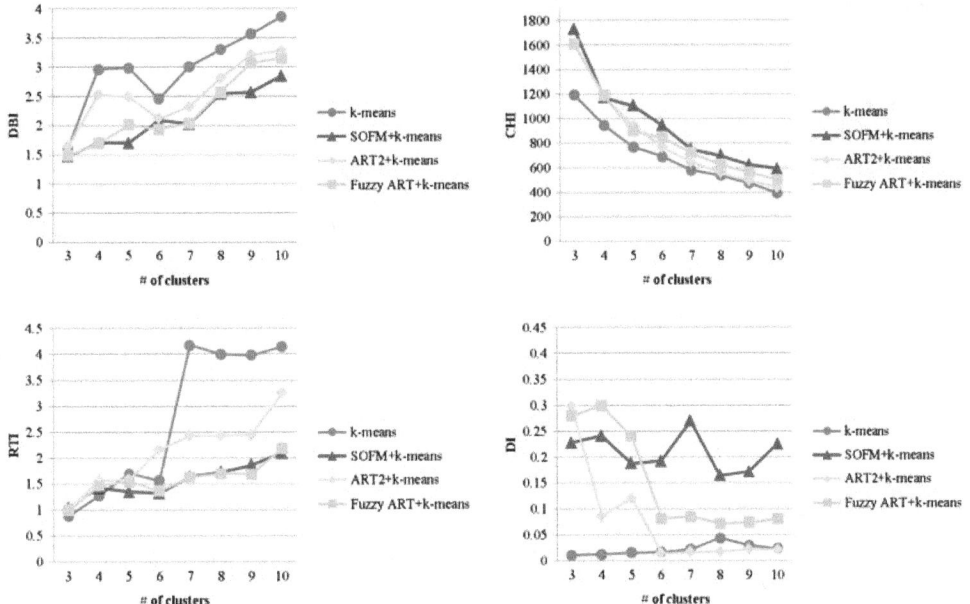

Figure 6. Cluster validations against number of clusters in different methods for marketing data-set.

Table 3. Clustering results of SOFM + k-means						
Index	Customer counts	Recency	Frequency	Monetary	RFM status	Strategic position
Cluster 1	1,723	2.80	2.74	140.07	R↓F↓M↓	New
Cluster 2	55	0.36	20.93	2,940.07	R↓F↑M↑	Loyal
Cluster 3	685	1.42	8.53	220.53	R↓F↑M↑	Loyal
Cluster 4	961	11.17	2.29	110.88	R↑F↓M↓	Vulnerable
Cluster 5	152	8.84	8.36	170.50	R↑F↑M↓	Potential
Cluster 6	994	20.94	1.86	120.35	R↑F↓M↓	Vulnerable
Cluster 7	297	0.67	18.61	330.82	R↓F↑M↑	Loyal
Total average		8.00	4.64	180.96		

defined clustering results than that of the direct method. Among the two-stage clustering procedures, the ART2 + k-means is the worst, whereas SOM + k-means is the best, supporting our observation in Section 3.2.1.

Each position of customer cluster is based on comparing its average RFM values with the total average (Ha & Park, 1998). If the average of a variable in a cluster is greater than the total average, an upward arrow is assigned to that variable; otherwise, a downward arrow is assigned. According to this rule, RFM status as well as strategic positions could be determined. We determine the number of clusters of the better method, SOFM + k-means, by the rule of thumb described in Section 3.2.1, suggesting that the ideal number of clusters is seven with respect to the marketing data-set. The result is summarized in Table 3. Clusters 2, 3, and 7, which have R↓F↑M↑, shall be considered as loyal customers who patronize and make a large purchase recently and frequently, especially Cluster 2 whose transaction amount is so huge that this cluster shall be further regarded as a golden customer cluster. Customers in Cluster 1, with R↓F↓M↓, may be new customers who recently visit the website. Cluster 5 possessing R↑F↑M↓ is treated as the potential cluster and top-priority target segment because each customer in this cluster may be promoted as a loyal customer. Vulnerable customers, with the status of R↑F↓M↓, are presented in Clusters 4 and 6 who are attracted by this website and may have churned.

4. Conclusions

Segments which exhibit both strong external isolation and tight internal cohesion are well defined. The motivation for two-stage clustering architectures was ignited by researched papers that surmount single-stage drawbacks. Four benchmark data-sets and a real-world marketing data-set are used for evaluation purposes. The benchmark data-sets are used for evaluating the clustering accuracy as well as for choosing number of clusters using different indexes, whereas the real-world data-set is used to compare the cluster validations under a series of number of clusters for different methods. The experimental results are unambiguous and agree with previous researches for three points:

(1) The two-stage clustering procedures surpass the direct clustering algorithm because of the intermediary of two-stage clustering procedure, i.e. ANN, which is capable of handling a wide range of messy data. The promises of noise removal and data complexity reduction make the homogeneous clusters easier to get.

(2) Comparing the discovery quality under various conditions, the SOFM + k-means has the lead, then fuzzy ART + k-means, and lastly ART2 + k-means. The SOFM + k-means can potentially improve the quality of decisions that require the cluster analysis, such as market segmentation, credit analysis, or quality grading, to maintain the competitive advantages.

(3) The identification of the number of clusters is one the most tricky problems in clustering analysis. None of the two-stage clustering procedures in this study can perfectly assist users to choose proper clustering number for a wide-ranged data-set.

A sensitivity analysis facilitates researchers and practitioners to use and calibrate a method. On the premise of the selection of multiple indexes as the clustering validations, however, doing sensitivity analysis has become an almost impossible mission since multiple parameters are difficult to hold a consistent decision under different validation indexes simultaneously. Among the mentioned two-stage clustering procedures, the SOFM + k-means has four parameters: arrangement type of neurons, number of epochs, learning rate, and smooth factor of neighbor function; the ART2 + k-means has eight parameters: number of epochs, five nameless parameters, learning rate, and vigilance value; and the fuzzy ART + k-means has four parameters: number of epochs, learning rate, constant, and vigilance value. The key idea of this study is to alleviate the issue of setting parameters, and we had tried our best to find out the default or suggested values that were widely examined by practical studies. Nevertheless, we still believe this study shall be examined by further studies.

Funding
This research is partially supported by the Ministry of Science and Technology, Taiwan [grant number MOST 103-2221-E-131-028].

Author details
Cheng-Ching Chang[1]
E-mail: ntuinformetrics@gmail.com
Ssu-Han Chen[2]
E-mail: ssuhanchen@mail.mcut.edu.tw
[1] Department of Library and Information Science, National Taiwan University, Taipei, Taiwan.
[2] Department of Industrial Engineering and Management, Ming Chi University of Technology, New Taipei City, Taiwan.

References
Abidi, S. S. R., & Ong, J. (2000). A data mining strategy for inductive data clustering: A synergy between self-organising neural networks and k-means clustering techniques. *Proceedings of IEEE TENCON, 2*, 568–573.

Bandyopadhyay, S., & Maulik, U. (2001). Nonparametric genetic clustering: Comparison of validity indices. *IEEE Transactions on Systems, Man and Cybernetics, Part C (Applications and Reviews), 31*, 120–125.

Bezdek, J. C., & Pal, N. R. (1998). Some new indexes of cluster validity. *IEEE Transactions on Systems, Man and Cybernetics, Part B (Cybernetics), 28*, 301–315.

Calinski, R. B., & Harabasz, J. (1974). A dendrite method for cluster analysis. *Communications in Statistics, 3*, 1–27.

Canetta, L., Cheikhrouhou, N., & Glardon, R. (2005). Applying two-stage SOM-based clustering approaches to industrial data analysis. *Production Planning & Control, 16*, 774–784.

Carpenter, G. A., & Grossberg, S. (1987). ART 2: Self-organization of stable category recognition codes for analog input patterns. *Applied Optics, 26*, 4919–4930.

Carpenter, G. A., Grossberg, S., & Rosen, D. B. (1991). Fuzzy ART: Fast stable learning and categorization of analog patterns by an adaptive resonance system. *Neural Networks, 4*, 759–771.

Chaimeun, O., & Srivihok, A. (2005). Clustering of Thai handcraft customers using combined SOM and k-means algorithm. *International Conference on of Databases and Applications*, 35–39.

Charrad, M., Lechevallier, Y., Ahmed, M. B., & Saporta, G. (2010). On the number of clusters in block clustering algorithms. *Proceedings of the Twenty-Third International Florida Artificial Intelligence Research Society Conference*, 392–397.

Chen, G., & Dai, Y. (2004). A new distance measurement for clustering time-course gene expression data. In *26th Annual International Conference of the IEEE EMBS* (pp. 2929–2932). San Francisco, CA.

Chen, A., Pan, Y., & Jiang, L. (2013). Improving k-means clustering method in fault diagnosis based on SOM network. *Journal of Networks, 8*, 680–687.

Davies, D. L., & Bouldin, D. W. (1979). A cluster separation measure. *IEEE Transactions on Pattern Analysis and Machine Intelligence, 1*, 224–227.

Ding, Y. X., Shi, Y., Shi, Y., & Jiang, J. Q. (2008). A hybrid clustering algorithm based on ART2 and its application in anomaly detection. *International Conference on Wavelet Analysis and Pattern Recognition*, 282–286.

Dunn, J. C. (1974). A fuzzy relative of the ISODATA process and its use in detecting compact well-separated clusters. *Journal of Cybernetics, 3*, 32–57.

Fisher, R. A. (1936). The use of multiple measurements in taxonomic problems. *Annals of Eugenics, 7*, Part II, 179–188.

Forina, M., Lanteri, S., Armanino, C., & Lauter, S. (1991). *PARVUS—An extendible package for data exploration, classification and correlation*. Genoa: Institute of Pharmaceutical and Food Analysis and Technologies.

Godin, N., Huguet, S., & Gaertner, R. (2005). Integration of the Kohonen's self-organising map and k-means algorithm for the segmentation of the AE data collected during tensile tests on cross-ply composites. *NDT&E International, 38*, 299–309.

Ha, S. H., & Park, S. C. (1998). Application of data mining tools to hotel data mart on the intranet for database marketing. *Expert Systems with Applications, 15*(1), 1–31.

Hayfron-Acquah, J. B., & Gyimah, M. S. (2014). Classification and recognition of fingerprints using self organizing maps (SOM). *International Journal of Computer Science Issues, 11*, 153–159.

Hughes, A. M. (1994). *Strategic database marketing*. Chicago, IL: Probus Publishing.

Hung, Y. S., Chen, K. L. B., Yang, C. T., & Deng, G. F. (2013). Web usage mining for analysing elder self-care behavior patterns. *Expert Systems with Applications, 40*, 775–783.

Juntunen, P., Liukkonen, M., Lehtola, M., & Hiltunen, Y. (2014). Characterization of alum floc in water treatment by image analysis and modeling. *Cogent Engineering, 1*, Article ID: 944767. Retrieved from http://dx.doi.org/10.1080/23311916.2014.944767

Khedairia, S., & Khadir, M. T. (2008). Self-organizing map and k-means for meteorological day type identification for the region of Annaba-Algeria. *7th Computer Information Systems and Industrial Management Applications*, 91–96.

Kohonen, T. (1990). Self-organizing map. *Proceedings of the IEEE, 78*, 1464–1480.

Park, S., Suresh, N. C., & Jeong, B. K. (2008). Sequence-based clustering for web usage mining: A new experimental framework and ANN-enhanced k-means algorithm. *Data & Knowledge Engineering, 65*, 512–543.

Ray, S., & Turi, R. H. (1999). Determination of number of clusters in k-means clustering and application in colour image segmentation. *Proceedings of the 4th International Conference on Advances in Pattern Recognition and Digital Techniques*, 137–143.

Sugiyama, A., & Kotani, M. (2002). Analysis of gene expression data by using self-organizing maps and k-means clustering. *Proceedings of International Joint Conference on Neural Networks*, 1342–1345.

Vesanto, J., & Alhoniemi, E. (2000). Clustering of the self-organizing map. *IEEE Transactions on Neural Networks, 11*, 586–600.

Weiss, S. M., & Indurkhya, N. (1998). *Predictive data mining: A practical guide*. San Francisco, CA: Morgan Kaufmann.

Wu, J., Xia, J., Chen, J. M., & Cui, Z. M. (2011). Moving object classification method based on SOM and k-means. *Journal of Computers, 6*, 1654–1661.

Xu, R., & Wunsch, II, D. (2005). Survey of clustering algorithms. *IEEE Transactions on Neural Networks, 16*, 645–678.

2

POEM: Practical ontology engineering model for semantic web ontologies

Shaukat Ali[1] and Shah Khusro[1]*

*Corresponding author: Shah Khusro, Department of Computer Science, University of Peshawar, Peshawar 25120, Pakistan

E-mail: khusro@upesh.edu.pk

Reviewing editor: Hsien-Tsung Chang, Chang Gung University, Taiwan

Abstract: Sundown of the twentieth century saw the emergence of the World Wide Web. A decade later, semantic web (SW) envisioned enriching of web-accessible information and services with machine-processable semantics to solve the problems of information management and sharing which are aroused by the success of the web. However, success of the SW largely depends on the availability of formal ontologies for representing and structuring information in different domains. To facilitate web ontology engineering (OE), methodologies are proposed by the researchers since years. However, OE particularly web OE is still immature and none of the methodologies is standardized for web OE projects as yet. This paper presents an evolutionary SW ontology engineering methodology called POEM. POEM presents a complete methodology comprising of various phases for performing conceptualization, designing, implementation, evaluation, and project management tasks. POEM exploits and incorporates the large experiences from the widely used software engineering standards to make the methodology more realistic and provide greater functionality. Due to its broad nature, POEM has the potential applicability in a wider range of OE projects. Comparison of POEM with other OE methodologies has ascertained POEM as more advantageous and easy methodology for SW ontology engineering.

ABOUT THE AUTHORS

Shaukat Ali is perusing his PhD degree in the area of Web Semantics at the Department of Computer Science, University of Peshawar, Pakistan. He received his MS degree from the same university in the year 2007. He is serving as a lecturer in Computer Science in the Department of Computer Science, University of Peshawar. He has published several papers in national and international journals and conferences. His current research interests include Ontology Engineering, Life-Logging, and Semantic Desktop.

   Shah Khusro received his PhD degree from the Institute of Software Technology & Interactive Systems, Vienna University of Technology, Austria in 2007. Previously, he received his MSc degree from the Department of Computer Science, University of Peshawar, Pakistan in 1997, where he is currently working as an assistant professor. He frequently publishes his work in national and international journals and conferences. His research interests include Web 2.0, Web Semantics, Life-Logging, Smartphones and Blind People.

PUBLIC INTEREST STATEMENT

Most of the development projects fail due to lack of proper methodologies and management. Semantic web (SW) turns the web of information into web of knowledge and enables people and computers to work in cooperation by giving well-defined meanings to web resources. However, success of the SW depends largely on the availability of web ontologies. Building SW ontology is a complex task and requires careful understanding, planning, and management like software development projects. Clearly, a comprehensive methodology is essential for handling the technicalities involved in an SW ontology engineering project. This paper presents a comprehensive methodology called POEM which consists of detailed steps from inception to implementation of SW ontology. POEM leverages valuable concepts and experiences from software engineering to provide an easy and practical approach. POEM outperforms the available methodologies by vibrantly supporting the ontology project management activities equally to the core ontology development activities.

Subjects: Algorithms & Complexity; Artificial Intelligence; Computer Science

Keywords: semantic web; ontology engineering; knowledge engineering; software engineering

1. Introduction

Ontology is old genie in a new bottle. The term ontology was first used in Philosophy in the nineteenth century where it gave an organized justification of being (Breitmann, Casanova, & Truszkowski, 2007) and is now a most relevant word in the knowledge engineering community (Corcho, Fernández-López, & Gómez-Pérez, 2003). A widely quoted definition of ontology in computer science literature is of Gruber's (Gruber, 1993): "An ontology is a formal, explicit specification of a shared conceptualization." Ontology has gained increasing popularity in the computer science fields (i.e. knowledge management and sharing, e-commerce, intelligent information integration, and database integration), where researchers believe of its significant role in the foreseeable future (Noy & McGuiness, 2001; Su & Ilebrekke, 2002). Ontology popularity is due to its promise of a shared and common understanding of some domain of interest for enhancing people and machines communication. Ontology may presume different formalisms but corresponds to a knowledge area (domain), where it give hierarchical description of explicitly defined concepts, detailed descriptions of concepts' attributes, and inter-relationships between the concepts that could be used for the domain interpretation.

Web is phenomenally a simple artifact providing new methods of information organization, retrieval, and sharing. Web simplicity is a great strength of the web and is an important factor of its popularity and growth (Horrocks, 2008). However, the exponential growth of the web resulting into information overload problem that is increasing the information interpretation burden of the human users. Semantic web (SW) envisions for making the web information more machine processable and understandable by mapping information into a rigorous structure using ontologies (Benslimane, Malki, Rahmouni, & Rahmoun, 2008). The term "ontology" is regularly quoted in SW literature, and it is believed that ontology will ease numerous types of information management tasks including information/knowledge engineering and management, information retrieval and integration, and information storage and sharing on the web. (Benslimane et al., 2008; Kapoor & Sharma, 2010). The quick and cheap development of formal domain-specific ontologies will serve as the major source of the SW success and proliferation (Benslimane et al., 2008; Vanitha et al., 2011). SW ontology allows for semantically enriching of web resources that is a pre-condition for developing novel advanced web services such as semantic search and web resources retrieval (De Nicola, Missikoff, & Navigli, 2009). Knowledge engineers (KEs) in cooperation with domain experts (DEs) builds SW ontologies which is a tedious, time-consuming, costly, and laborious task and might hinder the advancements of SW activities (Youn et al., 2004). To build a new ontology, one needs to answer a number of questions (related to contents, language, methodology, and tools) to guide and carry out the development process (Corcho et al., 2003). The automated SW ontology engineering tools are in their infancy, immature, and suffers with a number of shortcomings such as OWL 2 is designed to overcome some of the expressibility, syntax, and semantic problems of its prior version but it has lack of useful modeling constructs such as universal restriction (Rodrigues, Flores, & Rotta, 2015). Researchers have contributed a significant amount of research for analyzing and categorizing the available methodologies, tools, and languages for ontology building (Alam, Ali, Khan, Khusro, & Rauf, 2014; Corcho et al., 2003; Noy & McGuiness, 2001; Su & Ilebrekke, 2002).

An SW ontology building process is structurally and logically as complex as the production of a software artifact (De Nicola et al., 2009). Therefore, a cohesive and structured project development framework is needed for building SW ontologies which should ensure careful project planning, clear identification and definition of roles and tasks, and addressing of tones of crucial details for successful migration. In the past several years, several ontology engineering (OE) methodologies are proposed for helping researchers and organizations for successful development, implementation, and migration of ontologies. However, they are not suitable for SW OE where information are scattered, unknown, and requires integration and mapping of information in real time. None of the methodologies is widely acceptable due to a number of reasons including (Ashraf, Chang, Hussain, & Hussain, 2015; Corcho et al., 2003; De Nicola et al., 2009; Ferreira et al., 2007; Karapiperis & Apostolou, 2006): (1) none of them is accepted as a standard or not adopted widely to set as a standard in the foreseeable near future, (2) lacking with guidelines to engineer ontologies reusing and reengineering of ontological and non-ontological resources that are widely accepted in a domain, (3) do not describe OE process with the same fashion and granularity as the methodologies used for software engineering, (4) immature if compared with software engineering and knowledge engineering methodologies, (5) not unified that is each group is following its own approach and having variable degree of dependency of a developed ontology on its applications, (6) mostly focus on the centralized development of ontologies by employing KEs and DEs, however, methodologies are also proposed that advocates collaborative approaches for constructing ontologies, (7) targeted specifically for ontology developers and having no provenance for software developers to enhance their capabilities and understandings about ontology building for developing effective ontology-based applications, (8) primarily focusing on the core ontology development activities, especially on the ontology implementation and do not consider OE as a project by completely ignoring the project management-related activities such as project planning and scheduling, risk analysis, and usage analysis, and (9) most of them are used in a single domain and have not been used by external groups. A few of the methodologies are also proposed specifically for web-specific ontology engineering, but they are very shallow and superficial and could not handle the technical, development, and management tasks related with a web OE project. Web ontologies produced by the proposed methodologies would be light-weighted and would lack with detailed semantics of information in a domain. They are majorly based on heuristics and do not consider using of widely accepted scientific methods, necessary for ontology building as they are used in the software engineering and knowledge engineering disciplines. Therefore, none of the approaches presented is fully mature to meet the unique requirements and applications of SW ontologies.

Ontology-based software engineering is an emerging field where ontologies provide conceptual basis for extending and automating software engineering process including modularization, reuse, cross-cutting dependencies, standardization of domain knowledge, and distribution and integration of software components. In this paper, we have presented a methodology for SW ontology building called practical OE model for SW ontologies (POEM) that leverages the large valuable experiences and concepts from the widely accepted standards of software engineering and other state-of-the-art technologies. POEM is easy to conceptualize and use, and is aimed to provide greater functionality and interoperability. POEM consists of a sequence of activities for building SW ontologies form inception to deployment at any scale (i.e. lightweight or heavyweight). Goal of the POEM is similar to the software engineering: turning the process of SW ontology building from an art into an engineering discipline. Main objectives of the POEM are: (1) general enough in the sense to provide greater understandability and help to both software developers and ontology practitioners to build SW ontologies, (2) clear incorporation of software engineering processes or activities (i.e. requirements specifications, evaluation, evolution, risk analysis, and management activities) in SW OE and clear and precise definition of each process or activity stating its purpose, inputs and outputs, roles and responsibilities of the experts, and execution, (3) reduction of time and costs in the production of ontologies, (4) progressively testing of the incremental versions of the ontology for enhancing quality of the ontology, and (5) readily availability of the incremental version of the ontology for using in ontology-based applications. In reality, POEM is focused for SW ontology development, but its processing steps are broad and flexible enough to accommodate enterprise level ontology development and deployment projects. In the context of this paper, POEM focuses on centralized OE. However, POEM has the potential of supporting collaborative OE with certain extensions and refinements.

2. Related work
Apparently, ontology design seems similar to object-oriented design but designing classes and relations in ontology building is different from object-oriented programming. Therefore, an object-oriented program structure representing a domain is different from an ontology representing the same

domain (Noy & McGuiness, 2001). Knowledge from the fields of data modeling, object-oriented software analysis, and ontology modeling design patterns can be used for designing applicable principles for domain-specific ontology design patterns (Vujasinovic, Ivezic, & Kulvatunyou, 2015). Despite the emergence of several OE methodologies, none of them is succeeded in gaining significant marketplace and is accepted or going to be accepted as a standard in the foreseeable future. Therefore, OE is still much of an art (Ferreira et al., 2007). OE methodologies can be either centralized or collaborative. In centralized OE, all of the stockholders (i.e. ontology development team (ODT), DEs, and organization) work as a single group under a single roof at a single location with a single agenda. In collaborative OE, the stockholders work as decentralized groups at disperse geographical location with potentially divergent agendas and mutually established consensus (Simperl & Luczak-Rösch, 2013). These two schools of OE have support from the specifically designed and developed scenario processes, methodologies, and tools. POEM methodology could potentially support both of the paradigms but here mainly focuses on centralized OE. Scope of the paper includes centralized OE methodologies that are developed specifically for web ontology engineering and consisting of all the steps ranging from conceptualization to deployment. However, a slight review of the earlier centralized OE methodologies is also presented in the coming paragraphs.

2.1. General OE methodologies
Several OE methodologies are proposed by the researchers and organizations since years. However, research groups have no consensus and each group is using/applying his own methodology (Corcho et al., 2003; Noy & McGuiness, 2001). Some researchers believe that ontology development is an iterative process (Vanitha et al., 2011) starting with a rough initial version which would be progressively revised, evaluated, refined, and debugged using either application or problem-solving methods or arguing with DEs. The iterative process will continue throughout the life cycle of ontology (Kapoor & Sharma, 2010). Among the different alternative methodologies, the one to be selected largely depends on the application to be developed and the extensions that are anticipated (Noy & McGuiness, 2001). Generally, an ontology building methodology may include: identifying domain and scope of ontology, determining reuse of already available ontologies, identifying significant terms in the ontology, defining classes and the class hierarchies, identifying class properties (slots) and constraints, and defining instances of the classes (Kapoor & Sharma, 2010; Noy & McGuiness, 2001).

Uschold and King (1995) proposed a methodology for building Enterprise Ontology and is application independent. The methodology suggests four activities: (1) identifying purpose of ontology, (2) building ontology, (3) evaluating ontology, and (4) documenting ontology. Building activity encompasses knowledge acquisition, coding, and integrating other ontologies inside the current one. The methodology uses middle-out approach for identifying concepts and is application independent.

Grüninger and Fox (1995) proposed a methodology during the development of Toronto Virtual Enterprise (TOVE) project ontology for addressing business process and activities in a modeling domain. They proposed the use of first-order logic for the development of knowledge-based systems where informal description of ontological specifications needed to be defined earlier and then formalized. The methodology uses middle-out approach for identifying concepts and is semi-application dependents. To determine scope of the ontology, a set of competency questions (CQs) are identified. The CQs and their answers are used for the identification of main concepts, attributes, relations, and axioms in the ontology that can be properly encoded in first-order logic. It provides a good guideline for transforming informal scenarios into computable models.

SENSUS (Swartout, Patil, Knight, & Russ, 1996) methodology is developed at IST (Institute of Sciences Institute) which derives domain-specific ontology from a giant ontology using top-down approach and is semi-application dependent. A set of potential most relevant terms in a domain called "seed" terms are identified first. After identification, seed terms are manually located in broad-coverage ontology (i.e. SENSUS ontology that is containing more than 70,000 concepts). All the concepts coming up on the path from seed term to the top (root) of SENSUS are incorporated. A relevant term that is yet not appeared is manually added and this process is repeated until no term is missing.

A sub-tree entirely can be added if terms with large number paths are found or if majority of the nodes in a sub-tree are found relevant to the other nodes in the tree/sub-tree. This methodology prompts the usage of same base ontology for the development of many domain-specific ontologies.

KACTUS (Bernaras, Laresgoiti, & Corera, 1996) in KACTUS project proposed a methodology that follows top-down approach for identifying concepts and is application-dependent. Ontology can be built reusing existing relevant ontologies and the ontology can also be incorporated by later applications in their ontologies. Applying this criterion, ontology for applications can be built which would contain the required agreed knowledge.

METHONTOLOGY (Lopez, Gomez-Perez, Sierra, & Sierra, 1999) methodology has been created in the Artificial Intelligence Lab in the Polytechnic University of Madrid. This methodology proposes ontology building in different ways either from the scratch, reusing other ontologies, or by reengineering other existing ontologies. The METHONTOLOGY framework defines set of activities that should be performed while building ontology such as scheduling, control quality assurance, specification, knowledge acquisition, conceptualization, integration, formalization, implementation, evaluation, maintenance, documentation, and configuration management. The life cycle of ontology shows that ontology throughout of its life time should pass through which of the stages, and its interdependency with the life cycles of other ontologies. This methodology also identifies that which techniques have to be carried out in each activity, what should be the outputs of each activity, and how they have to be evaluated. METHONTOLOGY uses middle-out approach for identifying concepts and is application independent.

On-To-Knowledge (Staab, Studer, Schnurr, & Sure, 2001) methodology is application dependent, uses top-down approach for concepts identification strategy, and specifies the goals to be achieved by the management tools. The methodology includes steps: (1) kick-off: specify and capture ontology requirements, identify CQs, identify and study potentially reusable ontologies, and built an initial draft version of the ontology, (2) refinement: producing a mature and application-oriented ontology, (3) evaluation: checking requirements and CQs and testing ontology in application environment, and (4) ontology maintenance: carrying out activities related to ontology maintenance.

Detailed comparisons of the ontology building methodologies using IEEE 1074–1995 standard have been quoted in several relevant literatures (Gómez-Pérez, Fernández-López, & Corcho, 2007), but none of them is found fully mature if compared to software engineering methodologies. Each of the methodologies has certain enhancements and shortcomings such as On-To-Knowledge describes more activities but do not provide accurate descriptions of each activity (Gómez-Pérez et al., 2007). None of the methodologies covers all of the processes involved in ontology building. However, METHONTOLOGY is found as the most mature methodology which could be heavily used in for ontology building in different domains as recommended by FIPA for the ontology construction task (Casely-Hayford, 2003; Corcho et al., 2003). A state-of-the-art survey of classification and principles for domain-specific ontology design patterns development is presented in (Vujasinovic et al., 2015). Furthermore, several methodologies are proposed for other tasks as well such as ontology learning, ontology reengineering, ontology evolution, ontology evaluation, and ontology merging (Corcho et al., 2003). However, they are not discussed here because they do not fall into the scope of the paper.

2.2. Web OE methodologies

Web ontology describes metadata about resources in web documents. Web ontology makes web documents to be more processable by applications rather than only presented and interpreted by humans. A web ontology building process is also treated as an iterative process which starts with a rough first pass and is revised, refined, and more details are added in the subsequent iterations until a complete ontology has been formed. However, web ontology building is different from traditional ontology building due to non-standardized varying and scattered nature, and not readily availability of information. Devising of a specific methodology for web ontologies that should meet the unique nature, needs, and applications of web information has not received considerable response from the research community as yet.

Vanitha et al. (2011); Noy and McGuiness, (2001) proposes a simple iterative-based web ontology process model consisting of seven activities including: (1) determining the domain and scope of ontology, (2) reusing existing ontologies, (3) enumerating terms in the ontology, (4) defining classes and class hierarchy, (5) defining properties of classes, (6) defining facets (role restrictions) of the slots, and (7) creating instances. During the lifetime of ontology these activities would be repeated in circular fashion again and again until a functional ontological product has been obtained.

Kalyanpur, Hashmi, Golbeck, and Parsia (2004) proposes a life cycle for casual web ontology development process. The proposed methodology is similar to the standard web page development process, where users uses standard HTML editors (e.g. MS FrontPage) to quickly arrange and layout certain information they wish to deploy on the Web and creates links to the existing relevant information. The life cycle includes key stages including the use of shorthand key notation to draft ontology skeletons quickly, an effective ontology searching algorithm combining keyword with DL-based constructs to search-related concepts, an iterative copy–paste mechanism to borrow relevant fragments from a related existing ontology, and natural language-based presentation of terms to build and maintain ontologies effectively. An ontology development toolkit called SWOOPed is invented using these features and stages.

Some researchers have suggested using of semi-automatic approach of ontology extraction as the practical approach. Rules and methods have been suggested for ontology engineering by relational databases reverse engineering. (Stojanovic, Stojanovic, & Volz, 2002) approach suggests a set of rules for analysis of relations, keys, and inclusion dependencies for mapping relational databases constructs into semantically equivalent constructs in ontology. (Tijerino, Embley, Lonsdale, Ding, & Nagy, 2005) suggests understanding of HTML table structure and contents, constraints holding between the concepts, matching the recognized concepts with more general specifications of related concepts, and merging the resultant structure with other similar knowledge representation essential for web ontology building. (Astrova & Stantic, 2005) suggests construction of ontology by analysis of HTML forms for creating a model schema, transforming the schema into ontology, and creating ontological instances from data contained in the page. (Benslimane et al., 2008) suggests reverse engineering of data-intensive web sites into ontology based SW by analyzing the related HTML page for extracting the semantics of relational database, and merging the semantics with the captured relational schema to build ontology.

The proposed methodologies are valuable but are limited in scope due focusing mainly on the core web ontology building activities such as identifying classes, defining properties and relations between classes. They have no definitions of strategies for ontological constructs identifications and application dependency/independency, and have completely ignored management activities (i.e. schedule and quality assurance) as well as supporting activities (ontology integration, ontology evaluation, and ontology documentation, etc.) which are essential for web ontology building projects like any other software development project. Furthermore, the presented approaches are very shallow and providing no technical details of even prescribed engineering activities during a web ontology building process. Similarly, the reverse engineering approaches could also not produce an effective ontology for a domain modeling because the ontologies produced would not be semantically enriched due to absence of axioms, requirement of auxiliary information, and error-prone in analysis of tables' structures and schemas. Furthermore, they could also be very time consuming due to analysis of large data in a table or database. Thus, none of them is suitable for implication in a heavyweight web ontology building project.

3. An overview of POEM
A methodology has to answer what, who, and when questions about performing activities in a development process (Gómez-Pérez et al., 2007). IEEE defines methodology as "a comprehensive,

integrated series of techniques or methods creating a general system theory of how a class of thought intensive work ought to be performed" (IEEE, 1990). A methodology is composed of methods and techniques where methods are composed of processes, processes are composed of activities, and activities are composed of related tasks. Together, using the guidelines of IEEE and support from SW technologies can provide conceptualization for POEM. What distinguishes POEM from the other web OE methodologies is its software engineering compliance, evolutionary, incremental, and iterative nature. As an innovative aspect of the PEOM is the presentation of life cycle for web ontology building projects from their inceptions to live deployments which will help project team in focusing and achieving business values because no value can be realized until the solution is deployed and is operational. POEM believes in building ontologies in the same way of developing software and combines features from several of the software engineering industry standard methodologies into a single suit. Included features are: (1) stressing on the accomplishment of milestones from waterfall model, (2) coupling of the iterative nature of prototyping model with the systematic and controlled aspects of classical model from spiral model to accommodate changes as process progresses, (3) facilitating of system development through reusing of the existing prepackaged components from component-based development model, (4) supporting of system development using object-oriented concepts (e.g. classes, objects, and inheritance) from object-oriented process model, (5) emphasizing on verifications and validations from V-model, (6) rapid and continuous delivery of useful ontological product from agile model, and (7) using of UML for the preparation of all of ontology building blueprints.

SW ontology is also of evolutionary nature which like any complex system evolves over time with changes in the information domain. Moreover, the non-standardized and scattered nature, and readily unavailability of web information would make an SW ontology construction in a single go increasingly difficult. Therefore, a methodology making a straight line path to an end SW ontological product has unrealistic implication in the domain (Hesse, 2005). Furthermore, several other hidden factors (i.e. unpredictable in the early stages of a project) can also make completion of a comprehensive SW ontological product impossible; however, a limited version (i.e. based on a set of core product requirement) could be introduced to meet competitive and business needs. Therefore, a methodology is needed that has been explicitly designed to divide the development process into distinct and well-defined activities, and accommodate SW ontological products that evolve over the time. Methodologies with such characteristics are termed as evolutionary models in software engineering. Evolutionary approach is considered appropriate for ontology development (Hesse, 2005). Evolutionary models are iterative by nature which enables developers to develop increasingly more completed versions of a product in increasing number of iterations.

POEM is evolutionary by nature that would complete an SW ontology building project in a number of iterations as more and more information becomes available but is also incremental because at each iteration the ontology would be further detailed and extended in a stepwise fashion. POEM divides the ontology building methodology into several cycles (i.e. iterations), a cycle into phases (i.e. process), and a phase into activities for requirements specifications, project planning and scheduling, risk analysis, implementation, and testing. Each cycle ends with the release of a new incremental version of ontology. The activities can be divided into tasks (i.e. sub-activities), which will be smaller in number for a small/simple ontology project and larger in number for a large/complex ontology project. A sketchy representation of POEM model is presented in Figure 1. The ontology building process starts at the core of the model with the onetime processes of project identification and initiation, and feasibility analysis. The first iteration is of inception nature and majorly concerned with the identification/capturing of requirements in terms of the ontology requirements specifications (e.g. identifying domain, and scope of the ontology), concepts development and analysis, and initial planning and scheduling. This would not probably involve any implementation or testing processes and could take several other iterations as well, if required. The iteration would release ontology glossary that would contain terms from the domain of interest and their informal definitions. The subsequent iterations would include detailed conceptualization and designing, planning and scheduling, implementation and testing, feedback and roadmap for next iteration, and release of

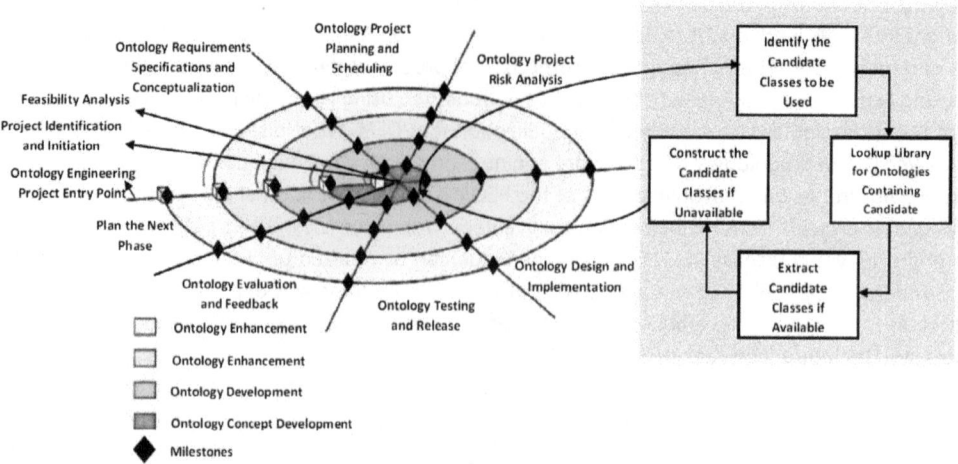

Figure 1. Top-level representation of POEM methodology.

incremental versions of ontology. The early iterations would end in the production of preliminary implementation to provide small skeletal blueprints of ontology. Stepwisely with enhancements and refinements, increasingly more sophisticated additive versions (increments) and eventually the final version of domain ontology would be released as the iterations proceeds further. Major versions of the ontology produced after the increasing iterations would have to be constantly aligned with the modeled reality. The later iterations will result increasingly in the ontology enhancements and maintenance. POEM is a milestone driven methodology where a milestone has to be produced at the end of every phase of each cycle containing the achievements and the criteria for accomplishing the phase. Each phase could have interim milestones which would help in achieving a phase's final milestone. Likewise, deliverables must be completed and produced where critical questions related to the development must be satisfactorily answered. In parallel to all these activities, umbrella activities such as ontology configuration management, ontology quality assurance, ontology development project tracking and control, formal technical reviews, and documents preparation and productions are to be carried out as well.

To demonstrate the practicality of POEM, the methodology is supported with a running proof-of-concept ontology building example of a web page in the web domain called Web Page Ontology (WPO). In the example, the ontology is chiefly concerned with semantic modeling of a web page structure and content, and tracking of a user's activities and interactions taking place while browsing a web page (e.g. downloading a picture from a web page by a user at an instant of time).

4. The POEM methodology
POEM is an evolutionary methodology, advocating for completion of ontology building process from inception to implementation in a number of iterations and incremental versions. Each of the iterations is composed of a number of phases. In the following subsections, detailed specific information about each of the phases is presented in reference to our WPO example.

4.1. Project identification and initiation
Identification of business needs yields in the identification of ontology building project. A business need may arise either due to some kid of "pain" within an organization (i.e. poor customer service levels or increase in competition) or an organization wants to take maximum advantages by leveraging the emerging IT technologies (e.g. cloud computing, radio frequency identification (RFID), and SW). Mostly, information system projects grow out of business process management (BPM) methodology used by organizations to improve their end-to-end business processes. Automating business process can bring several important benefits to organization by replacing ineffective information management process with technology components to gain cost efficiencies. Web has been proven as the rich information highway providing novel methods and opportunities for business processes improvements. Organization

can exploit novel SW technologies (i.e. ontologies) to provide high-valued services to their customers using the Web such as music CDs transitioning on the Web to provide enhanced searching, purchasing, and downloading services to customers. Ontology development team ODT[1] and business people needs to work conjunctively for finding ways to use ontologies to support business needs and bring ultimate real business objectives such as increasing sales, improving customer sales, and decreasing operating expenses.

The ontology project is properly initiated by issuing Ontology System Request Document (OSRD) describing the business reasons for building ontology and the values expected from the ontology to provide. An OSRD comprises five elements: project sponsor, business need, business requirements, business value, and special issue. Template of OSRD along with the description of each element is shown in Figure 2. Once the ontology system request got approval from the approval committee, the next step is the feasibility analysis.

4.2. Feasibility analysis

A knowledge management system needs to be properly integrated into its operating organization for functioning satisfactorily (Staab et al., 2001). Ontology building project success and failure can be attributed to a number of factors. Feasibility analysis analyzes these factors by firstly identifying the problem/opportunity areas and secondly putting them together into a wider organizational perspective. Feasibility study identifies the potential risks associated with ontology building project that must be managed before proceeding into the project. The feasibility analysis acts as a decision support system for determining technical and economical feasibility of ontology building project by selecting potential focus areas and target solutions. Technical feasibility (also called technical risks analysis) answers the question "Can we build it" by determining the extent to which the ontology can be successfully designed, developed, and implemented by ODT. Ontology technical feasibility is actually technical risk analysis that can endanger successful ontology building project completion (Dennis, 2012). The life-threatening risk includes level of ODT and DEs familiarity with the application and technology, accurate estimation of ontology project size (i.e. development team, time, and features), and compatibility of ontology with the technologies already existing in an organization. Economic feasibility (also called cost–benefit analysis) answers the question "Should we built the ontology?" by identifying and analyzing ontology building project's cost and benefits, assigning values to them, calculating future cash flows, and measuring the financial worthiness of ontology (Dennis, 2012). The format and approach of feasibility study vary according to an organization's business needs and processes. POEM incorporates feasibility analysis and uses the feasibility analysis approach proposed by CommonKADS methodology (Schreiber & Akkermans, 2000). The feasibility analysis activity needs to be performed before starting ontology building process and would serve as basis for the subsequent ontology project planning and scheduling, and risk analysis phases.

Ontology System Request Document	
1	**Project Sponsor**
	The person who initiates the SW ontology project and who serves as the primary point of contact for the project on the business side. For example, IT Manager, CEO, and Vice President of Marketing etc.
2	**Business Need**
	The business-related reasons for initiating the SW ontology project. For example, increasing sale, improving access to information, and improving customer service etc.
3	**Business Requirements**
	The business capabilities that the SW ontology will provide. For example, providing online access to information semantically, capturing and semantically organizing customer information, and providing semantic search capabilities etc.
4	**Business Values**
	The benefits that the SW ontology will create for the business. For example, 5% increase in sale, and $100,000 cost saving from removal of existing system etc.
5	**Special Issues**
	Issues relevant to the development and implementation of SW ontology. For example, ontology needed to be implemented before the Christmas etc.

Figure 2. Template of ontology system request document OSRD.

4.3. Ontology requirements specifications and conceptualization

The goal of this phase is to capture knowledge to be modeled in ontology in such a way to describe its universe of discourse, purpose and goal, contents and ingredients, users, and uses, etc., and to model the captured knowledge semantically to increase its conceptualization. This phase requires agreement and commitment between ODT, DEs, and end-users for establishing effective communication mediums and methods. Guidelines for building ontology and objectives of ontology from a user's point of view would be identified and laid down in the earliest meetings. However, detailed knowledge capturing needs to answer several questions related to the ontology to be developed including (Youn et al., 2004): (1) What is the domain of interest of ontology?, (2) What is the scope of ontology?, (3) What are the business purposes and economic benefits of ontology?, (4) Who are the intended users and what are the intended uses of ontology?, (5) Is there any other ontology existing in the domain?, (6) what are the questions to be answered by ontology?, (7) How would you describe "good" result that would be generated by a successful ontology?, and (8) Will any special performance issues or constrains affect the way the solution is approached?. During ontology building process, answers to these questions may vary, but, at any instant, of time they will help to constrain scope of ontology (Youn et al., 2004). Ontology Requirements Specification Document (ORSD) should be produced as output of this phase that would contain detailed description of requirements to be represented in ontology, facilitating searching of knowledge sources for reuse, intended uses and users of ontology, and ingredients for validation and verification of ontology, etc. Figure 3 shows template of the ORSD. The ORSC phase is divided into a number of activities to capture the required knowledge and answers the above questions. Figure 4 depicts the sequence of execution of the activities.

4.3.1. Ontology requirements specifications

Ontology requirements specifications (ORSs) summarizes the features and capabilities that the ontology would have to include, such as the ability to collect customer orders online or the ability for suppliers to receive inventory information as orders are placed and sales are made, etc. Users, DEs, and ODT work closely to carry out this activity by taking a set of ontological needs as input for identifying the ontological requirements. In this early stage, ODT would also look for already developed and potentially reusable ontologies as a starting point for the development of the domain ontology. Ontological requirements can be classified as non-functional requirements and functional

Ontology Requirements Specifications Document		
1	Purpose and Scope and Level of Formality	
	Main goals and objectives of the ontology should be defined in terms that what are the main functions or roles that that the ontology should provided in a domain of interest. The general coverage and the degree of detail of the ontology should be defined. The level of formality, and possible description languages and tools for the ontology development should be determined.	
2	Uses and End-Users	
	The intended uses and intended users of the ontology should be outlined. The application use cases determining the existing or prospective applications that might use the ontology presently or in the future.	
4	Relevant Ontologies and Components for Reuse	
	Interfaces and references to other existing relevant ontologies and components (prior, ancestor, descendent, neighbor, competing, and conflicting ones etc.) are determined, investigated, and outlined.	
5	Domain Lexicon	
	The collection of terminology mostly used in the domain of interest.	
6	Ontology Requirements	
	A Non-Functional Requirements	
	The general requirements or aspects that the ontology should fulfill, including optionally priorities for each requirement. Non-functional requirements are not related to the ontology content.	
	B Functional Requirements	
	Functional requirements are content specific requirements which refer to the particular knowledge to be represented in the ontology.	
	A Groups of Competency Questions	
	The content specific requirements that the ontology should fulfill in the form of groups of competency questions and their answers, including optional priorities for each group and for each competency question.	
7	Domain Glossary	
	The information definitions of the terms mostly used in the domain of interest that are taken from competency questions and their answers, and domain lexicon.	
8	Prioritizing Requirements and Use Cases Modeling	
	Assign priorities to competency questions and developing use cases for modeling requirements in competency questions.	

Figure 3. Template of ontology requirements specifications document ORSD.

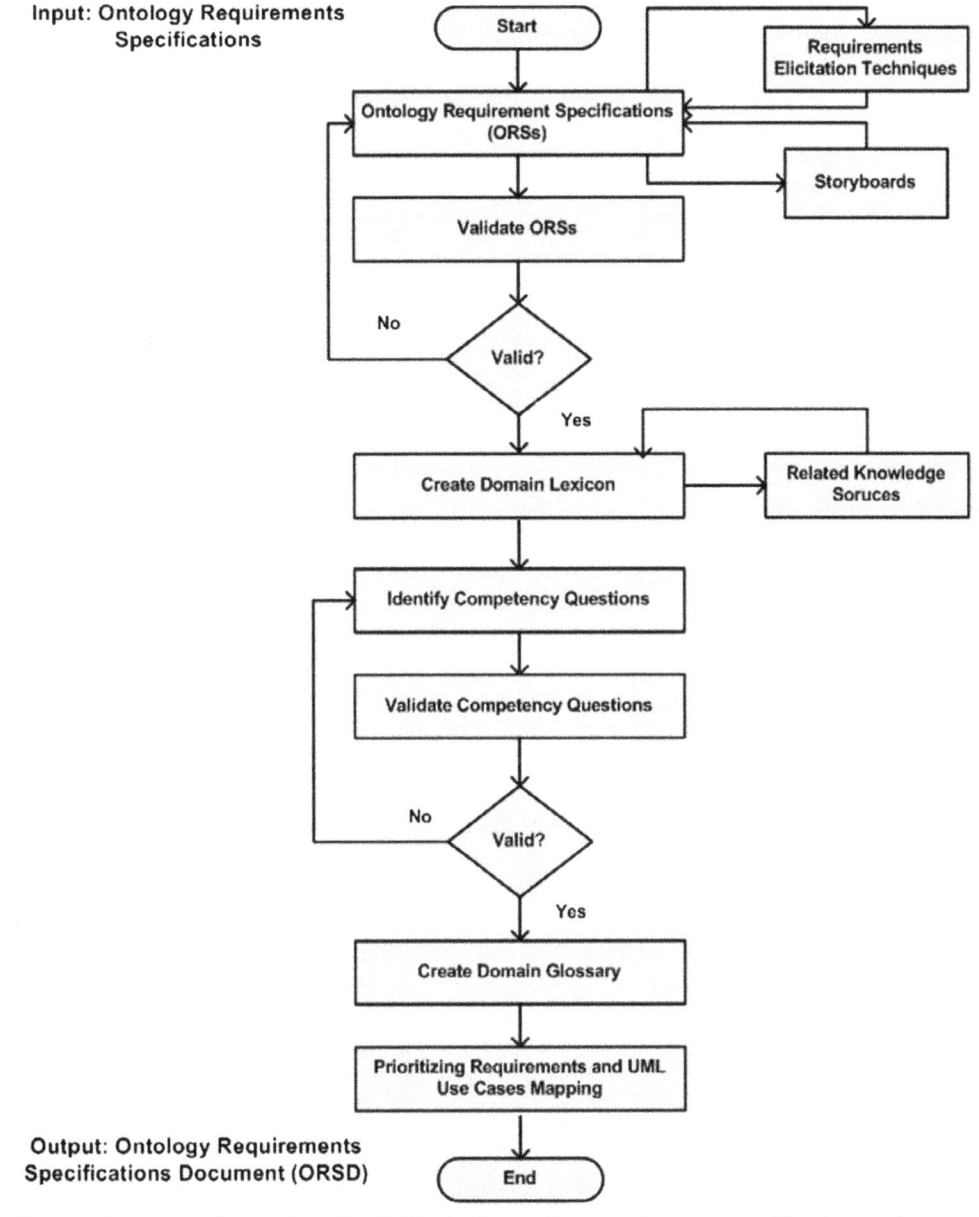

Figure 4. Sequence of execution of activities in the ontology requirements specifications and conceptualization phase.

requirements (Suarez-Figueroa & Gomez-Perez, 2009). Non-functional requirements are general requirements that the ontology should fulfill and are not related to the contents of ontology. Functional requirements are content-specific requirements which refer to the particular knowledge to be represented in ontology. Standard software engineering requirements elicitation methods (e.g. interviews, case studies, and simulation) can be employed in this activity to gather ontological requirements from DEs, and end-users. The DEs can be asked to write storyboards (narratives for modeling contexts and situations) by sketching sequence of activities that take place in different scenarios in the domain of interest. Technically, a storyboard corresponds to a particular scenario that is realizing one or more business purposes. In the context of our WPO, a storyboard would sound as follows:

> For downloading a research paper file, a researcher (user) sends a web page request to a web server using a URL. The web server processes the request and sends back the web page to the user browser's tab. The user analyzes the web page text, enter required information

(e.g. name and credit card number etc.) in the form elements (i.e. text boxes, and radio buttons etc.), and click the download button in the form or hyperlink from the menu in the header. The file is downloaded in the user's computer default download folder and information about date and time, and location of download is recorded in the browser's download log file.

The ontological requirements gathered in this activity would enable ODT to understand and specify the following aspects of ontology.

- *Domain of Interest, Purpose, Scope, and Level of Formality of Ontology:* Understanding and confining domain of interest is essential for concentrating focus of ODT to a specific fragment of reality to be modeled (De Nicola et al., 2009). A network of ontologies could be formed if the domain is large. In the context of this research paper, the domain used to validate POEM methodology is web page that is providing consensual semantic model of contents and actions for better understanding of the domain of interest by the semantic services (i.e. intelligent agents, and SW services) to serve its users. Purpose of ontology corresponds to the business needs and business values specified in the OSRD. Scope of ontology is laid out by identifying the most important concepts and their characteristics that will push the refinement to the suitable granularity. Scope determines coverage and granularity of ontology, and ontological commitments by bringing certain parts of domain into focus while neglecting the other parts. The degree of formality of ontology determines the implementation language to be used for codifying ontology.

- *Intended Users and Uses of Ontology:* Specifying reasons to have ontology and its potential uses and users corresponds to business process (De Nicola et al., 2009). DEs and ODT together carry out this activity and would use a set of ontological needs to identify potential users of ontology (Suarez-Figueroa & Gomez-Perez, 2009). The potential users of WPO could be both humans (e.g. web developers) and automatic systems (e.g. intelligent agents). Likewise, DEs and ODT would use a set of ontological needs to identify scenarios in which ontology would be used. Scenarios correspond to applications that will use ontology and describes the requirements that ontology should contain after being formally implemented (Suarez-Figueroa & Gomez-Perez, 2009). The scenarios can be expressed in natural language or modeled in UML use cases. The potential uses of WPO could be used in applications for web page modeling, user modeling, user adaptive interaction, and web page ranking and recommendations.

4.3.2. Validating ORSs
Once ontological requirements have been specified, they would have to validate for finding any conflict between requirements, missing requirements, and contradiction between requirements. POEM uses frameworks proposed by NeOn Methodology (Suarez-Figueroa & Gomez-Perez, 2009) for validating ontological requirements.

4.3.3. Creating domain lexicon
Domain lexicon (DL) is built by collecting the terminology used in the domain of interest (De Nicola et al., 2009). The specified and validated ontological requirements would serve as the main source for DL construction. However, additional domain-related resources (e.g. research papers, technical reports, glossaries, thesauri, standards, web resources, and relevant lexicons and ontologies) could also be contacted for gathering relevant terms into DL. The process of extracting and collecting of terms can be accomplished both manually and using automatic tools such as OntoLearn (Navigli & Velardi, 2004). In the WPO example, the DL is formed by extracting and collecting terms mainly from the relevant domain documents (i.e. research papers, books, technical reports, and web resources) and from DEs (i.e. web developers). Analysis of the information sources resulted in an extended set of DL that demanded for proper filtering. After consistently analyzing and filtering the collected terms using generic lexical database (e.g. WordNet), the DL is reduced to 293 most meaningful and specific terms. Figure 5 shows share of the different information sources in the construction of DL of WPO. An excerpt of WPO DL is reported in Table 1.

4.3.4. Create competency questions

Competency Questions (CQs) are informal (i.e. written in natural language) and conceptual-level (i.e. different from database query aiming at retrieving concepts rather than instances) questions defining ontology requirements that the ontology is needed to answer (Grüninger & Fox, 1995). CQs do not contribute to ontological commitments rather they are used to evaluate ontological commitments made by the ontology. Using the requirements gathered from DEs during interviews, end-users brainstorming, and terms gathered in DL, CQs can be outlined that could be used to evaluate the ontological commitments (i.e. coverage, consistency, and depth) during ontology testing process (De Nicola et al., 2009). To increase understandability, the knowledge workers can list the CQs into several groups either manually or automatically using tools such as MindMap and Cicero. CQs should be grouped in such a way that each category should contain questions specific to a particular feature of ontology. Once CQs are grouped, the next task is to validate the CQs to find any conflict between CQs, missing CQs, and continuation in CQs. This task is performed by end-users and DEs by taking a set of grouped CQs and answers at a time, and decides the validity of CQs using the gathered ontological requirements. Ontology Competency Questions Document (OCQD) should be produced containing the identified CQs and their respective answers for helping in further validations. In the WPO, total 53 CQs are identified and an excerpt of the CQs is presented in Table 2.

4.3.5. Creating domain glossary

Domain glossary (DG) is built by assigning informal definitions (i.e. natural language sentences) to the terms in a domain of interest for conceptualization purposes (De Nicola et al., 2009). The ODT carry out this task by taking DL, and CQs and their answers as input for identifying a list of the mostly

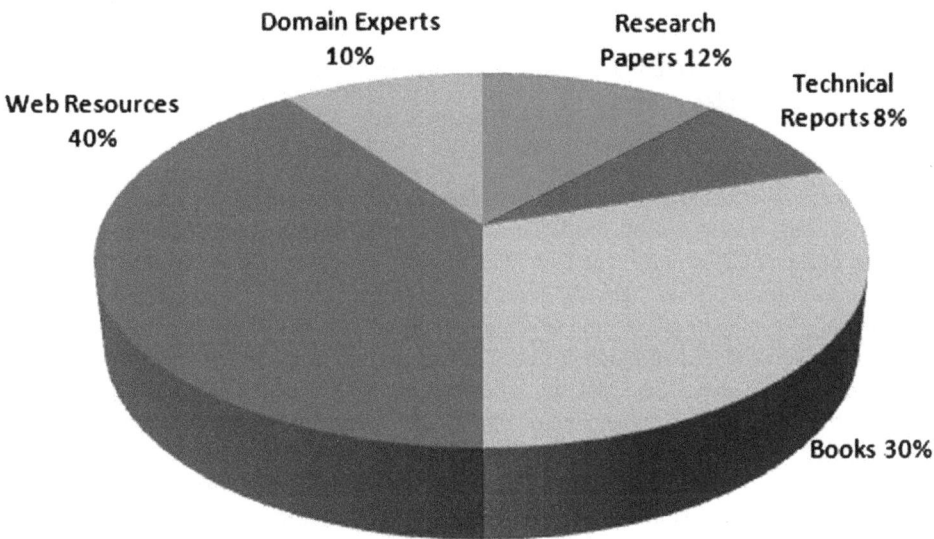

Figure 5. Share of data sources in WPO lexicon.

Table 1. An excerpt of the WPO domain lexicon				
WPO domain lexicon				
Web page	Title	Header	Footer	Hyperlink
Form	Button	Text box	Text	Breadcrumb
Border	Chat room	Comment	Web feed	Side bar
Label	Accordion	Tab	Audio	Video
Frame	Menu	Bookmark	Text	Metadata
URL text	Header image	Header text	Hyperlink URL	Frame scrolling
Label text	Element name	Footer menu	Footer text	Frame type

No.	WPO competency question
Table 2. An excerpt of the WPO competency questions	
CQ1	What is web page about?
CQ2	What is the title of web page?
CQ3	What is the URL of web page?
CQ4	What is visit time and date of a web page?
CQ5	How much time a user has spent on a web page?
CQ6	What type of multimedia a web page has?
CQ7	From which page picture X has been downloaded?
CQ8	Is web page is bookmarked?
CQ9	What type of menu is used in web page?
CQ10	What is the target URL of a hyperlink?
CQ11	Which activity would have to be performed before a user bookmarking web page?
CQ12	Is web page has breadcrumb?
CQ13	What are the tags associated with web page?

used terms and assigning one or more definitions to each term (Suarez-Figueroa & Gomez-Perez, 2009). DL and CQs should be used for extracting terminology (i.e. nouns, verbs, and adjectives) that could be used for formally representing concepts, attributes, and relations in ontology. Terminology extracted from answers of the CQs would be representing objects in the universe of discourse that could represent instances in ontology. Definitions to terminology should be assigned using domain-specific lexical databases and general lexical databases (e.g. WordNet) and common understandings of DEs and users. The WPO contains 90 entries in its DG at the time of writing this paper and an excerpt of the DG is presented in Table 3.

4.3.6. Prioritize requirements

The goal of this activity is to assign different priority levels to the different requirements identified in the different CQs groups (Suarez-Figueroa & Gomez-Perez, 2009). Users, DEs, and ODT carry out this task by taking group of CQs as input and assigning priorities to each group of CQs and to each CQ within a group. Prioritizing CQs will help ODT in identifying that which of the requirements should be addressed during the early iterations and which ones can be postponed. This specification would further guide the planning and development activities. If not prioritized, the team will model all of the requirements at the same time. UML use cases can be used to model CQs specifying the expected use of the ontology. The application of UML in OE is already shown in (Guizzardi, Herre, & Wagner, 2002) and found useful. In the ontologies, use cases would correspond to knowledge paths in ontology that would be followed for achieving business operations and addressing CQs. Use cases corresponding to particular CQs would be prioritized accordingly. Figure 6 shows a use case model and its corresponding CQ from the WPO.

4.4. Ontology project planning and scheduling

A successful ontology building project would deliver ontology according to the requirements of organization within the specified time and cost constraints. To properly manage OE project, ontology project planning and scheduling (OPPS) are related activities to be carried before formally starting ontology development. ORSD and other potential knowledge resources (i.e. historical data used for project planning and scheduling) serve as input to the OPPS phase. OPPS is the process of scoping, planning, staffing, organizing, directing, and controlling the development of an acceptable ontology at a minimum cost and within a specified time frame. A top-level view of OPPS process is shown in Figure 7 in algorithmic format. Application developers and ODT in collaboration with DEs and end-users carry out the task of defining an effective OPPS framework for OE project. The output of the phase is Ontology Project Plan Document (OPPD) describing an overall ontology building plan and a

Term	Description
Table 3. An excerpt of WPO domain glossary	
Web page	A web document written in HTML that is connected to the world wide web and viewable by anyone connected to the internet who has a web browser
Title	A heading that names a web page and may give a brief summary of the contents of the web page
Header	Header is the top portion of a web page that contains the company name and logos. Header may also contain a menu having hyperlinks for helping users to navigate other web pages
Hyperlink	A highlighted text or picture in a web page that user can click on with a mouse to go to another place in the same or a different web page
Bookmark	A bookmark is the record of a web page containing uniform resource locator (URL) of the web page that is stored for later retrieval
Text box	Text box is a rectangle shaped graphical control element intended to enable a user to input text information to be used by the program. A text box can be either single-line text box or multi-line text box
URL	URL stands for uniform resource locator and is the address of a web page. Each page has its own unique web address (URL). URL is used by the internet to locate the web page
Clicking	The process of placing mouse cursor on an object in a web page and pressing the mouse button
Browsing	The process of exploring the world wide web by following one interesting link to another, usually with a definite objective but without a planned search strategy. Browsing is the opposite of surfing
Web feed	A web feed (or news feed) is a data format used for providing users with frequently updated content. Content distributors syndicate a web feed, thereby allowing users to subscribe to it. A web feed is also sometimes referred to as a syndicated feed

Competency Question:

CQ11 - *What is the activity performed by a user before bookmarking a web page?*

Use Case Model:

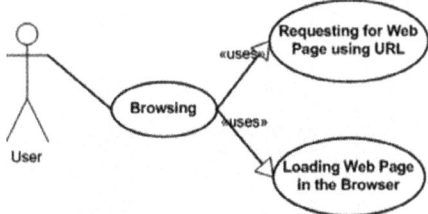

Figure 6. A use case model along with the corresponding CQ.

schedule strategy for monitoring and controlling the development and integration processes. The template of OPPD is shown in Figure 8. The OPPS phase can be mainly divided into two activities: ontology project planning and ontology project scheduling. Figure 9 shows the sequence of execution of the activities.

4.4.1. Determine ontology project planning

Objective of the ontology project planning (OPP) is to provide a framework for ODT to make reasonable estimates of resources, costs, and schedule. These estimations are identified within limited time frame at the beginning of ontology building project and should be updated regularly as the process progresses. Firstly, OPP proceeds by understanding ontology scope which would be already defined and documented in the feasibility analysis and ORSs phases. Secondly, the OPP estimates the resources required to accomplish ontology development efforts. Figure 10 illustrates the development resources as a pyramid. Each resource is described by providing description of the resource, statement of availability, time when the resource will be required, and duration of time that the resource will be used. Human is the primary resource and the number and skill of human resources required depends on the scope of the ontology building project. Integration and reusing of

```
1. Identify ontology project scope and establish the ontology project constraints
2. Make initial assessments of the ontology project parameters and available resources
3. Define ontology project milestones and deliverables
4. While (ontology project has not been completed or cancelled loop)
5.      Draw up ontology project schedule
6.      Initiate activities according to schedule
7.      Wait (for a while)
8.      Review ontology project progress
9.      Revise estimates of ontology project parameters
10.     Update the ontology project schedule
11.     Re-negotiate ontology project constraints
12.     if ( problems arise) then
13.             Initiate technical review and possible revision
14.     End if
15. End loop
```

Figure 7. Top-level view of OPPS process.

	Ontology Project Plan Document
1	**Introduction**
	Overview of the ontology project is noted here by specifying scope of the project, functional decomposition of the ontology, performance or behavioral issues, and management and technical constraints.
2	**Project Estimates**
	The ontology project cost, effort, and time (duration) estimates are noted here. People, hardware, software, tools, and other resources required to build the ontology is also presented here.
3	**Processes and Activities**
	Overview of selecting processes and activities, mapping of processes and activities into the development model phases, setting of order of processes and activities, and establishing of resources assignments to process and activities is presented here.
4	**Risk Management**
	The ontology project risk and the approaches to manage them are presented here. Name of risk, probability, impact, and RM3 (risk mitigation, monitoring, management) is noted here.
5	**Project Schedule**
	A complete ontology project schedule comprising of framework activities and task set, functional decomposition, tasks and their dependencies, and timeline chart is presented here.
6	**Staff Organization**
	Detailed description of staff which is organized, team structure, and mechanisms for progress reporting and inter/intra team communication is outline here.
7	**Tracking and Control Mechanisms**
	Techniques to be used for ontology project tracking and control are identified here. Overview of quality assurance and control, and change management and control is presented here.
8	**Appendix**
	Supplementary information is provided here.

Figure 8. Template of ontology project plan document OPPD.

ontological and non-ontological resources in ontology development can significantly reduce time and effort costs. However, OPP must clearly reflect the level of accuracy and confidence of the reusable resources, the amount of modification required, and the nature of associated risks. Environmental resources refer to the hardware and software tools that would be required for the development and implementation of ontology. Thirdly, the OPP estimates the cost required for ontology building project. Cost estimation includes both money and efforts estimates. Ontology cost and efforts can never be exact and many variables (i.e. human, technical, environmental, and political) can affect the ultimate cost and efforts estimations of ontology building project. However, OPP can use empirical estimation models and automatic estimation tools (CASE tools) for effective estimations of cost and efforts (Pressman, 2010).

4.4.2. Determining ontology project schedule

Ontology project scheduling (OPS) is similar to software engineering project scheduling and concerned with determining the timelines to be met by ontology development processes. OPS divides ontology building process into separate tasks and determines that how these tasks would be executed. OPS estimates the calendar time required, the efforts required, and the resources required for completing each task (Sommerville, 2006). However, the tasks should not be either too small or too large. OPS schedule tasks to be executed either in sequence or in parallel in such away to optimally

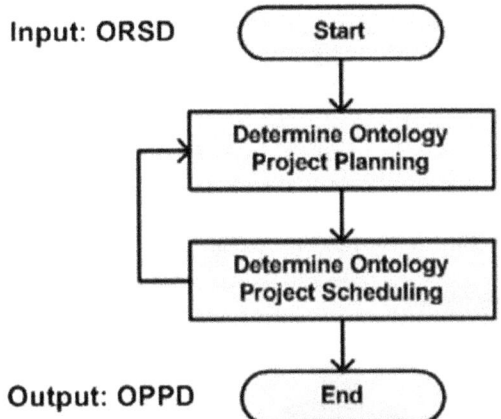

Figure 9. Sequence of execution of the activities in OPPS.

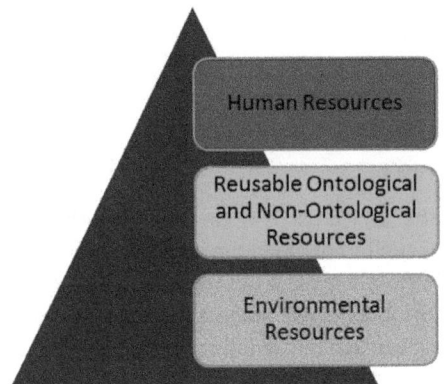

Figure 10. Development resources pyramid.

use the workforce and resources. Figure 11 illustrates the top-level view of OPS process. OPS provide mechanism for ODT to track and control a project progress by scheduling dates to which milestones and deliverable should be produced. CASE tools are developed that will take ontology building project information and produce OPS automatically in graphical notations in the shape of Gantt charts and activity networks (Sommerville, 2006). Bar chart (also called Gantt charts) shows that who is responsible for a task, the expected elapsed time for a task, and when a task is scheduled to begin and end. Activity network is a network diagram showing the dependencies between the different tasks making up a project. The initial OPS is created at the project startup phase and is refined and modified as the project progresses.

4.5. Risk analysis and management

Risk analysis and management (RAM) is a sequence of steps that helps ODT to identify and manage risks by drawing plans to minimize their effect on ontology building project. From software engineering perspectives, proper risk analysis can ensure product quality that is reasonably free of defects, delivered on time and within budget, meet requirements and expectations, and is maintainable. POEM uses proactive risk management approach where potential risks, their probability, and impacts are identified, assessed, and classified according to their importance long before any of the technical work is initiated. ODT team should try to avoid risks by actively accessing, monitoring, and managing potential risks until they are either handled or a contingency plan is prepared to handle unavoidable risks in a controlled and effective manner. POEM proposes an effective risk analysis and management framework (shown in Figure 12), which is inspired from MSF (Microsoft Solution Framework) risk management model and is a six-step logical model advocating managing current risk, planning and executing risk management strategies, and capturing knowledge for the enterprise. POEM has advantage over the other methodologies in risk management because of evaluating

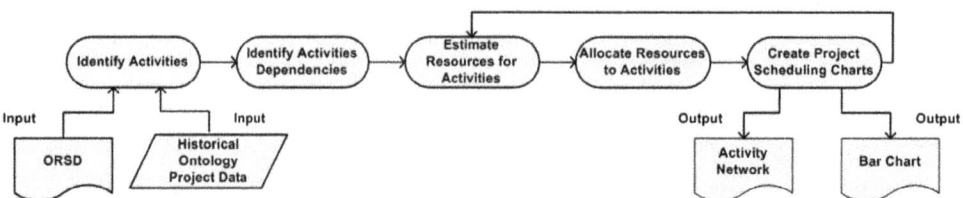

Figure 11. Top-level view of OPS process.

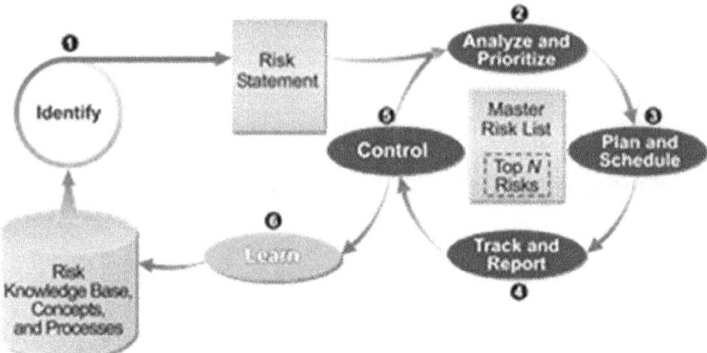

Figure 12. POEM risk management framework.

risks much earlier and providing opportunity to decide that which risk is to be handled with each cycle. POEM enables to deal with major obstacles and select alternatives in the earlier stages of the project, which is less expensive. ODT, DEs, and users work closely together to carry out risk analysis and management phase. Output of the phase will be a risk table that would be produced as an integral part of the OPPD as shown in Figure 9. Broadly, the activities to be carried out during this phase are risk identification, risk analysis, risk planning, and risk monitoring. Figure 13 illustrates the flow of execution of the activities.

4.5.1. Risk identification
Risk identification is a systematic process to specify threats to the OPP (i.e. estimates, schedule, and resource loading) (Pressman, 2010). Generic risks are easy to identify due to being potential threat to every ontology building project. Ontology-specific risks are hard to identify and can only be identified by those having clear understandings of the technology, the people, and the environment specific to the project. One way of identifying ontology-specific risks is to create a risk item checklist comprising of questions related to the categories: (1) ontology project size—overall size of the ontology to be built or modified, (2) business impact—due to constraints imposed by management or the marketplace, (3) user/DE characteristics—sophistication of the user/DE and ability of ODT to communicate with user/DE in a timely manner, (4) process definition—the degree of ontology development process definitions and being following by the ODT, (5) development environment—the availability and quality of tools to be used for building ontology, (6) technology to be built—the complexity and newness of ontology and system to be built, and (7) staff size and experience—overall technical and project experiences of ODT who do the work. Answer to these questions would help in identifying potential risks and the number of negative answers that would be directly proportional to the degree at which the project is at risk. Table 4 illustrates an excerpt of the risk identified along with corresponding categories for the WPO project.

4.5.2. Risk projection
Risk projection, also called risk estimation, attempts to determine likelihood or probability of a risk to occur and estimate the impacts and consequences associated with the risk (Pressman, 2010). Probability of a risk can be rated as very low, low, moderate, high, and very high. Impact of a risk can be rated as catastrophic, serious, tolerable, and insignificant. ODT in collaboration with technical staff workout risk projection by establishing a scale for perceiving probability of a risk, drawing

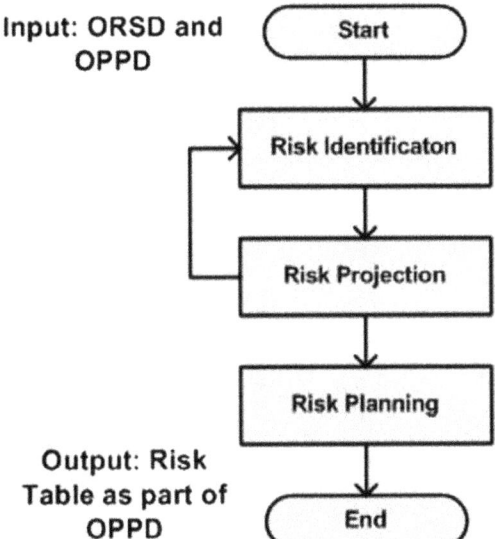

Figure 13. Sequence of execution of activities in the RAM phase.

consequences of a risk, delineating risk impacts on ontology building project and the resulting onto-logical product, and estimating accuracy of a risk projection to avoid any ambiguity. ODT can sim-plify risk projection process by developing a risk table with columns: risk ID, risk description, category, probability, impact, risk exposure, and risk planning. Probability and impact can be scaled numeri-cally where one might represent the lowest possible rate and n might represent the highest possible rate. Risk exposure is the product of these two rankings. Once the table is formed and sorted using risk exposure from high to low, the ODT can draw a cutoff line signifying the risks lying above the line are of the highest risk exposure (i.e. highest priority) and should be treated first. Risks coming below the line would be re-evaluated and treated in the second-order priority. Table 4 illustrates an excerpt of the risk table showing risk projection for the potential risk identified in the WPO project.

4.5.3. Risk planning
Risk management is concerned with developing strategies for dealing with a risk (Pressman, 2010). An effective strategy would include risk avoidance or risk management and contingency planning. For a proactive approach to risk management, risk avoidance is the best strategy by developing a risk monitoring plan to monitor factors that would provide information whether the risk is becoming more or less likely. A risk mitigation plan would be developed to either conquer or reduce the net effect of a risk. If risk mitigation plan is failed, the risk management and contingency plan is to be developed that would define strategy to deal with a risk and handle the risk smoothly and efficiently. Table 4 illustrates an excerpt of the risk planning strategies for the risks identified in the WPO project.

4.6. Ontology design and implementation
The goal of this phase is to give ontological structure to the ontological requirements gathered in the ORSD under the constraints and guidelines of OPPD. In essence, this phase takes the development process from linguistic dimension into conceptual dimension. Ontology design and ontology imple-mentation are closely related activities and the issues of one could severely affects the working of another such as implementation issues guides the decisions to be taken at the design development time. For simplicity to explain and understand, we divided this phase into two sub-phases: ontology design and ontology implementation.

4.6.1. Ontology design
Ontology design (OD) transforms the conceptual model of ontological requirements into a design model that would serve as a blueprint for ontology construction. The conceptualization phase figure

Table 4. An excerpt of the risks identified, projected, and planned in the WPO project

Risk ID	Risk description	Category	Probability	Impact	Risk exposure	Risk management planning
1	Ontology project scope and size is not stable	PS	4	3	12	Arrange efficient meetings with DEs and consult relevant domain literature
2	Possibility of recruiting staff with the skill for the project	ST	4	4	16	Arrange training sessions and developments courses for the available staff for improving their skills
3	Not sure about the potential applicability of the ontology	TC	3	4	12	Develop prototype to demonstrate feasibility
4	Reusable ontological and non-ontological components contain defects	PD	3	3	9	Replace defective components by either developing new components or make moderate changes to the available components or bought in new components of known reliability
5	Financial problems may force reduction in the ontology development project	BU	2	4	12	Prepare a brief document for the volunteer organizations showing how the project is making a very important contribution to the goals of the business domain
6	DE may propose changes in requirements that would require major design rework	PS	3	3	9	Derive traceability information to access requirements change impact and maximize information hiding in the design
7	Key and skilled staff may get ill at critical stage of the project	ST	3	3	12	Reorganize staff so that there is more overlap of work and people therefore understand each others' job
8	Lack of staff training on development tools	DE	4	3	12	Arrange training sessions and developments courses for the available staff for improving their skills

Notes: Category: PS—ontology project size, BU—business impact, CU—customer characteristic, PD—process definition, DE—development environment, TC—technology to be built, ST—staff size and skill.
Probability: 1—very low, 2—low, 3—moderate, 4—high, 5—very high.
Impact: 1—insignificant, 2—tolerable, 3—serious, 4—catastrophic.

out that what are the business needs and the design phase decides that how to build it. This is accomplished by refining the terms (representing entities, relationships, and processes) captured in the conceptualization phase, organizing the terms into conceptual hierarchies, and structuring them with attributes and axioms (De Nicola et al., 2009). Apart from devising structures and hierarchies (that could be possibly sub-ontologies) and interfaces as well as rules for commitment, mappings and translations of these conceptual constructs into "dialects" (i.e. Unified Modeling Language (UML)) are also provided in the ontology designing phase. UML has been used in several ontology building methodologies for ontology modeling (D'Antonio, Missikoff, & Taglino, 2007; De Nicola et al., 2009; Missikoff & Taglino, 2002). Researchers have demonstrated that how UML could be used to model lightweight ontologies and how UML models could be enriched by adding Object Constraint Language (OCL) expression to give explicit descriptions of specifications (Gómez-Pérez et al., 2007). UML class diagrams would represent concepts (and their attributes), relations between concepts (both taxonomic relationships and ad hoc ones), and axioms in OCL (e.g. cardinalities on object and datatype properties, and disjointness). Furthermore, UML object diagrams could be used to represent instances. Ontology development tools (e.g. Protege-2000 and WebODE) support exporting and importing of ontologies in UML format. ODT plays the key role in this phase by bringing concepts into taxonomic hierarchy but DEs can provide assistance for the required application and domain

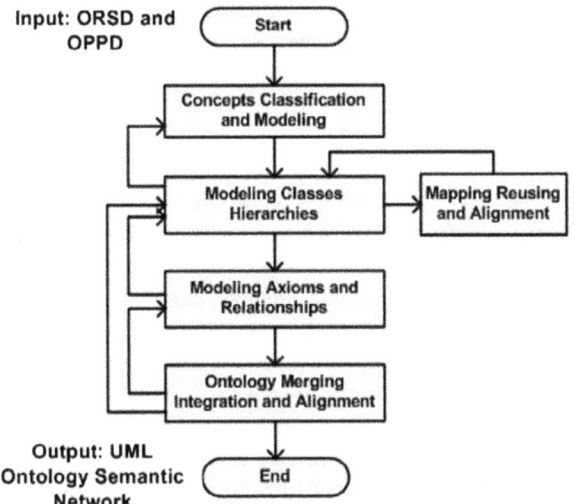

Figure 14. Sequence of execution of activities in the OD phase.

knowledge. The tasks in this phase are classified into concepts classification and modeling, modeling classes hierarchies, mapping reusing and alignment, modeling axioms and relationships, and ontology merging integration and alignment. Figure 14 shows the sequence of execution of the tasks. Output of the phase will be ontology semantic network in the UML format.

- *Concepts Classification and Modeling:* This activity starts by identifying concepts from glossary and UML use cases diagrams in the ORSD and works by classifying the concepts into different categories depending on their nature. Concepts can be classified using sameness that they have a common structure or exhibit a common structure. OPAL (Object, Process, and Actor modeling Language) (D'Antonio et al., 2007) is a UML- and an OWL-based ontology representation methodology that has provided common guidelines for classifying concepts into different categories that are deeply inspired from the primary modeling constructs of UML. These categories are business actor, business object, business process, messages, and attributes. A detailed discussion about these categories can be found at (D'Antonio et al., 2007). Before classifying concepts into categories, concepts are needed to be divided into four basis constructs (i.e. classes, object properties, datatype properties, and objects) that are necessary to complete a rich ontological representation of an observed reality.

Classes (also called concepts) in ontology are similar to UML classes that represent collections of similar entities (objects) serving the roles of business agents, business object, or business processes in a domain of discourse. Classes in a domain can be people, places, roles, things, organizational units, and occurrences or events. Classes in a domain are identified from the terms belonging to the noun or noun phrase classes of parts of speech. Classes in a domain will be related with each other due to either sharing or having some kind of semantic connection. Table 5 illustrates an excerpt of potential classes in WPO. Objects (also called instances) are occurrence of classes that are tangible and can be comprehended intellectually. In OE, classes are the logical modeling of a domain and objects are physical representation of classes. An ontology constituting classes together with a set of object forms a knowledgebase (Noy & McGuiness, 2001).

Properties represent characteristics of classes and will be used for relating classes with other classes or literals in the format of domain–range relationships pattern. Properties in a domain are identified from the terms belonging to the verb or verb phrase classes of parts of speech. In OE, properties can be either object properties or datatype properties. Object properties are similar to UML messages in a domain of discourse that represent information exchange during interactions between classes and representing relationships between instances of classes. Datatype properties are similar to UML attributes, characterizing the information structure of classes and representing relationships between instances of classes with instances of literals. A datatype property can be either atomic for modeling elementary information (e.g. URLText) or complex for modeling structured information (e.g. UserName is composed of first name, middle name, and last name). Table 5 illustrates an excerpt of object properties and datatype properties of WPO.

- *Modeling Classes Hierarchies:* In this stage, classes are organized into hierarchies that are conceptual clusters of classes using the criteria of sameness in their properties. Classes are classified into categories by first creating conceptual descriptions of categories and then classifying the classes according to the descriptions. A class hierarchy shows the existence of classes and their relationships in a logical view. A class hierarchy is created by relating classes in a category hierarchically using the generalization–specification (i.e. is-a) relations. Classes in a hierarchy are arranged in superclass–subclass pattern where superclass is general and subclass is specific. There are three ways to arrange classes in a hierarchy (Gómez-Pérez et al., 2007): (1) top-down (from general to specific that is from most abstract to most concrete), (2) bottom-up (from specific to general that is from the most concrete to the most abstract), and (3) middle-out (from the most relevant to the most abstract and most concrete). Middle-out approach tends to be more common and effective because concepts of the middle level are more informative about a domain. POEM uses middle-out approach by first identifying the salient concepts and then generalizing and specializing them. POEM encourages reusing of existing ontological and non-ontological resources. Therefore, once a candidate class is identified while constructing a class hierarchy, then mapping would be performed by searching the ontology library to find similar class in any of the existing ontologies. If yes, it will be reused via importing it in the developing ontology otherwise it would have to be engineered in the developing ontology. Alignment is not physical reusing of classes (i.e. importing of classes) rather ontology is connected with required classes in the existing ontologies via developing explicit relationships. POEM carries out this activity in accordance to NeOn Methodology (Suarez-Figueroa & Gomez-Perez, 2009) which provides a comprehensive framework for reusing ontological and non-ontological resources. The resulting class hierarchy can be extended with other UML relations such as part-of relations between classes using aggregation and composition. Conclusively, this task will convert the informal ontology representation into diagrammatic representation in the form of a set of UML class diagrams. Figure 15 illustrates an excerpt of the WPO UML class hierarchy.

- *Modeling Axioms and Relations:* The level and ability of ontologies to describe axioms and relations signifies their power. Axioms are logical assertions/constraints that are imposed by modeling reality and represent the complete theory that ontology is describing in its domain of discourse. Axioms are statement in the if-then (antecedent–consequent) format that constitutes the logical inferences which can be drawn from an assertion in a specific format. A simple example of axioms is disjointness that is classes in a category belonging to the same level are mutually disjointed (i.e. the object of one class in a disjointed set cannot be the object of another class in the same set). Properties of a class represent relationships/links of a class with other classes or literals in ontology. Linking classes using relations in an ontology exhibits that how object are related and how they interact with each other in the domain of discourse. Property restrictions (i.e. quantified, and cardinality) delegates business rules that defines rules needs to be followed while defining objects of classes in ontology (e.g. a person can be a student if he has exactly one occurrence of age property which value is greater than or equal to 5 years). In this stage, classes in a domain that are identified in concepts classification and modeling stage are needed to be enriched semantically by imposing different axioms and property restrictions from the domain of discourse. Figure 16 depicts an excerpt of relationships between the classes in WPO.

- *Ontology Merging Integration and Alignment:* POEM is iterative methodology and each iteration would produce a new incremental version of the ontology. The ontological model produced in a recent iteration needs to be merged and integrated with the ontological model produced in the previous iterations to obtain a single unified ontology that would have/include all the knowledge obtained from the domain so far. POEM supports the hypothesis of METHONTOLOGY that

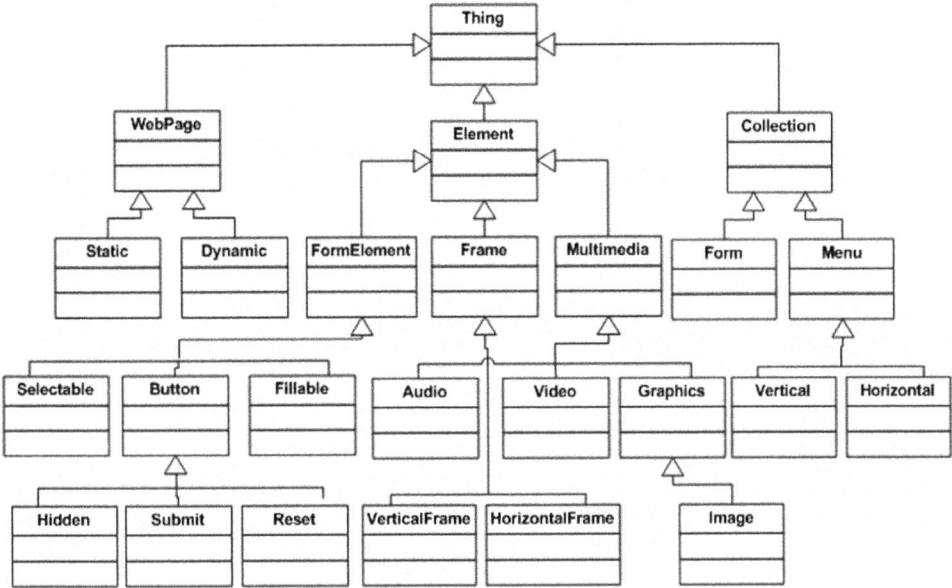

Figure 15. An excerpt of WPO class hierarchy.

integration should be carried out at knowledge level (i.e. in conceptualization) not at the symbol level (i.e. in formalization, when selecting the representation language) or implementation level (i.e. when the ontology is codified in the target language). At this stage, the ontology merging integration and alignment is performed by either simply defining relationships between the classes in new and previous versions of ontology or restructuring the class hierarchies at certain level and then defining relationships between the classes. Figure 17 illustrates the conceptual-level understanding of ontology merging integration and alignment in WPO.

4.6.2. Ontology implementation

At the ontology implementation (OI) phase, the ontology has to be codified in a formal ontology development language. This stage is concerned with transforming the conceptual ontological struc-tures created in the ontology designing phase into a formal and explicit format to be understandable by both machines and humans and directly usable by the applications. ODT plays the key role in this phase by bringing the conceptual models and designs into physical reality with minimal assistance of DEs for the required application and domain requirements. The activities in this phase are classi-fied into selection of representation language and tools, and codifying ontology. Figure 18 illustrate the sequence of execution of the tasks in this phase. Output of the activity is actual ontology code in a formal ontology representation language.

• *Selection of Representation Language and Tools:* In this task, appropriate formal representation language and tools are to be selected for the ontology development. However, certain factors related to ontology representation languages (i.e. expressiveness power, computational com-plexity of the associated reasoning, and level of acceptance within the community) as well as business requirements are needed to be considered while in selection of formal language for ontology. A number of formal languages are available for ontology developments varying in expressiveness power, computability, and decidability. Similarly, a number of automatic tools are also available that are providing features for the automatic and quick development and visu-alization of ontologies. Detailed surveys of ontology modeling languages, and OE tools and APIs are presented in (Alam et al., 2014; Corcho et al., 2003). Similarly, a number of serialization for-mats are also available for ontology developments and a detailed discuss about serialization formats can be found at (Alam, Khan, Ali, & Khusro, 2014). However, Web Ontology Language (OWL) is the W3C standard and is the most commonly used and accepted ontology

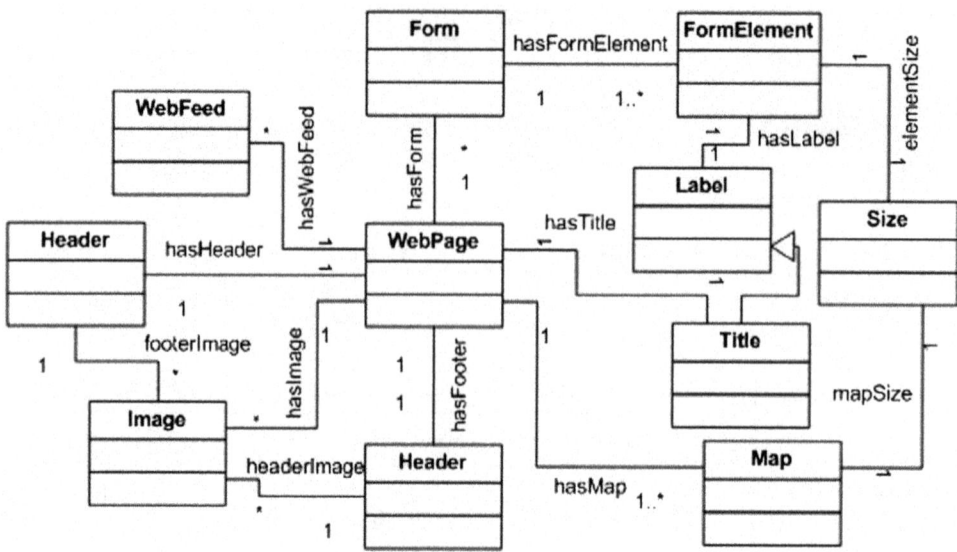

Figure 16. An excerpt of relationships between classes in WPO.

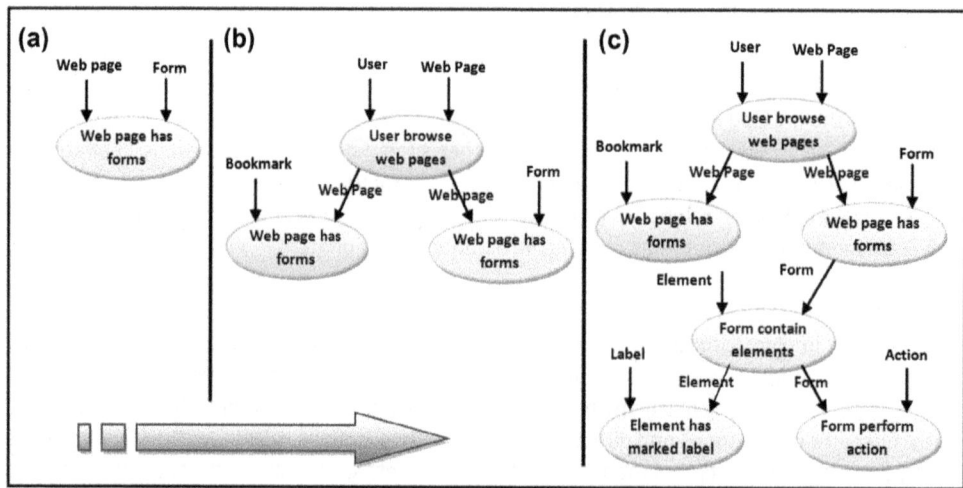

Figure 17. Conceptual-level model of merging and integration in WPO.

development language in the OE community. Similarly, Protégé is the most commonly used ontology editing tool.

• *Codifying Ontology:* In this task, ontology is codified using the selected formal ontology language and tools in accordance to the requirements gathered and designs produced. Results from sub-development cycles (regarding sub-ontologies, and previous versions) are integrated and a new version of ontology is created. The WPO is developed in OWL-DL dialect of the OWL in RDF/XML serialization format using Protégé 4.3 ontology editor. Figure 19 shows an excerpt of the WPO code in OWL.

4.7. Ontology quality testing and release

The architecture of POME results in a series of layered sub-ontologies (i.e. incremental versions) that encapsulates collaborating classes. Each of the ontological elements (i.e. sub-ontologies and classes) represents information that helps in achieving ontology requirement and business requirements indirectly. The objective of ontology quality testing is to uncover the greatest possible number of errors (i.e. arise due to classes collaborations within a sub-ontology) with a manageable amount of efforts applied over a realistic time span. Ontology quality testing is essential before releasing

Table 5. An excerpt of classes, object properties, and datatype properties of WPO

Classes

Web page	Header	Footer	Menu	Logo
Sidebar	Breadcumb	Bookmark	Image	Audio
Form	Button	Textbox	Textarea	Frame
Chatroom	Accodion	Comment	Feed	Border
URL	Text	Map	Tab	Popup
Hyperlink	Video	Submit	Column	Dynamic

Object properties

hasBreadcrumb	hasMenu	hasTab	hasURL	Accordiontext
Footerimage	Headerimage	HyperlinkURL	Hyperlinktarget	Tabmap
Logoimage	URLtext	Popupform	Sidebarmenu	hasForm
Popupform	hasTextarea	hasMap	hasComment	Commenttext
Feedfrom	hasChartroom	Tabform	Viewimage	Headertext

Datatype properties

hasTitle	hasText	hasVisittime	isSaved	Textcolor
hasName	hasValue	Menutype	isChecked	Titletext
Buttontype	isPrinted	hasColumns	Elementname	Formname
Formaction	Downloadtime	Downloadpath	Bookmarkname	Framename

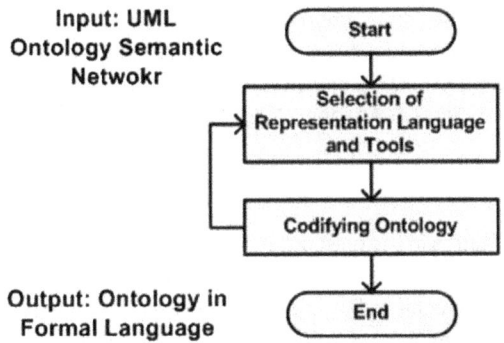

Input: UML Ontology Semantic Netwokr

Output: Ontology in Formal Language

Figure 18. Sequence of execution of activities in OI tasks.

ontology to customer for reducing the chances of experiencing frustrations associated with poor quality ontology. A set of quality matrices for ontology quality testing has been proposed in (Burton-Jones, Storey, Sugumaran, & Ahluwalia, 2005). The activities in this phase are classified into syntactic quality testing, semantic quality testing, pragmatic quality testing, and ontology release. Figure 20 illustrate the sequence of execution of the activities in this phase. Output of the phase is a tested incremental version of ontology and ontology release notes.

4.7.1. Syntactic quality testing

Syntactic quality testing employs measures to estimate the quality of ontology according to how it is written (Burton-Jones et al., 2005). Syntactic quality is measured in lawfulness and richness. Lawfulness is the degree to which ontology language syntactic rules have been followed. Richness is the degree to which features in ontology language are exploited for ontology development, the more the better. A set of quality matrices has been proposed and reused for syntactic quality testing from both software engineering and OE communities (Duque-Ramos et al., 2014). Matrices from software engineering community include response for a class, number of ancestor class, and number of children per class. Matrices from OE include lack of cohesion in method, property richness, attribute richness, and inheritance relationship richness. OntoQA (Tartir & Arpinar, 2007) is a

```
<Class rdf:about="&WPO;WebPage"/>
<Class rdf:about="&WPO;Dynamic">
    <rdfs:subClassOf rdf:resource="&WPO;WebPage"/>
    <disjointWith rdf:resource="&WPO;Static"/>  </Class>
<Class rdf:about="&WPO;Dynamic">
    <rdfs:subClassOf rdf:resource="&WPO;WebPage"/>
    <disjointWith rdf:resource="&WPO;Static"/>  </Class>
<Class rdf:about="&WPO;Element"/>
<Class rdf:about="&WPO;FormElement">
    <rdfs:subClassOf rdf:resource="&WPO;Element"/>  </Class>
<Class rdf:about="&WPO;Button">
    <rdfs:subClassOf rdf:resource="&WPO;FormElement"/>  </Class>
<Class rdf:about="&WPO;Hidden">
    <rdfs:subClassOf rdf:resource="&WPO;Button"/>  </Class>
<Class rdf:about="&WPO;Normal">
    <rdfs:subClassOf rdf:resource="&WPO;Button"/>  </Class>
<Class rdf:about="&WPO;Reset">
    <rdfs:subClassOf rdf:resource="&WPO;Button"/>  </Class>
<Class rdf:about="&WPO;Submit">
    <rdfs:subClassOf rdf:resource="&WPO;Button"/>  </Class>
```

Figure 19. An excerpt of WPO classes declarations in OWL.

feature-based ontology quality testing tool that uses the combination of these matrices for evaluating and analyzing ontologies from both schema and knowledge base perspective. Results of syntactic quality testing of WPO (i.e. after 2 iterations) using OntoQA is shown in Table 6. Interpretation of the matrices (i.e. using the information provided in (Tartir & Arpinar, 2007)) shows satisfactory results for WPO syntactic quality testing.

4.7.2. Semantic quality testing
Semantic quality testing evaluates the meaning of terms in the ontology in terms of interoperability, consistency, and clarity (Burton-Jones et al., 2005). Interoperability measure estimates the meaning of terms (i.e. classes and properties) in ontology and is achieved by checking the terms in the ontology in another independent semantic source (i.e. generic lexical database such as WordNet) using the formula $EI = W/C$ here C is the total number of terms used in the ontology and W is the number of terms having senses in WordNet. Clarity measures the context clarity of the terms in ontology and is estimated using the formula $CL = (\sum 1/A_i)/W$; here, A_i shows the number of meanings of every interoperable term in WordNet. Consistency measures whether terms have consistent meaning in ontology by finding any contradiction (i.e. declaring of an object of two disjointed classes) and correct use of molding constructs. To calculate consistency, the ontology has to pass through two major tests: sub-sumption test to check whether a class is a sub-class of another class or not, and the logical consistency check to see whether a class can have any instance or not. Consistency checking of the ontology can be achieved using a reasoner (e.g. Fact++, HerMiT, Pellet, and RacerPro). A reasoner works by taking a manually created class hierarchy (called asserted ontology) to automatically compute an inferred class hierarchy (called inferred ontology) using the descriptions of classes and relationships. Figure 21 depicts a snippet of the WPO asserted and inferred class hierarchies after reasoning using Fact++ in Protégé 4.3.

4.7.3. Pragmatic quality testing
Pragmatic quality testing evaluates the usefulness of ontology for its users irrespective of syntax and semantics (Burton-Jones et al., 2005). Pragmatic quality of ontology is measured in its accuracy, comprehensiveness, and relevancy. Accuracy checking determines that the asserted knowledge in ontology agrees with the experts' knowledge in the domain. Ontology with correct definitions and

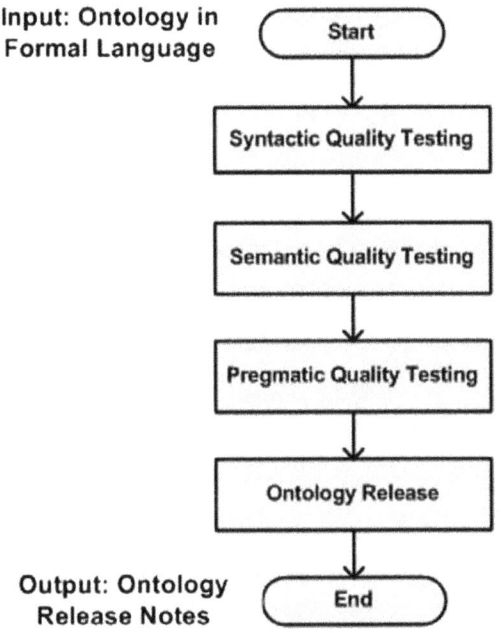

Input: Ontology in Formal Language

Output: Ontology Release Notes

Figure 20. Sequence of execution of activities in OQTR phase.

Table 6. Syntactic quality testing of WPO using OntoQA						
Ontology	Classes	Relationships	Relationships richness	Inheritance richness	Tree balance	Class richness
WPO	85	153	66.81	2.92	1.56	83.12

descriptions of classes, properties, and individuals will result into high accuracy. Recall and precision rate are the two primary measures used for evaluating the accuracy of ontology (Maynard, Peters, & Li, 2006). The accuracy of ontology can be measured by defining use cases. Use cases are concerned with CQs that are used for creating SPARQL queries to query ontology for retrieving relevant information. For example, a user might be interested in finding the URL of a particular web page which is the CQ3 of the WPO. A SPARQL query can be created on the basis of this use case and issued to WPO to answer with its content as shown in Figure 22. Relevance refers to coverage verifies that whether ontology satisfies a user's specific requirements. Relevancy checking, however, requires prior knowledge about a user's needs. Relevance can be checked in two ways: (1) semantically annotation and mapping of UML diagrams with the ontology contents by the DEs, and (2) using CQs to retrieve specific answers from the ontology contents. The second method is similar to querying ontology using SPARQL queries. Comprehensiveness refers to completeness and is a measure of the size of the ontology that whether the ontology satisfies the requirements and constraints of the problem it was meant to solve. Larger ontologies are more likely complete representation of their domains and provide more knowledge to their users. Comprehensiveness of the ontology can be evaluated using the domain goals, coverage of the ontology, and the degree of response to CQs.

4.7.4. Ontology release
Once ontology is thoroughly tested and approved against the specification provided in the requirements, it could be released for applications' uses. Like software engineering, ontology release notes documents should be produced at this stage that is shared with users, customers, and organizations. There is no standard format for release notes to be followed throughout the industry. However, ontology release notes details the general information and key issues about the current ontological version. The general information includes purpose, version number, type of release (e.g. final or not final release), release date, several statistics (e.g. number of classes, number of object properties,

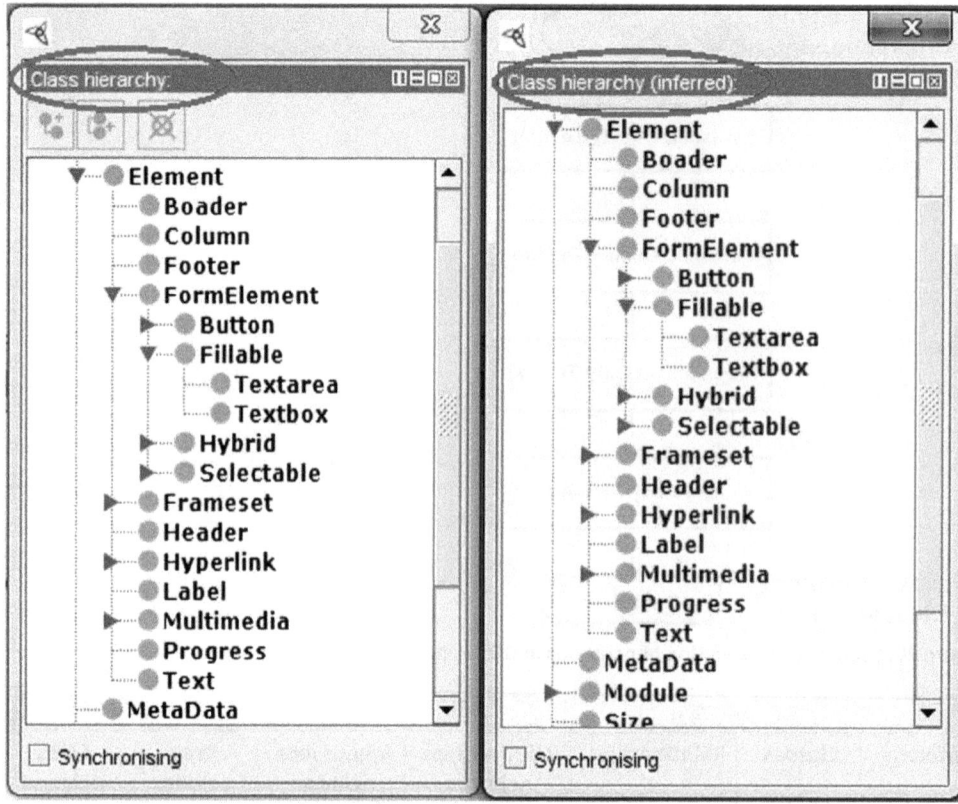

Figure 21. Asserted and inferred WPO class hierarchies after reasoning.

and number of datatype properties) about the total and newly added content, refactoring, license type, tests results and tests procedures, and potential applications about ontology. Key issues include the problems and errors identified in the testing process, bugs fixed, and novel methods of operations (e.g. how to perform a search process) about ontology. Ontology release notes are to be written by the ODT.

4.8. Ontology evaluation and feedback

After cold tests, the incremental version of ontology is provided for users' experiences using in different applications and problem solving methods. Although, ontology would have been tested in the previous phase, there could be still the possibilities of bugs, usability issues, and room for improvements which could only be identified if ontology is used in real-world scenarios. The activities to be carried out at this phase can be broadly classified into ontology evaluation and customer feedback. Figure 23 show the sequence of execution of activities at this phase.

4.8.1. Ontology evaluation

Ontology evaluation is the process of using ontology by the users with the intention of uncovering hidden errors and uncertainties. Ontology evaluation information will be helpful for ODT in more understandings about coverage, quality, reliability, and performance of ontology. Ontology evaluation will also provide information about ontology usage analysis that would help ontology developers in determining which parts of ontology could be used the most and which are not at all, and which parts of ontology are needed to be updated, deleted, or improved. A detailed review on the importance of ontology usage analysis is presented in (Ashraf et al., 2015). Ontology evaluation can be either open evaluation or closed evaluation. Open evaluation is uncontrolled where users are allowed to use ontology for all possible use cases and application scenarios. Close evaluation is controlled evaluation where some specific use cases would be outlined for evaluation of ontology by the ODT, DEs, and end-users. POEM uses close approach due to producing ontological products in

```
Competency Question:

    CQ3 - What is the URL of Google home page?

SPARQL Query:

    PREFIX xsd: <http://www.w3.org/2001/XMLSchema#>
    PREFIX wp: <http://www.semanticweb.org/imimam/ontologies/2015/11/webpageontology#>
    SELECT ?WebPage ?Address
        WHERE        {
                            ?WebPage wp:pageName ?pageName.
                            FILTER (?pageName = "GoogleHomePage"^^xsd:string).
                            ?WebPage wp:hasURL ?URL.
                            ?URL wp:addressURL ?Address.
                        }

Answer:
```

WebPage	Address
GoogleHomePage	http://www.google.com.pk

Figure 22. Competency question and associated SPARQL query and answer.

Figure 23. Sequence of execution of activities in ontology evaluation and feedback phase.

increments where each increment would be addressing a specific aspect of ontology and the ODT and DEs would be interested in evaluation of ontology in that specific aspect (i.e. completeness, accuracy, clarity, and relevancy).

4.8.2. User feedback

User feedback is the process of collecting information about users' experiences of using ontology after the evaluation process. User feedback can be either evaluation-specific or unfolding aspects of ontology which has not yet been discovered. Different techniques have been proposed for taking and valuing user feedbacks in the field of software engineering. Criteria-based assessment is a quantitative assessment technique that is derived from ISO/IEC 9126 Software Engineering—Product Quality standard providing information about usability, sustainability and maintainability areas of a product. POEM encourages the using of the same technique for ontology evaluation and taking users' feedbacks. All that is required in the methods is the creation of questionnaire consisting of questions from each area of ontology and rating of the answer options. The summary score of each criterion will indicate clear understanding of the strength or weakness of ontology in an area.

4.9. Plan the next iteration

Testing and evaluation of incremental versions of ontology will not only determine the degree of completeness of ontology but will also highlight a number of issues that will require immediate attention from the ODT. Planning next iteration needs to detail what is to be done in the next iteration in a fine-grained way. This would be a fine-grained plan for a next single iteration and would be developed under the ontology project plan. However, it could affect the ontology project plan. The ontology project plan plans out the entire project into detailed iterations in advance but the project unfolds as iterations progresses and plans changes using the feedbacks obtained after delivery of the incremental versions of ontology. For next iteration planning, POEM uses the idea of iteration or sprint plan from agile software engineering methodology that emphasizes on changing and articulating new plan as per situations. Like agile process, POEM makes honest plans based on the users' feedbacks. However, plans should not be of short duration because that could affect the ontology project plan. Plan for the next iteration will determine the current status of the ontology project, results of the current iteration, list of scenarios and use cases that must be completed by end of the next iteration, a list of risk that must be addressed by end of the next iteration, and list of changes (i.e. bug fixes, and changes in requirements) that must be incorporated in the current version of the ontology. Output of the phase is Next Iteration Plan Document (NIPD) comprising of different sections about needs of the next iteration, tasks to be achieved in the next iteration, and objective achieved in the current iteration. Template of NIPD is shown Figure 24.

5. POEM assessment

The focus is on assessing the comprehensiveness and effectiveness of POEM. We have divided the quantitative assessments of POEM into two sessions: (1) experiment for comparing the features offered by POEM with other OE methodologies using a criterion extending IEEE standard, and (2) experiment for evaluating effectiveness of POEM by how POEM improves the quality of the result (i.e. ontologies). The sessions are separated in time and each session involves a different criteria, objective, and participants. Below we describe the experiments settings, the participants, and the criterions we have applied in order to assess POEM.

5.1. First session experiment settings and results

POEM exploits the large experiences drawn from the widely used standards in the software engineering for building SW ontologies. In order to compare POEM with different ontology building methodologies generally and web ontology building methodologies specifically, a comparison framework has been established that is majorly using the framework presented by Fernández-López and Gómez-Pérez (Gómez-Pérez et al., 2007) based on the IEEE 1074–1955 standard for software development life cycle. Two different criterions are used for comparing POEM with other sister proposals and are shown in Tables 7 and 8 respectively. The criterion included in Table 7 is of subjective features whose values are determined by contacting and analyzing the mother or relevant literature sources. The criterion included in Table 8 is empirical and an empirical study is conducted for the determination of values of the features. The subjects of the study are twenty (20) participants who are voluntarily selected from the junior researchers (i.e. master students) specializing in areas of Web Semantics and Web Engineering in the Department of Computer Science, University of Peshawar. The criterion for selection of the participants is their familiarity, understanding, and having much experience of the ontologies and OE phenomenon. Anyhow, for accurate estimations, first the students are trained with the available ontology building methodologies (including POEM) for a week and then they are asked to fill a questionnaire consisting of questions regarding the criterion features of each methodology. The questionnaire is close-ended where each question is given with four potential answer options. The options were: (1) not proposed—the criterion feature is not referenced at all, (2) proposed—the criterion feature is referenced only, (3) described—the criterion feature is included but no detailed technique is proposed, and (4) fully described—the criterion feature is include and detailed technique is proposed, respectively to cover all of the possible features in a methodology. For numerical analysis the options are weighted with 0, 1, 2, and 3 ranks respectively. The value of a criterion feature is computed by taking arithmetic mean of the corresponding answers reported by the participants using the formula shown in Equation (1) where n is the sample size ($n = 20$) and A_i is answer of the ith participant. The overall maturity of a methodology is shown in summary score that is computed by taking sum of all of criterion feature values using the formula shown in Equation (2) where m is the total count of criterions and C_i is criterion value of the ith criterion feature.

Next Iteration Plan Document	
1	**Objectives and Goals of Next Iteration**
	Objectives and goals of the next iteration are to be presented here. For example, what is to be achieved in the next iteration? etc.
2	**Need of Next Iteration**
	Factors determining the initiation of next iteration is to he presented here. For example, a reason of next iteration could be the discovery of hidden and important requirements for the ontology in the current iteration, and identification of factious units of requirements etc.
3	**Status of the Project**
	Status of the project is to be reported here. For example, on track, late, large number of problems, and requirements creep etc.
4	**Achievements and Losses of the Current Iteration**
	Overall mirror of the current iteration is to be mentioned here. It is to be stated in light of the iteration's objectives and goals. For example, schedule slip, and failed in achieving the degree of completeness etc.
5	**Test Results and User's Feedback**
	Information obtained tests (.i.e., noted in ontology release notes) and user's feedback has to be presented here. This will highlight the total quality of the current incremental version of the ontology.
6	**Recommendations for Next Iteration**
	Strategies for the next iteration are to be recommended here. It is should be pointed out that which of the next phases needs more attention?, what important set of features (.i.e., use cases, and scenarios etc.) are to be included in the next iteration?, Which type of estimation needed to be redesigned? etc.
7	**Appendix**
	Supplementary information is provided here.

Figure 24. Template of next iteration plan document NIPD.

$$Criterion\ Value = \frac{\sum_{i=n}^{i=1} Ai}{n}. \tag{1}$$

$$Summary\ Score = \sum_{i=m}^{i=1} Ci \tag{2}$$

Table 7 compares the methodologies using the construction strategy used for ontologies by the methodologies. Comparatively, POEM provides satisfactory results by following approaches that are most commonly supported by the researchers and practitioners for the ontology engineering. For example, POEM is using the prevailing evolving life cycle model, using the most commonly used middle-out approach for identifying concepts in ontology taxonomy, and supporting incremental-based development which grows a developing ontology by layers and new definitions would be included when a new version is planned, etc. Rest of the information in the table are self-explanatory.

Table 8 empirically compares the methodologies using an extended version of the framework proposed by the IEEE 1074–1995 standard. The framework is extended with certain additional features especially project management (e.g. project planning and scheduling, risk analysis, and merging and alignment) to provide an extended comparison. POEM realizes the complexity of an SW ontology building project and incorporates pre/post project management activities equally to core development activities. POEM suggest the proper ontology project initiation, feasibility analysis, project planning and scheduling, risk analysis and management, taking users' feedback, laying plan for the next incremental version, installation, maintenance, and retirement that makes POEM advantageous over its competitors especially METHONTOLOGY and UPON. Particularly, the risk analysis and management provides a measuring tool to both ODT and DEs that earlier methodologies do not have. Another advantage is, like UPON, POEM has strong roots in UML and suggests using of UML tools (e.g. Rational Rose, and Microsoft Visio) for diagramming and documentation for ontology requirements and designs, etc. Another broad aspect of POEM is its milestone- and deliverable-oriented nature emphasizing on the production of enough documentations at each phase and activity (properly approved by the ontology quality assurance group) for helping ODT and DEs in understanding, guiding, and control the ontology building process.

Table 7. Comparison POEM with earlier methodologies using construction strategy

Methodologies	Details of methodology	Recommendation of formalization	Strategy for building applications	Strategy for identifying concepts	Recommended life cycle	Reusing existing ontologies	Collaborative development	Use of core ontology	Interoperability support
Uschold	Low	None	Application independent	Middle-out	Non-proposed	Yes	No	No	No
TOVE	Medium	Yes (Logic)	Application semi-independent	Middle-out	Evolving prototypes or Incremental	No	No	No	No
METH-ONTOLOGY	High	None	Application independent	Middle-out	Evolving prototypes	Yes	No	Depends on the available resources	No
KACTUS	Low	None	Application dependent	Top-down	Evolving prototypes	Yes	No	No	No
SENSUS	Low	None	Application semi-independent	Top-down	Non-proposed	No	Yes	Yes	Yes
On-to-Knowledge	Low	None	Application dependent	Top-down Bottom-up Middle-out	Incremental	Yes	No	Depends on the available resources	No
UPON	High	None	Application dependent	Middle-out	Incremental	No	No	No	No
Vanitha	Low	None	Application independent	Top-down	Evolving	Yes	No	Depends on the available resources	No
Noy	Low	None	Application independent	Top-down	Non-proposed	Yes	No	No	No
Kalyanpur	Low	Yes (Logic)	Application dependent	Top-down	Non-proposed	Yes	No	No	No
POEM	High	None	Application independent	Middle-out	Incremental	Yes	No	Depends on the available resources	Yes

Table 8. Comparison of POEM with earlier methodologies using extended IEEE 1074–1955 framework

Feature		Uschold	TOVE	KACTUS	METH-ONTOLOGY	SENSUS	On-To-Knowledge	UPON	Vanitha	Noy	Kalyanpur	POEM
Project management processes	Project initiation	0	0	0	0	0	1	0	0	0	0	1
	Project monitoring and control	0	0	0	1	0	1	0	0	0	0	2
	Ontology quality management and assurance	0	0	0	1	0	1	0	0	0	0	1
	Project planning and scheduling	0	0	0	1	0	2	0	0	0	0	2
	Risk analysis	0	0	0	0	0	0	0	0	0	0	2
Ontology development-oriented processes	Pre-development processes — Feasibility study	0	0	0	0	0	2	0	0	0	0	1
	Environment study	0	0	0	0	0	1	1	0	0	0	1
	System (resources) allocation	0	0	0	0	0	0	0	0	0	0	1
	Development processes — Requirements specification	1	3	1	3	1	3	3	0	0	1	3
	Design	0	3	1	3	0	1	3	1	1	1	3
	Formalization	0	3	2	2	0	2	2	0	0		3
	Implementation	1	2	1	3	2	2	3	0	0	0	3
	Post-development processes — Installation	0	0	0	0	0	0	0	0	0	0	1
	Operation	0	0	0	0	0	1	0	0	0	0	0
	Support/feedback	0	0	0	0	0	0	0	0	0	0	2
	Maintenance	0	0	0	1	0	1	1	0	0	0	1
	Retirement	0	0	0	0	0	0	0	0	0	0	0
Ontology support activities	Knowledge acquisition	1	1	0	3	0	2	3	0	0	0	3
	Evaluation	1	3	0	3	0	1	2	0	0	0	3
	Ontology configuration management	0	0	0	2	0	1	0	0	0	0	2
	Documentation	1	1	0	3	0	2	1	0	0	0	3
	Training	0	0	0	0	0	0	0	0	0	0	1
	Integration	1	1	1	1	0	1	0	1	1	1	2
	Merging and alignment	1	0	1	1	0	1	1	1	1	1	2
Summary score		7	17	7	28	3	26	20	3	3	4	43

Notes: Ranks: 0—Not proposed, 1—Proposed, 2—Described, 3—Fully described.

5.2. Second session experiment settings and results

For effectiveness assessment of POEM, another empirical experiment is designed for the second session. The subjects of the second session are 15 participants who are either having substantial experience or directly involved in developing ontologies using POEM including ontology developers mainly PhD students, DEs, and end-users. The data for the empirical experiment is collected from the participants using a questionnaire consisting of 30 questions. Questions in the questionnaire are propositions whoes answers are selected from a 5-point Likert-scale, ranging from "strongly disagree" to "strongly agree." The questions describing the methods and measures for assessing effectiveness of the POEM are included in the questionnaire to exploit experiences of the personals and characteristics of the ontologies developed using POEM. The questions analyzes POEM with respect to its neutrality, coverage of problem, usability, usefulness, solving tasks faster, modeling mistakes, results quality, and using of software engineering experiences for OE. Table 9 summarizes statistics of the participants' responses to the questions. About 73.78% of the participants (31.56% strongly agree and 42.22% agree) agreed in effectiveness of POEM and showed their confidence, whereas, only 17.11% of the participants (6.89% strongly disagree and 10.22% disagree) did not.

The data collected using Likert-scale is of ordinal scale. With ordinal scale, the order of the values is important and significant but the difference between each one is not really known. For analyzing Likert-scale data with descriptive statistics, we combined the five response categories (i.e. strongly disagree, disagree, neutral, agree, and strongly agree) into two nominal categories (i.e. disagree, and agree) for allowing to carry out Chi-Square test. Table 10 shows the distribution of response categories into nominal categories and their percentage values in the nominal categories and in the total. To check whether POEM provides an effective approach for developing SW ontologies, we have performed a Chi-Square test on the data collected in the second session using SPSS 16.0. The null and alternative hypotheses are respectively:

H_0: POEM is not an effective methodology for SW ontology engineering.
H_1: POEM is an effective methodology for SW ontology engineering.

Table 11 shows results of Chi-Square test, where Pearson Chi-Square statistic χ^2 = 71.20, and $p < 0.001$. The null hypothesis is rejected, since $p < 0.05$ (i.e. in fact $p < 0.001$). Therefore, the alternative hypothesis is significant, which signifies that POEM is an effective methodology for SW ontology engineering.

5.3. Additional comments

Apart from the frameworks comparisons, several related valuable characteristics of POEM are observed in the process. These includes: (1) flexibility for empowering ODT in determining the development phases according to nature and complexity of ontology building project, (2) flexibility for accommodating changes at any stage of the ontology building life cycle, (3) supporting reuse of ontological and non-ontological resources to accelerate the ontology building process, increase probability of producing high quality ontological product, save time, and reduce costs, (4) blurring the difference between ontology development and ontology maintenance results into the production of a highly customizable ontological product, and (5) applicability in complex domains where information would be difficult to extract and understand, and may be not readily available. Despite potential advantages, POEM also has several weaknesses/challenges including: (1) requiring active and timely involvement and commitment from the ODT, DEs, and end-users to finish ontology building project within the defined timeframe and constraints, (2) communication and coordination skills plays major role in a project progress, (3) a confusion may arise due to informal demands of improvements after each phase—controlled mechanisms need to be develop to handle subsequent requests, (4) success of a project is highly dependent on the proper project planning and scheduling, and risk analysis and management—requiring high level of expertise to carry out these tasks, (5) correct division and estimation of a project into increments requires prior clear and complete definition of the whole requirements and applications which might not be readily available, (6) applicable

Table 9. Statistics of the participants' responses for the questions in second session

Questions * sample	Likert-scale	Frequency	Percent	Valid percent	Cumulative percent
30 *15	Strongly dis-agree	31	6.89	6.89	6.89
	Disagree	46	10.22	10.22	17.11
	Neutral	41	9.11	9.11	26.22
	Agree	190	42.22	42.22	68.44
	Strongly agree	142	31.56	31.56	100
	Total	450	100	100	

Table 10. Distribution of response categories into nominal categories and their percentage values

Groups	Group wise distribution	Likert-scale responses					Total
		Strongly disagree	Disagree	Neutral	Agree	Strongly agree	
Disagree	Count	31	46	41	0	0	118
	(%) Group disagree	26.3	39.0	34.7	0	0	100.0
Agree	Count	0	0	0	190	142	332
	(%) Group agree	0	0	0	57.2	42.8	100.0
Total	Count	31	46	41	190	142	450
	(%) Groups	6.9	10.2	9.1	42.2	31.6	100.0

Table 11. Results of the Chi-Square test using SPSS

Descriptive statistic	Value	df	p-Value
Pearson chi-square	$4.500E2°$	4	.000
Likelihood ratio	517.832	4	.000
Linear-by-linear association	340.427	1	.000
N of valid cases	450		

°0 cells (0%) have expected count less than 5. The minimum expected count is 8.13.

but not suitable for small ontology building projects, and (7) requiring strong technological support that tools should extend either full or partial to the methodology.

6. POEM and collaborative OE

Collaborative OE is a consensus building process that involves collaboration and participation of geographically distributed stockholders to develop useful and economically feasible ontologies in an incremental and asynchronous fashion (Simperl & Luczak-Rösch, 2013). Collaborative OE is the result of intensive theoretical and research within the fields of SW and supporting technologies (e.g. Web 2.0). Stakeholders in collaborative OE use Wikis and similar communication platforms as the most important technological components to exchange ideas and discuss modeling decisions. OE methodologies varies for centralized and collaborative OE. A collaborative OE methodology has the phases (Karapiperis & Apostolou, 2006): (1) preparatory and analysis phase that defines the criteria of analysis of the domain to be captured in the ontology by agreeing stockholders on the requirements and their priorities for guiding and assessing its success, (2) anchoring phase to develop initial version of ontology that will seed next phase, (3) iterative development phase for revising ontology until consensus is reached through a consensus building technique, and (4) application phase to apply the final ontology structure to demonstrate its uses. The two fundamental roles in collaborative OE are ontology editors and ontology contributors where the former have the authority to perform changes in the ontology and the later give feedback and suggests changes based on new and evolving requirements of their particular settings (Simperl & Luczak-Rösch, 2013). POEM, by nature, is a comprehensive methodology proposing an extended list of activities that have the potential to fulfill the phases of collaborative OE methodology, as described above. However, in the context of this paper, POEM is experimented and used for centralized OE. Furthermore, the ontologies developed using POEM, are all based on centralized approach. As collaborative OE has emerged as an independent research topic in the OE community, therefore, POEM is to be experimented in the collaborative OE paradigm and may be enhanced or restructured accordingly to provide full potential support.

7. Conclusion and future work

A number of OE methodologies are reported in the literature for OE generally and web OE specifically. However, none of them has been accepted as a standard nor used commonly to be adopted as a standard in the near foreseeable future. Therefore, OE is still much of an art and not an engineering discipline. Building ontology is not the same as developing a software system, but the steps and phase used for software systems development can be equally applied to ontologies development.

In this paper, we have presented a methodology for SW ontology building called practical ontology engineering model (POEM) that leverages the large valuable experiences and concepts from the widely accepted standards of software engineering and other state-of-the-art technologies. POEM is an evolutionary incremental methodology that consists of sequence of phases and activities for guiding SW ontology building projects from inception to deployment. The strength of the methodology lies in the clear incorporation of software engineering experiences for SW ontology engineering and its vibrant support for ontology project management activities equally to the core ontology building activities within a single suit. The phases and activities within the phases are comprehensive enough to provide enough opportunities to project the need and feasibility of the project, to understand domain of interest and scope and complexity of the ontology, to properly plan and schedule the project for effective utilization of resources and skill of the experts under the project's constraints, to effectively anticipate the risk which could hinder the project and ultimately the quality of the ontology to be developed, to correctly transform conceptual models into semantic networks for achieving extreme accuracy at implementation, and to design effective testing and feedback strategies to fuel plan for the next iterations. The methodology is flexible enough allowing ODT to scale and customize the phases and activities according to the natures and contexts of projects. Theoretical and empirical evaluations of POEM have shown that POEM has all of the features of the best solutions and in some cases outclass them by providing features which they do not have. In addition to SW ontology building, PEOM has the potential application for a wide range of ontology building projects at enterprise level. Practicality of POEM has been demonstrated by developing WPO as proof-of-concept in this paper. Apart from it, POEM has been experimented in a few of the ontology building activities (e.g. used in the ontology building project for supporting the automation of hospital management systems of KP, Pakistan) of the WISE (Web Information and System Engineering) research group projects at the University of Peshawar. POEM, however, is a pragmatic approach and do not claim to be an orthogonal, complete, and universally acceptable one. It, therefore, needs attention from the academia and industry for its usage in technically high and large scale ontology building projects to effectively evaluate its strengths and weaknesses.

POEM has almost all of the phases and activities that are needed for collaborative OE, but focused on centralized OE in this paper. In the future, we are considering to use POEM within the collaborative OE and may integrating the missing collaborative OE activities within the POEM to provide full potential support.

Acknowledgment
This research work has been undertaken by the first author as a partial fulfillment of PhD degree with support of the Higher Education Commission (HEC) of Pakistan.

Funding
The authors received no direct funding for this research.

Author details
Shaukat Ali[1]
E-mail: shoonikhan@upesh.edu.pk
Shah Khusro[1]
E-mail: khusro@upesh.edu.pk
ORCID ID: http://orcid.org/0000-0002-7734-7243
[1] Department of Computer Science, University of Peshawar, Peshawar 25120, Pakistan.

Note
1. ODT would consist of personals belonging to the different groups such as KEs, ontology developers, and project managers

References
Alam, F., Ali, S., Khan, M. A., Khusro, S., & Rauf, A. (2014). A comparative study of RDF and topic maps development tools and APIs. *BUJICT Journal, 7*(1), 1–12.

Alam, F., Khan, M. A., Ali, S., & Khusro, S. (2014). The jigsaw of resource description framework (RDF) and topic maps serialization formats: A survey. *Proceedings of the Pakistan Academy of Sciences, 51*, 101–114.

Ashraf, J., Chang, E., Hussain, O. K., & Hussain, F. K. (2015). Ontology usage analysis in the ontology lifecycle: A state-of-the-art review. *Knowledge-Based Systems, 80*, 34–47. http://dx.doi.org/10.1016/j.knosys.2015.02.026

Astrova, I., & Stantic, B. (2005). *An HTML-form-driven approach to reverse engineering of relational databases to ontologies*. Paper Presented at the Databases and Applications. Retrieved from http://dblp.uni-trier.de/db/conf/dba/dba2005.html#AstrovaS05

Benslimane, S., Malki, M., Rahmouni, M., & Rahmoun, A. (2008). Toward ontology extraction from data-intensive web sites: An HTML forms-based reverse engineering approach. *The International Arab Journal of Information Technology, 5*, 34–44.

Bernaras, A., Laresgoiti, I., & Corera, J. M. (1996). *Building and reusing ontologies for electrical network applications*. Paper presented at the 12th European Conference on Artificial Intelligence ECAI'96. Retrieved from http://dblp.uni-trier.de/db/conf/ecai/ecai96.html#BernarasLC96

Breitmann, K. K., Casanova, M. A., & Truszkowski, W. (2007). *Semantic web: Concepts*. London: Springer-Verlag.

Burton-Jones, A., Storey, V. C., Sugumaran, V., & Ahluwalia, P. (2005). A semiotic metrics suite for assessing the quality of ontologies. *Data & Knowledge Engineering, 55*, 84–102. http://dx.doi.org/10.1016/j.datak.2004.11.010

Casely-Hayford, L. (2003). *A comparative analysis of methodologies, tools and languages used for building ontologies*. Warrington: CCLRC Daresbury Laboratories.

Corcho, O., Fernández-López, M., & Gómez-Pérez, A. (2003). Methodologies, tools and languages for building ontologies, Where is their meeting point? *Data & Knowledge Engineering, 46*, 41–64. http://dx.doi.org/10.1016/S0169-023X(02)00195-7

D'Antonio, F., Missikoff, M., & Taglino, F. (2007). *Formalizing the OPAL eBusiness ontology design patterns with OWL*. Paper presented at the IESA. Retrieved from http://dblp.uni-trier.de/db/conf/iesa/iesa2007.html#DAntonioMT07

De Nicola, A., Missikoff, M., & Navigli, R. (2009). A software engineering approach to ontology building. *Information Systems, 34*, 258–275. http://dx.doi.org/10.1016/j.is.2008.07.002

Dennis, A. (2012). *Systems Analysis and Design* (5th ed.). Hoboken, New Jersey, NJ: Wiley Publishing.

Duque-Ramos, A., Boeker, M., Jansen, L., Schulz, S., Iniesta, M., & Ferna'ndez-Breis, J. T. S. (2014). Evaluating the good ontology design guideline (GoodOD) with the ontology quality requirements and evaluation method and metrics (OQuaRE). *PLoS ONE, 9*(8), 1–14.

Ferreira, C. R., Marques, P., Martins, A. L., Rita, S., Grilo, B., Araújo, R., ... Pinto, H. S. (2007). Ontology design risk analysis. In R. Meersman, Z. Tari, & P. Herrero (Eds.), *On the move to meaningful internet systems 2007: OTM 2007 workshops: OTM confederated international workshops and posters, AWeSOMe, CAMS, OTM academy doctoral consortium, MONET, OnToContent, ORM, PerSys, PPN, RDDS, SSWS, and SWWS 2007, Vilamoura, Portugal, November 25–30, 2007, Proceedings, Part I* (pp. 522–533). Berlin: Springer, Berlin.

Gómez-Pérez, A., Fernández-López, M., & Corcho, O. (2007). *Ontological Engineering: With examples from the areas of knowledge management, e-Commerce and the semantic web. (Advanced information and knowledge processing)*. New York, NY: Springer-Verlag.

Gruber, T. R. (1993). A translation approach to portable ontology specifications. *Knowledge Acquisition, 5*, 199–220. http://dx.doi.org/10.1006/knac.1993.1008

Grüninger, M., & Fox, M. S. (1995). *Methodology for the design and evaluation of ontologies*. Paper presented at the International Joint Conference on Artificial Inteligence (IJCAI95), Workshop on Basic Ontological Issues in Knowledge Sharing. Retrieved from http://citeseerx.ist.psu.edu/viewdoc/summary?doi=10.1.1.44.8723

Guizzardi, G., Herre, H., & Wagner, G. (2002). Towards ontological foundations for UML conceptual models. In R. Meersman & Z. Tari (Eds.), *On the move to meaningful internet systems 2002: CoopIS, DOA, and ODBASE: Confederated International Conferences CoopIS, DOA, and ODBASE 2002 Proceedings* (pp. 1100–1117). Berlin: Springer, Berlin.

Hesse, W. (2005). *Ontologies in the software engineering process*. Paper presented at the Enterprise Application Integration (EAI' 05), Marburg, Germany.

Horrocks, I. (2008). Ontologies and the semantic web. *Communications of the ACM, 51*, 58–67. http://dx.doi.org/10.1145/1409360

IEEE. (1990, December 31). IEEE standard glossary of software engineering terminology. *IEEE Std 610.12-1990*, 1–84. doi: http://dx.doi.org/10.1109/IEEESTD.1990.101064. Retrieved August 25, 2015 from www.mit.jyu.fi/ope/kurssit/TIES462/Materiaalit/IEEE_SoftwareEngGlossary.pdf

Kalyanpur, A., Hashmi, N., Golbeck, J., & Parsia, B. (2004). *Lifecycle of a casual web ontology development process*. Paper presented at the WWW Workshop on Application Design, Development and Implementation Issues in the Semantic Web. Retrieved from http://dblp.uni-trier.de/db/conf/www/wwwsw2004.html#KalyanpurHGP04

Kapoor, B., & Sharma, S. (2010). A Comparative study of ontology building tools in semantic web applications. *International Journal of Web & Semantic Technology, 1,* 1–13.

Karapiperis, S., & Apostolou, D. (2006). Consensus building in collaborative ontology engineering processes. *Journal of Universal Knowledge Management, 1,* 199–216.

Lopez, M. F., Gomez-Perez, A., Sierra, J. P., & Sierra, A. P. (1999). Building a chemical ontology using methontology and the ontology design environment. *IEEE Intelligent Systems, 14,* 37–46. http://dx.doi.org/10.1109/5254.747904

Maynard, D., Peters, W., & Li, Y. (2006). *Metrics for evaluation of ontology-based information extraction.* Paper presented at the WWW, Workshop on Evaluation of Ontologies for the Web(EON). Edinburgh.

Missikoff, M., & Taglino, F. (2002). Business and enterprise ontology management with SymOntoX. In I. Horrocks & J. Hendler (Eds.), *The semantic web—ISWC 2002: First international semantic web conference Sardinia, Italy, June 9–12, 2002 proceedings* (pp. 442–447). Berlin: Springer, Berlin. http://dx.doi.org/10.1007/3-540-48005-6

Navigli, R., & Velardi, P. (2004). Learning domain ontologies from document warehouses and dedicated web sites. *Computational Linguistics, 30,* 151–179. http://dx.doi.org/10.1162/089120104323093276

Noy, N. F., & McGuiness, D. L. (2001). *Ontology development 101: A guide to creating your first ontology.* Stanford, CA: Stanford University Knowledge Systems Laboratory Technical Report KSL-01-05.

Pressman, R. (2010). *Software engineering: A practitioner's approach.* New York, NY: McGraw-Hill.

Rodrigues, F. H., Flores, C. D., & Rotta, L. N. (2015, February 7–9). *An ontology design pattern to represent universal relationships.* Paper presented at the Semantic Computing (ICSC), 2015 IEEE International Conference.

Schreiber, G. T., & Akkermans, H. (2000). *Knowledge engineering and management: the CommonKADS methodology.* London: MIT Press, Cambridge.

Simperl, E., & Luczak-Rösch, M. (2013). Collaborative ontology engineering: A survey. *The Knowledge Engineering Review, 29,* 101–131.

Sommerville, I. (2006). Software engineering: (Update) *International Computer Science* (8th ed.). Boston, MA: Addison-Wesley Longman.

Staab, S., Studer, R., Schnurr, H. P., & Sure, Y. (2001). Knowledge processes and ontologies. *IEEE Intelligent Systems, 16,* 26–34. http://dx.doi.org/10.1109/5254.912382

Stojanovic, L., Stojanovic, N., & Volz, R. (2002). *Migrating data-intensive web sites into the semantic web* (pp. 1100–1107). Paper presented at the Proceedings of the 2002 ACM symposium on Applied computing, Madrid, Spain.

Su, X., & Ilebrekke, L. (2002). *A Comparative Study of Ontology Languages and Tools.* Paper presented at the Proceedings of the 14th International Conference on Advanced Information Systems Engineering, Toronto, Ontario, Canada.

Suarez-Figueroa, M. C., & Gomez-Perez, A. (2009). *NeOn methodology for building ontology networks: A scenario-based methodology.* Paper presented at the Proceedings of the International Conference on Software, Services & Semantic Technologies (S3T 2009), Sofia, Bulgaria.

Swartout, B., Patil, R., Knight, K., & Russ, T. (1996). *Towards distributed use of large-scale ontologies.* Paper presented at the Proceedings of the 10th, Knowledge Acquisition for Knowledge-Based Systems Workshop. Retrieved from http://ksi.cpsc.ucalgary.ca/KAW/KAW.html

Tartir, S., & Arpinar, I. B. (2007). *Ontology evaluation and ranking using OntoQA.* Paper presented at the Proceedings of the International Conference on Semantic Computing, Irvine, California, CA.

Tijerino, Y. A., Embley, D. W., Lonsdale, D. W., Ding, Y., & Nagy, G. (2005). Towards ontology generation from tables. *World Wide Web, 8,* 261–285. http://dx.doi.org/10.1007/s11280-005-0360-8

Uschold, M., & King, M. (1995, August 20–25). *Towards a methodology for building ontologies.* Paper presented at the Workshop on Basic Ontological Issues in Knowledge Sharing, held in conjunction with IJCAI-95, Montreal.

Vanitha, K., Yasudha, K., Venkatesh, M. S., Ravindra, K., Lakshmi, S. V., & Soujanya, K. N. (2011). The development process of the semantic web and web ontology. *(IJACSA). International Journal of Advanced Computer Science and Applications, 2,* 122–125.

Vujasinovic, M., Ivezic, N., & Kulvatunyou, B. (2015). A survey and classification of principles for domain-specific ontology design patterns development. *Applied Ontology, 10,* 41–69.

Youn, S., Arora, A., Chandrasekhar, P., Jayanty, P., Mestry, A., & Sethi, S. (2004). Survey about ontology development tools for ontology-based knowledge management. Retrieved 2012, November 20 from www.scf.usc.edu/~csci586/projects/ontology-survey.doc

3

A recursive algorithm for computing the inverse of the Vandermonde matrix

Youness Aliyari Ghassabeh[1]*

*Corresponding author: Youness Aliyari Ghassabeh, Toronto Rehabilitation Institute (UHN), 550 University Avenue, Toronto, Canada M5G 2A2

E-mail: aliyari@cs.toronto.edu

Reviewing editor: Jenhui Chen, Chang Gung University, Taiwan

Abstract: The inverse of a Vandermonde matrix has been used for signal processing, polynomial interpolation, curve fitting, wireless communication, and system identification. In this paper, we propose a novel fast recursive algorithm to compute the inverse of a Vandermonde matrix. The algorithm computes the inverse of a higher order Vandermonde matrix using the available lower order inverse matrix with a computational cost of $O(n^2)$. The proposed algorithm is given in a matrix form, which makes it appropriate for hardware implementation. The running time of the proposed algorithm to find the inverse of a Vandermonde matrix using a lower order Vandermonde matrix is compared with the running time of the matrix inversion function implemented in MATLAB.

Subjects: Applied Mathematics; Linear & Multilinear Algebra; Numerical Algebra

Keywords: Vandermonde matrix; recursive algorithm; matrix inversion

1. Introduction

The Vandermonde matrix and its inverse have been widely used in many applications, such as polynomial interpolation (Phillips, 2003), curve fitting (Wilf, 1958), system identification (Barker, Tan, & Godfrey, 2004), signal reconstruction (Olkkonen & Olkkonen, 2010), wireless communication (Wang, Scaglione, Giannakis, & Barbarossa, 1999), and signal processing (Ryan & Debbah, 2009). Computing the inverse of a Vandermonde matrix has been extensively studied over the last four decades. Tou

ABOUT THE AUTHOR

Youness Aliyari Ghassabeh received the BS degree in electrical engineering from the University of Tehran, Tehran, Iran, in 2004, the MS degree from K.N. Toosi University of Technology, Tehran, in 2006, and the PhD degree in mathematics and engineering from Queen's University, Kingston, ON, Canada, in 2013. He was a postdoctoral fellow at the Toronto Rehabilitation Institute, University Health Network, Toronto, ON between 2013 to 2014. He is currently a manager in Operational Risk Methodology group at Bank of Montreal, Toronto, ON, Canada. His main research interests include machine learning, statistical pattern recognition, probability theory and stochastic processes, image/signal processing, source coding and information theory.

PUBLIC INTEREST STATEMENT

The Vandermonde matrix and its inverse have been widely used in many applications, such as polynomial interpolation and signal processing. In this paper, a fast recursive algorithm is proposed to find the inverse of a Vandermonde matrix. We show that the inverse of a $(n + 1) \times (n + 1)$ Vandermonde matrix can be computed recursively using the inverse of a reduced size $n \times n$ Vandermonde matrix. The size of $n \times n$ Vandermonde matrix can be further reduced until we reach to a size small enough that the inverse can be computed easily.

Furthermore, the proposed algorithm can be used for finding the inverse Vandermonde matrix when the entries are observed sequentially. The proposed algorithm in each iteration uses the new entry and the previous inverse matrix to compute the inverse of the increased size Vandermonde matrix.

(1964) and Wertz (1965) used the Lagrange interpolation formula and expressed the elements of the inverse of a Vandermonde matrix as the coefficients of a polynomial. Explicit formulas for finding the inverse of the Vandermonde matrix are given in Kaufman (1969), Neagoe (1996), El-Mikkawya (2003), Respondek (2016). Authors in Gautschi and Inglese (1988) found lower bounds for the condition number of the Vandermonde matrices and showed that the bounds grow exponentially as the size of the matrix increases. Therefore, the Vandermonde matrices are usually ill conditioned and the methods proposed in Kaufman (1969), Neagoe (1996), El-Mikkawya (2003) may fail to accurately compute the elements of the inverse matrix. In later works, fast algorithms are derived in $O(n^2)$ and $O(n^3)$ to compute the elements of the inverse of the Vandermonde matrix (Eisinberg & Fedele, 2006; Gohberg & Olshevsky, 1997).

In this paper, we propose a novel recursive algorithm for computing the inverse of the Vandermonde matrix. We show that the inverse of a $(n + 1) \times (n + 1)$ Vandermonde matrix can be computed recursively using the inverse of a reduced size $n \times n$ Vandermonde matrix. The size of $n \times n$ Vandermonde matrix can be further reduced until we reach to a size small enough that the inverse can be computed easily. One of the advantages of the proposed recursive algorithm is its capability to update the inverse matrix when the size of the matrix increases due to observing new incoming entries. The entries of the Vandermonde matrix can be considered as a sequence such that by observing each new entry, the size of the matrix increases by one. In the real-world applications, we may confront situations where a complete set of the entries is not available in advance and the matrix entries are observed sequentially (Aliyari Ghassabeh & Abrishami Moghaddam, 2013; Aliyari Ghassabeh, Rudzicz, & Abrishami Moghaddam, 2015). The proposed techniques in Kaufman (1969), Neagoe (1996), El-Mikkawya (2003), Gohberg and Olshevsky (1997), Eisinberg and Fedele (2006) require to have access to the whole entries in advance to find the inverse matrix. In contrast to the previously mentioned methods, the proposed recursive algorithm has the ability to observe the entries sequentially and update the new (increased size) inverse matrix simultaneously. The computational cost for computing the inverse of $(n + 1) \times (n + 1)$ Vandermonde matrix using $n \times n$ dimensional inverse matrix after observing the new entry is $O(n^2)$, which is considerably less than the usual matrix inversion techniques. Furthermore, the proposed recursive algorithm is presented in a matrix form that makes it suitable for hardware implementation and reduces the computational time and complexity.

The paper is organized as follows: Section 2 introduces the new recursive algorithm for computing the inverse of a Vandermonde matrix. The simulation results are given in Section 3, where the running time of the proposed algorithm for computing the inverse of a Vandermonde matrix is compared with the running time of the inverse function implemented in MATLAB. The concluding remarks are given in Section 4.

2. Proposed recursive algorithm

Let $\mathbf{A}_n - \mathbf{A}(a_1, a_2, \ldots, a_n), n \geq 1$ denote an $n \times n$ Vandermonde matrix defined over the set of all complex numbers $\mathbb{C}$,

$$\mathbf{A}(a_1, a_2, \ldots, a_n) = \begin{pmatrix} 1 & 1 & \ldots & 1 \\ a_1 & a_2 & \ldots & a_n \\ \vdots & \vdots & \ldots & \vdots \\ a_1^{n-1} & a_2^{n-1} & \ldots & a_n^{n-1} \end{pmatrix}, \qquad a_i \in \mathbb{C}, i = 1, \ldots, n.$$

The determinant of $\mathbf{A}_n^{-1}$ is given by $|\mathbf{A}| = \prod_{1 \leq i < j \leq n}(a_j - a_i)$ (Mirsky, 2011). Therefore, the Vandermonde matrix is nonsingular if and only if the parameters $a_i, i = 1, \ldots, n$ are distinct.

Definition 1   Let $\mathbf{B}_n = \mathbf{B}(a_1, a_2, \ldots, a_n), n \geq 1$ be an $n \times n$ matrix defined by

$$\mathbf{B}_n = \mathbf{B}(a_1, a_2, \dots, a_n) = \begin{pmatrix} a_1 & a_2 & \dots & a_n \\ a_1^2 & a_2^2 & \dots & a_n^2 \\ \vdots & \vdots & \dots & \vdots \\ a_1^n & a_2^n & \dots & a_n^n \end{pmatrix}, \qquad a_i \in \mathbb{C}, i = 1, \dots, n.$$

Then we have the following proposition

PROPOSITION 1   (Horn & Johnson, 1990) *Suppose that $\mathbf{A}_n$ and $\mathbf{B}_n$ are defined as above. Let $d \neq 0$ denote the determinant of the Vandermonde matrix $\mathbf{A}_n$, i.e. $|\mathbf{A}_n| = d$. Assume $a_i \neq 0, i = 1, \dots, n$, then $|\mathbf{B}_n| = d \prod_{i=1}^n a_i$ and $\mathbf{B}_n^{-1}$ is given by*

$$\mathbf{B}_n^{-1} = \frac{1}{d} \begin{pmatrix} \frac{cof\ A_{n_{11}}}{a_1} & \frac{cof\ A_{n_{21}}}{a_1} & \dots & \frac{cof\ A_{n_{n1}}}{a_1} \\ \frac{cof\ A_{n_{12}}}{a_2} & \frac{cof\ A_{n_{22}}}{a_2} & \dots & \frac{cof\ A_{n_{n2}}}{a_2} \\ \vdots & \vdots & \dots & \vdots \\ \frac{cof\ A_{n_{1n}}}{a_n} & \frac{cof\ A_{n_{2n}}}{a_n} & \dots & \frac{cof\ A_{n_{nn}}}{a_n} \end{pmatrix},$$

where $cof\ A_{n_{ij}}$ denotes the ijth cofactor of the matrix $\mathbf{A}_n$.

Therefore, if $\mathbf{A}_n^{-1}$ is available then $\mathbf{B}_n^{-1}$ can be computed with complexity $O(n^2)$ using Proposition 1.[2] Now we are in a position to prove the following lemma that introduces a recursive algorithm for finding the inverse of a Vandermonde matrix

LEMMA 1   *Let $\mathbf{A}_{n+1} = \mathbf{A}(a_1, a_2, \dots, a_{n+1})$ denote an $(n+1) \times (n+1)$ Vandermonde matrix such that $a_i \neq 0, i = 1, \dots, n+1$. Let $\mathbf{B}_n = \mathbf{B}(a_1, a_2, \dots, a_n)$ be an $n \times n$ matrix according to Definition 1. Let $\mathbf{I}_n$ denote the identity matrix of order n. Furthermore, let b_{ij} denote the ijth element of $\mathbf{B}_n^{-1}$. Then the inverse of the Vandermonde matrix $\mathbf{A}_{n+1}$ is given by the following recursive formula*

$$\mathbf{A}_{n+1}^{-1} = \mathbf{E}_{n+1} \mathbf{C}_{n+1} \mathbf{D}_{n+1},$$

where

$$\mathbf{D}_{n+1} = \begin{pmatrix} 1 & 0 \dots & & 0 \\ 0 & & & \\ \vdots & & \mathbf{B}_n^{-1} & \\ 0 & & & \end{pmatrix}, \quad \mathbf{C}_{n+1} = \begin{pmatrix} 1 & -1 & -1 & \dots & -1 & -1 \\ -1 & 2 & 1 & \dots & 1 & 1 \\ -1 & 1 & 2 & \dots & 1 & 1 \\ \vdots & \vdots & \vdots & \dots & \vdots & \vdots \\ -1 & 1 & 1 & \dots & 1 & 2 \end{pmatrix}, \quad \mathbf{E}_{n+1} = \begin{pmatrix} \frac{1}{c_1} & & 0 \dots & 0 \\ \frac{-c_2}{c_1} & & & \\ \frac{-c_3}{c_1} & & & \\ \vdots & & \mathbf{I}_n & \\ \frac{-c_{n+1}}{c_1} & & & \end{pmatrix},$$

where $\mathbf{B}_n^{-1}$ is computed using Proposition 1, $\mathbf{C}_{n+1}$ is a constant matrix, and $c_i, i = 1, \dots, n+1$ are given by

$$\begin{cases} c_1 = 1 - a_{11} - a_{21} - a_{31} \dots - a_{n1}, \\ c_{i+1} = a_{i1} - c_1, i = 1, \dots, n \\ a_{i1} = b_{i1} a_{n+1} + b_{i2} a_{n+1}^2 + \dots + b_{in} a_{n+1}^n, i = 1, \dots, n. \end{cases} \tag{1}$$

Remark 1

(a) The last two equations in 1 can be rewritten in matrix form as follows

$$
\begin{pmatrix} a_{11} \\ a_{21} \\ \vdots \\ a_{n1} \end{pmatrix} = \mathbf{B}_n^{-1} \begin{pmatrix} a_{n+1} \\ a_{n+1}^2 \\ \vdots \\ a_{n+1}^n \end{pmatrix}, \qquad \begin{pmatrix} c_2 \\ c_3 \\ \vdots \\ c_{n+1} \end{pmatrix} = \mathbf{B}_n^{-1} \begin{pmatrix} a_{n+1} \\ a_{n+1}^2 \\ \vdots \\ a_{n+1}^n \end{pmatrix} - c_1 \begin{pmatrix} 1 \\ 1 \\ \vdots \\ 1 \end{pmatrix}. \tag{2}
$$

(b) For a two dimensional Vandermonde matrix $\mathbf{A}_2 = \mathbf{A}(a_1, a_2)$, where a_1 and a_2 are nonzero and distinct, $\mathbf{D}_2, \mathbf{C}_2$, and $\mathbf{E}_2$ are given as follows[3]

$$
\mathbf{D}_2 = \begin{pmatrix} 1 & 0 \\ 0 & \frac{1}{a_2} \end{pmatrix}, \ \mathbf{C}_2 = \begin{pmatrix} 1 & -1 \\ -1 & 2 \end{pmatrix}, \ \mathbf{E}_2 = \begin{pmatrix} \frac{a_2}{a_2 - a_1} & 0 \\ \frac{-2a_1 + a_2}{a_2 - a_1} & 1 \end{pmatrix}. \tag{3}
$$

By multiplying these three matrices, we obtain

$$
\mathbf{E}_2 \mathbf{C}_2 \mathbf{D}_2 = \frac{1}{a_2 - a_1} \begin{pmatrix} a_2 & -1 \\ -a_1 & 1 \end{pmatrix} = \mathbf{A}_2^{-1},
$$

which is the well-known formula for the inverse of a 2×2 Vandermonde matrix $\begin{pmatrix} 1 & 1 \\ a_1 & a_2 \end{pmatrix}$.

(c) To compute $\mathbf{E}_n$, it appears that c_1 cannot be zero. The following lemma guarantees that c_1 is always non-zero.

LEMMA 2   *The coefficient c_1 defined in (1) is always a non-zero number.*

Expressing the equations in a matrix form reduces the running time and makes the hardware implementation easier. Note that the coefficients $c_i, i = 2, \ldots, n + 1$ are needed to construct $\mathbf{E}_{n+1}$ and using (2) they can be computed in $O(n^2)$. The complexity of computing the matrix product $\mathbf{C}_{n+1} \mathbf{D}_{n+1}$ is $O(n^2)$ and the complexity of multiplying the result by $\mathbf{E}_{n+1}$ is $O(n)$, therefore the inverse of a $(n + 1) \times (n + 1)$ Vandermonde matrix $\mathbf{A}_{n+1}^{-1}$ can be found using $\mathbf{A}_n^{-1}$ in $O(n^2)$. The required steps for finding $\mathbf{A}_{n+1}^{-1} = \mathbf{A}^{-1}(a_1, a_2, \ldots, a_{n+1})$ from $\mathbf{A}_n^{-1} = \mathbf{A}^{-1}(a_1, a_2, \ldots, a_n)$ is given as follows

(a) Compute $\mathbf{B}_n^{-1}$ using Proposition 1.

(b) Construct $\mathbf{C}_{n+1}, \mathbf{D}_{n+1}$, and $\mathbf{E}_{n+1}$ using (1) and (2).

(c) The inverse matrix is the product of the matrices in step (b), i.e. $\mathbf{A}_{n+1}^{-1} = \mathbf{E}_{n+1} \mathbf{C}_{n+1} \mathbf{D}_{n+1}$. If the inverse of $\mathbf{A}_n$ is not available, we can represent $\mathbf{A}_n^{-1}$ as a function of $\mathbf{A}_{n-1}^{-1}$ and continue the recursion procedure. The recursion continues until we reach a Vandermonde matrix with a known inverse matrix.

The recursive algorithm for finding the inverse of an $n \times n$ Vandermonde matrix, $\mathbf{A}_n^{-1}$, can be summarized as follows

Algorithm 1: Recursive algorithm for finding the inverse of the Vandermonde matrix

Input : $\mathbf{A}_n = \mathbf{A}(a_1, a_2, \ldots, a_n)$, Vandermonde matrix.
Output: $\mathbf{A}_n^{-1}$, the inverse matrix.

Function RecVandermonde $(\mathbf{A}_n)$
    if $n = 1$ **then**
        return 1;
    else
        RecVandermonde $(\mathbf{A}_{n-1})$;
        Compute $\mathbf{B}_{n-1}^{-1}$ using Proposition 1;
        Construct $\mathbf{C}_n, \mathbf{D}_n$, and $\mathbf{E}_n$ using Lemma 1 and Equation (2);
        return $\mathbf{E}_n \mathbf{C}_n \mathbf{D}_n$;
        /* From Lemma 1, $\mathbf{A}_n^{-1} = \mathbf{E}_n \mathbf{C}_n \mathbf{D}_n$ */

Note that we also can start with a 2×2 Vandermonde matrix $\mathbf{A}_2$, increase the dimension of the Vandermonde matrix by one in each iteration and compute its inverse using Lemma 1. The iterations stop until the Vandermonde matrix has the desired size. In the next section, we compare the running time of the proposed algorithm with the running time of the matrix inversion function implemented in MATLAB.

3. Simulation results

In the following simulations we compute the running time of the proposed algorithm to find the inverse of a Vandermonde matrix in an adaptive manner for polynomial interpolation. The running time is compared with the inverse function implemented in MATLAB. The algorithm is implemented in MATLAB and the simulations run on a PC with Intel Pentium 4, 2.6 GHZ CPU, and 2048 Mb RAM.

Given a set of n observations $(x_i, y_i), i = 0, 1, \ldots, n-1$, where x_is are distinct and $x_i \neq 0, i = 0, 1 \ldots, n-1$, we can find a unique polynomial p of degree $n-1$ such that $p(x_i) = y_i, i = 0, 1, \ldots, n-1$ (Phillips, 2003). Suppose that the interpolation polynomial p is given by $p(x) = a_0 + a_1 x + a_2 x \ldots + a_{n-1} x^{n-1}$. Then the problem can be written in the following matrix form

$$
\begin{pmatrix}
1 & x_0 & \cdots & x_0^{n-2} & x_0^{n-1} \\
1 & x_1 & \cdots & x_1^{n-2} & x_1^{n-1} \\
\vdots & \vdots & \cdots & \vdots & \vdots \\
1 & x_{n-1} & \cdots & x_{n-1}^{n-2} & x_{n-1}^{n-1}
\end{pmatrix}
\begin{pmatrix}
a_0 \\
a_1 \\
\vdots \\
a_{n-1}
\end{pmatrix}
=
\begin{pmatrix}
y_0 \\
y_1 \\
\vdots \\
y_{n-1}
\end{pmatrix}.
\tag{4}
$$

It is a system of n linear equations and the unknown coefficients $a_i, i = 0, 1, \ldots, n-1$ are given by

$$
\begin{pmatrix}
a_0 \\
a_1 \\
\vdots \\
a_{n-1}
\end{pmatrix}
= (\mathbf{A}_n^{-1})^t
\begin{pmatrix}
y_0 \\
y_1 \\
\vdots \\
y_{n-1}
\end{pmatrix},
\tag{5}
$$

where $\mathbf{A}_n = \mathbf{A}(x_0, x_1, \ldots, x_{n-1})$ is an $n \times n$ Vandermonde matrix. It is clear from (5) that finding the unknown coefficients involves computing the inverse of the associated Vandermonde matrix and multiplying it by $[y_0, y_1, \ldots, y_{n-1}]^t$.

In the following simulations we assume that the observations are made sequentially and the observed data are used to find the polynomial p that passes through the given points. We assume that the input data are observed in an increasing order, i.e. $0 < x_0 < x_1 < \ldots < x_{n-1}$. As the number of observed data increases the degree of the polynomial p also linearly increases. For example, if we have k pairs of input data, the degree of the polynomial p is $k-1$ and by observing the next pair of the data the degree of the polynomial increases to k. In other words, upon arrival of each observation the size of the associated Vandermonde matrix increases by one and we are required to compute the inverse of the new increased size Vandermonde matrix. After each observation, the current matrix inversion algorithms need the whole data set to compute the inverse of the Vandermonde matrix (e.g. the matrix inverse function in MATLAB requires the whole observations to find the inverse matrix). But the proposed algorithm uses only the current observation and the previous inverse matrix to update the inverse of the higher order Vandermonde matrix. As mentioned before, the computational cost for updating the Vandermonde matrix using the proposed algorithm is $O(n^2)$, which is much less than most regular matrix inversion techniques.

We compute the required time for updating the Vandermonde matrix using the proposed algorithm as a function of the size of the matrix. The results are compared with the running time of the function implemented in MATLAB for computing the inverse matrix. For each matrix size, we repeated the experiment 100 times and the average running time was found. The initial size of the Vandermonde matrix is 10 and by adding new entries (observing new data) it gradually increases to 80. For the sake of simplicity, the input elements of a $k \times k$ Vandermonde matrix are assumed to be

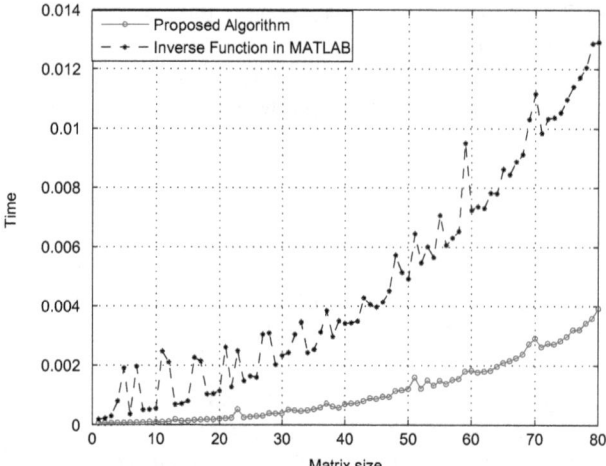

Figure 1. Comparison between the running times of the proposed algorithm and the matrix inversion function in MATLAB. The size of the Vandermonde matrix increases from 10 to 80, and in each iteration the time required to find the inverse function is computed.

$1, 2, \ldots, k$, i.e., $\mathbf{A}_k = \mathbf{A}(1, 2, \ldots, k)$. As mentioned before, for finding the polynomial p with degree $n - 1$ we need n pairs of observations (x_i, y_i), $i = 1, 2, \ldots, n$. Since our goal here is to test the performance of the proposed algorithm for finding the inverse of the Vandermonde matrix, we just need the first element of each observation. Figure 1 compares the running times of the proposed algorithm with the MATLAB inverse function for finding the inverse of a Vandermonde matrix as a function of the matrix size. The x-axis in Figure 1 is the size of the Vandermonde matrix, and y-axis is the requires time (second) to find the inverse matrix. It can be observed from Figure 1 that the proposed algorithm is faster than the matrix inversion function in MATLAB.[4]

4. Conclusion

Computing the inverse of a Vandermonde matrix arises in many applications such as polynomial interpolation, curve fitting, and signal processing. In this paper, we proposed a fast recursive algorithm to find the inverse of a Vandermonde matrix. The proposed algorithm in each iteration uses the new entry and the previous inverse matrix to compute the inverse of the increased size Vandermonde matrix. The proposed algorithm can be implemented as a recursive function to find the inverse of a Vandermonde matrix recursively. The running times of the proposed algorithm to find the inverse of a Vandermonde matrix are compared with the inverse function implemented in MATLAB and the simulation results showed that for a sequential data the proposed algorithm is faster than the inverse function in MATLAB.

Funding
The author received no direct funding for this research.

Author details
Youness Aliyari Ghassabeh[1]
E-mail: aliyari@cs.toronto.edu
[1] Toronto Rehabilitation Institute (UHN), 550 University Avenue, Toronto, Canada M5G 2A2.

Notes
1. For the sake of simplicity, hereafter we use $\mathbf{A}_n$ to refer to an $n \times n$ Vandermonde matrix $\mathbf{A}(a_1, a_2, \ldots, a_n)$.
2. Note that $cofA_{n_{ij}}/d, i, j = 1, \ldots, n$ is jith element of $\mathbf{A}_n^{-1}$ (Horn & Johnson, 1990).
3. We assume that the new entries are added from the left to the Vandermonde matrix. So, for a 2×2

Vandermonde matrix $\mathbf{A}_2 = \mathbf{A}(a_1, a_2)$, we have $\mathbf{A}_1 = 1$ and $\mathbf{D}_1 = a_2$. For the general $n \times n$ case, see the Proof of Lemma 1 in Appendix.
4. Note that for the proposed algorithm, the required time for finding the inverse matrix using the previous inverse matrix and the new entry is reported.
5. Otherwise, the determinant of the Vandermonde matrix is zero and the inverse does not exist.

References
Aliyari Ghassabeh, Y., & Abrishami Moghaddam, H. (2013). Adaptive linear discriminant analysis for online feature extraction. *Machine Vision Applications, 24*, 777–794.
Aliyari Ghassabeh, Y., Rudzicz, F., & Abrishami Moghaddam, H. (2015). Fast incremental LDA feature extraction. *Pattern Recognition, 31*, 1999–2012.
Barker, H. A., Tan, A. H., & Godfrey, K. R. (2004). Optimal levels of perturbation signals for nonlinear system identification. *IEEE Transactions on Automatic Conrol, 49*, 1404–1407.
El-Mikkawya, M. E. A. (2003). Inversion of a generalized Vandermonde matrix. *International Journal of Computer Mathematics, 80*, 759–765.

Eisinberg, A., & Fedele, G. (2006). On the inversion of the Vandermonde matrix. *Applied Mathematics and Computation, 174*, 1384–1397.

Gautschi, W., & Inglese, G. (1988). Lower bounds for the condition number of Vandermonde matrix. *Numerische Mathematik, 52*, 241–250.

Gohberg, I., & Olshevsky, V. (1997). The fast generalized Parker-Traub algorithm for inversion of Vandermonde and related matrices. *Journal of Complexity, 13*, 208–234.

Horn, R. A., & Johnson, C. R. (1990). *Matrix analysis*. Cambridge: Cambridge University Press.

Kaufman, I. (1969). The inversion of the Vandermonde matrix and transformation to the Jordan canonical form. *IEEE Transactions on Automatic Control, 14*, 774–777.

Mirsky, L. (2011). *An introduction to linear algebra*. New York, NY: Dover Publications.

Neagoe, V. (1996). Inversion of the Van der Monde matrix. *IEEE Signal Processing Letters, 3*, 119–120.

Olkkonen, H., & Olkkonen, J. T. (2010). Sampling and reconstruction of transient signals by parallel exponential filters. *IEEE Transactions on Circuits and Systems - Part II: Express Briefs, 57*, 426–429.

Phillips, G. M. (2003). *Interpolation and approximation by polynomials*. New York, NY: Springer Verlag.

Ryan, O., & Debbah, M. (2009). Asymptotic behaviour of random Vandermonde matrices with entries on the unit circle. *IEEE Transaction on Information Theory, 55*, 3115–3147.

Respondek, J. S. (2016). Incremental numerical recipes for the high efficient inversion of the confluent Vandermonde matrices. *Computers & Mathematics with Applications, 71*, 489–502.

Wertz, H. (1965). On the numerical inversion of a recurrent problem: The Vandermonde matrix. *IEEE Transactions on Automatic Control, 10*, 492.

Wang, Z., Scaglione, A., Giannakis, G., & Barbarossa, S. (1999). Vandermonde–Lagrange mutually orthogonal flexible transceivers for blind CDMA in unknown multipath. In *Proceedings of 2nd IEEE Workshop on Signal Processing Advances in Wireless Communications* (pp. 42–45). Minneapolis, MN.

Wilf, H. S. (1958). Curve-fitting matrices. *The American Mathematical Monthly, 65*, 272–274.

Tou, J. (1964). Determination of the inverse Vandermonde matrix. *IEEE Transactions on Automatic Control, 9*, 314.

Appendix 1

Proof of Lemma 1

Proof We show that $\mathbf{E}_{n+1}\mathbf{C}_{n+1}\mathbf{D}_{n+1}\mathbf{A}_{n+1} = \mathbf{I}_{n+1}$, where $\mathbf{I}_{n+1}$ is a $(n+1)\times(n+1)$ identity matrix. To achieve this goal, we start by computing the product of $\mathbf{D}_{n+1}$ and $\mathbf{A}_{n+1}$,

$$
\mathbf{D}_{n+1}\mathbf{A}_{n+1} =
\begin{pmatrix}
1 & 0\ldots & & 0 \\
0 & & & \\
\vdots & & \mathbf{B}_n^{-1} & \\
0 & & &
\end{pmatrix}
\begin{pmatrix}
1 & 1 & 1 & \ldots & 1 \\
a_{n+1} & a_1 & a_2 & \ldots & a_n \\
\vdots & \vdots & \vdots & \ldots & \vdots \\
a_{n+1}^n & a_1^n & a_2^n & \ldots & a_n^n
\end{pmatrix}.
$$

It is straightforward to show that

$$
\mathbf{D}_{n+1}\mathbf{A}_{n+1} =
\begin{pmatrix}
1 & 1 & 1 & \ldots & 1 \\
a_{11} & 1 & 0 & \ldots & 0 \\
a_{21} & 0 & 1 & \ldots & 0 \\
\vdots & \vdots & \vdots & \ldots & \vdots \\
a_{n1} & 0 & 0 & \ldots & 1
\end{pmatrix}
=
\begin{pmatrix}
1 & 1 & & 1 & \ldots & 1 \\
a_{11} & & & & & \\
a_{21} & & & & & \\
\vdots & & \mathbf{I}_n & & & \\
a_{n1} & & & & &
\end{pmatrix},
$$

where

$$
\begin{cases}
a_{11} = b_{11}a_{n+1} + b_{12}a_{n+1}^2 + \ldots + b_{1n}a_{n+1}^n, \\
a_{21} = b_{21}a_{n+1} + b_{22}a_{n+1}^2 + \ldots + b_{2n}a_{n+1}^n, \\
\vdots = \quad \vdots \\
a_{n1} = b_{n1}a_{n+1} + b_{n2}a_{n+1}^2 + \ldots + b_{nn}a_{n+1}^n.
\end{cases}
\tag{6}
$$

The above equations can be written in the following compact matrix form

$$\begin{pmatrix} a_{11} \\ a_{21} \\ \vdots \\ a_{n1} \end{pmatrix} = \mathbf{B}_n^{-1} \begin{pmatrix} a_{n+1} \\ a_{n+1}^2 \\ \vdots \\ a_{n+1}^n \end{pmatrix}. \tag{7}$$

Now, we evaluate $\mathbf{C}_{n+1}\mathbf{D}_{n+1}\mathbf{A}_{n+1}$,

$$\mathbf{C}_{n+1}\mathbf{D}_{n+1}\mathbf{A}_{n+1} = \begin{pmatrix} 1 & -1 & -1 & -1 & \dots & -1 & -1 \\ -1 & 2 & 1 & 1 & \dots & 1 & 1 \\ -1 & 1 & 2 & 1 & \dots & 1 & 1 \\ \vdots & \vdots & \vdots & \dots & & \vdots & \vdots \\ -1 & 1 & 1 & 1 & \dots & 1 & 2 \end{pmatrix} \begin{pmatrix} 1 & 1 & 1 & \dots & 1 \\ a_{11} & 1 & 0 & \dots & 0 \\ a_{21} & 0 & 1 & \dots & 0 \\ \vdots & \vdots & \vdots & \dots & \vdots \\ a_{n1} & 0 & 0 & \dots & 1 \end{pmatrix}.$$

It is simple to show that

$$\mathbf{C}_{n+1}\mathbf{D}_{n+1}\mathbf{A}_{n+1} = \begin{pmatrix} c_1 & 0 & 0 & \dots & 0 & 0 \\ c_2 & 1 & 0 & \dots & 0 & 0 \\ c_3 & 0 & 1 & \dots & 0 & 0 \\ \vdots & \vdots & & \dots & \vdots & \vdots \\ c_n & 0 & 0 & \dots & 1 & 0 \\ c_{n+1} & 0 & 0 & \dots & 0 & 1 \end{pmatrix} = \begin{pmatrix} c_1 & & 0\dots & & 0 \\ c_2 & & & & \\ \vdots & & & \mathbf{I}_n & \\ c_{n+1} & & & & \end{pmatrix}, \tag{8}$$

where

$$c_1 = 1 - a_{11} - a_{21} - a_{31} \cdots - a_{n1}, \tag{9}$$

$$\begin{cases} c_2 = -1 + 2a_{11} + a_{21} + a_{31} \dots a_{n1} = a_{11} - c_1, \\ c_3 = -1 + a_{11} + 2a_{21} + a_{31} \dots a_{n1} = a_{21} - c_1, \\ c_4 = -1 + a_{11} + a_{21} + 2a_{31} \dots a_{n1} = a_{31} - c_1, \\ \vdots \quad = \qquad\qquad \vdots \qquad\qquad = \quad \vdots \\ c_{n+1} = -1 + a_{11} + a_{21} + a_{31} \dots 2a_{n1} = a_{n1} - c_1. \end{cases} \tag{10}$$

The above equalities can be written in the following matrix

$$\begin{pmatrix} c_2 \\ c_3 \\ \vdots \\ c_{n+1} \end{pmatrix} = \begin{pmatrix} a_{11} \\ a_{21} \\ \vdots \\ a_{n1} \end{pmatrix} - c_1 \begin{pmatrix} 1 \\ 1 \\ ! \\ 1 \end{pmatrix}. \tag{11}$$

It remains to show that $\mathbf{E}_{n+1}\mathbf{C}_{n+1}\mathbf{D}_{n+1}\mathbf{A}_{n+1} = \mathbf{I}_{n+1}$. Using Equation (8), we obtain

$$\mathbf{E}_{n+1}\mathbf{C}_{n+1}\mathbf{D}_{n+1}\mathbf{A}_{n+1} = \underbrace{\begin{pmatrix} \frac{1}{c_1} & & 0\dots & & 0 \\ \frac{-c_2}{c1} & & & & \\ \frac{-c_3}{c1} & & & & \\ \vdots & & & \mathbf{I}_n & \\ \frac{-c_{n+1}}{c_1} & & & & \end{pmatrix}}_{\mathbf{E}_{n+1}} \underbrace{\begin{pmatrix} c_1 & & 0\dots & & 0 \\ c_2 & & & & \\ \vdots & & & \mathbf{I}_n & \\ c_{n+1} & & & & \end{pmatrix}}_{\mathbf{C}_{n+1}\mathbf{D}_{n+1}\mathbf{A}_{n+1}} = \mathbf{I}_{n+1}. \tag{12}$$

Therefore,

$$\mathbf{E}_{n+1}\mathbf{C}_{n+1}\mathbf{D}_{n+1} = \mathbf{A}_{n+1}^{-1}.$$

Proof of Lemma 2

Proof We use contradiction to show $c_1 \neq 0$. Assume the coefficient c_1 is zero, i.e. $c_1 = 0$. Then using Equations (1) and (2), we have

$$a_{11} + a_{21} + \dots + a_{n1} = 1 \tag{13}$$

$$\mathbf{B}_n \begin{pmatrix} a_{11} \\ a_{21} \\ \vdots \\ a_{n1} \end{pmatrix} = \begin{pmatrix} a_{n+1} \\ a_{n+1}^2 \\ \vdots \\ a_{n+1}^n \end{pmatrix}. \tag{14}$$

By combining Equations (9) and (10), we obtain

$$\begin{pmatrix} 1 & 1 & \dots & 1 & 1 \\ a_1 & a_2 & \dots & a_n & a_{n+1} \\ a_1^2 & a_2^2 & \dots & a_n^2 & a_{n+1}^2 \\ \vdots & \vdots & \dots & \vdots & \vdots \\ a_1^n & a_2^n & \dots & a_n^n & a_{n+1}^n \end{pmatrix} \begin{pmatrix} a_{11} \\ a_{21} \\ \vdots \\ a_{n1} \\ -1 \end{pmatrix} = \begin{pmatrix} 0 \\ 0 \\ \vdots \\ 0 \\ 0 \end{pmatrix}. \tag{15}$$

The first matrix in (15) is a $(n+1) \times (n+1)$ Vandermonde matrix $\mathbf{A}_{n+1}$. Since $a_i, i = 1, \dots, n+1$ are distinct,[5] therefore $\mathbf{A}_{n+1}$ is a nonsingular matrix and its inverse exists. By multiplying both sides of Equation (15) by $\mathbf{A}_{n+1}^{-1}$, we obtain

$$\begin{pmatrix} a_{11} \\ a_{21} \\ \vdots \\ a_{n1} \\ -1 \end{pmatrix} = \begin{pmatrix} 0 \\ 0 \\ \vdots \\ 0 \\ 0 \end{pmatrix}. \tag{16}$$

The above equality implies that our assumption, $c_1 = 0$, is not correct. Therefore, $c_1 \neq 0$. $\qquad\square$

4

Evolutionary algorithm for analyzing higher degree research student recruitment and completion

Ruhul Sarker[1]* and Saber Elsayed[1]

*Corresponding author: Ruhul Sarker, School of Engineering and Information Technology, University of New South Wales at Canberra, Northcott Drive, Canberra 2600, Australia

E-mail: r.sarker@adfa.edu.au

Reviewing editor: Jenhui Chen, Chang Gung University, Taiwan

Abstract: In this paper, we consider a decision problem arising from higher degree research student recruitment process in a university environment. The problem is to recruit a number of research students by maximizing the sum of a performance index satisfying a number of constraints, such as supervision capacity and resource limitation. The problem is dynamic in nature as the number of eligible applicants, the supervision capacity, completion time, funding for scholarships, and other resources vary from period to period and they are difficult to predict in advance. In this research, we have developed a mathematical model to represent this dynamic decision problem and adopted an evolutionary algorithm-based approach to solve the problem. We have demonstrated how the recruitment decision can be made with a defined objective and how the model can be used for long-run planning for improvement of higher degree research program.

Subjects: Evolutionary Computing; Intelligent Systems; Operations Research

Keywords: higher degree research student recruitment; differential evolution; evolutionary algorithms

ABOUT THE AUTHORS

Ruhul Sarker and Saber Elsayed are with the School of Engineering and Information Technology at University of New South Wales, Canberra, Australia. Ruhul Sarker's research interests are on evolutionary computation, optimization and their interfaces. Saber Elsayed's research interests include design of evolutionary computation-based algorithms and optimization. Jointly they have developed a number of high performing evolutionary algorithms for solving different optimization problems. Their contributions have been recognized through publications in high impact journals in the field such as *IEEE Transactions on Evolutionary Computation*, *IEEE Transactions on Industrial Informatics*, and *Computers & Operations Research*. The research reported in this paper includes a new dynamic optimization problem from a higher education institution and a solution approach for solving such a complex problem. There are many situations in practice where similar problems can be found. So the solution approach developed in this research will help to solve those problems.

PUBLIC INTEREST STATEMENT

The authors are well-known from their contributions in the field of evolutionary computation and optimization. They have applied their developed algorithms in solving many different practical problems. In this paper, they have introduced an interesting practical problem and solved it using an evolutionary algorithm. Practical problems from different domains, with similar characteristics, can be solved using the algorithms applied in this paper. This would benefit many organizations and community.

1. Introduction

Many real-world decision problems, such as project scheduling, production planning, and resource allocation, are multi-period and dynamic (Sarker & Newton, 2007). In these problems, it is required to make the decisions for many periods in the future repeatedly. In some cases, firstly, the multi-period problem is solved as a static problem based on the anticipated parameters and then the solutions are updated at a regular interval with the availability of new information. In some other cases, the problem is solved only for the current period as the data and information for future periods are hardly available in the current period. In the literature, similar problems are solved as optimization problems.

In this paper, we introduce a problem of higher degree research student recruitment (HDRSR) process. In the process, we recruit the best possible set of students considering the eligibility of students, their ability for timely completion, supervision capacity, funding availability, and other resource limitation. As all these information are available at the time of the application process, the decision problem is to allocate the eligible students to some supervisors or a group of supervisors in different disciplines using a department, school or faculty specific decision criteria. Examples of decision criteria are maximizing the throughput, minimizing the average completion time, maximizing the quality of output, minimizing the overall cost, and maximizing the return on investment. The HDRSR problem looks like a single-period static optimization problem that must be solved in each period (or session or semester) with period dependent parameters and data.

To analyze the recruitment pattern or the performance over a number of future periods, it is required to solve the problem for many periods, where the parameters are either stochastic or dynamic. That means, this is a dynamic optimization problem where the timing of parameter change is known, but their magnitude must be either calculated or predicted using historical data and derived functions. For better results, such a model must be run in each period on a rolling horizon basis.

In this research, we have defined a HDRSR as an optimization problem and developed a mathematical model to represent the problem. The mathematical model has been solved using a differential evolution (DE) algorithm. The representative data were taken from a research intensive school/department considering five research focus areas. The model has been solved using DE algorithm for a single semester as a static optimization problem and for several semesters in the future as a dynamic optimization problem. The performance of each research focus area has been analyzed and their combined affect has also been reported.

The rest of this paper is organized as follows: Section 2 presents the problem definition and mathematical model of HDRSR. Section 3 gives an overview of DE. The details of the algorithm used to solve the problem are given in Section 4, while Section 5 presents the computational results. Finally, conclusions are elaborated in Section 6.

2. Problem definition and mathematical modeling

In this paper, we consider an academic unit, such as a department, school or research centre, within a higher degree institution/university. As a part of the academic activities, the selected academic unit offers higher degree research program, such as Doctor of Philosophy (PhD). The unit has a number of research focus areas and each area has limited qualified academics to supervise HDR students. The unit has its own scheme to fund scholarships to high quality HDR students. There may be some additional funding available under special projects and from external sources. The eligible students apply for admission to conduct research in a research area of his/her interest and at the same they apply for scholarships. In the HDRSR problem, for simplicity, we aim to allocate the research students to a group of supervisors, having similar research interests, by maximizing the sum of a performance index that emphasizes on quick completion as well as high quality output. However, one can consider the allocation to individual supervisors or school and faculty level. Such a problem requires input from the academic unit, such as supervision capacity in each research focus area in each semester, the number of scholarships available in each semester, the number of eligible applicants under each area in each semester, and any special condition imposed by the unit, such as supervision performance of each research area. The output expected is the allocation of students to each research area and performance analysis for each area and the unit as a whole.

We assume that all applicants eligible for enrollment will apply for scholarships. Here, the scholarship means living allowance paid by the individual research group, or the academic unit. This assumption can be relaxed depending on the mix of applicants. For example, a group of students may require only supervision not funding. We consider two types of scholarships: (1) common pool—applicants from any research group can apply and (2) special scholarships—funded by individual research group for their own applicants. We also assume that the expected completion time for a PhD program is 3.5 years (seven semesters).

The constraints considered here are the number of eligible applicants, the supervision capacity in each research area, and the availability of funding for scholarships (converted to the number of scholarships) in both general pool and special scholarships.

To develop the mathematical model for the HDRSR problem, we define a set of decision variables and parameters, as presented in Table 1.

The objective is to maximize the sum of a performance index subject to a set of constraints, such that

$$\text{Maximize } f(x) = \sum_{i}^{n} \left(\frac{W}{ACT_{it} - D} \right) x_{it} \tag{1}$$

Subject to:

$$x_{it} \leq NA_{it}, \quad \forall i, t \tag{2}$$

$$x_{it} \leq SC_{it}, \quad \forall i, t \tag{3}$$

$$y_{it} \leq SS_{it}, \quad \forall i, t \tag{4}$$

Table 1. List of abbreviations used

Index	Meaning
i	A research group
t	Time period (equal to a semester)
k	An applicant (eligible research student)
x_{it}	Number of students recruited to start in t with i
y_{it}	Number of students selected for special scholarships in t with i
NS_t	Number of scholarships available in the general pool in t
SS_{it}	Number of special scholarships available in i at semester t
NA_{it}	Number of eligible applicants in i at t
SC_{it}	Supervision capacity available (number of students that can be supervised) in i at t
$SCom_{it}$	Number of students successfully completed their degree from i at t
$NPub_{it}$	Number of elite papers published from student research in group i in semester t
DES_{kit}	Number of semesters taken to complete by a student k from i (who completes in semester t)
ACT_{it}	Average completion time of students of group i as calculated in semester t
D	The minimum number of semesters allowed by the university for thesis submission−1
QI_{it}	Quality index of students' research in group i in semester t
n	The number of groups
W	The weight

$$\sum_{i}^{n}(x_{it} - y_{it}) \leq NS_t, \quad \forall t \tag{5}$$

$$x_{it}, y_{it} \geq 0 \text{ and integer}, \quad \forall i, t \tag{6}$$

where the constraint inequalities Equations 2–6 represent the limit on eligible applicants, supervision capacity, limit on special scholarships, limit on general pool of scholarships, and non-negativity of variables, respectively. Firstly, the applicants are ranked based on their qualifications, research experiences, and publications, and then the number of short-listed applicants set the limit on eligible applicants used in the constraint. The supervision capacity is determined based on the number of students that can be supervised by the research area in a semester. The number of scholarships is calculated based on the funding available. The average completion time is calculated, and updated at each t, using the following equation that considers the completions of the past S semesters

$$ACT_{it} = \frac{\sum_{t-S}^{t-1} \sum_{k} DES_{kit}}{\sum_{t-S}^{t-1} SCom_{it}} \tag{7}$$

For simplicity, in this paper, the quality index is measured as the high quality publications produced per unit supervision capacity, which is expressed as follows:

$$QI_{it} = \frac{N\,Pub_{it}}{SC_{it}} \tag{8}$$

W is a sum of three components as follows:

$$W = A_i ACT_{it} + B_i y_{it} + C_i QI_{it} \tag{9}$$

where A_i, B_i, and C_i are the given parameters. A higher value of A_i ensures a higher weight for average early completion, a higher value of B_i ensures higher weight for the group having own funding for scholarships, while a higher value of C_i provides higher weight for the group's quality index. The quality index may include other achievements, such as quality of theses and external recognition.

3. Differential evolution

DE is a powerful global search algorithm for real parameter optimization. It combines the concept of using larger population from a GA and self-adapting mutation from evolution strategy (Storn & Price, 1995). DE differs from other EAs mainly in its generation of new vectors by adding the weighted difference vector between two individuals to a third individual (Storn & Price, 1995). We have selected DE in this paper because of its superior search ability in solving complex practical problems, and it does not require the satisfaction of any mathematical properties of a problem on hand (Sarker & Newton, 2007; Elsayed, Sarker, & Essam, 2013a). Also, the HDRSR problem is dynamic, so using flexible algorithms like DE can guarantee better performance in comparison with deterministic methods (Sarker, Kamruzzaman, & Newton, 2003). The rest of this section gives an overview of DE's operators and parameters.

3.1. Mutation

A mutant vector is generated by multiplying F by the difference between two random vectors and the result is added to a third random vector (DE/rand/1) as

$$\vec{V}_z = \vec{X}_{r_1,j} + F(\vec{X}_{r_2,j} - \vec{X}_{r_3,j}) \tag{10}$$

where r_1, r_2, and r_3 are different random integer numbers $\in [1, PS]$ and none of them is similar $z = 1, 2, \ldots, PS$, PS is the population size. The type of mutation operator has a great effect on the performance of DE. As a consequence, many mutation types have been introduced over the last era, such as: DE/best/1 (Storn & Price, 1997), DE/rand-to-best/1 (Qin, Huang, & Suganthan, 2009) and DE/current-to-best (Zhang & Sanderson, 2009).

3.2. Crossover

There are two well-known crossover schemes, exponential and binomial. In an exponential crossover, firstly, an integer index, l, is randomly selected from a range $[1, n]$, where n is the problem dimension. This index acts as an initial position in the target vector from where an exchange of variables with the donor vector begins. An integer index, L, that defines the number of components the donor vector contributes to the target vector, is randomly selected, such that $L \in [1, n]$. Subsequently, a trial vector ($\overline{u}$) is calculated such that

$$u_{z,j} = \begin{cases} v_{z,j} & \text{for } j = \langle l \rangle_n, \langle l+1 \rangle_n, \ldots, \langle l+L-1 \rangle_n \\ x_{z,j} & \forall j \in [1, n] \end{cases} \tag{11}$$

where $j = 1, 2 \ldots, D$, and $\langle l \rangle_n$ denotes a modulo function with a modulus of n and a starting location of l.

On the other hand, the binomial crossover is conducted on every variable with a predefined crossover probability, such that:

$$u_{z,j} = \begin{cases} v_{z,j} & \text{if } (rand \leq Cr | j = j_{rand}) \\ x_{z,j} & \text{otherwise} \end{cases} \tag{12}$$

$j_{rand} \in 1, 2, \ldots, D$ is a randomly selected index, which ensures $\vec{u_z}$ gets at least one component from $\vec{v_z}$.

3.3. Selection

The selection process is simple, in which an offspring will be survived to the next generation, if it is better than its parent, based on its objective value and/or constraints violation.

Over the last two decades, many DE variants have been proposed to adapt DE parameters and/or operators.

Storn and Price (1997) recommended a population size of $5n - 20n$ (and an F value of 0.5, while Rönkkönen (2009) indicated that F is typically between 0.40 and 0.95, with $F = 0.9$ being a good first choice. Abbass (2002) proposed generating F using a Gaussian distribution $N(0, 1)$. This technique was then modified in Elsayed, Sarker, and Essam (2011). Qin et al. (2009) proposed a novel DE algorithm (SaDE), where F was approximated by a normal distribution $N(0.5, 0.3)$, and was truncated to the interval $(0, 2]$. Cr was randomly generated according to an independent normal distribution with mean Cr_m and standard deviation 0.1. The Cr_m values were fixed for five generations before the next regeneration. Cr_m was initialized to 0.5, and it was updated every 25 generations based on the recorded successful Cr values since the last Cr_m update.

Using fuzzy logic controllers, Liu and Lampinen (2005) presented a fuzzy adaptive DE. Brest, Greiner, Boskovic, Mernik, and Zumer (2006) proposed a self-adaptation scheme for the DE control parameters, where in it, a set of F and Cr values were assigned to each individual in the population, thus augmenting the dimensions of each vector. Zhang and Sanderson (2009) introduced an adaptive DE algorithm with optional external memory (JADE). In it, at each generation, Cr_z of each individual was independently generated according to a normal distribution of mean μ_{Cr} and standard deviation of 0.1. μ_{Cr} was initialized at a value of 0.5 and was latter updated. Similarly, F_z of each individual was independently generated according to a Cauchy distribution with location parameter (μ_F) and scale parameter 0. μ_F was initialized at a value of 0.5 and was subsequently updated at the end of each generation.

Sarker, Elsayed, and Ray (2014) proposed a DE algorithm that used a mechanism to dynamically select the best performing combinations of parameters Cr and F for a problem during the course of a single run. The performance of the algorithm was judged by solving three well-known sets of optimization test problems (two constrained and one unconstrained). The results demonstrated that the proposed algorithm was superior to other state-of-the-art algorithms. Elsayed et al. (2011) proposed an algorithm that divides the population into four sub-populations. Each sub-population uses one combination of search operators. During the evolutionary process, the sub-population sizes were adaptively varied, such that the sub-population size of each successful operator was increased, and at the same time the sub-population size of the unsuccessful operators was shrunk. The measure of success and failure of any combination of operators was decided based on changes in the fitness values, constraint violations, and the feasibility ratio of the sub-populations individuals. The algorithm performed well on a set of constrained problems. The algorithm was then extended and improved in Elsayed, Sarker, and Essam (2012, 2013b).

Algorithm 1 General framework of DE considered

1: Generate an initial random population. The variables of each individual $(\vec{x_z})$ must be within its boundaries;
2: Calculate the fitness value and constraint violation of $(\vec{x_z})$;
3: **while** $iter < iter_{max}$ **do**
4:    **for** $z = 1 : PS$ **do**
5:       Generate a new individual $(\vec{u_z})$;
6:       Calculate the fitness value and constraint violation of $(\vec{u_z})$;
7:       **if** $\vec{u_z}$ is better than $\vec{x_z}$ **then**
8:          $\vec{u_z}$ is survived to the next generation;
9:       **end if**
10:       Update and sort the new population.
11:    **end for**
12:    $iter \leftarrow iter + 1$
13: **end while**

Zamuda and Brest (2012) proposed an algorithm that incorporated two multiple mutation strategies into a self-adaptive DE (jDE) (Brest et al., 2006) and a population reduction methodology which was introduced in Brest and Maučec (2008). The algorithm was tested on 22 real-world applications, and showed better performance than two other algorithms. Brest et al. (2013) also proposed a DE algorithm which embedded a self-adaptation mechanism for parameter control. In it, the population was divided into sub-populations to apply more DE strategies, and a population diversity mechanism was also introduced. The algorithm was tested on a set of unconstrained problems.

4. A DE algorithm for HDRSR
The general framework of the DE algorithm used in this research is presented in Algorithm 1.

Firstly, instead of encoding two initial populations, one for x and one for y, each individual of a length n, a single population is encoded, of size PS, and each individual with a length $2n$, where the first n components represent x, while the subsequent n components are for y. For simplicity, instead on saying $2n$ as the problem dimension, we name it to n. For simplicity, we will use x to represent the decision variables. Each individual must be within its range, such that

$$x_{z,j} = \underline{x}_{z,j} + rand \times (\bar{x}_{z,j} - \underline{x}_{z,j}) \qquad (13)$$

where $\underline{x}_{z,j}, \bar{x}_{z,j}$ are the lower and upper bounds of the decision variable x_j, and $rand$ is a random number $\in [0, 1]$. As we deal with an integer optimization problem, each $x_{z,j}$ is rounded to an integer number, as depicted in Figure 1.

Subsequently, DE takes place to generate new individuals. DE/current-to-best (Zhang & Sanderson, 2009) is used, along with the binomial crossover, such that

| 7 | 4 | 9 | 0 | 0 | 2 | 6 | 4 | 8 | 3 |

Figure 1. Representation of a DE individual.

| Generated offspring | 0.746835 | 9.471519 | 10.563291 | 9.379747 | 8.598102 | 1.908228 | 7.563291 | 3.218354 | 4.091772 | 1.436709 |

$$\downarrow$$

Generated offspring (rounded) | 1 | 9 | 11 | 9 | 9 | 2 | 8 | 3 | 4 | 1 |

$$
u_{z,j} = \begin{cases} x_{z,j} + F_z \cdot (x_{best,j} - x_{z,j} + x_{r_1,j} - x_{r_2,j}) \\ \qquad\quad if(rand \le cr_z | j = j_{rand}) \\ x_{z,j} \qquad\qquad\qquad otherwise \end{cases} \tag{14}
$$

Figure 2. Representation of a possible generated offspring.

where $x_{best,j}$ is the jth variable of the best individual within the current population, a possible representation of one individual is represented in Figure 2.

If $\bar{u}_z$ is better than $\bar{x}_z$, it will survive to the next generation; otherwise keep $\bar{x}_z$ in the next generation. The process continues until a stopping criterion is met. The definition of superiority is based on the superiority of feasible solutions technique (Deb, 2000), as it does not require user-defined parameters. In it, three conditions exist: (1) between two feasible candidates, the fittest one (according to fitness function) is selected; (2) a feasible point is always better than an infeasible one; and (3) between two infeasible solutions, the one with a smaller sum of constraint violations (Θ) is chosen.

5. Experimental results

For the current semester t, the optimization model presented in Section 2 is a simple static problem, where all the relevant data and parameters can be calculated and generated using the historical data and based on the goal of the administration. For analyzing multiple periods in the future, some parameters (such as ACT_{it} and QI_{it}) are dynamically changed with relation to their earlier activities and performances, and some other parameters (such as NA_{it} and NS_t) are basically random variables. For multiple periods analysis, we ran the model for a single period, update the parameters, and then re-ran it for the next period. The process continues until all T periods are completed. For the

Table 2. Data generation	
n	5 groups for x and the same is for y, hence $n = 10$
NS_t	Randomly generated between 20 and 30
SS_{it}	Randomly between 0 and 3
NA_{it}	Randomly between 25 and 40
$MaxSC_{i,L}$	48 for each group (8 supervisors, with a maximum supervision limit of 6 of each one)
SC_{it}	Randomly between 0 and $MaxSC_{i,t} - SCom_{i,t-1}$
$SCom_{it}$	Randomly between 0 and $k_{i,t-6}$
$k_{i,t}$	Randomly between 0 and $MaxSC_{i,t} - SCom_{i,t-1}$
DES_{kit}	Randomly generated 5 and 10
D	3
QI_{it}	1 to 5, where 5 is assigned for the best group.
S	6
t	7
T	18
A	10
B	5
$\underline{x}_{z,j}$	0
$\bar{x}_{z,j}$	NA_{it}

t	Best	Mean	Std.
Table 3. Function values obtained at each semester			
7	2.1362E+02	2.1362E+02	0.000E+00
8	1.7674E+02	1.7674E+02	0.000E+00
9	1.2170E+02	1.2170E+02	0.000E+00
10	1.2655E+02	1.2655E+02	0.000E+00
11	1.2205E+02	1.2205E+02	0.000E+00
12	1.3513E+02	1.3513E+02	0.000E+00
13	1.3941E+02	1.3941E+02	0.000E+00
14	1.2122E+02	1.2122E+02	0.000E+00
15	1.1663E+02	1.1663E+02	0.000E+00
16	1.2524E+02	1.2524E+02	0.000E+00
17	1.2930E+02	1.2930E+02	0.000E+00
18	1.4790E+02	1.4790E+02	0.000E+00

experimental study, we used random values for some parameters within their ranges observed in the past. Alternatively, the predicted values can be used which can then be changed with the availability of updated information, as shown in Table 2.

Regarding DE parameters, both $F \in [0.4 - 0.95]$, while Cr was set at a value of 0.95 (Sarker et al., 2014). The algorithm was run for 25 times at each period. The best and mean objective values were recorded along with the standard deviation, as shown in Table 3. From this table, it is clear that the algorithm is robust, in which it was able to obtain the same solution, in all 25 runs, at each semester.

Furthermore, Figure 3 shows the number of students that may be recruited during each semester for the subsequent 12 semesters. This figure shows that the numbers of students, in each group, will be close to each other in the long run if they have similar supervision capacity. In the optimization

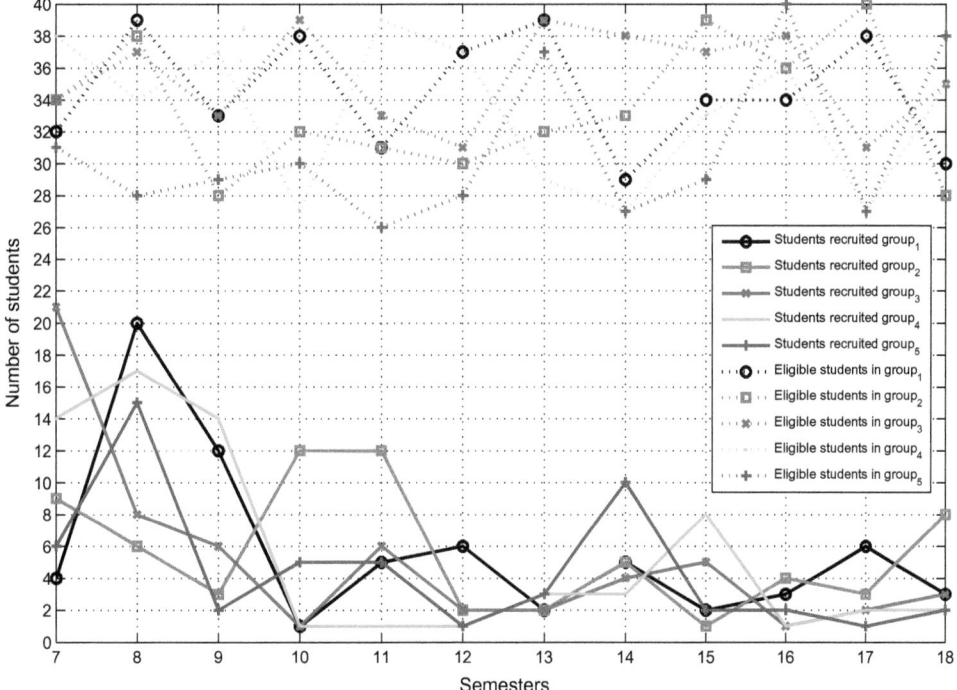

Figure 3. Number of students recruited and eligible students over 12 semesters.

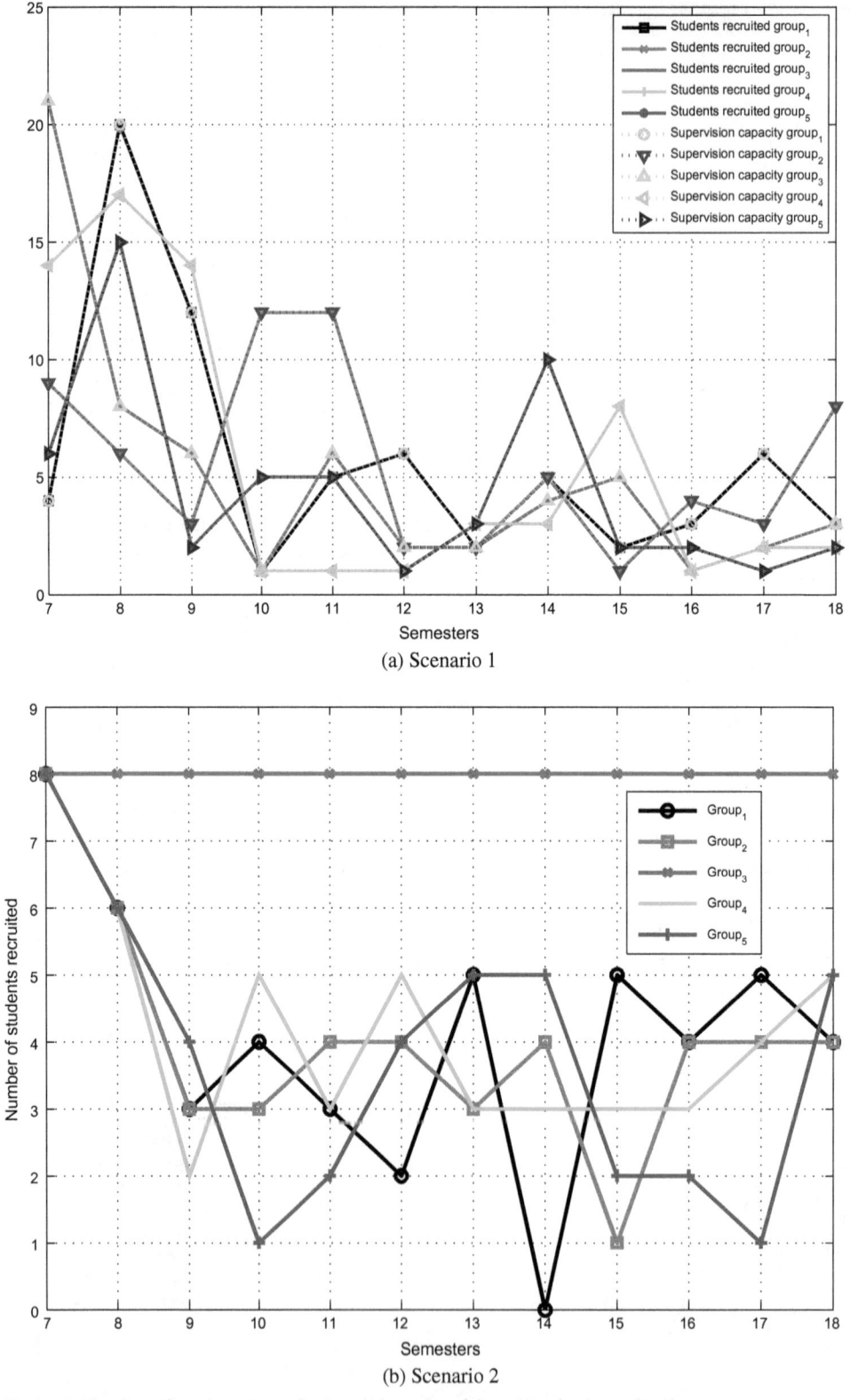

Figure 4. Number of students recruited and the supervision capacity in each group.

process, the students will be assigned to high performing groups first and then to the remaining capacity in other groups if the constraints permit.

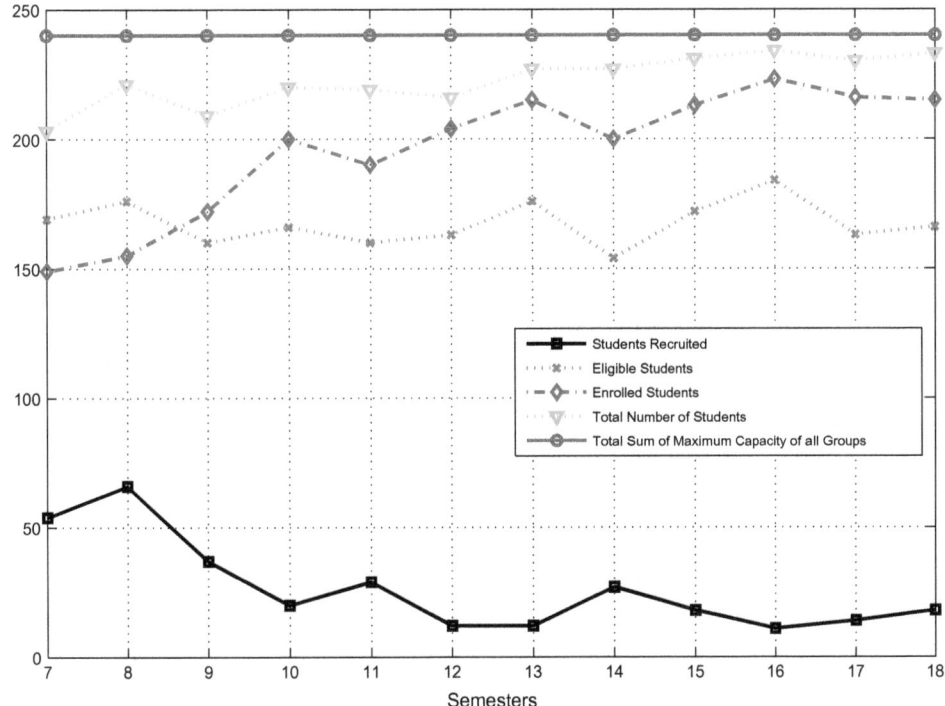

Figure 5. Aggregated summary of students currently enrolled and recruited in each semester.

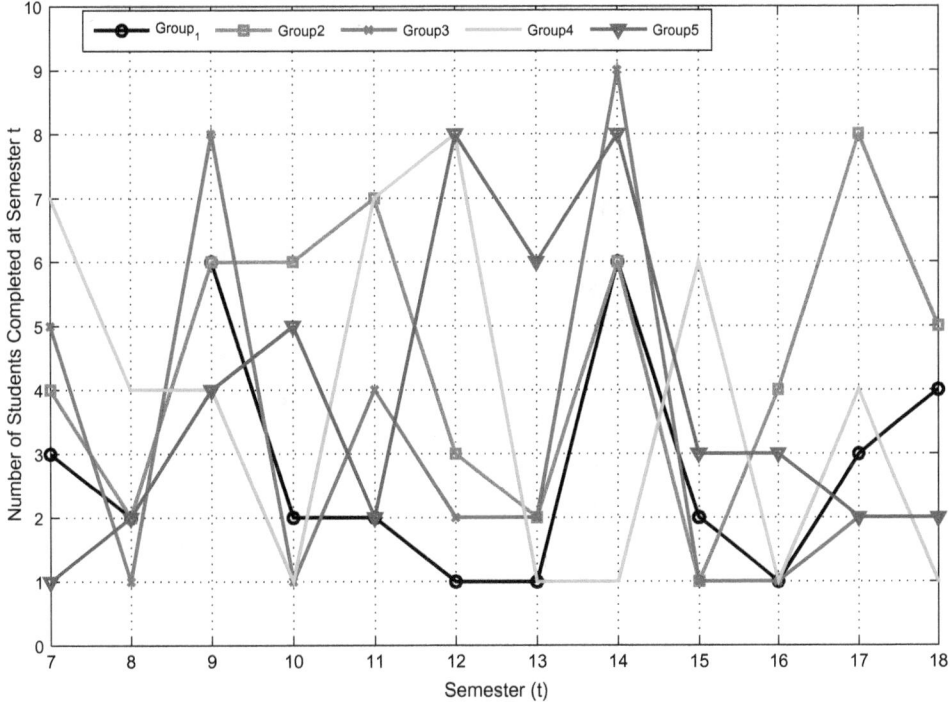

Figure 6. Number of students who completed their studies at each semester.

Figure presents two scenarios. In scenario 1, we assume that there are many scholarships in each semester and in scenario 2 only a few scholarships are available in each semester. In Figure 4, we present the number of students recruited in each group, at each semester, and the supervision capacity. From this figure, it is clear that the numbers of students recruited are optimized to be identical to the supervision capacity in each group, while Figure shows that the best performing group will receive more students compared to other groups due to the limited number of scholarships.

Figure 5 provides a summary of the total sum of enrolled and recruited students in all groups.

Lastly, Figure 6 is presented to give an overview of the performance of each group, in terms of the number of students who completed their studies at each semester.

5.1. Comparison to other algorithms

In this section, we compare the results obtained with other methods which are well-known in the literature (1) GA, and (2) branch and bound (BB) technique. Both of them are available in Matlab. The results obtained are shown in Table 4, and a comparison summary is presented in Table 5. From the results obtained, it was found that all algorithms were able to obtain the same best results. However, considering the average results achieved, it was shown that DE was the best. This gives a conclusion that DE is more robust than the other two algorithms in solving the problem under consideration in this paper.

Also, the Wilcoxon signed rank test (Corder & Foreman, 2009) is considered to statistically compare between both algorithms. As a null hypothesis, it is assumed that there is no significant difference between the best and/or average results of two samples, while the other hypothesis is that there is a significant difference in the best and/or mean fitness values of the two samples. Using a significance level of 5%, one of three signs (+, –, and $\approx$) is assigned for the comparison of any two algorithms, where the "+" sign means that the first algorithm is significantly better than the second, the "–"sign means that the first algorithm is significantly worse, and the "$\approx$" sign means that there

Table 4. Function values obtained at each semester

t	Best results			Mean results			Std.		
	DE	GA	BB	DE	GA	BB	DE	GA	BB
7	2.1362E+02	2.1362E+02	2.1362E+02	2.1362E+02	1.9935E+02	2.1362E+02	0.000E+00	1.1610E+01	1.1369E-13
8	1.7674E+02	1.7674E+02	1.7674E+02	1.7674E+02	1.6996E+02	1.7652E+02	0.000E+00	6.5558E+00	1.0743E+00
9	1.2170E+02	1.2170E+02	1.2170E+02	1.2170E+02	1.1293E+02	1.2170E+02	0.000E+00	5.3008E+00	4.2633E-14
10	1.2655E+02	1.2655E+02	1.2655E+02	1.2655E+02	1.1993E+02	1.2640E+02	0.000E+00	4.5200E+00	7.2354E-01
11	1.2205E+02	1.2205E+02	1.2205E+02	1.2205E+02	1.1312E+02	1.2205E+02	0.000E+00	5.4741E+00	0.0000E+00
12	1.3513E+02	1.3513E+02	1.3513E+02	1.3513E+02	1.2765E+02	1.3479E+02	0.000E+00	3.8629E+00	1.6330E+00
13	1.3941E+02	1.3941E+02	1.3941E+02	1.3941E+02	1.3128E+02	1.3941E+02	0.000E+00	5.0925E+00	5.6843E-14
14	1.2122E+02	1.2122E+02	1.2122E+02	1.2122E+02	1.1576E+02	1.2122E+02	0.000E+00	4.3298E+00	2.8422E-14
15	1.1663E+02	1.1663E+02	1.1663E+02	1.1663E+02	1.0939E+02	1.1495E+02	0.000E+00	5.0459E+00	5.6770E+00
16	1.2524E+02	1.2524E+02	1.2524E+02	1.2524E+02	1.2020E+02	1.2217E+02	0.000E+00	4.3455E+00	1.5053E+01
17	1.2930E+02	1.2930E+02	1.2930E+02	1.2930E+02	1.2275E+02	1.2890E+02	0.000E+00	5.7719E+00	1.7739E+00
18	1.4790E+02	1.4790E+02	1.4790E+02	1.4790E+02	1.3930E+02	1.4739E+02	0.000E+00	7.0395E+00	2.4815E+00

Table 5. A comparison summary of DE against GA and BB

Algorithms	Results	Better	Similar	Worse	Decision
DE vs. GA	Best	0	12	0	$\approx$
	Mean	12	0	0	+
DE vs. SQP	Best	0	12	0	$\approx$
	Mean	7	5	0	+

is no significant difference between the two algorithms. The results are shown in Table 5. From this table, it was found that DE was statistically better than both other algorithms only based on the average results.

6. Conclusions and future work

In this paper, we have introduced an interesting optimization problem arising from HDRSR process and completion in a university environment. The problem is to maximize a user given performance index by satisfying supervision capacity and resource limitation constraints. This is basically a dynamic optimization problem where many parameters not only vary from period to period but also they are difficult to predict in advance. In this research, we have presented a mathematical model to represent this problem and applied DE algorithm to solve the model. Different analysis related to recruitment and completion has been provided. This model can be used for long-run recruitment planning of higher degree research programs based on the forecasted number of applications and scholarships.

For future work, we intend to (1) study the problem in different academic units and institutions, (2) consider different objective functions, (3) consider simultaneous optimization of more than one objective function, and (4) consider many units under an institutions with limited budget constraint.

Funding
The authors received no direct funding for this research.

Author details
Ruhul Sarker[1]
E-mail: r.sarker@adfa.edu.au
Saber Elsayed[1]
E-mail: s.elsayed@adfa.edu.au
[1] School of Engineering and Information Technology, University of New South Wales at Canberra, Northcott Drive, Canberra, 2600 Australia.

References
Abbass, H. A. (2002). The self-adaptive pareto differential evolution algorithm. In *IEEE Congress on Evolutionary Computation (CEC)* (Vol. 1, pp. 831–836). Honolulu, HI: IEEE.
Brest, J., Boskovic, B., Zamuda, A., Fister, I., & Mezura-Montes, E. (2013). Real parameter single objective optimization using self-adaptive differential evolution algorithm with more strategies. In *IEEE Congress on Evolutionary Computation (CEC)* (pp. 377–383). Cancun: IEEE.
Brest, J., Greiner, S., Boskovic, B., Mernik, M., & Zumer, V. (2006). Self-adapting control parameters in differential evolution: A comparative study on numerical benchmark problems. *IEEE Transactions on Evolutionary Computation, 10*, 646–657.
Brest, J., & Maučec, M. S. (2008). Population size reduction for the differential evolution algorithm. *Applied Intelligence, 29*, 228–247.
Corder, G. W., & Foreman, D. I. (2009). *Nonparametric statistics for non-statisticians: A step-by-step approach*. Hoboken, NJ: Wiley.
Deb, K. (2000). An efficient constraint handling method for genetic algorithms. *Computer Methods in Applied Mechanics and Engineering, 186*, 311–338.
Elsayed, S. M., Sarker, R. A., & Essam, D. L. (2011). Multi-operator based evolutionary algorithms for solving constrained optimization problems. *Computers & Operations Research, 38*, 1877–1896.
Elsayed, S. M., Sarker, R. A., & Essam, D. L. (2012). On an evolutionary approach for constrained optimization problem solving. *Applied Soft Computing, 12*, 3208–3227.
Elsayed, S. M., Sarker, R. A., & Essam, D. L. (2013a). Self-adaptive differential evolution incorporating a heuristic mixing of operators. *Computational Optimization and Applications, 54*, 771–790.
Elsayed, S. M., Sarker, R. A., & Essam, D. L. (2013b). An improved self-adaptive differential evolution algorithm for optimization problems. *IEEE Transactions on Industrial Informatics 9*, 89–99.
Liu, J., & Lampinen, J. (2005). A fuzzy adaptive differential evolution algorithm. *Soft Computing, 9*, 448–462.
Qin, A. K., Huang, V. L., & Suganthan, P. N. (2009). Differential evolution algorithm with strategy adaptation for global numerical optimization. *IEEE Transactions on Evolutionary Computation, 13*, 398–417.
Rönkkönen, J. (2009). *Continuous multimodal global optimization with differential evolution-based methods*. Lappeenranta, FL: Lappeenranta University of Technology.
Sarker, R., Elsayed, S., & Ray, T. (2014). Differential evolution with dynamic parameters selection for optimization problems. *IEEE Transactions on Evolutionary Computation, 18*, 689–707.
Sarker, R., Kamruzzaman, J., & Newton, C. (2003). Evolutionary optimization (evopt): A brief review and analysis. *International Journal of Computational Intelligence and Applications, 3*, 311–330.
Sarker, R. A., & Newton, C. S. (2007). *Optimization modelling: A practical approach*. Boca Raton, FL: CRC Press.
Storn, R., & Price, K. (1995). *Differential evolution-a simple and efficient adaptive scheme for global optimization over continuous spaces* (Vol. 3). Berkeley, CA: ICSI.
Storn, R., & Price, K. (1997). Differential evolution-a simple and efficient heuristic for global optimization over continuous spaces. *Journal of Global Optimization, 11*, 341–359.
Zamuda, A., & Brest, J. (2012). Population reduction differential evolution with multiple mutation strategies in real world industry challenges. In L. Rutkowski, M. Korytkowski, R. Scherer, R. Tadeusiewicz, L. Zadeh, & J. Zurada (Eds.), *Swarm and evolutionary computation* (pp. 154–161). Zakopane: Springer.
Zhang, J., & Sanderson, A. C. (2009). Jade: Adaptive differential evolution with optional external archive. *IEEE Transactions on Evolutionary Computation, 13*, 945–958.

5

Petri net modeling and simulation of pipelined redistributions for a deadlock-free system

Stavros I. Souravlas[1]* and Manos Roumeliotis[1]

*Corresponding author: Stavros I. Souravlas, Department of Applied Informatics, University of Macedonia, Thessaloniki, Greece

E-mail: sourstav@uom.gr

Reviewing editor: Jenhui Chen, Chang Gung University, Taiwan

Abstract: The growing use of multiprocessing systems has given rise to the necessity for modeling, verifying, and evaluating their performance in order to fully exploit hardware. The Petri net (PN) formalism is a suitable tool for modeling parallel systems due to its basic characteristics, such as parallelism and synchronization. In addition, the PN formalism allows the incorporation of more details of the real system into the model. Examples of such details include contention for shared resources (like memory) or identification of blocked processes (a definition for blocked processes is found in the Introduction section). In this paper, PNs are considered as a modeling framework to verify and study the performance of parallel pipelined communications. The main strength of the pipelines is that if organized in a proper way, they lead to overlapping of computation, communication, and read/write costs that incur in parallel communications. Most of the well-known pipelined schemes have been evaluated by theoretical analysis, queueing networks, and simulations. Usually, the factors taken into account are scheduling, message classification, and buffer spacing. To the best of our knowledge, there is no work in the literature that uses PN as a modeling tool for verification of the pipeline-based scheme. Apart from verification, a more accurate and complete model should also consider other factors, such as contentions and blocked processes. These factors have a high impact on the performance of a parallel system. The PN model presented in this paper accurately

ABOUT THE AUTHORS

Stavros Souravlas and Manos Roumeliotis are faculty members of the Department of Applied Informatics at the University of Macedonia. They are the authors of three books in the field of Digital Logic Design, Digital Systems Modeling and Simulation with VHDL, and Simulation Techniques. Also, Stavros Souravlas Manos Roumeliotis are members of the Computer and Network Systems Technologies (CNST) group at the University of Macedonia. This group conducts research on the fields of digital systems design, parallel and distributed processing, communication networks, hardware description languages, and modeling and simulation of computer and network systems. This work is a part of a general research project ran by the CNST group on the possible faults that incur when applying parallel algorithms on a multiprocessor network.

PUBLIC INTEREST STATEMENT

This paper presents a Petri net-based model used to verify and evaluate the performance of pipelined parallel distributions. It precisely captures the behavior of a pipeline-based parallel communication system. The model considers message scheduling and message classification, while it is deadlock and contention free. Because it is symmetric, it can easily be used for larger systems only with minor changes.

The model is composed of two subnetworks: the reading subnetwork and the pipeline execution subnetwork. The reading subnetwork implements the task of preparing the necessary pipeline tasks. The pipeline execution subnetwork implements the actual communication by executing the series of tasks. The model (and thus the real system) maintains its safety by preventing a pipeline from starting until all pipeline tasks have been formed. Also, it avoids deadlocks by preventing a new communication to start before all the other segments have been assigned the proper tasks.

captures the behavior of the pipeline-based parallel communication system. The model considers synchronization, message scheduling, and message classification, while it is proven to be free of deadlocks and contentions. Also, the model is characterized by symmetry, so it can be used for large and complex systems.

Subjects: Systems & Computer Architecture; Design; Systems Architecture

Keywords: Petri nets; parallel systems; pipeline; performance evaluation; block cyclic redistributions

1. Introduction-related work

The problem of data distribution between several processors is very important, affecting the efficiency of parallel algorithms. As a parallel program is being executed, it may require a different distribution of data between the processors or *redistribution*.

The principal issues that need to be considered to model a pipeline-based communication are (1) *total redistribution cost*, (2) *message scheduling*, (3) *message classification*, (4) *load balancing*, (5) *contentions*, and (6) *blocked processes*.

(a) *Total redistribution cost*: It is the total cost to redistribute data between several processors. It is composed of the **index computation overhead**, the **total communication overhead**, and the **R/W** (or **I/O**) overhead. The index computation overhead refers to computing the target processor and the memory positions where each data element will be located. The total communication overhead incurs during data distribution between parallel processors. The R/W overhead refers to the time consumed by R/W operations.

(b) *Message scheduling*: The term refers to the organization of message exchanges into structured communication steps, such that the total redistribution cost is minimized.

(c) *Message classification*: The term refers to dividing the data to be redistributed into homogeneous (in terms of communication cost) groups to effectively organize their redistribution.

(d) *Load balancing*: The ability of having all communication links equally or nearly equally loaded to avoid network congestions.

(e) *Contention*: This refers to conflicting transferring processes that distribute data to the same target processor at the same time.

(f) *Blocked processes*: A process is blocked if it waits for the execution of another process that never occurs.

Several pipeline-based techniques have been propo.sed in the literature (King, Chou, & Ni, 1990; Preud'homme, Sopena, Thomas, & Folliot, 2012; Rodrigues, Wheeler, & Kogge, 2008). The pipeline techniques have been widely studied (Caron & Desprez, 2005; Jayachandran & Abdelzaher, 2007; Kashif, Gholamian, Pelizzoni, Patel, & Fischmeister, 2013; Kuntraruk, Pottenger, & Ross, 2005; Souravlas & Roumeliotis, 2004, 2014 among others) and used to schedule interprocessor communication. In Caron and Desprez (2005), pipelining is combined with out-of-core techniques (OOC) to overlap the computation, communication, and R/W overheads. Scheduling is based on dividing memory into three memory blocks and then loading three blocks of data into memory. These blocks are three times smaller than what should be loaded without this segmentation. The communication costs overlap because during each period, the first memory block performs I/O, computation is performed on the data stored in the second block, and data from the third block is distributed to a nearby processor. No actual message classification incurs. Data are just fragmented into three pieces and transferred. Based on scheduling, no contentions should occur. During anytime, a memory block clearly receives one data block. The communication model does not take into account the issue of blocked processes. Assuming that there is a proper synchronization of the pipeline segments (so that no process can block the execution of another process), the communication tasks pass from one segment to another and delays are introduced on the writing processes to avoid idle times. A similar approach is presented in Jayachandran and Abdelzaher (2007), but it imposes a restriction on the usage of the pipelines: every task should finish before proceeding to the next pipeline segment.

In Kashif et al. (2013), the worst-case response times of real-time applications on multiprocessor systems are computed. The proposed technique schedules a simple pipelined communication operation for data distribution. The model consists of a set of processing resources interconnected with pipelined communication resources (CRs). Data transmitted on the CRs travel through the first segment followed by the next, and so on. Simultaneous transmission of data on segments is allowed. This means that while data are being transmitted on a later segment, new data can be transmitted on an earlier segment in parallel. However, if this situation is not handled carefully, it can lead to blocked processes. Pipeline segments should be carefully released first, before handling new transmissions.

The work in Kuntraruk et al. (2005) addresses the problem of developing a resource estimation model for applications executed within a parallel pipeline model of execution. The model estimates the computation and communication complexities for parallel pipelined applications. It includes two components: the ones that execute pipelined application tasks and the ones that perform merge operations. In the beginning, there are P tasks processed on P processors, one task per processor. Afterwards, at every step, the tasks are reduced in half since half of the processors are merging data received from the previous step. The model pays no attention to conflicts that could easily arise when different data volumes are carried over the network of processors. Also, there is no concern about possible blocked processes.

An interesting approach for modeling pipeline parallelism is given in Navarro et al. (2009). The authors develop a series of analytical models based on queueing theory for several parallel pipeline templates, which are modeled as closed or open queueing systems. Specifically, each pipeline segment is treated as a $M/M/c_i/N/K$ queue (for closed systems) or as a $M/M/c_i$ queue (for open systems). The models assure load balancing over the network. Since the proposed models are based on queues, contention is *not* avoided between messages that try to enter the queue. Things deteriorate if there is not much space in the queues. Necessarily, these models (unlike most of the models described) have to take into account the limited memory (buffer space). Simulations on real systems were used to verify that the queuing pipeline models capture the behavior of parallel systems faithfully. A related approach in Ties et al. (2007) marks the pipeline segments and tries to track the data communications performed in each of them. Also, an open system approach model is proposed by Liao et al. (2004), with the same factors taken into account. The latest approaches mentioned do not guarantee load balancing between processor sets.

Many other pipeline-based parallel communication models have been presented in the literature (King et al., 1990; Proud'homme et al., 2012; Rodrigues et al., 2008; Zhang & Deng, 2002). Generally, the models presented are basically concerned with maintaining some load balancing on the network during the pipelined distributions, with little or no attention paid on the problem of contentions and blocked processes. All these models also use simulation as the verification and performance study tool. Table 1 summarizes the factors addressed by the pipeline communication models discussed in this section. Note that all of the models involve some communication scheduling and load balancing (the messages distributed are of the same size) and none of them considers blocked processes. Also, most of the models assume that buffer space is enough to handle the distributed data and do not include a straightforward contention-preventing mechanism.

This paper introduces a Petri net (PN) model for modeling and simulating pipelined and deadlock-free parallel communications. PNs are used to examine the sequence of executed tasks (Granda, Drake, & Gregorio, 1992). The study of the process sequence is very important to avoid faults such as **deadlocks** [(some very general ideas about modeling pipelined parallel communication with PN can be found in Zhao, Liu, Dou, and Yang (2012)]. A deadlock-free scheme enhances the performance of

Table 1. Pipeline-based communication models in the literature and the factors they incorporate

Paper	Model	Verification	Factors incorporated					
			Scheduling	Message classification	Contentions	Blocked processes	Memory space	Load balance
Caron and Desprez (2005), Jayachandran and Abdelzaher (2007)	OOC and pipelining	Simulation	√	X	√	X	X	√
Kashif et al. (2013)	Pipelining	-Mathematics	√	X	X	X	X	√
		- Simulation						
Kuntraruk et al. (2005)	Pipelining	Simulation	√	X	X	X	X	√
Liao, Choundary, Weiner, and Varshney (2004), Navarro, Asenjo, and Tabik (2009), Ties, Chandrasekhar, and Amarasinghe (2007)	-Pipelining	Simulation	√	X	X	X	√	√
	-Queues							
This work	-Pipelining	Petri net, Simulation	√	√	√	√	X	√
	-Block cyclic							

any communication system. Generally, deadlocks occur when processes stay blocked for ever (waiting for an event caused by another process that never occurs) and in such cases, probably the whole system needs to be restarted. A block cyclic redistribution scheme can suffer from deadlock situations since each target block is formed during *runtime* and after a series of interrelated processes, which are described in Section 4.

The rest of the paper is organized as follows: Section 2 presents the background of the model, which is based on block cyclic(*r*) to block cyclic(*s*) distributions. Section 3 describes the pipelined communication, which is modeled via PN in Section 4. Section 5 presents some simulations for the complete PN model of Section 5, for three different communication scenarios. Section 6 concludes this paper.

2. Background
The model presented in this work has it is mathematical background on the well-known block cyclic redistribution problem, so this section briefly introduces the definitions required.

Definition 1   *Data array* is an array of size *M* used to represent the redistributed data. An *array element* is an element of the redistributed data indexed with *i*. Indexing begins from zero, thus, $i \in [0 \dots M - 1]$.

Definition 2   A processor grid can be represented by a two-dimensional (2D) table called *communication grid* Π: $\Pi = \{(p,q) \in [0 \dots P - 1] \times [0 \dots Q - 1]\}$. Obviously, *p* is the *source processor index*, *q* is the *destination processor index*, while *P, Q* represent the total number of sending and receiving processors, respectively.

Definition 3   Data distributed in a block cyclic fashion are divided into *data blocks*. If each data block has *r* elements, then, provided that *M* divides *r*, the data array will be divided into M_b blocks where: $M_b = \frac{M}{r}$. If *M* does not divide *r*, then $M_b = \frac{M}{r} + 1$. We use variable *l* as a *block index* that relates data blocks to the processors of the communication grid in a cyclic manner. Therefore, *l* lies in $\left[0 \dots \frac{M_b}{P}\right)$

or $\left[0 \dots \frac{M}{Pr}\right)$ (since $M_b = \frac{M}{r}$). Finally, variable x indexes the local position of an element inside a block. This means that $0 \le x < r$.

Definition 4   The *source distribution* $R(i, p, l, x)$ is the mapping of a data array element with index i to a processor index p, a block index l, and a local position inside the block x, where $i = (lP + p)r + x$.

Definition 5   Consider an element that is distributed cyclic(s) on Q processors. The number of blocks created is $M'_b = \frac{M}{s}$, where s is the block size. Variable m relates data blocks to the processors and its bounds are found in the interval $\left[0 \dots \frac{M'_b}{Q}\right)$ or $\left[0 \dots \frac{M}{Qs}\right)$ (because $M'_b = \frac{M}{s}$). The *target distribution* $R'(j, q, m, y)$ is defined similarly to the source redistribution. Parameters (j, q, m, y) have the same meaning as (i, p, l, x) of the source distribution. We can derive an equation for the distribution of element j: $j = (mQ + q)s + y$.

Definition 6   Suppose that data are a redistributed array from cyclic(r) on P processors to cyclic (s) on Q processors. In this case, changes will occur for all elements as far as their processor, block, and local position indices are concerned. These changes are described by: $R(i, p, l, x) = R'(j, q, m, y)$ or:

$$(lP + p)r + x = (mQ + q)s + y \tag{1}$$

This linear Diophantine equation is subject to the following restrictions: $0 \le p < P$, $0 \le q < Q$, $0 \le l < \frac{L}{Pr}$, $0 \le m < \frac{L}{Qs}$, $0 \le x < r$, $0 \le y < s$, where L is the least common multiplier of Pr, Qs, that is, $L = LCM(Pr, Qs)$.

Definition 7   The cost of transferring a message from a sending processor p to a receiving processor q is called *communication cost*, $C_{(p,q)}$. To compute the communication cost for a processor pair (p, q), one needs to find the number of quadruples (l, m, x, y) that satisfy Equation 1, given the number of sending (P) and receiving (Q) processors, and the block sizes of the source (r), and the target (s) redistribution.

Definition 8   Consider the following function:

$$f(p, q) = (pr - qs) \bmod g, \tag{2}$$

where $g = gcd(Pr, Qs)$ is the greatest common divisor of Pr and Qs. A pair of processors (p, q) belongs to a communication class (Desprez, Dongarra, Petitet, Randriamaro, & Robert, 1998a) k if:

$$f(p, q) = k \text{ or } (pr - qs) \bmod g = k \tag{3}$$

As Equation 3 indicates, all pairs of processors that communicate belong to a class of $(pr - qs) \bmod g$. The number of existing classes is at most g. Table 2 summarizes the variables used in this paper.

Table 2. Definitions of variables in this paper			
Variable	**Definition**	**Variable**	**Definition**
P	Number of sending nodes	s	Target distribution block size
Q	Number of receiving nodes	l	Source distribution block index
M	Size of data array	m	Target distribution block index
R	Source distribution	x	Source distribution element position
R'	Target distribution	y	Target distribution element position
p	Source processor index	g	Greatest common divisor of Pr, Qs
q	Destination processor index	L	Least common multiplier of Pr, Qs
r	Source distribution block size		

3. Pipelined communication

This section presents the pipelined interprocessor communication. Each pipeline includes a number of tasks responsible for the communication between carefully selected processor pairs. The main properties of the pipeline operations and their tasks are:

(1) Each pipeline task handles the transmission of data between processor pairs that have the same communication cost.

(2) A pipeline operation cannot include more than one task that handles message transmissions of a cost.

(3) The time required for the execution of a task equals the communication cost of the processor pairs it includes.

(4) The time required for the execution of a pipeline operation equals the execution time of its longest task.

(5) All tasks are scheduled in such a way that receiving processors get one message at a time, thus congestions on the receiving ports are avoided.

(6) The pipeline will include a number of segments (the role of segments in the communication will be explained in Section 3.3) equal to the number of different costs that exist in the scheme.

(7) The time the processors remain idle is minimized.

The pipelined data distribution is composed of three stages: (1) generating the pipeline tasks, (2) reading messages from memory, and (3) transferring the messages and writing them to the target processors' memory. In the next sections, details for each stage are presented.

3.1. Stage 1: Generating the pipeline tasks

The pipeline tasks must be scheduled in such a way that receiving processors get one message at a time. To satisfy this requirement, each task must include a number of distributions of **same** cost to **different** destination processors. Therefore, classes are used to group all the communicating processor pairs with respect to the cost of such communication. A processor pair lies in class $b(k)$, if $k = (pr - qs) \bmod g$. The class processor table (CPT) shows the class of each processor pair and the communication cost of this class. Consider a redistribution with $P = Q = 9, r = 4$, and $s = 5$. In this case, $g = 9$. The CPT for this redistribution example is shown in Table 3. For example, if $(p, q) = (4, 3)$, then $pr - qs = 16 - 15 = 1$. Thus, $(pr - qs) \bmod g = 1 \bmod 9 = 1$. This means that the processor pair (4,3) belongs to the class $k = 1$. The cost of communication for each class is computed as the number of quadruples (x, y, l, m) that satisfy Equation 1, for a given set (p, q).

Having defined the classes, it remains to: (1) find the number of pipeline operations and the number of their tasks, (2) define an upper bound for the number of processor pairs selected from each class for a pipeline task, and (3) define the number of classes from which the processor pairs are selected to have a minimum of Q transmissions (one message for each destination processor) in each pipelined communication.

Class	Processor pairs	Communication cost
b(0)	(0, 0), (8, 1), (7, 2), (6, 3), (5, 4), (4, 5), (3, 6), (2, 7), (1, 8)	4
b(1)	(7, 0), (6, 1), (5, 2), (4, 3), (3, 4), (2, 5), (1, 6), (0, 7), (8, 8)	4
b(2)	(5, 0), (4, 1), (3, 2), (2, 3), (1, 4), (0, 5), (8, 6), (7, 7), (6, 8)	4
b(3)	(3, 0), (2, 1), (1, 2), (0, 3), (8, 4), (7, 5), (6, 6), (5, 7), (4, 8)	4
b(4)	(1, 0), (0, 1), (8, 2), (7, 3), (6, 4), (5, 5), (4, 6), (3, 7), (2, 8)	4
b(6)	(6, 0), (5, 1), (4, 2), (3, 3), (2, 4), (1, 5), (0, 6), (8, 7), (7, 8)	4
b(7)	(4, 0), (3, 1), (2, 2), (1, 3), (0, 4), (8, 5), (7, 6), (6, 7), (5, 8)	4
b(8)	(2, 0), (1, 1), (0, 2), (8, 3), (7, 4), (6, 5), (5, 6), (4, 7), (3, 8)	4

Table 3. CPT for $P = Q = 9, r = 4$, and $s = 5$

To minimize the time the processors remain idle, each pipeline must be scheduled to have a maximum number of tasks; in other words, to transfer as much data as possible with a single pipeline operation. If the number of different communication costs found in all classes is d, then a pipeline operation has at most d tasks and can satisfy up to dQ message transmissions, without contentions.

Theorem 1 (for proof see Desprez et al., 1998a) is used to define an upper bound for the number of processor pairs in class $b(k)$ that will be added in a pipeline task. Initially, we set $s'' = gcd(s, P)$ and $r' = gcd(r, Q)$. Since s' divides P and r' divides Q, there exist integers P' and Q' such that: $P = P's'$ and $Q = Q'r'$. Also, we set $g_0 = gcd(P', Q')$.

THEOREM 1 Each class includes exactly $\frac{PQ}{g} = \frac{P'Q'}{g_0}$ processor pairs. Theorem 1 leads to the following corollaries:

(1) The number of sending requests to a destination inside a class is P'/g_0.
(2) There are exactly Q' different destinations inside each class, thus a pipeline task can satisfy no more than Q' communications between processor pairs of a class because this would cause contentions.

To define the number of classes from which processor pairs are selected for a minimum of Q transmissions for a pipeline operation, Proposition 1 will be used.

Proposition 1 For a pipeline operation with minimum number of Q communications, the communicating processor pairs must be selected from r' different classes.

The minimum number of message exchanges for a pipeline operation corresponds to "one message for each destination processor", that is, Q messages in total. A pipeline task can satisfy at most Q' communications from one class, otherwise contentions will occur. From the relationship $Q = Q'r'$, one can easily conclude that the processor pairs must be selected from r' classes to complete Q transmissions. The generation of the pipeline operations and their tasks can be described in a series of well-defined steps as follows:

Step 1: Solve (Equation 3) for all processor pairs (p, q) to define the processor classes and create the CPT.

Step 2: Find the total communication cost for each $b(k)$ by computing the number of quadruples (l, m, x, y) that satisfy Equation 1. Since each class includes messages of the same cost, only one computation is needed for a pair (p, q). All other processor pairs in the same class would have the same cost. Afterwards, define the value of different costs that exist for this distribution, d.

Step 3: Start from the class $b(k)$, for which the communication cost $C_{b(k)}$ is minimum, and get Q' processor pairs. If the pairs selected from $b(k)$ can form a task of Q transmissions, that is, if $Q = Q'$, move to Step 4. Otherwise, check if there is a class of the same cost as $b(k)$ to add up to $Q - Q'$ pairs. In either case, the processor pairs that task T_i should include must be such that all destination processor indices differ: $T_i = (p_{\lambda_0}, q_{\mu_0}), (p_{\lambda_1}, q_{\mu_1}), \ldots (p_{\lambda_p}, q_{\mu_Q})$, where $\mu_0 \neq \mu_1 \neq \ldots \neq \mu_Q$.

Step 4: Find the class $b(k)$ with the next communication cost and repeat Step 3. Tasks with the same communication cost are not allowed in the same pipeline operation. Once a pipeline includes dQ message exchanges, it is completed. Go to Step 5.

Step 5: Check the value of d to find the number of different costs for the rest of the processor pairs and use Steps 3 and 4 to create the next pipeline operation.

Step 6: When all processor pairs are added in a pipeline operation, terminate, if not, return to Step 1. Consider the redistribution for $P = Q = 9$, $r=4$, and $s = 5$. In this case, $g = 9$. The CPT is shown in

Table 3. Also (see the last column of Table 3), $d = 4$ since there are four different communication costs in the scheme varying from 1 to 4 time units. According to Step 3, we get $Q' = 9$ processor pairs from $r' = 1$ class to create a task of $Q = 9$ transmissions. We can select pairs from any of the two classes $b(4)$ and $b(6)$ since they have the same communication cost of one time unit. Suppose that we select from class $b(4)$. These processor pairs will form the first task T_0 of the first pipeline operation.

According to Step 4, the processor pairs of class $b(6)$ cannot be used in any of the tasks for this pipeline because the same communication cost of one unit will appear twice for all destinations. For the same reason, the classes $b(2)$ and $b(8)$, $b(0)$ and $b(1)$, and $b(3)$ and $b(7)$ are mutually exclusive. The tasks of the first pipeline include processor pairs from $b(0)$, $b(2)$, $b(3)$, and $b(4)$.

In Step 5, the value of d is checked to find the number of different costs in the remaining classes $b(1)$, $b(6)$, $b(7)$, and $b(8)$. We have $d = 4$. Therefore, Steps 3 and 4 are used to create the second pipeline (the two pipeline operations are shown in Table 4).

Once the pipeline operations and their tasks are scheduled, the messages must be read from local processor memories and prepared for distribution. This stage is described in the next section.

3.2. Initialization—reading messages from memory

This stage involves computing the local memory positions where the data to be distributed reside. Using the terms of Table 1 and Equation 1, one can describe the reading stage as follows: the reading stage computes the local positions x of the data elements to be redistributed. These elements reside in block l of the source processors' (p) memory. All this information can be easily obtained when (Equation 1) is solved. As an example, consider the transfer of data blocks towards processor $q = 0$ in a redistribution problem with parameters $P = Q = 9$, $r = 4$, and $s = 5$. Table 5 gives solutions of equation (Equation 1) when $q = 0$ and $p \in [0, 8]$.

Suppose that we want to know the position of the data elements scheduled to be distributed from source processor $p = 7$ to target processor $q = 0$. As shown in Table 5, these elements reside in block $l = 0$ and their local position inside the block is defined by x, that is, 0, 1, 2, and 3. The upper part of Figure 1 shows all the elements that will move to $q = 0$ and their initial position in the source processors. These positions are computed from Equation 1, as shown in Table 5. Once the initialization computations are done, the pipelines are ready for execution.

3.3. Transferring the messages and writing to the target processors' memory

When the pipelines execute, they generate a number of communications between several processors. It is important to note that pipeline operations are executed sequentially (one after the other) but their

Table 4. Pipeline operations and its tasks for $P = Q = 9$, $r = 4$, and $s = 5$		
Pipeline Task	**Communicating Processor Pairs (p,q)**	**Communication Cost**
First pipeline		
T_0	(1, 0), (0, 1), (8, 2), (7, 3), (6, 4), (5, 5), (4, 6), (3, 7), (2, 8)	1
T_1	(3, 0), (2, 1), (1, 2), (0, 3), (8, 4), (7, 5), (6, 6), (5, 7), (4, 8)	2
T_2	(5, 0), (4, 1), (3, 2), (2, 3), (1, 4), (0, 5), (8, 6), (7, 7), (6, 8)	3
T_3	(7, 0), (6, 1), (5, 2), (4, 3), (3, 4), (2, 5), (1, 6), (0, 7), (8, 8)	4
Second pipeline		
T_0	(6, 0), (5, 1), (4, 2), (3, 3), (2, 4), (1, 5), (0, 6), (8, 7), (7, 8)	1
T_1	(4, 0), (3, 1), (2, 2), (1, 3), (0, 4), (8, 5), (7, 6), (6, 7), (5, 8)	2
T_2	(2, 0), (1, 1), (0, 2), (8, 3), (7, 4), (6, 5), (5, 6), (4, 7), (3, 8)	3
T_3	(0, 0), (8, 1), (7, 2), (6, 3), (5, 4), (4, 5), (3, 6), (2, 7), (1, 8)	4

(p, q)	l	m	x	y	(p, q)	l	m	x	y	Cost
Table 5. Solutions of Equation 1 for $P = Q = 9, r = 4$, and $s = 5$										
(0, 0)	0	0	0	0	(7, 0)	3	3	0	1	4
	0	0	1	1		3	3	1	2	
	0	0	2	2		3	3	2	3	
	0	0	3	3		3	3	3	4	
(1, 0)	0	0	0	4	(6, 0)	3	3	3	0	1
(2, 0)	1	1	1	0	(5, 0)	2	2	0	2	3
	1	1	2	1		2	2	1	3	
	1	1	3	2		2	2	2	4	
(3, 0)	1	1	0	3	(4, 0)	2	2	2	0	2
	1	1	1	4		2	2	3	1	

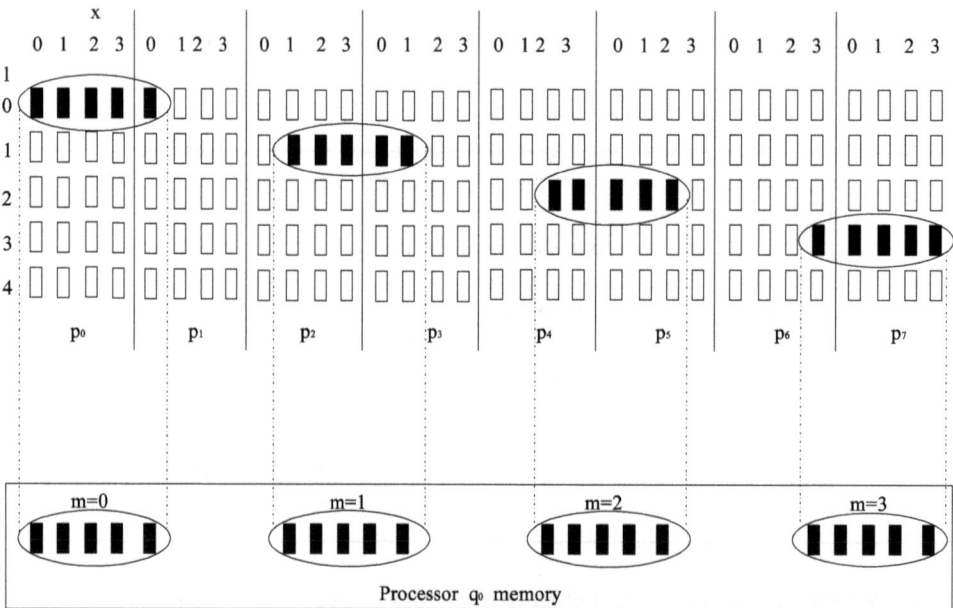

Figure 1. Reading from source processors' memories and writing to target processors' memories.

tasks are parallel. Figure 2 shows the execution of the two pipeline operations for the redistribution with parameters $P = Q = 9, r = 4$, and $s = 5$. Each pipeline operation is composed of four tasks ($T_0 - T_3$).

The horizontal axis displays the time in time units, while the vertical axis gives the pipeline segment. The role of a segment is to handle the distribution process performed by a pipeline task T_j. When a task is handled by the nth out of d segments, it is scheduled to be the nth to complete its distribution job. For example, in Figure 2, there are four segments that handle four transferring tasks. As tasks move "downwards" from segment 4 to segment 1, they are approaching their completion. Apparently, in this figure, T_0 is to finish first, as it is the "cheapest" task (one time unit, see Table 4). The time required for the execution of a task equals the communication cost of the processor pairs it includes. From the previous discussion in Section 3.1, it is obvious that the pipeline tasks are completed at different times. Since each task cannot contain more than a message to a specific destination, contentions at the receiving processors' ports are avoided. To make it more clear, consider the four tasks shown in Table 4. All tasks handle messages to the same target nodes; however, congestions are avoided since these tasks complete at different times.

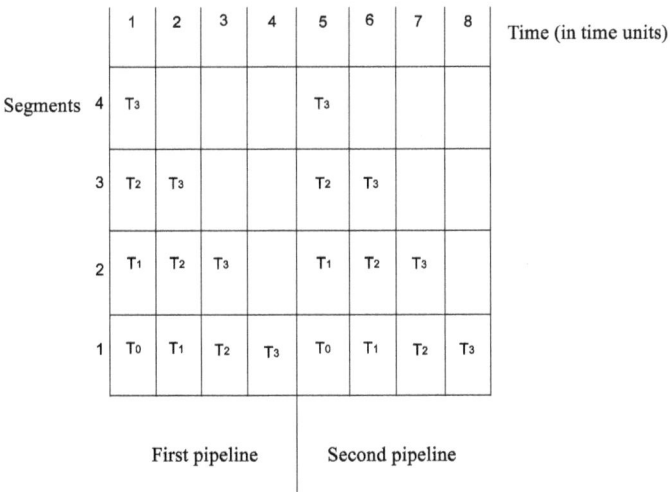

Figure 2. R/W for P=Q=9,r=4, and s=5.

Each of the tasks performs a partial transferring job, that is, it "adds" elements to data blocks at a certain time. Now, let us examine how these task are executed during communication to processor $q = 0$. Suppose that communication starts at time $t = 0$. By the end of time $t = 1$, the first task T_0 is complete (see Figure 2). This means that one element from source $p = 1$ (note in Table 4 that $p = 1$ sends data to $q = 0$ during execution of T_0) is transferred to its new location. By the end of time time $t = 2$ two more elements are added from $p = 3$. The first pipeline operation completes at $t = 4$ time units. In the very same manner, the second pipeline operation starts execution at time $t = 5$. At each time unit, a task completes and adds elements to $q = 0$. At $t = 8$, the distribution to $q = 0$ is complete. Similarly, all destination processors receive their data blocks during the same period of time.

When pipeline execution completes, the distributed elements become parts of newly formed blocks indexed by m in the memories of the target processors q. Their new local position inside the blocks is defined by y. For example, the lower part of Figure 1 shows the newly formed blocks in the memory of $q = 0$. It is clear that each new block has five elements. The block $m = 0$ is formed by four elements transferred from $p = 0$ and one element transferred from $q = 1$. The local position of these five data elements in the newly formed block is given by y, that is, 0, 1, 2, 3 (for elements from $p = 0$), and 4 (for the one element from $p = 1$). The lower part of Figure 1 shows the new position of the elements distributed to $q = 0$ in their new blocks $m = 0, 1, 2,$ and 3. Figure 3 shows the formulation of these blocks over time, during the execution of the pipeline tasks included in the two pipeline operations shown in Table 4. Assuming that communication starts at time $t = 1$, at $t = 2$, the first task will be completed. Therefore, the target processor $q = 0$ will have received one data block from the sending processor $p = 1$ (see task T_0 of the first pipeline in Table 4). According to the results in Table 5, for $(p, q) = (1, 0)$, this block will be stored in position $y = 4$ of the target block $m = 0$ (recall that block positions indexes start from 0, so this element occupies the last position of the block). Similarly, at $t = 2$, task 2 is completed. Therefore, the target processor $q = 0$ will have received two data blocks from the sending processor $p = 3$ (see task T_0 of the first pipeline in Table 4). According to the results in Table 5, for $(p, q) = (3, 0)$, this block will be stored in positions $y = 3$ and $y = 4$ of the target block $m = 1$.

4. The PN pipelined communication model

As described in Section 2, the pipeline based models of communication in the literature do not consider the problem of deadlocks (blocked processes), while they seldom take into account the contentions. The goal here is twofold: (1) use the PN model as a tool to verify that the communication model of Section 3 is deadlock and conflict-free and (2) obtain the performance metrics for three different distribution scenarios from the PN model via a discrete event simulations.

The system model under consideration comprises of a number of pipeline tasks in a single pipeline operation that execute as described in Sections 3.1–3.3. Apparently, a distribution problem can

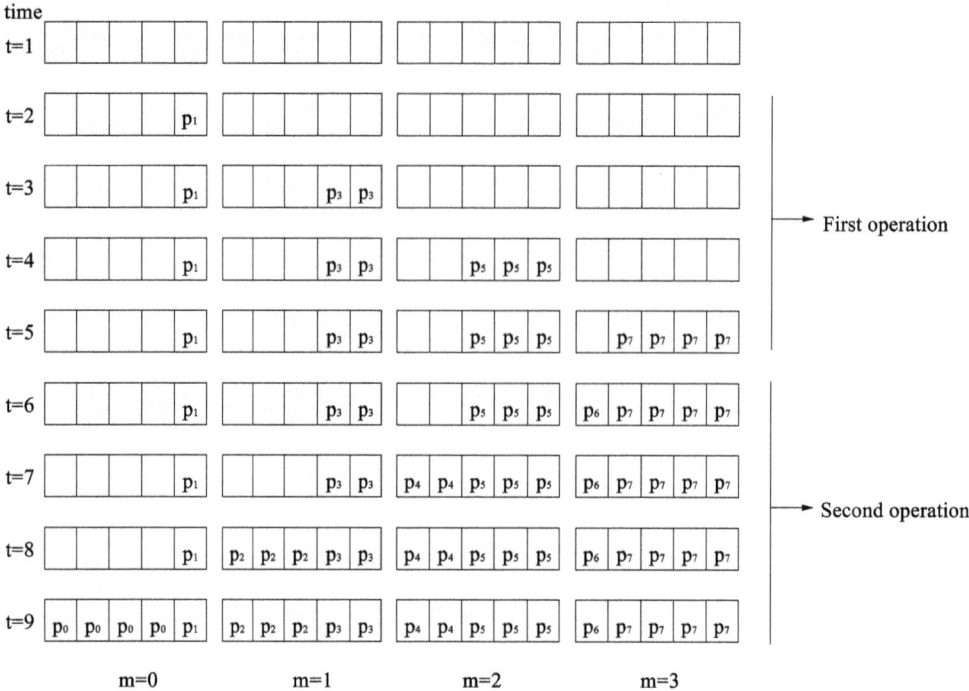

Figure 3. Memory writing over time for P=Q=9, r=4, and s=5.

include a variable number of operations with a variable number of tasks. Since all pipeline operations can follow the same pattern (execute a number of parallel tasks), it is important to design a symmetric model, so that it can be applied for variable number of tasks with minor changes. From a modeling perspective, there are three occurrences of interest: (1) generation of the pipeline tasks, (2) execution of the pipelines, and (3) handling the pipeline segments. This section presents a fully symmetric PN model for these occurrences and performs deadlock and safeness analyses to verify that the models (and consequently the pipeline communication schedule) do not suffer from blocked processes or contentions. Notice that occurrences (2) and (3) are closely related, thus presented in the same subsection. Before that some preliminaries regarding PN are required.

4.1. PN preliminaries

This subsection briefly presents the basic PN notations required in this work. A PN is a set of two different types of nodes: *places* (pictured with circles) and *transitions* (pictured with bars). Places and transitions are connected via directed arcs from places to transitions and vice versa. If an arc is directed from node *A* to node *B*, then *A* is an input to *B*. The *state* of a PN changes when it is *executed*. The execution is controlled by the *tokens* placed inside nodes. When the PN is executed, a number of tokens are removed from their current place and are located in different places. The distribution of tokens in the places defines the *state* of the net. This distribution is referred as *marking* of the PN. Apparently, when a system is initialized, it must have an initial state or *initial marking*. In this paper, every marking (initial or later) is denoted by $\mu_i = (P_i, \ldots P_{i+k}, \ldots P_n)$, where i is the marking index ($i = 1$ denotes the initial marking), n is the number of places, and P_i is every place that has a token in this marking.

A change of a PN's state (that is, the movement of tokens) occurs when the transitions are *enabled* to *fire* and this is true when all of its input places have a token. To describe that fact that a transition's firing changed the marking from μ_i to μ_{i+1}, the following notation is used: $\mu_i \xrightarrow{t_j} \mu_{i+1}$ or $(P_i, \ldots P_{i+k}, \ldots P_n) \xrightarrow{t_j} (P_i, \ldots P_{i+k}, \ldots P_n)'$, where $()'$ indicates the new set of token-holding places. As an example, consider the PN of Figure 4(a). The initial marking is $\mu_1 = (P_3, P_4)$ and the only enabled transition is t_4 (t_2 is not enabled, although P_2 has a token because its input place P_5 has no token). When t_4 fires, the token will be removed from P_4 and two new tokens will be placed, one in P_3 and one in P_1, resulting in $\mu_2 = (P_2, P_3, P_4)$.

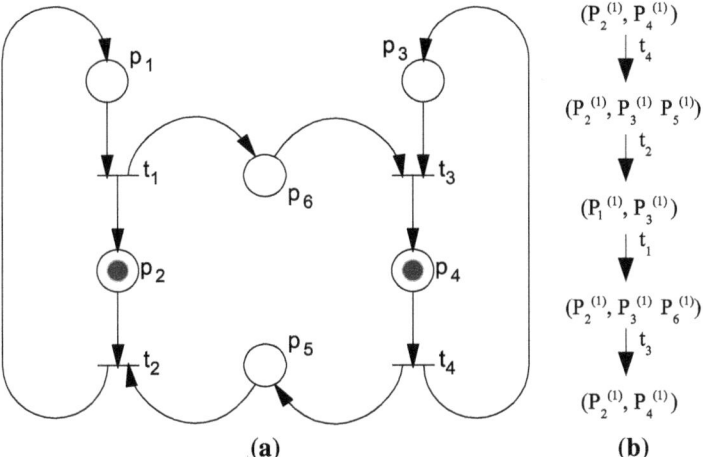

$(\text{P}_2^{(1)}, \text{P}_4^{(1)})$

$\downarrow t_4$

$(\text{P}_2^{(1)}, \text{P}_3^{(1)} \ \text{P}_5^{(1)})$

$\downarrow t_2$

$(\text{P}_1^{(1)}, \text{P}_3^{(1)})$

$\downarrow t_1$

$(\text{P}_2^{(1)}, \text{P}_3^{(1)} \ \text{P}_6^{(1)})$

$\downarrow t_3$

$(\text{P}_2^{(1)}, \text{P}_4^{(1)})$

(a)   **(b)**

Figure 4. (a) A PN example and (b) Reachability tree

A very important issue about PN is that a sequence of firings can result in a marking μ, where no transition is enabled. This would drive the model in a deadlock (process being blocked by another process). This means that there are a number of unwanted states that can lead to a deadlock. Spotting these states is a very important issue when modeling because it uncovers the sequence of executing events that can lead the model, and consequently the real system, to deadlock. The tool used to analyze the PN model for deadlocks is called *reachability tree*. A reachability tree is a set of nodes that represents all possible markings of a net (if the set is finite) caused by the firing of transitions. Figure 4(b) shows the reachability tree for the example of Figure 4(b). The transition that causes every new marking is written near the arrows. The parentheses above places 0 show the number of tokens in every place. If no parentheses are included, the number of tokens is 1. In the case of Figure 4(b), no place does store more than one token, but this is not always the case.

Peterson (1997) introduced two basic rules for the reachability analysis: (1) if a newly formed marking is equal to an existing one on the path from the root (which is an initial marking) to this new marking, then this marking is a *terminal node*. This means that if a new marking is equal to a previous one, then all markings reachable from it are already added to the reachability tree, and (2) if a newly formed marking y is greater than a previous marking x, then all possible firings from marking x are also possible from marking y. In this case, the components of y which are greater than the corresponding components of x are replaced by the symbol ω, where ω is a value arbitrarily large compared to a natural number α. Also, the sequence of firings that lead from x to y can be repeated endlessly, resulting every time in an increase of the number of tokens in the corresponding positions P_i. The symbol ω is used to denote an arbitrarily large number of tokens in P_i, and the notation $P_i^{(\omega)}$ is used. From Peterson's rules, we derive Proposition 2 that gives a condition under which a model does not reach a deadlock.

Proposition 2   A PN model will never reach a deadlock if for all markings that are roots to subtrees formed on the reachability tree, it is possible to find a terminal node or a marking greater than the root.

In a PN model, the places represent conditions, while the transitions represent events. The presence of a token in a place shows that a condition is true. Since a condition is either true or false, there is no point in having more than a token in a place. Thus, especially when modeling hardware, one of the most important characteristic of PN is *safety*. A place of a PN is safe if its tokens are never more than one. In other words, therefore, safeness is violated when a sequence of firings puts two or more tokens in a place. In a parallel pipelined communication model, safeness ensures that there are no conflicting processes. Two or more processes are in conflict if, at the same time, they try to read the data blocks from the same source processors or to distribute and write data to the same target processors. The reachability analysis can show if multiple tokens are put in one place. Deadlock and safety analyses are provided for the proposed models in the next subsections.

4.2. Modeling the pipeline generation

The background and the steps required to generate the pipelines were presented in Section 3.1. Figure 5(a) presents the PN model and Figure 5(b) shows the pipeline generation in pseudo-code form. The part in the square is the *reading subnetwork*. Out of the reading subnetwork, there are two places, P_E and P_G and two transitions, t_E and t_G, their roles described in the following. The places and transitions of the model are described as follows:

Places

P_G:	Generation request
P_E:	Transfer request (pipeline execution)
P_1:	Lowest cost class
P_2:	Q' messages
P_3:	While condition
P_4:	If condition
P_5:	Unread messages from lowest cost class
P_6:	End System available to generate new operation

Transitions

t_G:	Get lowest cost class
t_1:	Read $Q - Q'$ messages
t_2:	Check condition $Q' < Q$
t_3:	Assign FALSE to condition
t_4:	Assign TRUE to condition
t_5:	Terminate reading
t_6:	Get to next lowest cost class
t_7:	Read unread messages from a same cost class

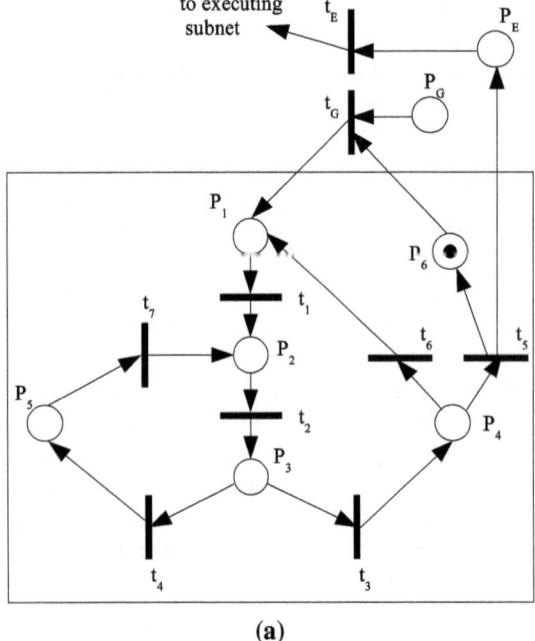

Generating the Pipeline Tasks

1. *Get Q' communicating pairs from a minimum communication cost class.*
2. *While $Q'<Q$ do*
   {
        Get next class with equal cost
        Add another Q' communications
   }

// Q communications completed

3. *If there is a class not added*
        Get it and go to Step 3.
   else end;
   // All classes added to pipelines

(a)   (b)

Figure 5. Pipeline generation model.

The pipeline generation of model of Figure 5 is a repeating process which is initialized by a generation request provided that there is no pipeline generation in process. The initial marking, $\mu_1 = (P_6)$, indicates that the system is available to generate a new pipeline operation. Once P_G gets a token, t_G is enabled to fire and cause a series of firings. Firing of t_G will cause one token from P_G and one from P_6 to be removed and one token to be placed to P_1 (the lowest cost class is defined). This will produce $\mu_2 = (P_1)$ and enable t_1. Once t_1 fires, a token is removed from P_1 and one token is be placed to P_2 (Q' messages generated). The new marking is $\mu_3 = (P_2)$ and t_2 is enabled. Then, a while condition should be checked to decide if more messages are required from the same class. When t_2 fires, a token is placed in P_3 [marking $\mu_4 = (P_3)$]. This enables two transitions (t_3 and t_4), but only one can fire. It should be stressed that PN does not have a mechanism to decide which of the enabled transitions will fire. This depends on the designer of the model. When t_4 is selected, there is a cyclic execution of firings, which repeats until $Q = Q'$ and creates repeatedly the markings $\mu_5 = (P_5)$, $\mu_6 = (P_2)$, and $\mu_7 = (P_3)$. When t_3 is selected, a token is placed to P_4 (marking $\mu_8 = (P_4)$. As with the while condition, the system now has to check if there is a class of a specific cost not added. If so, t_6 fires to cause $\mu_9 = (P_1)$. This means that the sequence of firings described will be repeated. If not, t_5 fires to cause $\mu_9 = (P_6, P_E)$. This means that the system has terminated the pipeline generation and it is available to generate a new one. Also, a transfer request is activated (pipelines can be executed, as described in Section 4.3).

At this point, an anti-paradigm is necessary to stress the importance of modeling. Assume that the arc from P_6 to t_G is removed. Also, assume that a pipeline generation is in process (say, is checking the while statement, that is, a token is in P_3). If a second generation request is made, the system will have to start a new operation, starting with a new lower cost class. Thus, a token is placed in P_1. Then, a sequence of firings t_3, t_6 will result in having two tokens stored in P_1. The system is not safe and it can start a pipeline generation with two different distribution parameters (lowest cost class). This is a conflict and the problem can be resolved only by restarting the system. To avoid this, t_G is enabled only if there is a request (token in P_G) and the system is available (token in P_6).

4.3. Execution of the pipelines handling the segments
Once the reading stage is completed, the actual communication can start. To execute the pipelined communication, the system control requires the following sequence of events:

- Output of segment 1 (lowest segment that handles the lowest cost task) is ready. Thus, the lowest cost messages are to arrive at the target nodes.
- Messages from segment 1 are written to the memories of the target nodes.
- Output of segment 2 is ready. The task handled by segment 2 is now handled ("moves to") by the lowest segment 1.
- Segment 2 is free (ready to accept a task from the upper segment 3) and segment 1 now handles communication previously handled by segment 2 (these are the next messages to arrive to the target nodes).
- Output of segment 3 is ready. The task handled by segment 3 moves to segment 2.
- Segment 3 is free.
- Output of segment 4 is ready. The task handled by segment 4 moves to segment 3.
- The same pattern repeats until all d segments "move down" to segment 1 and complete communication.

As described in the previous subsection, once node P_E receives a token, the execution stage can start. This is done by firing t_E. When t_E fires, one token is removed from P_E and put in *all places that indicate the output of one pipeline segment is ready*. Since a distribution problem has d different costs (thus, d pipeline tasks), the model requires a maximum of d segments; thus, d places receive a token by firing t_E. Figure 6(a) shows the model of the *pipeline execution subnetwork* (recall that place and transition numbering continue from the reading subnetwork) and Figure 6(b) shows the marking that arises by firing t_E. This marking is $\mu_1 = (P_7, P_{13}, P_{14}, P_{18}, \ldots P_{m+1})$, where P_{m+1} is the place showing that the output of segment

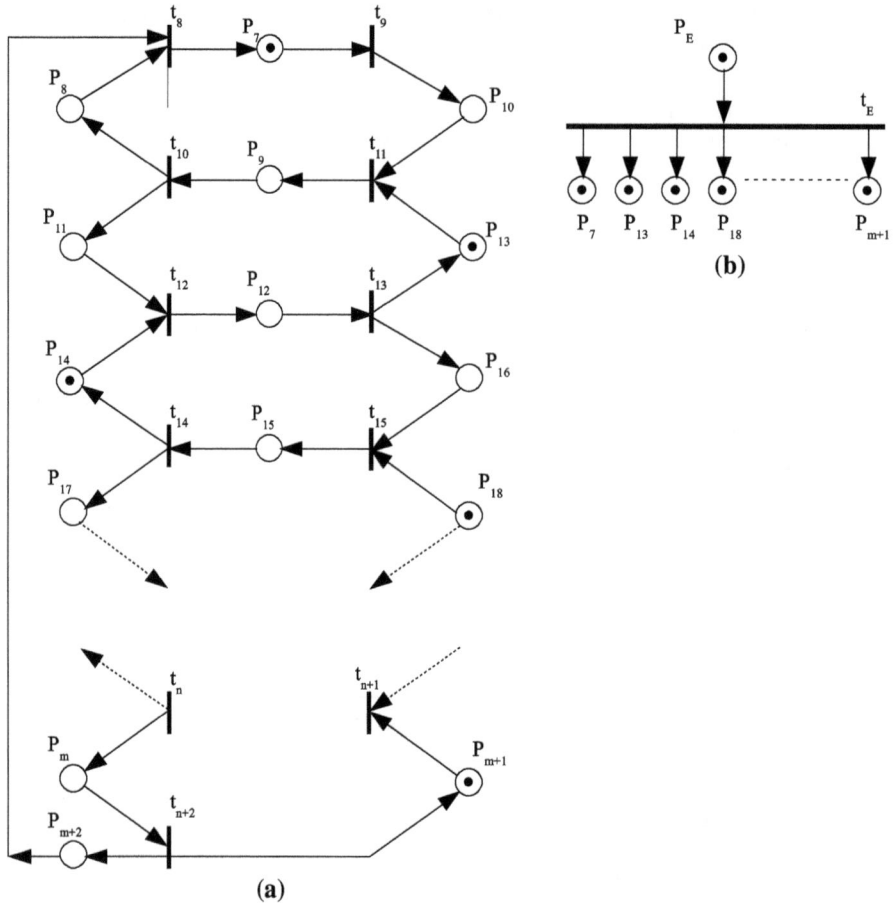

Figure 6. Pipeline execution model.

d is ready. Clearly, the model suggests that segments correspond with "circles" of places and transitions, which are clearly formed in Figure 6(a). Transfer between segments is implemented via firing the dual input transitions. Also, note that the circles are symmetric, with the only exception being the last segment where there is one node missing for the simple reason that there is no other segment to move down to *d*. The dashed arrows indicate that the pattern repeats until the last segment *d*. The places and transitions of the model are described as follows:

Places

P_7:   Output of segment 1 is ready
P_8:   Segment 1 busy
P_9:   Segment 2 in segment 1
P_{10}:   Lowest cost communication done
P_{11}:   Segment 2 empty
P_{12}:   Segment 3 in segment 2
P_{13}:   Segment 2 output ready
P_{14}:   Segment 3 output ready
P_{15}:   Segment 4 in segment 3
P_{16}:   Segment 3 empty
P_{17}:   Segment 4 empty
P_{18}:   Segment 4 output ready

P_m: Segment d empty
P_{m+1}:   Segment d output ready
P_{m+2}:   Lower segment communication continues

Transitions

t_8:   Unpack messages
t_9:   Write to receiving processors' memory
t_{10}:   Reset segment 2
t_{11}:   "Move" segment 2 to segment 1
t_{12}:   "Move" segment 3 to segment 2
t_{13}:   Reset segment 3
t_{14}:   Reset segment 4
t_{15}:   "Move" segment 4 to segment 3
t_{16}:   "Move" segment 5 to segment 4
t_{17}:   Reset segment 5
t_n: Reset segment d
t_{n+1}:   "Move" segment d to segment $d-1$
t_{n+2}:   Proceed communication in lower segment

The proposed model is fully symmetric and it can be used easily for any number of states. Now, we are going to perform a test for the small distribution problem with parameters $P = Q = 9, r = 4$, and $s = 5$ presented in Section 3. This test will help us understand fully the execution of the model. Based on the CPT (Table 3), there are two pipeline operations, each including four tasks $(T_0) - T_3$ (see Table 4). The "movement" of these tasks across the pipeline segments is shown in Figure 2. The model for this distribution would include four circles formed by places and transitions and it is in shown in Figure 7(a).

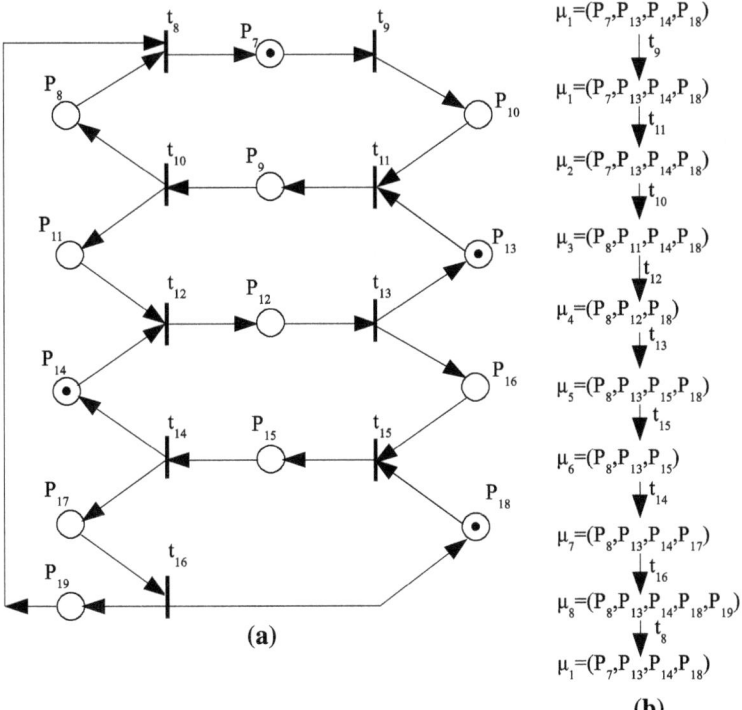

Figure 7. Pipeline execution model for P=Q=9, r=4, and s=5.

Initially, there are four places having a token, so $\mu_1 = (P_7, P_{13}, P_{14}$, and $P_{18})$. Thus, the only enabled transition is t_9. Once t_9 fires, a token is removed from P_7 and placed in P_{10}, resulting in $(P_{10}, P_{13}, P_{14}$, and $P_{18})$. From the real system's point of view, this describes event **completion of communications performed by task T_0(1)** (T_0 is handled by segment 1, see Figure 2). Now, t_{11} is the only transition enabled. When it fires, it produces $\mu_2 = (P_9, P_{14}$, and $P_{18})$ (tokens are removed from P_{10}, P_{13} and one token is placed in P_9. In the real system event, **task T_1 is assigned to segment 1 (2)** (because segment 2 moves to segment 1). Next, only transition t_{10} can fire, resulting in $\mu_3 = (P_8, P_{11}, P_{14}$, and $P_{18})$. We have two events now: **segment 2 is empty (3)** and **segment 1 is now busy with T_1 (4)**. At this point, there is a synchronization issue: if t_8 is enabled, the same pattern will be executed continuously. In the first of this series of executions, segment 1 will deliver some messages to the source processors, but afterwards there will be no messages to deliver because it will have to *wait for tasks from segment 2 that do not come since segment 2 is empty waiting for upper segments*. Practically, this means that the system stays idle for as long as this repeating execution continues and if this sequence does not change, the system **reaches a deadlock** and transmission has to start from scratch. Also, if t_{12} does not fire in the meantime, more than one token will be placed on P_{11} rendering the system unsafe. The solution we give with this model is to enable $t_8$only *after t_{16} fires*, which, for the real system, means that segment 1 can finish another distribution task only when all the remaining tasks are assigned to segments ("move downwards" as can be seen in Figure 2). When t_{16} fires, a token is put in place P_{19} and this enables t_8. However, t_{16} can fire only after $t_{10}, t_{12}, t_{13}, t_{13}$, and t_{15} have fired, so all the tasks have been properly assigned to segments. That is, the model indicates that there must be a synchronization between segments (and consequently between the tasks they include) to avoid deadlocks.

Continuing the description, t_{12} is the only enabled transition. Once it fires, it produces $\mu_4 = (P_8, P_{12}$, and $P_{18})$. This indicates that event **task T_2 is assigned to segment 2 (5)** (segment 3 moves to segment 2). Now, t_{13} is enabled. Once it fires, the new marking is $\mu_5 = (P_8, P_{13}, P_{16}$, and $P_{18})$. Now, there are two events: **output of segment 2 is ready (6)** and **segment 3 is empty (7)**. Event 6 means that T_2 is ready to move to segment 1 after the completion of T_1 executed there. From marking μ_5, it is obvious that only t_{15} can fire, resulting in $\mu_6 = (P_8, P_{13}$, and $P_{15})$. For the real system, event **task T_3 is assigned to segment 3 (8)** (because segment 4 moves to segment 3). Now, t_{14} is enabled. When it fires, the new marking is $\mu_7 = (P_8, P_{13}, P_{14}$, and $P_{17})$. The two real system events are: **output of segment 3 is ready (9)** (meaning that when T_1 finishes from segment 1 and T_2 is pushed from segment 2 to segment 1, T_3 will move to segment 2) and **segment 4 is empty (10)**. Now t_{16} is enabled. When it fires, the new marking is $\mu_8 = (P_8, P_{13}, P_{14}, P_{18}$, and $P_{19})$. With a token in P_{19}, transition t_8 is enabled again because all segments have moved as explained previously. When this firing occurs, there is one event: **completion of communications performed by task T_1 (11)**. Also, the new marking produced is μ_1, meaning that the same sequence of firings repeats. Therefore, another transfer (task T_1) can be completed in the lowest segment 1 and the segments will move downwards again, repeating the same execution cycle. Next, the sequence of events produced by the model's execution is listed (the events written boldfaced in the analysis above).

(1) Completion of communications performed by task T_0

(2) Task T_1 is assigned to segment 1

(3) Segment 2 is empty

(4) Segment 1 is now busy with T_1

(5) Task T_2 is assigned to segment 2

(6) Output of segment 2 is ready

(7) Segment 3 is empty

(8) Task T_3 is assigned to segment 3

(9) Output of segment 3 is ready

(10) Segment 4 is empty

(11) Completion of communications performed by task T_0

(12) Same pattern repeats

Based on the above analysis, it is easy to get the reachability tree of Figure 7(b). Obviously, the PN model has no deadlocks since there is no sequence of firings that can disable a transition and the pattern is proven to repeat itself. As an anti-paradigm, suppose that the at least one of the places P_7, P_{13}, P_{14}, and P_{18}, say P_{13} is not initially marked. When t_9 fires, a token will move to P_{10}, but since P_{13} has no token, t_{11} is disabled causing a deadlock. For the real system, this means that segment 2 cannot move down to segment 1, simply because its output is not, and will never be, ready. This will halt the system causing unwanted effects (e.g. communication restart).

4.4. Advantages of the proposed model
At this point, it is important to summarize some of the advantages of the proposed model.

(a) *Optimal in terms of complexity*: The complexity of the model is $O(n)$, where n is the number of states examined. Clearly, this is the best that can be achieved as any other method would have to examine every state, so the complexity would at least be $O(n)$.

(b) *Symmetry*: As stated before, the model can be used for any redistribution problem (that is, any number of states) due to its symmetry. Thus, generally, there are no applicability limitations.

(c) *Precision*: The model includes all the main processes involved in a redistribution problem (as described in Section 3): generation of the pipeline tasks, initialization and reading messages from memory, transferring, and writing back to memory. Thus, it is precise and models the real problem with high accuracy.

Remark   When the second cycle is executed, segment 4 will be found empty (from the execution of t_{14} in the first cycle). This means that segment 4 can now be used to put the lowest cost task of the next pipeline communication. In this case, when t_{15} fires, the lowest task of the next pipeline can move to segment 3. Similarly, when the third cycle executes, segment 3 will be found empty (from the execution of t_{13} in the second cycle). So, the lowest cost task of the second pipeline can move from segment 4 to segment 3, while the next lowest cost task can enter segment 4. However, it must be pointed out that the communication model is not designed to take advantage of the empty segments in an organized manner. Maybe, an idea would be to create and pipeline groups of classes to assure some kind of transfer homogeneity. This is a subject of future research.

5. Experiments
In this section, the accuracy of the model is verified via simulations. Based on the PN model, a small pipeline simulator (PPN simulator) was implemented to serve the purpose of this work. The simulator simply executes the well-defined sequence of processors described in Section 3.3. The simulations performed are not restricted by the assumption that there is adequate bandwidth and enough buffer space imposed for the sake of the model. Instead, different bandwidth sizes are used and simulations were performed considering the fact that buffers may or may not have enough size for the data volume carried over the network. Different scenarios are studied in terms of buffer space, bandwidth, and data volumes. The interprocessor communication is performed via all to all links. Each link has a bandwidth of B MB/sec bandwidth. Considering that each node sends a number of messages at each communication step, the bandwidth available to a node would be:

$$\text{bandwidth}_p = B \times \frac{\ell}{h} \tag{4}$$

where B MB is the link bandwidth, ℓ is the number of links to a node p, and h is the average number of intermediate hops required for the communication between two processors. Assuming that there is only one link for each node and since h depends on the logarithmic value of P, Equation 4 becomes:

$$\text{bandwidth}_p = B \times \frac{1}{\log_2(P)} \tag{5}$$

To run the simulations, the theoretical block size s of the target distribution must be converted to real time. By multiplying s to an assumed vector size, the message size transferred between two processors at a step is produced. For example, if the target distribution block size $s = 5$ and vector size is 1 MB, then processor p will send a message of 5 MB to processor q. Since the bandwidth is B Mb/sec, it is easy to estimate the time required for the transmission. In the following, the vector sizes will also be variable. In half of the simulations ran, the buffer spaces available were considered to be, on the average, u% less than the maximum bandwidth. For the remaining half simulations, the buffer sizes were considered to have enough space to accommodate the data.

5.1. Scenario 1
The parameters and their values for the first scenario are as follows:

(1) $r = 7$ and $s = 11$
(2) Number if processors $P = 8$.
(3) Vector size: ranging from 128 Kb to 2 Mb
(4) Real data volumes distributed: 1408 Kb–22 MB
(5) $B = 50$, so the bandwidth available is $\frac{50}{\log_8}$
(6) u is 0 or 40 (when it is 0, the buffer space is enough)

Figure 8(a) shows the simulation results. The bandwidth available for a processor p is computed as $\text{bandwidth}_p = \frac{50}{\log(8)} \approx 16.66$ MB. The vector size varies from 128 Kb to 2 MB. The upper line gives the results on the basis that the buffers have, on the average, 40% less capacity than the maximum bandwidth ($u = 40$), in this case, ≈ 10 MB. The lower line assumes that the buffers have enough space to accommodate the messages ($u = 0$). For vector sizes less than 128 Kb, the buffers can accommodate the messages arrived because each sending processor p sends a maximum of

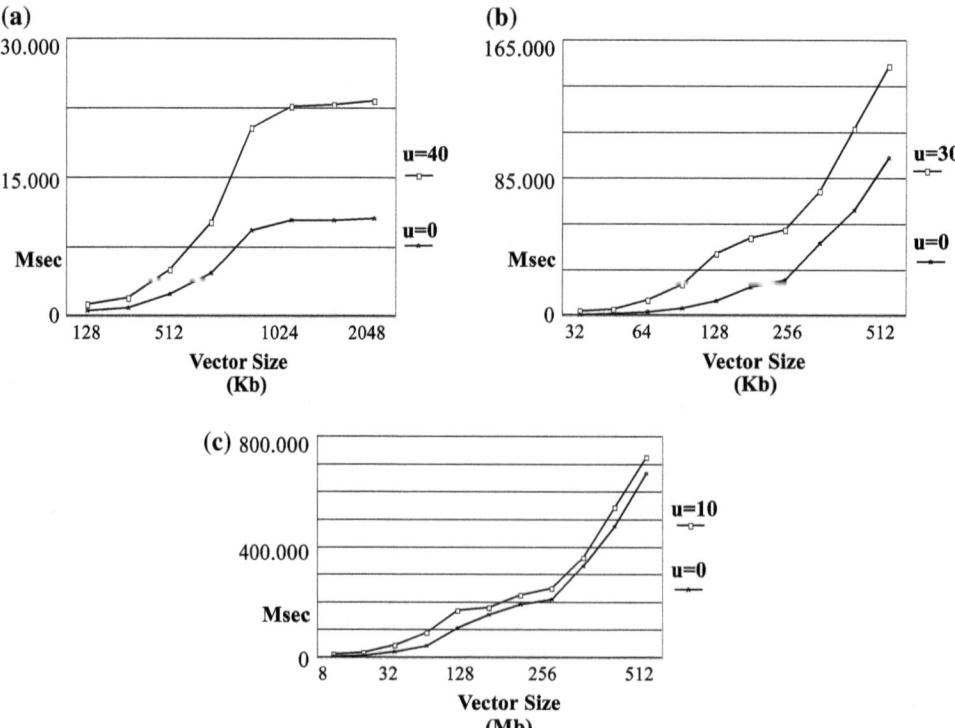

Figure 8. Experiments for various parameters.

$128 \times 11 = 1408$ KB to a receiver q. Since the maximum number of sending processors towards q is 8, q can receive a maximum of approximately 8×1408 Kb = 11 Mb. As the vector size increases, the gap between the two lines increases.

5.2. Scenario 2

In the second scenario, the vector size ranges from 32 to 512 Kb and the number of processors is $P = Q = 16$. The parameters and their values for the first scenario are as follows:

(1) $r = 7$ and $s = 11$

(2) Number if processors $P = Q = 16$.

(3) Vector size: ranging from 32 to 512 Kb

(4) Real data volumes distributed: 352 Kb–5.5 MB

(5) $B = 50$, so the bandwidth available is $\frac{50}{\log_{16}}$

(6) u is 0 or 30

Figure 8(b) shows the simulation results. The bandwidth available for a processor p is computed as $\text{bandwidth}_p = \frac{50}{\log(16)} \approx 8.33$ MB. The upper line gives the results on the basis that the buffers have, on the average, 30% less capacity than the maximum bandwidth ($u = 30$), in this case, ≈ 5.8 MB. The lower line assumes that the buffers have enough space to accommodate the messages ($u = 0$). For vector sizes less than 32 Kb, the buffers can accommodate the messages arrived because each sending processor p sends a maximum of $32 \times 11 = 352$ KB to a receiver q. Since the maximum number of sending processors towards q is 16, q can receive a maximum of approximately 16×352 Kb = 5.5 Mb. As the vector size increases, the gap between the two lines increases. In this scenario, m decreases by 10% compared to the first scenario. This means that the memory can accommodate higher percentages of the total data volumes (recall that as the number of processors increases, the available bandwidth drops off). Thus, the two lines converge more compared to the first scenario.

5.3. Scenario 3

In the second scenario, the vector size ranges from 8 to 512 Kb and the number of processors is $P = Q = 64$. The parameters and their values for the first scenario are as follows:

(1) $r = 7$ and $s = 11$

(2) Number if processors $P = Q = 64$.

(3) Vector size: ranging from 8 to 512 Kb

(4) Real data volumes distributed: 88 Kb–5.5 MB

(5) $B = 50$, so the bandwidth available is $\frac{50}{\log 64}$

(6) u is 0 or 10

Figure 8(b) shows the simulation results. The bandwidth available for a processor p is computed as $\text{bandwidth}_p = \frac{50}{\log(64)} \approx 6.25$ MB. The upper line gives the results on the basis that the buffers have, on the average, 10% less capacity than the maximum bandwidth ($u = 10$), in this case, ≈ 5.6 MB. The lower line assumes that the buffers have enough space to accommodate the messages ($u = 0$). For vector sizes less than 8 Kb, the buffers can accommodate the messages arrived because each sending processor p sends a maximum of $8 \times 11 = 88$ KB to a receiver q. Since the maximum number of sending processors towards q is 64, q can receive a maximum of approximately 64×88 Kb = 5.5 Mb. As the vector size increases, the gap between the two lines increases. Again, notice that m decreases by another 20% compared to the second scenario, meaning that the memory can accommodate higher percentages of the total data volumes. Thus, the two lines are closer compared to the second scenario.

As an observation, one can state that the results the model produces for the three scenarios corroborate each other. In the first scenario, the local processors' memories were not capable of storing a good percentage of the data carried over the network. While u keeps on reducing and the number of processors increases (thus, reducing the bandwidth and the data volumes distributed), the two lines shown in each of the three graphs are converging. The correctness of the results verifies the validity of the model.

6. Conclusions—future research

This paper presents a PN-based model used to verify and evaluate the performance of pipelined parallel distributions. It precisely captures the behavior of a pipeline-based parallel communication system. The model considers message scheduling and message classification, while it is deadlock and contention free. Because it is symmetric, it can easily be used for larger systems only with minor changes. This is one of its biggest strengths.

Future work can include the study of pipelined systems on certain topologies. It is interesting to check if the proposed model (perhaps with minor changes) can be used to study the performance of a data distribution over a torus or mesh network. Also, as already mentioned in the remark of Section IV, an implementation that can take advantage of any empty segments that incur during the distribution is of particular interest. An idea would be the introduction of *superclasses* (groups of classes).

Funding
The authors received no direct funding for this research.

Author details
Stavros I. Souravlas[1]
E-mail: sourstav@uom.gr
Manos Roumeliotis[1]
E-mail: manos@uom.gr
[1] Department of Applied Informatics, University of Macedonia, Thessaloniki, Greece.

References
Caron, E., & Desprez, F. (2005). Out-of-core and pipeline techniques for wavefront algorithms. In *Proceedings of the 19th IEEE International Parallel and Distributed Symposium (IPDPS'05)*. Denver, CO.

Chung, Y.-C., Hsu, C.-H., & Bai, S.-W. (1998). A basic-cycle calculation technique for efficient dynamic data redistribution. *IEEE Transactions on Parallel and Distributed Systems, 9*, 359–377.

Desprez, F., Dongarra, J., Petitet, A., Randriamaro, C., & Robert, Y. (1998a). Scheduling block-cyclic array redistribution. *IEEE Transactions on Parallel and Distributed Systems, 9*, 192–205.

Desprez, F., Dongarra, J., Petitet, A., Randriamaro, C., & Robert, Y. (1998b). More on scheduling block-cyclic array redistribution. In *Proceedings of the 4th Workshop on Languages, Compilers, and Run-time Systems for Scalable Computers, volume 1511 of Lecture Notes in Computer Science* (pp. 275–287). Pittsburgh, PA: Springer-Verlag.

Granda, M., Drake, J. M., & Gregorio, J. A. (1992). Performance evaluation of parallel systems by using unbounded generalized stochastic Petri nets. *IEEE Transactions on Software Engineering, 18*, 55–70.

Jayachandran, P., & Abdelzaher, T. (2007). A delay composition theorem for real-time pipelines. In *Proceedings of the 19th Euromicro Conference on Real-Time Systems, ECRTS '07* (pp. 29–38). Washington, DC: IEEE Computer Society.

Kashif, H., Gholamian, S., Pelizzoni, R., Patel, H. D., & Fischmeister, S. (2013, April). ORTAP: An offset-based response time analysis for a pipelined communication resource model. In *Proceedings of the 19th Real-Time and Embedded Technology and Applications Symbosium (RTAS)*. Philadelphia, PA.

Kaushik, S. D., Huang, C. H., Johnson, R. W. & Sadayappan, P. (1994, July). An approach to communication-efficient data redistribution. In *Proceedings of the 8th ACM International Conference on Supercomputing*. Manchester.

King, C. T., Chou, W. H., & Ni, L. M. (1990). Pipelined data-parallel algorithms: Part I: Concept and modeling. *IEEE Transactions on Parallel and Distributed Systems, 1*, 470–485.

Kuntraruk, J., Pottenger, W. M., & Ross, A. M. (2005). Application resource requirement estimation in a parallel pipeline model of execution. *IEEE Transactions on Parallel and Distributed Systems, 16*, 1154–1165.

Liao, W.-K., Choundary, A., Weiner, D., & Varshney, P. (2004). Performance evaluation of a parallel pipeline computational model for space-time adaptive processing. *Journal of Supercomputing, 31*, 137–160.

Navarro, A., Asenjo, R., & Tabik, S. (2009, September). Analytical modeling of pipeline parallelism. In *Proceedings of the 18th International Conference on Parallel Architectures and Compilation Techniques*. Raleigh, NC.

Peterson, J. L. (1997). Petri nets*. *ACM Computing Surveys (CSUR), 9*, 223–252.

Preud'homme, T., Sopena, J., Thomas, G., & Folliot, B. (2012). An improvement of openMP pipeline parallelism with the BatchQueue algorithm. In *Proceedings of the 18th IEEE International Conference on Parallel and Distributed Systems (ICPADS)*. Singapore.

Rodrigues, A., Wheeler, K., & Kogge, P. (2008). Fine-grained message pipelining for improved MPI performance. In *Proceedings of IEEE Conference on Cluster Computing*. Barcelona.

Souravlas, S. I., & Roumeliotis, M. (2004). A pipeline technique for dynamic data transfer on a multiprocessor grid. *International Journal of Parallel Programming, 32*, 361–388.

Souravlas, S. I., & Roumeliotis, M. (2014, March). Verification & performance evaluation of parallel pipelined communications using Petri nets. In *IEEE, UKSIM-AMSS, 16th International Conference on Computer Modeling and Simulation* (pp. 398–403). Cambridge.

Ties, W., Chandrasekhar, V., & Amarasinghe, S. (2007). A practical approach to exploiting coarse-grained pipeline parallelism in C programs. In *MICRO'07* (pp. 356–369). Chicago, IL.

Zhang, P., & Deng, Y. (2002). Design and analysis of pipelined broadcast algorithms for the all-port interlaced bypass torus networks. *IEEE Transactions on Parallel and Distributed Systems, 23*, 2245–2253.

Zhao, Z., Liu, X., Dou, W., & Yang, K. (2012, October 19–22). Research on data parallel and scheduling mechanism based on Petri nets. In *11th International Symposium on Distributed Computing and Applications to Business, Engineering & Science (DCABES)* (pp. 36–39). Guilin.

6

A hybrid guided neighborhood search for the disjunctively constrained knapsack problem

Mhand Hifi[1]*, Sagvan Saleh[1] and Lei Wu[1]

*Corresponding author: Mhand Hifi, Université de Picardie Jules Verne, EPROAD-EA 4669, 7 rue du Moulin Neuf, 80000 Amiens, France

Email: hifi@u-picardie.fr

Reviewing editor: Jenhui Chen, Chang Gung University, Taiwan

Abstract: In this paper, we investigate the use of a hybrid guided neighborhood search for solving the disjunctively constrained knapsack problem. The studied problem may be viewed as a combination of two NP-hard combinatorial optimization problems: the weighted-independent set and the classical binary knapsack. The proposed algorithm is a hybrid approach that combines both deterministic and random local searches. The deterministic local search is based on a descent method, where both building and exploring procedures are alternatively used for improving the solution at hand. In order to escape from a local optima, a random local search strategy is introduced which is based on a modified ant colony optimization system. During the search process, the ant colony optimization system tries to diversify and to enhance the solutions using some informations collected from the previous iterations. Finally, the proposed algorithm is computationally analyzed on a set of benchmark instances available in the literature. The provided results are compared to those realized by both the Cplex solver and a recent algorithm of the literature. The computational part shows that the obtained results improve most existing solution values.

Subjects: Applied Mathematics; Computer Engineering; Computer Science

Keywords: combinatorial optimization; hybridation; integer programming; knapsack; neighborhood

ABOUT THE AUTHORS

Mhand Hifi is a full professor of Computer Science and Operations Research at the University of Picardie Jules Verne (UPJV), France. He is the head of the laboratory EPROAD of the UPJV. His research interest is NP Hard combinatorial optimization applied to logistic and OR problems.

Sagvan Saleh is a PhD student at the UPJV, France. He received his B.S. in Computer Science at the University of Nahrain. He got his M.S. in Mathematic Computer Science from the University of le Havre, France.

Lei Wu is an associate professor of Computer Science and Operations Research at the UPJV, France. He is the head of the team ROAD of EPROAD (UPJV). He got his PhD. in Computer Science from UPJV, France. His research interest is NP Hard combinatorial optimization.

PUBLIC INTEREST STATEMENT

Cutting, packing, and knapsack problems belong to the family of natural combinatorial optimization problems. These problems are admitted in numerous real-world applications from industrial engineering, logistics, manufacturing, production process, automated planning, etc.

This paper tackles the disjunctive constrained knapsack (belonging to the knapsack family) with a hybrid guided search-based method.

Such a problem can be encountered as a subproblem for solving a well-known two-dimensional bin packing problem, belonging to the cutting and packing family.

1. Introduction

Integer and mixed-inter programming play a central role in modeling NP-hard combinatorial optimization problems. Such models generally serve as a guide to design effective exact methods. However, exact methods derived from these models are often difficult to use, especially when tackling large-scale problems. In this case, the availability of effective approximative methods, like heuristics, meta-heuristics and hybrid methods, are of paramount importance.

In this paper, we investigate the use of an effective hybrid guided neighborhood search (HGNS) for solving a special 0–1 knapsack problem known as *Disjunctively Constrained Knapsack Problem* (DCKP). An instance of DCKP is characterized by a knapsack of fixed capacity c, a set I containing n items and a set E of incompatible items, where $E \subseteq \left\{ (i,j) \in I \times I, \ i < j \right\}$. Furthermore, each item $i, \forall i \in I$, is characterized by a weight w_i and a profit p_i. The aim of DCKP is to maximize the total profit of items that can be placed into the knapsack without exceeding its capacity and all items included in the knapsack must be compatible. The integer linear program of DCKP can be written as follows:

$$(P_{DCKP}) \quad \max \sum_{i \in I} p_i x_i \tag{1}$$

$$\text{s.t.} \sum_{i \in I} w_i x_i \leq c \tag{2}$$

$$x_i + x_j \leq 1 \quad \forall \, (i,j) \in E \tag{3}$$

$$x_i \in \{0,1\} \quad \forall \, i \in I,$$

where the decision variable $x_i, \forall \, i \in I$, is equal to 1 if item i is included in the knapsack (solution) and 0 otherwise (out of the solution). Inequality (Equation 2) represents the knapsack constraint of capacity c and inequalities (Equation 3) denote the disjunctive constraints, which ensure that all items belonging to a feasible solution must be compatible. Note that the knapsack's polytope can be obtained by combining Inequality (Equation 2) with integral constraints $x_i \in \{0,1\}, \ \forall i \in I$, and the polytope of the weighted-independent set problem can be obtained by associating inequalities (Equation 3) with the integral constraints. In the following we assume, we assume that

- all input data c, p_i, $w_i, \forall \, i \in I$, are nonnegative integers and,
- item $\sum_{i \in I} w_i > c$.

The remainder of the paper is organized as follows. Section 2 reviews some previous works on the DCKP. Section 3 presents the principle of the HGNS for approximately solving the DCKP. Section 3.1 introduces the first procedure which builds a DCKP's feasible solution from an independent set solution. Section 3.2 presents a modified ant colony optimization system which is used to guide the neighborhood search toward high-quality solutions. Section 3.3 details a descent method which is used as a local search around the current local (optimal) solution. Section 3.4 gives an overview of the proposed hybrid algorithm. Section 4 evaluates the performance of the proposed HGNS on instances taken from the literature, and analyzes the obtained results. Finally, Section 5 summarizes the contents of the paper.

2. Related work

The DCKP is an NP-hard combinatorial optimization problem. It reduces to the maximum *weighted-independent set* problem (Garey & Johnson, 1979) when the knapsack's capacity constraint is omitted, and the *classic knapsack* problem when $E = \emptyset$. It is easy to show that DCKP is a more complex extension of the multiple-choice knapsack problem which arises either as a stand-alone problem or as a component of more difficult combinatorial optimization problems. For example, DCKP was used in Dantzig–Wolfe's decomposition formulation for the two-dimensional bin packing problem (Pisinger & Sigurd, 2007). It served as a local optimization subproblem that needs to be solved for solving the pricing subproblem, which consists in finding a feasible packing of a single bin yielding smallest reduced cost.

Due to the complexity and hardness of the DCKP, most results on this topic are based on heuristics. The first paper addressing the resolution of DCKP is due to Yamada, Kataoka, and Watanabe (2002) and, Yamada and Kataoka (2001), where approximate and exact methods have been proposed. The approximate algorithm generates an initial feasible solution and improves it using a 2-opt neighborhood search. The exact algorithm starts its search from the solution obtained by the approximate algorithm and undertakes an implicit enumeration combined with an interval reduction technique. The exact algorithm solves uncorrelated instances containing from 100 to 1,000 items with a density varying from 0.001 to 0.020 (which is equivalent to a maximum of 10,000 disjunctive constraints).

Hifi and Michrafy (2007) proposed three exact algorithms in which reduction strategies, an equivalent model and a dichotomous search cooperate to solve the DCKP. The first algorithm reduces the size of the original problem by starting with a lower bound and successively solving relaxed DCKPs. The second algorithm combines a reduction strategy with a dichotomous search in order to accelerate the search process. The third algorithm tackles instances with a large number of disjunctive constraints.

Hifi and Michrafy (2006) proposed a three-step reactive local search. The first step of the algorithm provides an initial solution using a greedy procedure that iteratively introduces an item into the knapsack until filling it and sets it to the current solution. The second step is based on an intensification procedure in the neighborhood of the current solution where a neighboring solution is obtained by removing an item from the solution and inserting other ones. It adopts a memory list that stores swaps and/or the hashing function; thus, forbids cycling. The third step diversifies the search process by accepting to temporarily degrade the quality of the solution in hope of escaping from local optima. The reactive local search repeats the last two steps until satisfactory solution is reached.

Pferschy and Schauer (2009) presented pseudopolynomial algorithms for several special cases of the disjunctively knapsack problem which is mainly based on a graph representation: trees, graphs with bounded tree-width and chordal graphs. Furthermore, the authors extended their algorithms for establishing fully polynomial time approximation schemes (FPTAS).

Hifi, Negre, and Ould Ahmed Mounir (2009) investigated the use of the rounding solution procedure and an effective local branching. The method can be viewed as a combination of two complementary approaches: (1) a rounding solution procedure and (2) a restricted exact solution procedure. The performance of the approach was evaluated on the existing instances of the literature and it was remarked that this approach was able to improve several best-known solutions from the literature, but an increasing runtime is needed because the Cplex solver was used as a black box in the algorithm.

Hifi and Otmani (2011, 2012) investigated the use of the scatter search for approximately solving the DCKP. The approach tried to explore some characteristics of two problems in order to tackle the DCKP: the independent set problem and the single knapsack problem. The performance of the approach was evaluated on the same instances as considered in Hifi et al. (2009) and showed that such approach was able to improve the solution quality of some instances.

Finally, in Hifi (2014) an iterative rounding search (IRS)-based algorithm has been proposed. The method can be viewed as a cooperative approach between the methods proposed in Hifi et al. (2009) and Hifi and Otmani (2012), where three strategies were combined: (1) the variable-fixing technique using the rounding method applied to the linear relaxation of the DCKP, (2) the injection of successive valid constraints, and (3) a neighbor search around solutions characterizing a series of reduced subproblems. The aforementioned steps are iterated until satisfying some stopping criteria.

3. A hybrid guided neighborhood search
This section discusses the main principle of the proposed algorithm, which can be viewed as a HGNS approach. Neighborhood search is an approximative approach that has proven to be effective on a wide range of combinatorial optimization problems. Generally, neighborhood search-based algorithms are composed of two complementary procedures: (1) a building procedure and (2) an exploring

procedure. The building procedure serves to yield a reduced solution space while the goal of the exploring procedure is to find a local optimum in the yielded space.

Moreover, two classes of neighborhood searches may be distinguished: (1) the descent methods and the random neighborhood searches. The descent methods are often recognized as the family containing the k-optimization, the local branching, the feasibility pump, etc. Generally, such methods apply the deterministic strategies in order to build a neighborhood of a given solution. Next, the local optimum is improved using enumerative methods. Then, both building and exploring procedures are successively employed until no further improvement occurs. However, the size of the neighborhood adopted in the descent method should not be large when the exploring procedure uses an enumerative method. Unlike the descent method, which often falls into a local optimum, a random neighborhood search method applies some nondeterministic strategies in order to yield a large size neighborhood. It also uses either exact methods or heuristics for exploring the resulting search space.

In our study, the proposed hybrid algorithm is composed of three procedures: an *outer search procedure*, a *conversion procedure*, and an *inner search procedure*. The outer search procedure is based on a modified ACO system (a random neighborhood search), which provides a series of independent set solutions. Through the execution of the outer search procedure, the conversion procedure is used in order to transform a current independent set to a feasible solution of DCKP while the inner search procedure uses a descent method for improving the DCKP's feasible solution. In what follows, we first introduce the conversion procedure used to compute a DCKP's solution from an independent set.

3.1. Building a DCKP's solution from an independent set
This section shows how a DCKP's feasible solution can be built from an independent set. In order to simplify mathematical expressions, all integer linear program models will be illustrated as a graphical representation with discrete points. We also adopt the following notations:

$Po(P)$: denotes the set of solutions of the problem P.
S_P: represents a feasible solution of P.
Opt_P: is an optimal solution of P.
IS^r: denotes an independent set which respects the disjunctive constraints of type (Equation 3) of P_{DCKP}.

Indeed, the DCKP is a combination of the *weighted independent set problem* (noted P_{WIS}) and the *classical binary knapsack problem* (noted P_K). P_{WIS} is obtained from P_{DCKP} by removing the capacity constraint (Equation 2) and by setting the profit of all items to one. Formally, the resulting problem can be rewritten as follows:

$$(P_{WIS}) \quad \max \sum_{i \in I} x_i$$
$$\text{s.t.} \quad x_i + x_j \le 1 \quad \forall (i,j) \in E$$
$$x_i \in \{0,1\} \quad \forall i \in I.$$

Let $S_{IS} = (s_1, \ldots, s_n)$ be a feasible solution of P_{WIS}, where s_i denotes the binary value assigned to x_i, $\forall i \in I$. Let $IS^r \subseteq I$ be a subset of S_{IS} such that, for all items included in IS^r, their decision variables are fixed to 1. However, S_{IS} may violate the capacity constraint (Equation 2) of P_{DCKP}. In order to make it feasible for the DCKP, the following problem is solved:

$$(P_K^r) \quad u(x) = \max \sum_{i \in IS^r} p_i x_i$$
$$\text{s.t.} \quad \sum_{i \in IS^r} w_i x_i \le c,$$
$$x_i \in \{0,1\}, \quad \forall i \in IS^r. \tag{4}$$

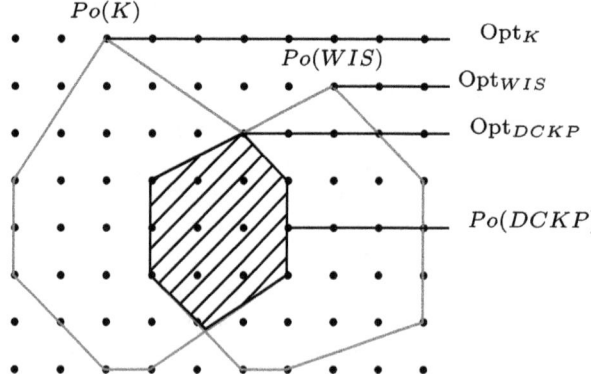

Figure 1. Representation of the sets of feasible solutions of P_K's, P_{WIS}'s, and P_{DCKP}'s respectively, and their corresponding optimal solutions.

In order to explain the decomposition strategy, we represent the set of solutions related to P_{DCKP}, P_{WIS}, and P_K^r by a graph, as illustrated in Figure 1: we can observe that all feasible solutions of P_{DCKP} belong to both $Po(K)$ and $Po(WIS)$, because $Po(K)$ is characterized by constraints (Equations 2 and 4) whereas $Po(WIS)$ is characterized by constraints (Equations 3 and 4). Differently stated, P_K dominates P_{DCKP} and the optimal solution Opt_{DCKP} of P_{DCKP} is one of P_{WIS}'s feasible solutions. Consequently, the convex hull of P_{DCKP} is the result of the intersection between the convex hull of both P_K and P_{WIS}.

Algorithm 1 shows how a feasible DCKP solution can be computed using IS^r (a feasible independent solution of P_{WIS}). It starts by checking whether S_{IS} (an independent set) respects the capacity constraint (Equation 2) of P_{DCKP} or not. If the capacity constraint is satisfied, S_{IS} is considered as a feasible solution of P_{DCKP}. Otherwise, P_K^r is solved using the exact algorithm proposed by Martello, Pisinger, and Toth (1999). Let S_K be a feasible solution of P_K^r: a DCKP's feasible solution can be obtained by setting the decision variables, whose values are fixed to 1 in S_{IS} but 0 in S_K, to 0. In other words, in order to make S_{IS} feasible, Algorithm 1 tries to remove certain items belonging to IS^r.

3.2. Using ACO to build a series of independent sets

It is well known that P_{WIS} is an NP-hard combinatorial optimization problem (cf. Garey & Johnson, 1979). On the one hand, determining an optimal solution of such a problem may be time-consuming. On the other hand, our objective is to yield a feasible solution of P_{WIS} (an independent set), which may contain a high-quality solution of DCKP. So, instead of solving P_{WIS} exactly, we apply an ACO system for approximately solving P_{WIS}.

We recall that ACO is a simple and efficient population-based metaheuristic. It has been first introduced in Colorni, Dorigo, and Maniezzo (1991) for approximately solving some large-scale instances of combinatorial optimization problems, like the traveling salesman problem. Its principle is based on the observation of real ants which are able to find the shortest path using the pheromone trails deposited by other ants. In term of optimization, let P be a combinatorial optimization problem which is characterized by a set of decision variables. Assume that for each feasible solution of P there always exists a path for ants toward it. The main idea of ACO is to determine an auto-updating system that

---

Algorithm 1 : A feasible DCKP solution via a classical knapsack problem
---
Input: IS^r, an independent set of P_{WIS}, and S_{IS}, a solution of P_{DCKP}.
Output: S_{DCKP}, a feasible DCKP solution.
  1: **if** S_{IS} satisfies the capacity constraint (2) of P_{DCKP} **then**
  2:    Set $S_{DCKP} = S_{IS}$;
  3: **else**
  4:    Let P_K^r be the resulting knapsack problem for IS^r;
  5:    Solve P_K^r by using an exact method and let S_K be the optimum solution;
  6:    Update S_{DCKP} according to S_K and S_{IS};
  7: **end if**
  8: **return** S_{DCKP} as a feasible solution of DCKP.

highlights the path so that the ants find the most interesting solution. As shown in Colorni et al. (1991), after a sufficient number of iterations, the most of ants move onto the same path which represents the stability of the system.

An ACO-based algorithm is generally composed of two components: a *path building strategy* and a *pheromone updating strategy*. The path building strategy represents a solution as a path and finds a way of selecting arcs to build the path. The pheromone updating strategy contains two keys: the enhancement and the evaporation of pheromone. On the one hand, the enhancement ensures that the more interesting the path is, the more the ants tend to move onto such a path. On the other hand, in order to avoid that the search procedure converges quickly to a local optima, the pheromone trail evaporates with the time passing.

Following the mechanism used by Fidanova (2005), a similar algorithm was introduced for solving P_{WIS}. Indeed, Figure 2 illustrates the mechanism adopted: a directed graph $G = (V, A)$, where V denotes its vertex set (i.e. $V = \{v_0, v_1, \ldots, v_n\}$) and A is the set of arcs (i.e. $A = \{(v_i, v_{i+1})^k \mid \forall \, v_i \in V \text{ and } k \in \{0, 1\}\}$). For any travel from vertex i to $i + 1$, either $(v_i, v_{i+1})^0$ or $(v_i, v_{i+1})^1$ can be chosen, but not at the same time. For all i, $i \in I$, the vertex i indicates the state of the decision variable x_i of P_{WIS}. In this case, x_i is fixed to 1 if $(v_{i-1}, v_i)^1$ is selected; x_i is unfixed otherwise. Further, x_i is fixed to 0 if and only if the item i is incompatible with one of the items whose decision variables have already fixed to 1. Once the vertex x_i is fixed to 0 (resp. 1), the ant must select the arc $(v_{i-1}, v_i)^0$ (resp. $(v_{i-1}, v_i)^1$) to follow. Such building continues when all decision variables of P_{WIS} are fixed. Note that if the ant has arrived to the n-th vertex with some unfixed variables, then it restarts the selection process from the vertex 0.

Algorithm 2 : Determining of an independent set as a solution for P_{WIS}

Input: an instance I of P_{DCKP}.
Output: a feasible solution (independent set) IS^r for P_{WIS}.
 1: **Initialization:** set $IS^r = \emptyset$ and $S = \{1, \ldots, n\}$.
 2: Rank all items of S following the non-increasing order of their reduced costs; set $i = 1$;
 3: **while** $S \neq \emptyset$ **do**
 4:     Randomly select an arc $(v_{i-1}, v_i)^k$ $(k = 0, 1)$ related to item i;
 5:     **if** $(v_{i-1}, v_i)^1$ is selected **then**
 6:        Set $IS^r = IS^r \cup \{i\}$; remove i from S; remove all incompatible items with i from S;
 7:     **end if**
 8:     If $i = n$ and $S \neq \emptyset$, reset i as the first item included in S;
 9: **end while**
10: **return** IS^r as a feasible solution of P_{WIS}.

In our study, all items are ranked in nonincreasing order of their reduced costs which can be obtained by solving the linear relaxation of P_{DCKP} with the simplex method. Instead of ranking items according to the profit per weight or the degree, we favor the reduced cost because it combines informations related to the objective function (Equation 1), the capacity constraint (Equation 2), and all disjunctive constraints (Equation 3). Algorithm 2 starts by initializing IS^r to an empty set (a feasible solution of P_{WIS}) and ranking all items of S in nonincreasing order of their reduced costs. In the main loop, an ant selects an item with a certain probability, and removes the selected item i and all its incompatible items from S. The selection procedure iterates until no item can be added to the current independent set IS^r and the algorithm stops with a feasible solution IS^r of P_{WIS}.

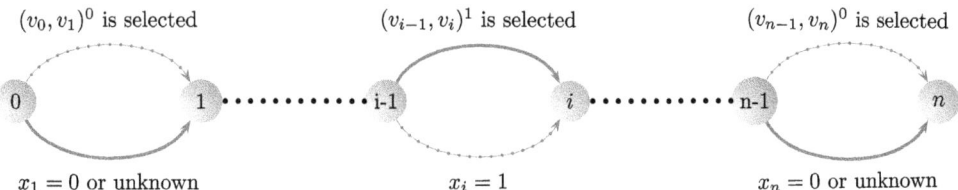

Figure 2. Representation of an independent set solution through the use of the path building strategy.

However, while building a solution or a path, the probability of the selection of an arc made by an ant depends on the density of pheromone deposited on the arc by the other ants. Here n, for the path building strategy, the following tunings are considered. First of all, the items are ranked in non-increasing order of their reduced costs. Let τ_{ik}^t be the amount of pheromone deposited on the arc $(v_{i-1}, v_i)^k$, $\forall i$, $i \in I$, and $k \in \{0, 1\}$ at the t-th iteration. The probability of selecting the arc $(v_{i-1}, v_i)^k$ at the t-th iteration can be defined as follows:

$$p_{ik}^t = \frac{\tau_{ik}^t}{\tau_{i0}^t + \tau_{i1}^t}.$$

Indeed, the ant randomly selects arcs to traverse the graph, but the probability of selecting arcs is dynamically updated at the end of each iteration. The pheromone updating strategy generally depends on the local optima obtained from previous iterations and the number of iterations already completed. Formally, at the end of the t-th iteration, the amount of pheromone on the arc (i, j) is updated according to the following equality:

$$\tau_{ik}^{t+1} = (1 - \rho) \cdot \tau_{ik}^t + \Delta_{ik}^t, \quad \forall i \in I \text{ and } k \in \{0, 1\},$$

where $0 < \rho < 1$ is the evaporation parameter and Δ_{ik}^t denotes the reinforcement value on the arc $(v_{i-1}, v_i)^k$ at the t-th iteration. Note that the evaporation parameter ρ adjusts the diversity of solutions computed by ACO, whereas the reinforcement value Δ_{ik}^t adjusts the convergence of ACO to a local optima. However, the right choice of both parameters can lead the ant system to good local optima. Unfortunately, the values of both parameters are experimentally determined. Our limited computational results showed that the following adjustments realized a good behavior for the convergence of ACO: $\rho = 0.999$ and $\forall i$, $i \in I$, and $k \in \{0, 1\}$,

$$\Delta_{ik}^t = \begin{cases} f(u^t) & \text{if } (v_{i-1}, v_i)^k \text{ is selected at the } t\text{-th iteration} \\ 0 & \text{otherwise,} \end{cases}$$

where u^t (resp. u^*) is the current solution value (resp. the best solution value found) and $f(.)$ is a function of u^t such that:

$$f(u^t) = \frac{e^{g(u^t) \cdot P}}{Q}, \quad \text{where} \quad g(u^t) = \frac{u^t}{u^* + (u^* - u^t)}. \tag{5}$$

Note that the parameter P of Formula (5) is used for adjusting the growth rate of u^t and so, that of $f(u^t)$. The parameter Q is used for adjusting the equilibrium between reinforcement and evaporation of pheromones. Differently stated, according to the parameters used in Formula (5), the better solution is, the more pheromones are deposited on the corresponding arcs.

3.3. The descent method as a local search

In order to improve a current solution of P_{DCKP}, this section presents a descent method which is based on a deterministic building procedure and an exact exploring procedure. Figure 3 illustrates the main principle of the descent method that we applied to DCKP. The "dark area" of Figure 3 represents a neighborhood of a feasible DCKP solution. Such an area, a subsolution space, can be obtained by removing a percentage of items whose decision variables have already been fixed in S_{DCKP} (i.e. the value of each variable is equal either to 1 or 0). Therefore, the descent method (cf. Algorithm 3) consists in building and exploring a series of such areas until no further improvement occurs.

Let S_{DCKP} be a feasible DCKP solution provided by Algorithm 1 and α, where $\alpha \in [0, 100]$, be the percentage of the unassigned decision variables. Then, we consider $S^{(\alpha)}$ as the unassigned items set associated to S_{DCKP} and $\overline{S^{(\alpha)}}$ as the complementary set of $S^{(\alpha)}$ such that $S^{(\alpha)} \cup \overline{S^{(\alpha)}} = I$ (i.e. $\overline{S^{(\alpha)}}$ is the assigned items set associated to S_{DCKP}). Therefore, the descent method (cf. Algorithm 3) consists in building and solving the following equivalent integer linear program:

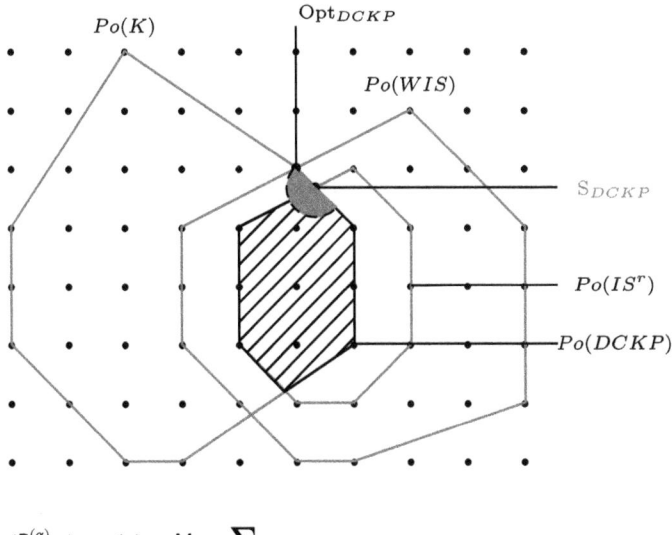

$$(P_{DCKP}^{(\alpha)}) \quad u(x) = \text{Max} \sum_{i \in S^{(\alpha)}} p_i x_i$$

$$\text{s.t.} \sum_{i \in S^{(\alpha)}} w_i x_i \leq c^{(\alpha)}$$

$$x_i + x_j \leq 1 \quad \forall (i,j) \in E^{(\alpha)}$$

$$x_i \in \{0,1\} \quad \forall i \in S^{(\alpha)},$$

Figure 3. Illustration of the neighborhood of a feasible DCKP solution.

where $E^{(\alpha)}$ denotes the subset of incompatible items belonging to $S^{(\alpha)}$ and $c^{(\alpha)}$ is the residual capacity such that $c^{(\alpha)} = c - \sum_{i \in \overline{S^{(\alpha)}}} x_i w_i$. From Figure 3, we can observe that a local optimal solution is used like an interior point of $Po(DCKP)$ to generate a $P_{DCKP}^{(\alpha)}$ by erasing the value of $\alpha\%$ of the variables. Further, a new local optimal solution can be reached by exactly solving the resulting problem $P_{DCKP}^{(\alpha)}$ (in dark area).

Algorithm 3 : Descent local search procedure

Input: S_{DCKP}, a starting solution of DCKP.
Output: $S_{DCKP}^{\star}$, an improved solution of DCKP.
1: Set $u(S_{DCKP}^{\star}) = -\infty$.
2: **while** $\left(u(S_{DCKP}) > u(S_{DCKP}^{\star}) \right)$ **do**
3:    Update $S_{DCKP}^{\star}$ with S_{DCKP}.
4:    Let $S^{(\alpha)}$ (resp. $\overline{S^{(\alpha)}}$) be the set of unassigned (resp. assigned) variables according to S_{DCKP}.
5:    Let $P_{DCKP}^{(\alpha)}$ be a restricted subproblem according to $S^{(\alpha)}$.
6:    Solve $P_{DCKP}^{(\alpha)}$ and let $S_{DCKP}^{(\alpha)}$ be its solution.
7:    Update S_{DCKP} according to $\overline{S^{(\alpha)}}$ and $S_{DCKP}^{(\alpha)}$.
8: **end while**
9: **return** $S_{DCKP}^{\star}$.

According to the presentation detailed above, we now describe the principle of the decent method (cf. Algorithm 3). The algorithm starts with a feasible DCKP solution (noted S_{DCKP}) reached by applying Algorithm 1. The main loop (cf. lines 2–8) describes the main steps of the descent method. At line 3, $S_{DCKP}^{\star}$ is updated with S_{DCKP}, an improved DCKP solution provided in the last iteration. Line 4 determines a set $S^{(\alpha)}$ of $\alpha\%$ unassigned variables from the current solution S_{DCKP}, where items with highest degree (i.e. items having the greatest number of incompatible items) are favored. Then, the reduced problem $P_{DCKP}^{(\alpha)}$ related to $S^{(\alpha)}$ is defined and solved (lines 5 and 6). We use $S_{DCKP}^{(\alpha)}$ to denote the optimal solution of $P_{DCKP}^{(\alpha)}$. At line 7, S_{DCKP} is updated according to the assigned items set $\overline{S^{(\alpha)}}$ and the optimal solution $S_{DCKP}^{(\alpha)}$ related to the unassigned items set $S^{(\alpha)}$. The main loop is iterated until no better solution is obtained. Finally, Algorithm 3 stops with the best solution $S_{DCKP}^{\star}$ of value $u(S_{DCKP}^{\star})$ found so far.

Table 1. Characteristics of the medium and large scale instances									
# Inst.	n	c	ρ	$|E|$	# Inst.	n	c	ρ	$|E|$
1IAx	500	1,800	0.10	12,475	6IAx	1,000	2,000	0.06	29,970
2IAx	500	1,800	0.20	24,950	7IAx	1,000	2,000	0.07	44,955
3IAx	500	1,800	0.30	37,425	8IAx	1,000	2,000	0.08	39,960
4IAx	500	1,800	0.40	49,900	9IAx	1,000	2,000	0.09	44,955
5IAx	1,000	1,800	0.05	24,975	10IAx	1,000	2,000	0.10	49,950

3.4. An overview of the HGNS

In this section, the main steps of the HGNS are detailed. HGNS can be considered as a hybrid neighborhood search which combines two complementary neighborhood strategies: (1) a random neighborhood search and (2) a deterministic neighborhood search. In order to combine both random and deterministic strategies, we propose to decompose the DCKP into two complementary problems, i.e. the weighted independent set and the classical binary knapsack. A series of these complementary problems are iteratively solved for reaching a final solution for the DCKP. More precisely, the random strategy mimics an ACO system to provide a series of independent sets containing high-quality solutions of DCKP. For each obtained independent set, a conversion procedure is used in order to convert an independent set to a feasible solution of DCKP. Once a feasible solution is obtained, the deterministic neighborhood search applies a descent method for improving the current solution. Finally, the DCKP's solution provided by the descent method is used to update the ACO system.

Algorithm 4 : Hybrid guided neighborhood search for the DCKP: HGNS

Input: An instance I of DCKP.
Output: A near-optimal solution for the DCKP.
 1: **Initialization:** set $S^*_{DCKP} = \emptyset$.
 2: **while** stopping criteria is not satisfied **do**
 3:   Set $i = 0$ and $S^{\circ}_{DCKP} = \emptyset$;
 4:   **while** $\left(i < m \right)$ **do**
 5:     Set $S^{local}_{DCKP} = \emptyset$;
 6:     The i-th ant applies Algorithm 2 to build the solution IS^r of P_{WIS} according to the current state of the pheromones laid on the arcs.
 7:     Let S_{DCKP} be a new DCKP solution reached by Algorithm 1 according to IS^r.
 8:     **If**$\left(u(S_{DCKP}) > u(S^{local}_{DCKP})\right)$, **then** set $S^{local}_{DCKP} = S_{DCKP}$.
 9:   **end while**
10:   Let S°_{DCKP} be the solution provided by Algorithm 3 when considering S^{local}_{DCKP}.
11:   **If** $\left(u(S^{\circ}_{DCKP}) > u(S^*_{DCKP})\right)$, **then** set $S^*_{DCKP} = S^{\circ}_{DCKP}$.
12:   According to the best local solution S^{local}_{DCKP}, determine a new independent set solution IS'.
13:   Update the pheromones according to $u(S^*_{DCKP})$, $u(S^{\circ}_{DCKP})$ and IS'.
14: **end while**
15: **return** S^*_{DCKP}, the best solution found for the DCKP.

Algorithm 4 describes the main steps of HGNS. At step 1, the best solution of DCKP is initialized to the empty set ($S^*_{DCKP} = \emptyset$). Then, the main loop of HGNS (steps 2–14) describes the principle of the proposed ACO system. It stops when the stopping criteria are performed. In the main loop, the inner loop (steps 4–9) is represented by m ants, where each of them applies Algorithm 2 to provide an independent set IS', and uses Algorithm 1 to compute a feasible solution of DCKP from IS'. The best solution of DCKP realized by m ants is then saved in S^{local}_{DCKP}. Step 10 calls Algorithm 3 for improving the current local solution S^{local}_{DCKP} using a descent local search (the best solution found so far is noted by S°_{DCKP}). Step 11 updates S^*_{DCKP} according to the current solution S°_{DCKP}. At step 12, we extend S°_{DCKP}, the best solution reached by the descent method, to an independent set IS' by adding the items which are compatible with the items belonging to S°_{DCKP}. Step 13 updates the pheromones used by the ACO system according to the current best objective value $u(S^*_{DCKP})$, the current local optimal objective value $u(S^{\circ}_{DCKP})$, and the independent set IS' related to the current optimal solution. Finally, the main loop is iterated until performing the stopping criteria, and the algorithm stops with the best solution S^*_{DCKP} for the DCKP.

Table 2. Effect of the descent local search

		Algorithm 3: *the descent local search*			
		Variation of α			
Algorithm	**Algorithm 1**	**5**	**10**	**15**	**20**
Av. Sol.	1,413.38	2,129.98	2,188.80	2,232.36	2,217.04
Av. Imp.		33.64	35.43	36.69	36.25
Av. time	0.32	0.47	2.03	19.72	118.30

4. Computational results

This section investigates the effectiveness of the proposed *Guided Neighborhood Search* (HGNS) on two groups of instances (taken from Hifi and Michrafy (2006) and generated following Yamada et al.'s (2002) and, Yamada and Kataoka (2001)). As detailed in Table 1, the first group, labeled from 1IAx to 4IAx with $1 \le x \le 5$, contains 20 medium instances with $n = 500$ items, a capacity $c = 1,800$, and different densities ρ (assessed in terms of the number of disjunctive constraints $|E|$). The second group, labeled from 5IAx to 10IAx with $1 \le x \le 5$, contains 30 large instances, where each instance contains 1,000 items, with $c = 1,800$ or 2,000 and with various densities. The algorithm HGNS was coded in C++ and tested on an Intel Pentium Core i5-2,500 with 3.3 GHz.

4.1. Effect of the descent method

This section evaluates the effect of the descent local search (cf. Algorithm 3). We recall that the method begins with a starting solution and improves it by alternatively applying both building and exploring procedures. Here n, the reduced problems provided by the building procedure are solved by using the Cplex solver.[1] In order to provide a starting solution, as an input for Algorithm 3, we first apply Algorithm 1 on the independent set built by applying the following simple greedy procedure: (1) from the current problem select an unassigned item with the highest reduced cost, (2) add the selected item to the current independent set, (3) remove the selected item with its incompatible items to get a reduced problem, and (4) repeat steps from (1) to (3) until reducing the problem to the empty set.

Table 2 shows the variation of Av Sol (the average solution values provided by the considered algorithm over all instances), Av Imp (the percentage improvement relative to the starting solution values), and Av time (the average runtime required by each algorithm for reaching the results). In order to evaluate the impact of α on the behavior of the descent method, Algorithm 3 is performed by varying the value of α in the discrete interval $\{5, 10, 15, 20\}$. From Table 2, we observe what follows.

(1) First, Algorithm 1 is able to provide the interesting results even if the average runtime remains rather small (0.32 s).

(2) Second, by setting $\alpha = 5$, Algorithm 3 is able to improve the quality of the solutions realized by Algorithm 1. Indeed, it obtains an average improvement of 33.64% whereas it consumes an average runtime of 0.47 s; that is slightly larger than that of Algorithm 1.

(3) Third, by increasing the value of α to either 5 or 10, Algorithm 3 is able to provide more interesting results. Moreover, this adjustment consumes a longer runtime even if it can be considered as reasonably small (it needs an average of 2.03 s).

TAble 3. A comparative study between Cplex, IRS and HGNS

	Cplex				HGNS: *variation of α*					
	3,600	**10,000**	**IRS**	**cpu**	**10%**	**9%**	**8%**	**7%**	**6%**	**5%**
				t_1	48	47	44	40	34	34
nb_{best}	3	4	15							
				t_2	48	47	47	47	46	43

Instance	Best	V_{Cplex}		V_{IRS}	Guided Neighborhood Search: V_{HGNS}			
					First runtime t_1		Second runtime t_2	
	Best	3,600	10,000	V_{IRS}	10%	9%	10%	9%
1I1	2,567*	2,567*	2,567*	2,567*	2,567*	2,567*	2,567*	2,567*
1I2	2,594*	2,594*	2,594*	2,594*	2,594*	2,594*	2,594*	2,594*
1I3	2,320	2,320	2,320	2,320	2,320	2,320	2,320	2,320
1I4	2,310	2298	2,300	2,303	2,310	2,310	2,310	2,310
1I5	2,330	2,310	2,320	2,310	2,330	2,330	2,330	2,330
2I1	2,118	2,080	2,080	2,100	2,118	2,117	2,118	2,118
2I2	2,110	2,070	2,080	2,110	2,110	2,110	2,110	2,110
2I3	2,132	2,098	2,098	2,128	2,132	2,132	2,132	2,132
2I4	2,109	2,070	2,080	2107	2,109	2,109	2,109	2,109
2I5	2,114	2,090	2,090	2,103	2,110	2,114	2,110	2,114
3I1	1,845	1,667	1,845	1,840	1,845	1,845	1,845	1,845
3I2	1,795	1,681	1,681	1,785	1,795	1,795	1,795	1,795
3I3	1,774	1,461	1,588	1,742	1,774	1,774	1,774	1,774
3I4	1,792	1,567	1,753	1,792	1,792	1,792	1,792	1,792
3I5	1,794	1,563	1,772	1,772	1,794	1,794	1,794	1,794
4I1	1,330	1,053	1,187	1,321	1,330	1,330	1,330	1,330
4I2	1,378	1,199	1,223	1,378	1,378	1,378	1,378	1,378
4I3	1,374	1,212	1,318	1,374	1,374	1,374	1,374	1,374
4I4	1,353	1,066	1,284	1,353	1,353	1,353	1,353	1,353
4I5	1,354	1,229	1,268	1,354	1,354	1,354	1,354	1,354
5I1	2,690	2,680	2,680	2,690	2,690	2,690	2,690	2,690
5I2	2,700	2,690	2,690	2,690	2,700	2,700	2,700	2,700
5I3	2,690	2,670	2,680	2,689	2,690	2,690	2,690	2,690
5I4	2,700	2,680	2,680	2,690	2,700	2,700	2,700	2,700
5I5	2,680	2,660	2,660	2,680	2,680	2,680	2,680	2,670
6I1	2,850	2,820	2,820	2,840	2,850	2,850	2,850	2,850
6I2	2,830	2,800	2,820	2,820	2,820	2,830	2,830	2,829
6I3	2,830	2,790	2,790	2,820	2,820	2,820	2,830	2,830
6I4	2,829	2,790	2,800	2,800	2,820	2,829	2828	2,829
6I5	2,830	2,800	2,810	2,810	2,829	2,830	2,830	2,830
7I1	2,780	2,700	2,727	2,750	2,780	2,770	2,780	2,770
7I2	2,770	2,720	2,720	2,750	2,770	2,770	2,770	2,770
7I3	2,760	2,718	2,740	2,747	2,760	2,760	2,760	2,760
7I4	2,800	2,728	2,750	2,773	2,790	2,790	2,790	2,800
7I5	2,770	2,730	2,750	2,757	2,760	2,770	2,760	2,760
8I1	2,720	2,638	2,686	2,720	2,720	2,720	2,720	2,720
8I2	2,720	2,659	2,690	2709	2,720	2,720	2,720	2,720
8I3	2,740	2664	2,690	2,730	2,730	2,740	2,740	2,740
8I4	2,720	2,620	2,670	2,710	2,719	2,710	2,719	2,720
8I5	2,710	2644	2,659	2,710	2,710	2,710	2,710	2,710
9I1	2,677	2,589	2,600	2,650	2,677	2,670	2,677	2,670

Table 4. Performance of HGNS vs Cplex and IRS on the benchmark instances of the literature

(Continued)

Table 4. (*Continued*)					Guided Neighborhood Search: V_{HGNS}			
		V_{Cplex}			First runtime t_1		Second runtime t_2	
Instance	Best	3,600	10,000	V_{IRS}	10%	9%	10%	9%
9I2	2,666	2,580	2,620	2,640	2,660	2,660	2,660	**2,666**
9I3	2,670	2,580	2,620	2,635	2,660	2,660	2,669	**2,670**
9I4	2,668	2,540	2,620	2,630	2,659	2,660	2,660	**2,668**
9I5	2,670	2,594	2,610	2,630	2,660	2,660	2,660	**2,670**
10I1	2,620	2,500	2,570	2,610	2,610	2,617	2,618	**2,620**
10I2	2642	2549	2578	**2642**	2,630	2,620	2,630	2,630
10I3	2,620	2527	2,580	2618	**2,620**	2,610	**2,620**	**2,620**
10I4	2621	2509	2560	**2621**	2,610	2,620	2,618	2,618
10I5	2,630	2530	2550	2,606	**2,630**	2,620	**2,630**	**2,630**
Av. Sol.	2401.92	2,317.88	2,354.74	2,390.40	2399.26	2399.36	2,400.56	2,400.86

*Used method reaches an optimal solution value.

(4) Fourth and last, Algorithm 3 with both $\alpha = 15$ and $\alpha = 20$ realized better average solution quality, even though the results of the first assignment ($\alpha = 15$) dominate those of the second assignment ($\alpha = 20$). These results are achieved by consuming a much longer runtime. Indeed, Algorithm 3 with $\alpha = 15$ consumes an average runtime close to 20 s whereas with $\alpha = 20$ it needs an average runtime of 120 s.

Recall that Algorithm 3 is generally used in order to refine the solutions yielded by the ACO system. Therefore, it is interesting to find a judicious compromise between the quality of solutions reached by the descent method and the used runtime. Then, in order to maintain a reasonable runtime for HGNS, the choice with α varying in the interval [5, 10] is adopted for the remainder of this paper.

4.2. Performance of HGNS
In order to evaluate the performance of the proposed method, we first compare HGNS with Cplex solver (version 12.4) and IRS proposed in Hifi (2014) (one of the most recent methods in the literature). Because of the high complexity of DCKP, two runtime limits of Cplex are considered: 3,600 s and 10,000 s. For HGNS, two runtime limits are considered: $t_1 = 500$ and $t_2 = 1,000$ (measured in seconds).

We recall that HGNS is based on an ant colony optimization system which is performed with certain parameters (cf. Section 3.2). Here n, we tried to find a good tuning that ensures a balance between the convergence of ACO and its solutions' quality. Then, after different trials, two tunings are used. Indeed, for the first runtime t_1, ACO uses the following tunings: $\rho = 0.999, m = 10, P = 10$, and $Q = 500$. For the second runtime t_2, it uses the following values: $\rho = 0.9995, m = 10, P = 10$, and $Q = 500$. Further, for each considered runtime limit, HGNS is performed with different values of α varying from 5 to 10. Because of the stochastic aspect of the ACO system, 10 independent trials of HGNS were performed for all considered instances.

Table 3 exposes the number of the best solutions reached by each considered approach (cf. Table 4). Columns 2 and 3 (resp. column 4) show nb_{best}, the number of the best solutions matched by the Cplex solver (resp. IRS). Column 5 displays the runtime limits used by HGNS, i.e. with $t_1 = 500$ and $t_2 = 1,000$ s. For each runtime limit, columns from 6 to 11 give the number of the best solutions realized by HGNS when varying α. From Table 3, we observe what follows.

(1) First, on the one hand, we can observe the inferiority of Cplex because it only matches three (resp. four) instances over 50 within 3,600 (resp. 100,000) s. It represents a percentage of 6%

(resp. 8%) of the best solutions of the literature. On the other hand, the most recent method of the literature provides 15 best solutions out of 50, representing a percentage of 30% of the best solutions. Note that among the best solutions, HGNS matches 2 optimal solutions (as shown in Table 4: instances 1I1 and 1I2 have been optimally solved by the Cplex solver within 10,000 s—solutions marked with the symbol "*").

(2) Second, for the first runtime $t_1 = 500$, the number of the best solutions reached by HGNS increases. Indeed, for $\alpha = 10$ (resp. 9) HGNS reaches 48 (resp. 47) best solutions out of 50, representing a percentage of 96% (resp. 94%) of the best solutions.

(3) Third, for the second runtime $t_2 = 1,000$, the quality of the solutions provided by HGNS becomes more interesting. Indeed, for $\alpha = 8$ (resp 7, 6, and 5), the percentage of nb_{best} increases from 88 to 94% (resp. from 80 to 94%, from 68 to 92% and, from 68 to 86%, respectively).

Because HGNS is able to provide better solutions for $\alpha = 9$ and $\alpha = 10$, both values are adopted for the rest of the paper.

Table 4 shows the solution values reached by Cplex, IRS, and HGNS. Column 1 displays the data labels and column 2 reports the best solutions found by the considered algorithms. Columns 3 (resp. column 4) reports the solution values (V_{Cplex}) reached by Cplex v12.4 within 3,600 (resp. 10,000) s. Column 5 displays the best-known solution values available in the literature, noted by V_{IRS}. For the first runtime $t_1 = 500$, the best value $V_{HGNS_{(10)}}$ (resp. $V_{HGNS_{(9)}}$) realized by HGNS with $\alpha = 10$ (resp. $\alpha = 9$), for 10 independent trials, is displayed on column 6 (resp. 7). Similarly, columns 8 and 9 show the solution values reached by HGNS for the second runtime $t_2 = 1,000$. We note that the value in "boldface" means that the best solution value has been obtained by the considered algorithm, the value in italic indicates that HGNS reaches a better solution value than IRS, and the value with the symbol "*" means that the method reaches the optimal solution value.

In order to evaluate the behavior of HGNS, which includes a probabilistic procedure, 10 trials of HGNS were considered. According to these trials, Table 5 shows the average results of the solution values reached by these trials and those displayed in Table 4. From Table 5, we observe what follows:

(1) The average value of 2,400.86 confirms the superiority of HGNS when both values t_2 and $\alpha = 9$ are used. The average solution values corresponding to the couple $(cpu, \alpha)=(t_2, 10)$ remains very competitive because it realizes an average solution value of 2,400.56 which is very close to the best average solution values, i.e. the value 2,400.86 realized by the couple $(t_2, 9)$.

(2) Both tunings $(t_1, 9)$ and $(t_1, 10)$ remain interesting when compared to the best average solution values realized by both Cplex (2,317.88 with 3,600 s and 2,354.74 with 10,000 s) and the best average solution values taken from the literature (2,390.40).

(3) Over 10 trials, with the first runtime limit t_1, HGNS maintains its superiority over Cplex and the best solutions of the literature. Indeed, its average value is equal to 2,394.02 for $\alpha = 10$ and increases slightly to 2,394.84 for $\alpha = 9$.

(4) Globally, by doubling the runtime limit (i.e. $t_2 = 1,000$), the behavior of HGNS becomes more interesting. Indeed, in this case, the proposed algorithm realizes an average value of 2,397.54 for $\alpha = 10$ and 2398.87 for $\alpha = 9$.

Table 5. Behavior of HGNS vs Cplex and IRS							
	Cplex			Guided Neighborhood Search			
				First runtime limit t_1		Second runtime limit t_2	
	3,600	10,000	V_{IRS}	10%	9%	10%	9%
Av. best Sol.	2,317.88	2,354.74	2,390.40	2399.26	2399.36	2,400.56	2,400.86
Av. Sol. 10 trials				2394.02	2,394.84	2,397.54	2398.87

Table 6. Impact of the parameter used by HGNS on the average solution quality				
	t_1		t_2	
Trial	10	9	10	9
1	2,391.48	2,391.32	2,394.58	2,396.62
2	2,390.66	2,393.74	2,391.82	2,397.54
3	2,390.80	2,392.04	2,392.28	2,395.90
4	2,392.92	2,393.16	2,394.08	2,396.72
5	2,391.52	2,394.98	2,394.14	2,397.26
6	2,392.20	2,391.58	2,393.72	2,395.74
7	2,391.80	2,393.38	2,393.22	2,396.60
8	2,392.30	2,393.16	2,393.66	2,396.50
9	2,392.14	2,392.84	2,394.66	2,397.60
10	2,390.92	2,393.64	2,394.20	2,396.94
G. Av.	2,391.67	2,392.99	2,393.64	2,396.74

4.3. Detailed results

This section provides a detailed study of the results reached by HGNS over 10 trials. Indeed, we have already mentioned that 10 trials of the HGNS have been performed for each of the 50 problem instances. These trials are performed for both $\alpha = 9$ and $\alpha = 10$ and each trial is stopped when the runtime limit t_1 (resp. t_2) is performed.

Table 6 shows the average quality of the solutions reached by HGNS over the 10 trials and the detailed results are exposed in Tables A1- A4, as shown in Appendix.

Line 1 (resp. line 2) of Table 6 displays the runtime limits (resp. the value of the parameter α). Lines from 3 to 12 display the average solution quality over all instances, line 13 shows the average solution quality over the 10 trials. The analysis of Table 6 shows what follows:

(1) For the first couple of values $(t_1, 10)$, on the one hand, HGNS realizes an average solution value varying from 2,390.66 (trial 2) to 2,392.92 (trial 4). On the other hand, the smallest average solution value realized by HGNS is still greater than the best average value realized by IRS (that is equal to 2,390.40—cf. Table 4). The same observation holds for $(t_1, 9)$, where the minimum average solution value realized by HGNS is equal to 2,391.32 while its maximum average solution value is equal to 2,394.98.

(2) By increasing the runtime limit (i.e. using t_2 instead of t_1), for either $\alpha = 10$ or $\alpha = 9$, one can observe that HGNS realizes better average solution qualities. Indeed, for the parameter $\alpha = 10$ (resp. $\alpha = 9$), it reaches a minimum average solution value of 2,391.82 (resp. 2,395.74) and a maximum average solution value of 2,394.66 (resp. 2,397.60).

5. Conclusions

In this paper, we proposed a HGNS for solving the disjunctively constrained knapsack problem. The proposed algorithm applies an ant colony optimization (ACO) system to guide a neighborhood search procedure toward high-quality solutions. In order to improve the quality of the solutions provided by ACO, a descent local search procedure is introduced. Both ACO and the descent method are based on building and exploring a series of neighborhoods related to a series of local optima. The performance of the proposed algorithm was computationally analyzed on a set of benchmark instances taken from the literature. The provided results were compared to those realized by both the Cplex solver and a recent algorithm available in the literature. The obtained results show that the guided neighborhood search was able to improve most existing solutions.

Acknowledgements
The authors thank the anonymous referees for their helpful comments and suggestions which contributed to the improvement of the contents of this paper.

Funding
The authors received no direct funding for this research.

Author details
Mhand Hifi[1]
E-mail: hifi@u-picardie.fr
Sagvan Saleh[1]
E-mail: sagvanhajani@yahoo.com
Lei Wu[1]
E-mail: lei.wu@u-picardie.fr
[1] Université de Picardie Jules Verne, EPROAD-EA 4669, 7 rue du Moulin Neuf, 80000 Amiens, France.

Note
1. The Cplex solver is a commercial software developed by IBM in order to solve (mixed)integer linear programming problems. The current version is based on the branch-and-cut framework in which a set of local search procedures are used for enhancing its performance.

References
Colorni, A., Dorigo, M., & Maniezzo, V. (1991). Distributed optimization by ant colonies. In F. Varlea & P. Bourgine (Eds.), *Proceedings of the First European Conference on Artificial Life* (pp. 134–142). Paris: Elsevier.
Fidanova, S. (2005). Ant colony optimization for multiple knapsack problem and model bias. *Numerical Analysis and its Applications, Lecture Notes in Computer Science, 3401,* 280–287.
Garey, M. R., & Johnson, D. S. (1979). *Computers and intractability: A guide to the theory of NP-completeness.* San Francisco, CA: W.H. Freeman.
Hifi, M. (2014). An iterative rounding search-based algorithm for the disjunctively constrained knapsack problem. *Engineering Optimization, 46,* 1109–1122.
Hifi, M., & Michrafy, M. (2006). A reactive local search algorithm for the disjunctively constrained knapsack problem. *Journal of the Operational Research Society, 57,* 718–726.
Hifi, M., & Michrafy, M. (2007). Reduction strategies and exact algorithms for the disjunctively constrained knapsack problem. *Computers & Operations Research, 34,* 2657–2673.
Hifi, M., Negre, S., & Ould Ahmed Mounir, M. (2009). Local branching-based algorithm for the disjunctively constrained knapsack problem. *IEEE Proceedings of the International Conference on Computers & Industrial Engineering,* 279–284.
Hifi, M., & Otmani, N. (2011). An algorithm for the disjunctively constrained knapsack problem. *IEEE International Conference on Communications, Computing and Control Applications,* 1–6.
Hifi, M., & Otmani, N. (2012). An algorithm for the disjunctively constrained knapsack problem. *International Journal of Operational Research, 13,* 22–43.
Martello, S., Pisinger, D., & Toth, P. (1999). Dynamic programming and strong bounds for the 0–1 knapsack problem. *Management Science, 45,* 414–424.
Pferschy, U., & Schauer, J. (2009). The knapsack problem with conflict graphs. *Journal of Graph Algorithms and Applications, 13,* 233–249.
Pisinger, D., & Sigurd, M. (2007). Using decomposition techniques and constraint programming for solving the two-dimensional bin-packing problem. *INFORMS Journal on Computing, 19,* 36–51.
Yamada, T., & Kataoka, S. (2001). *Heuristic and exact algorithms for the disjunctively constrained knapsack problem. EURO 2001* (pp. 9–11). Rotterdam.
Yamada, T., Kataoka, S., & Watanabe, K. (2002). Heuristic and exact algorithms for the disjunctively constrained knapsack problem. *Information Processing Society of Japan Journal, 43,* 2864–2870.

Appendix A

Detailed results on 10 trials of HGNS

Table A1. The quality of the solutions reached by the 10 trials of HGNS for $\alpha = 10$ and t_1

Inst.	1	2	3	4	5	6	7	8	9	10	AV. Sol.	Max
1I1	2,567	2,567	2,567	2,567	2,567	2,567	2,567	2,567	2,567	2,567	2,567.00	2,567
1I2	2,594	2,594	2,594	2,594	2,594	2,594	2,594	2,594	2,594	2,594	2,594.00	2,594
1I3	2,320	2,320	2,320	2,320	2,320	2,320	2,320	2,320	2,320	2,320	2,320.00	2,320
1I4	2,310	2,310	2,310	2,310	2,310	2,310	2306	2,310	2,310	2,310	2309.60	2,310
1I5	2,330	2,330	2,330	2,330	2,330	2,330	2,330	2,330	2,330	2,330	2,330.00	2,330
2I1	2,115	2,117	2,110	2,117	2,114	2,115	2,117	2,115	2,118	2,117	2,115.50	2,118
2I2	2,110	2,110	2,110	2,110	2,110	2,110	2,110	2,110	2,110	2,110	2,110.00	2,110
2I3	2,115	2,111	2,111	2,110	2,111	2112	2108	2,132	2,118	2,110	2113.80	2,132
2I4	2,100	2,109	2,109	2,100	2,100	2,100	2,100	2,109	2105	2107	2,103.90	2,109
2I5	2,110	2,110	2,110	2,110	2,110	2108	2108	2,109	2108	2,110	2,109.30	2,110
3I1	1,743	1,720	1,714	1,845	1,845	1,845	1,778	1,845	1,845	1,778	1,795.80	1,845
3I2	1,779	1,757	1,795	1,779	1,779	1,779	1,795	1,795	1,757	1,757	1,777.20	1,795
3I3	1,774	1,718	1,712	1,774	1,774	1,774	1,774	1,711	1,774	1,774	1,755.90	1,774
3I4	1,792	1,753	1,792	1,753	1,753	1,757	1,792	1,753	1,792	1,753	1,769.00	1,792
3I5	1,775	1,775	1,748	1,794	1,721	1,794	1,735	1,775	1,777	1,794	1,768.80	1,794
4I1	1,330	1,330	1,330	1,330	1,330	1,330	1,330	1,330	1,330	1,330	1,330.00	1,330
4I2	1,378	1,378	1,378	1,378	1,378	1,378	1,378	1,378	1,378	1,378	1,378.00	1,378
4I3	1,374	1,334	1,374	1,374	1,354	1,334	1,334	1,374	1,318	1,374	1,354.40	1,374
4I4	1,353	1,353	1,353	1,353	1,353	1,353	1,353	1,353	1,353	1,353	1,353.00	1,353
4I5	1,332	1,332	1,354	1,321	1,354	1,318	1,354	1,354	1,330	1,354	1,340.30	1,354
5I1	2,680	2,690	2,690	2,680	2,690	2,689	2,680	2,680	2,690	2,680	2,684.90	2,690
5I2	2,700	2,700	2,700	2,699	2,700	2,700	2,700	2,698	2,700	2,700	2,699.70	2,700
5I3	2,690	2,690	2,690	2,690	2,690	2,690	2,690	2,690	2,690	2,690	2,690.00	2,690
5I4	2,700	2,700	2,700	2,700	2,700	2,700	2,690	2,700	2,690	2,699	2697.90	2,700
5I5	2,669	2,670	2,670	2,670	2,670	2,660	2,680	2,670	2,680	2,670	2,670.90	2,680
6I1	2,840	2,850	2,850	2,850	2,850	2,850	2,850	2,840	2,840	2,830	2,845.00	2,850
6I2	2,810	2,820	2,820	2,820	2,820	2,818	2,820	2,820	2,810	2,820	2,817.80	2,820
6I3	2,810	2,820	2,820	2,820	2,819	2,820	2,819	2,820	2,810	2,820	2,817.90	2,820
6I4	2,820	2,820	2,820	2,820	2,819	2,810	2,820	2,820	2,820	2,810	2,817.90	2,820
6I5	2,820	2,820	2,820	2,820	2,820	2,820	2,820	2,820	2,829	2,820	2,820.90	2,829
7I1	2769	2,780	2,770	2,780	2769	2,760	2,770	2,760	2,768	2,780	2,770.60	2,780
7I2	2764	2,770	2769	2,760	2,760	2,770	2,770	2,770	2,760	2,760	2765.30	2,770

(Continued)

Table A1. (Continued)

Inst.	1	2	3	4	5	6	7	8	9	10	AV. Sol.	Max
7I3	2,740	2,750	2,750	2,750	2,750	2,750	2,760	2,750	2758	2,750	2,750.80	2,760
7I4	2,780	2,790	2,780	2,770	2,770	2,780	2,790	2787	2,780	2,780	2,780.70	2,790
7I5	2,760	2,760	2,760	2,750	2,760	2754	2,750	2,760	2,750	2,760	2756.40	2,760
8I1	2,720	2,720	2,700	2,710	2,710	2,720	2709	2,710	2,720	2,710	2712.90	2,720
8I2	2709	2,720	2,710	2,710	2,720	2,710	2,720	2,710	2,710	2,710	2712.90	2,720
8I3	2,720	2,730	2,730	2,730	2,730	2,720	2,729	2,730	2,730	2,719	2726.80	2,730
8I4	2,719	2,710	2,700	2,710	2707	2,700	2,710	2,700	2,700	2,700	2705.60	2,719
8I5	2,690	2,710	2,710	2,700	2,700	2,700	2,710	2697	2695	2,700	2701.20	2,710
9I1	2,659	2,660	2,660	2,660	2,660	2,670	2,670	2,660	2,677	2,659	2,663.50	2,677
9I2	2,657	2,660	2,650	2,660	2,660	2,659	2,660	2,660	2656	2,660	2,658.20	2,660
9I3	2,660	2,650	2,660	2,660	2,660	2,660	2,650	2,650	2,660	2,650	2656.00	2,660
9I4	2,650	2,655	2,650	2,649	2,650	2,659	2,650	2,650	2,640	2,659	2,651.20	2,659
9I5	2,650	2,660	2,660	2,650	2,650	2,659	2,650	2,649	2,650	2,650	2652.80	2,660
10I1	2,610	2,610	2,610	2,610	2,600	2,600	2,600	2,610	2,600	2,610	2,606.00	2,610
10I2	2,630	2,630	2,620	2,610	2,610	2,620	2,620	2,620	2,610	2,610	2,618.00	2,630
10I3	2,620	2,620	2,610	2,610	2,614	2609	2,600	2,610	2,620	2,610	2,612.30	2,620
10I4	2,610	2,610	2,610	2,610	2,600	2,610	2,610	2,600	2,600	2,610	2,607.00	2,610
10I5	2,617	2,630	2,630	2,619	2,610	2,615	2,610	2,610	2,630	2,600	2,617.10	2,630
Average	2,391.48	2,390.66	2,390.80	2,392.92	2,391.52	2,392.20	2,391.80	2,392.30	2,392.14	2,390.92	2,391.67	2399.26

Table A2. The quality of the solutions reached by the 10 trials of HGNS for $\alpha = 9$ and t_1

Inst.	1	2	3	4	5	6	7	8	9	10	AV. Sol.	Max.
1I1	2,567	2,567	2,567	2563	2,567	2,567	2,567	2,567	2,567	2,567	2566.60	2,567
1I2	2,594	2,594	2,594	2,594	2,594	2,594	2,594	2,594	2,594	2,594	2,594.00	2,594
1I3	2,320	2,320	2,320	2,320	2,320	2,320	2,320	2,320	2,320	2,320	2,320.00	2,320
1I4	2,310	2306	2,310	2,300	2,310	2,310	2,310	2306	2,310	2309	2308.10	2,310
1I5	2,330	2,330	2,330	2,330	2,330	2,330	2,330	2,330	2,330	2,330	2,330.00	2,330
2I1	2,115	2,117	2,115	2,114	2,117	2,117	2,115	2,115	2,110	2,117	2,115.20	2,117
2I2	2,110	2,110	2,110	2,110	2,110	2,110	2,110	2,110	2,110	2,110	2,110.00	2,110
2I3	2119	2,132	2108	2,110	2,115	2,111	2,115	2,110	2122	2,132	2,117.40	2,132
2I4	2,100	2,100	2,100	2,100	2,100	2107	2,100	2,109	2,100	2,100	2101.60	2,109
2I5	2,110	2,110	2,110	2107	2,109	2,110	2,110	2,110	2,114	2106	2,109.60	2,114
3I1	1,845	1,778	1,845	1799	1,845	1,743	1,845	1,845	1799	1,845	1818.90	1,845
3I2	1,779	1,779	1,779	1,795	1,779	1,795	1,795	1,795	1,795	1,757	1,784.80	1,795
3I3	1750	1,735	1,774	1,774	1,774	1,774	1,755	1,755	1,774	1,774	1763.90	1,774
3I4	1734	1,792	1689	1,792	1,792	1,792	1,792	1,753	1,757	1,792	1,768.50	1,792
3I5	1,748	1,775	1,748	1,775	1,794	1,748	1,794	1,777	1,775	1,794	1,772.80	1,794
4I1	1,330	1,330	1,330	1,330	1,330	1,330	1,330	1,330	1,330	1,330	1,330.00	1,330
4I2	1,378	1,378	1,378	1,378	1,378	1,378	1,378	1,378	1,378	1,378	1,378.00	1,378
4I3	1,374	1,374	1,374	1,374	1,374	1,374	1,334	1,374	1,374	1,374	1370.00	1,374
4I4	1,353	1,353	1,353	1,353	1,353	1,353	1,353	1,353	1,353	1,353	1,353.00	1,353
4I5	1,321	1,354	1,354	1,354	1,332	1,321	1,330	1,354	1,332	1,330	1338.20	1,354
5I1	2,689	2687	2,680	2,680	2,689	2,689	2,680	2,690	2,680	2,680	2,684.40	2,690
5I2	2,690	2,700	2,690	2,700	2,690	2,700	2,690	2,698	2,700	2,700	2695.80	2,700
5I3	2,690	2,690	2,690	2,690	2,690	2,690	2,690	2,690	2,690	2,690	2,690.00	2,690
5I4	2,690	2,700	2,700	2,690	2,700	2,700	2,690	2,690	2,690	2,700	2695.00	2,700
5I5	2,680	2,660	2,670	2,660	2,677	2,660	2,670	2,670	2,670	2,660	2,667.70	2,680
6I1	2,850	2,850	2,850	2,850	2,840	2,850	2,850	2839	2,850	2,850	2847.90	2,850
6I2	2,820	2,820	2,810	2,820	2,820	2,817	2,810	2,820	2,830	2,820	2,818.70	2,830
6I3	2,820	2,820	2,820	2,820	2,820	2,820	2,820	2,820	2,820	2,820	2,820.00	2,820
6I4	2,829	2,820	2,820	2,819	2,820	2,820	2,820	2,820	2,820	2,820	2,820.80	2,829
6I5	2,820	2,820	2,820	2,830	2,820	2827	2,820	2,820	2,820	2,830	2822.70	2,830
7I1	2,770	2,770	2,770	2,760	2,770	2,760	2,770	2,760	2,750	2,750	2763.00	2,770
7I2	2,760	2,770	2,760	2,770	2,770	2,760	2,760	2,770	2,750	2,770	2764.00	2,770
7I3	2,750	2,750	2,750	2,760	2,750	2,760	2,750	2,750	2,760	2,750	2753.00	2,760

(Continued)

Table A2. (Continued)

Inst.	1	2	3	4	5	6	7	8	9	10	AV. Sol.	Max.
7I4	2,780	2,790	2,788	2,780	2,780	2,780	2,790	2,780	2,780	2,780	2782.80	2,790
7I5	2,750	2,750	2,750	2,750	2,770	2753	2,760	2,750	2,750	2,750	2753.30	2,770
8I1	2,710	2,720	2709	2709	2,710	2,710	2,710	2,720	2,710	2,720	2712.80	2,720
8I2	2,710	2,719	2,720	2,720	2,720	2,710	2,720	2,710	2,720	2,710	2715.90	2,720
8I3	2,720	2,730	2,730	2,720	2,730	2,720	2,720	2,729	2,740	2,740	2,727.90	2,740
8I4	2,700	2,710	2,710	2709	2,710	2,700	2,710	2,710	2,710	2,700	2706.90	2,710
8I5	2,700	2,700	2,710	2702	2,700	2,710	2709	2,700	2701	2,710	2704.20	2,710
9I1	2,660	2,669	2,670	2,660	2,660	2,660	2,670	2,660	2,669	2,660	2,663.80	2,670
9I2	2,650	2,659	2,660	2,660	2,650	2,650	2,660	2,660	2,660	2,660	2656.90	2,660
9I3	2,650	2,660	2,660	2,660	2,660	2,660	2,649	2,649	2,660	2,660	2656.80	2,660
9I4	2,660	2,660	2,659	2,650	2,650	2,660	2,659	2,650	2,650	2,650	2654.80	2,660
9I5	2,660	2,660	2,650	2,660	2,660	2,660	2,660	2,650	2,660	2,650	2,657.00	2,660
10I1	2,614	2,610	2,610	2,610	2,610	2,610	2,617	2,610	2,610	2,610	2611.10	2,617
10I2	2,617	2,620	2,619	2,610	2,620	2,620	2,620	2,620	2,610	2,610	2616.60	2,620
10I3	2,610	2609	2609	2,610	2,610	2,610	2,600	2,610	2,608	2,610	2,608.60	2,610
10I4	2,620	2,610	2,610	2,610	2,610	2609	2,608	2,608	2,620	2,600	2,610.50	2,620
10I5	2,610	2,620	2,620	2,617	2,620	2,620	2,610	2,620	2,610	2,610	2,615.70	2,620
Average	2,391.32	2,393.74	2,392.04	2,393.16	2,394.98	2,391.58	2,393.38	2,393.16	2,392.84	2,393.64	2,392.984	2399.36

Table A3. The quality of the solutions realized by the 10 trials of HGNS for $\alpha = 10$ and t_2

Inst.	1	2	3	4	5	6	7	8	9	10	AV. Sol.	Max.
1I1	2,567	2,567	2,567	2,567	2,567	2,567	2,567	2,567	2,567	2,567	2,567.00	2,567
1I2	2,594	2,594	2,594	2,594	2,594	2,594	2,594	2,594	2,594	2,594	2,594.00	2,594
1I3	2,320	2,320	2,320	2,320	2,320	2,320	2,320	2,320	2,320	2,320	2,320.00	2,320
1I4	2,310	2,310	2,310	2,310	2,310	2,310	2306	2,310	2,310	2,310	2309.60	2,310
1I5	2,330	2,330	2,330	2,330	2,330	2,330	2,330	2,330	2,330	2,330	2,330.00	2,330
2I1	2,115	2,117	2,110	2,117	2,114	2,115	2,117	2,115	2,118	2,117	2,115.50	2,118
2I2	2,110	2,110	2,110	2,110	2,110	2,110	2,110	2,110	2,110	2,110	2,110.00	2,110
2I3	2,115	2,111	2,111	2,110	2,111	2112	2108	2,132	2,118	2,110	2113.80	2,132
2I4	2,100	2,109	2,109	2,100	2,100	2,100	2,100	2,109	2105	2107	2,103.90	2,109
2I5	2,110	2,110	2,110	2,110	2,110	2108	2108	2,109	2108	2,110	2,109.30	2,110
3I1	1,743	1,720	1,714	1,845	1,845	1,845	1,778	1,845	1,845	1,845	1802.50	1,845
3I2	1,779	1,757	1,795	1,779	1,779	1,779	1,795	1,795	1,757	1,757	1,777.20	1,795
3I3	1,774	1,718	1,712	1,774	1,774	1,774	1,774	1,711	1,774	1,774	1,755.90	1,774
3I4	1,792	1,753	1,792	1,753	1,792	1,757	1,792	1,753	1,792	1,753	1,772.90	1,792
3I5	1,775	1,775	1,748	1,794	1,721	1,794	1,775	1,775	1,794	1,794	1,774.50	1,794
4I1	1,330	1,330	1,330	1,330	1,330	1,330	1,330	1,330	1,330	1,330	1,330.00	1,330
4I2	1,378	1,378	1,378	1,378	1,378	1,378	1,378	1,378	1,378	1,378	1,378.00	1,378
4I3	1,374	1,334	1,374	1,374	1,354	1,334	1,334	1,374	1327	1,374	1355.30	1,374
4I4	1,353	1,353	1,353	1,353	1,353	1,353	1,353	1,353	1,353	1,353	1,353.00	1,353
4I5	1,354	1,354	1,354	1,330	1,354	1,332	1,354	1,354	1,354	1,354	1349.40	1,354
5I1	2,680	2,690	2,690	2,680	2,690	2,689	2,680	2,680	2,690	2,680	2,684.90	2,690
5I2	2,700	2,700	2,700	2,699	2,700	2,700	2,700	2,698	2,700	2,700	2,699.70	2,700
5I3	2,690	2,690	2,690	2,690	2,690	2,690	2,690	2,690	2,690	2,690	2,690.00	2,690
5I4	2,700	2,700	2,700	2,700	2,700	2,700	2,690	2,700	2,690	2,699	2697.90	2,700
5I5	2,669	2,670	2,670	2,670	2,670	2,660	2,680	2,670	2,680	2,670	2,670.90	2,680
6I1	2,850	2,850	2,850	2,850	2,850	2,850	2,850	2,840	2,840	2,850	2848.00	2,850
6I2	2,830	2,820	2,820	2,829	2,820	2,820	2,820	2,830	2,820	2,820	2822.90	2,830
6I3	2,820	2,820	2,820	2,820	2,820	2,830	2,820	2,820	2,820	2,820	2821.00	2,830
6I4	2,820	2,820	2828	2,820	2,819	2,820	2,820	2,820	2,820	2,820	2,820.70	2828
6I5	2,820	2,820	2,820	2,820	2,820	2,820	2,820	2,830	2,829	2,820	2821.90	2,830
7I1	2,780	2,780	2,770	2,780	2,770	2,760	2,770	2,768	2,768	2,780	2772.60	2,780
7I2	2,770	2,770	2,770	2,760	2,770	2,770	2,770	2,770	2,760	2,770	2,768.00	2,770
7I3	2,750	2,750	2,750	2,750	2,750	2,760	2,760	2,750	2,760	2,750	2753.00	2,760

(Continued)

Table A3. (Continued)

Inst.	1	2	3	4	5	6	7	8	9	10	AV. Sol.	Max.
7I4	2,780	2,790	2,790	2,770	2,790	2,790	2,790	2,789	2,780	2,780	2,784.90	2,790
7I5	2,760	2,760	2,760	2,750	2,760	2754	2,750	2,760	2,750	2,760	2756.40	2,760
8I1	2,720	2,720	2715	2,720	2,710	2,720	2,710	2,710	2,720	2,710	2715.50	2,720
8I2	2,710	2,720	2,710	2,710	2,720	2,710	2,720	2,719	2,710	2,710	2713.90	2,720
8I3	2,740	2,740	2,740	2,730	2,730	2,720	2,729	2,730	2,730	2,720	2,730.90	2,740
8I4	2,719	2,710	2708	2,710	2707	2,700	2,710	2,700	2,700	2,700	2706.40	2,719
8I5	2,710	2,710	2,710	2,700	2,710	2,700	2,710	2,700	2,700	2,700	2705.00	2,710
9I1	2,660	2,663	2,660	2,670	2,677	2,670	2,670	2,663	2,677	2,666	2,667.60	2,677
9I2	2,659	2,660	2654	2,660	2,660	2,660	2,660	2,660	2,660	2,660	2,659.30	2,660
9I3	2,660	2,660	2,660	2,660	2,660	2,660	2656	2,653	2,660	2,669	2,659.80	2,669
9I4	2,660	2,660	2,660	2,650	2,660	2,659	2,650	2,650	2,649	2,659	2,655.70	2,660
9I5	2,660	2,660	2,660	2,659	2,660	2,659	2,655	2,659	2,660	2,650	2,658.20	2,660
10I1	2,610	2,618	2,610	2,610	2,600	2,618	2609	2,610	2,606	2,610	2,610.10	2,618
10I2	2,630	2,630	2,620	2,620	2,610	2,620	2,620	2,620	2,620	2,610	2,620.00	2,630
10I3	2,620	2,620	2,610	2,610	2,620	2,610	2609	2,610	2,620	2,610	2613.90	2,620
10I4	2,610	2,610	2,618	2,610	2,608	2,610	2,610	2,610	2,610	2,610	2,610.60	2,618
10I5	2,619	2,630	2,630	2,619	2,610	2,615	2,610	2,610	2,630	2,630	2,620.30	2,630
Average	2,394.58	2,391.82	2,392.28	2,394.08	2,394.14	2,393.72	2,393.22	2,393.66	2,394.66	2,394.20	2,393.64	2,400.56

Table A4. The quality of the solutions reached by the 10 trials of HGNS for $\alpha = 9$ and t_2

Inst.	1	2	3	4	5	6	7	8	9	10	AV. Sol.	Max.
111	2,567	2,567	2,567	2,567	2,567	2,567	2,567	2,567	2,567	2,567	2,567.00	2,567
112	2,594	2,594	2,594	2,594	2,594	2,594	2,594	2,594	2,594	2,594	2,594.00	2,594
113	2,320	2,320	2,320	2,320	2,320	2,320	2,320	2,320	2,320	2,320	2,320.00	2,320
114	2,310	2,310	2,310	2,310	2,310	2,310	2,310	2309	2,300	2,310	2308.90	2,310
115	2,330	2,330	2,330	2,330	2,330	2,330	2,330	2,330	2,330	2,330	2,330.00	2,330
211	2,118	2,118	2,118	2,118	2,118	2,118	2,118	2,118	2,118	2,118	2,118.00	2,118
212	2,110	2,110	2,110	2,110	2,110	2,110	2,110	2,110	2,110	2,110	2,110.00	2,110
213	2119	2,132	2,132	2,132	2119	2122	2,132	2,132	2122	2,132	2127.40	2,132
214	2,109	2,109	2,109	2,109	2,109	2,109	2,109	2,109	2,109	2,109	2,109.00	2,109
215	2,114	2,110	2,110	2,114	2,114	2,110	2,110	2,110	2,114	2,110	2,111.60	2,114
311	1,845	1,845	1,845	1,845	1,845	1799	1,845	1,845	1,845	1,845	1,840.40	1,845
312	1,795	1,795	1,779	1,758	1,795	1,779	1,795	1,771	1,795	1,779	1,784.10	1,795
313	1,774	1,774	1,774	1,774	1,774	1,774	1,774	1,774	1,774	1,774	1,774.00	1,774
314	1,792	1,792	1,792	1,792	1,792	1,792	1,792	1,792	1,792	1,792	1,792.00	1,792
315	1,775	1,777	1,794	1,777	1,794	1,775	1,794	1,794	1,775	1,775	1783.00	1,794
411	1,330	1,330	1,330	1,330	1,330	1,330	1,330	1,330	1,330	1,330	1,330.00	1,330
412	1,378	1,378	1,378	1,378	1,378	1,378	1,378	1,378	1,378	1,378	1,378.00	1,378
413	1,374	1,374	1,334	1,374	1,374	1,374	1,374	1,374	1,374	1,374	1370.00	1,374
414	1,353	1,353	1,353	1,353	1,353	1,353	1,353	1,353	1,353	1,353	1,353.00	1,353
415	1,332	1,354	1,332	1,354	1,332	1,330	1,332	1,354	1,354	1,354	1342.80	1,354
511	2,680	2687	2,680	2,680	2,689	2,690	2,680	2,680	2,690	2,680	2683.60	2,690
512	2,690	2,690	2,698	2,690	2,700	2,700	2,690	2,700	2,690	2,690	2693.80	2,700
513	2,690	2,690	2,690	2,690	2,690	2,690	2,690	2,690	2,690	2,690	2,690.00	2,690
514	2,700	2,700	2,700	2,700	2,700	2,700	2,700	2,700	2,700	2,700	2,700.00	2,700
515	2,670	2,660	2,670	2,670	2,660	2,670	2,660	2,660	2,660	2,660	2664.00	2,670
611	2,850	2,850	2,850	2,850	2,850	2,850	2,850	2,850	2,850	2,850	2,850.00	2,850
612	2,829	2,820	2,820	2,820	2,820	2,829	2,820	2,820	2,820	2,820	2821.80	2,829
613	2,820	2,830	2,820	2,830	2,829	2,820	2,829	2,829	2,820	2,830	2825.70	2,830
614	2,820	2,829	2,820	2,820	2,820	2,829	2,820	2,820	2,829	2,820	2822.70	2,829
615	2,820	2,820	2,820	2,820	2,829	2,830	2,829	2,820	2,820	2,820	2822.80	2,830
711	2,760	2,770	2,770	2,770	2,770	2,770	2,760	2,770	2,770	2,770	2,768.00	2,770
712	2,770	2,770	2,770	2,770	2,770	2,770	2,770	2,770	2,770	2,770	2,770.00	2,770
713	2,760	2,760	2,750	2,760	2,760	2,760	2759	2,760	2,760	2,760	2758.90	2,760

(Continued)

Table A4. (Continued)

Inst.	1	2	3	4	5	6	7	8	9	10	AV. Sol.	Max.
7I4	2,790	2,780	2,800	2,790	2,790	2,780	2,780	2,790	2,790	2,790	2,788.00	2,800
7I5	2,760	2,760	2759	2759	2,750	2,760	2,760	2759	2,760	2,760	2758.70	2,760
8I1	2,710	2,720	2,710	2,710	2,720	2,720	2,710	2,710	2,720	2,720	2715.00	2,720
8I2	2,720	2,719	2,720	2,720	2,720	2,719	2,719	2,714	2,710	2,710	2,717.10	2,720
8I3	2,728	2,730	2,719	2,730	2,728	2,730	2,730	2,730	2,740	2,740	2,730.50	2,740
8I4	2,720	2,710	2,710	2,710	2,710	2,710	2,710	2,710	2,710	2,710	2711.00	2,720
8I5	2,700	2,700	2,700	2,710	2,700	2,710	2,710	2,700	2,710	2,710	2705.00	2,710
9I1	2,670	2,670	2,670	2,670	2,670	2,670	2,670	2,662	2,660	2,667	2,667.90	2,670
9I2	2,660	2,660	2,650	2,660	2,660	2,660	2,660	2,660	2,660	2,666	2,660.60	2,666
9I3	2,670	2,670	2,650	2,660	2,670	2,660	2,660	2,660	2,669	2,660	2,663.90	2,670
9I4	2,658	2,660	2,658	2,668	2,660	2,660	2,660	2,658	2,658	2,660	2,660.00	2,668
9I5	2,660	2,660	2,650	2,660	2,660	2,650	2,660	2,669	2,670	2,650	2,659.90	2,670
10I1	2,610	2,620	2,620	2,610	2,610	2,610	2,610	2,610	2,620	2,610	2613.00	2,620
10I2	2,620	2,620	2,620	2,620	2,620	2,620	2,620	2,620	2,630	2,630	2622.00	2,630
10I3	2,619	2,610	2,620	2,610	2,610	2,606	2,620	2,610	2,610	2,610	2,612.50	2,620
10I4	2,618	2,610	2,610	2,610	2,610	2,610	2,607	2,610	2,610	2,610	2,610.50	2,618
10I5	2,620	2,630	2,630	2,630	2,630	2,630	2,620	2,620	2,630	2,630	2,627.00	2,630
Average	2,396.62	2,397.54	2,395.9	2,396.72	2,397.26	2,395.74	2,396.6	2,396.5	2,397.6	2,396.94	2,396.74	2,400.86

7

Restoration of lost connectivity of partitioned wireless sensor networks

Virender Ranga[1]*, Mayank Dave[1] and Anil Kumar Verma[2]

*Corresponding author: Virender Ranga, Department of Computer Engineering, National Institute of Technology, Kurukshetra, Haryana, India

E-mail: virendersinghmtech@gmail.com

Reviewing editor: YangQuan Chen, University of California Merced, USA

Abstract: The lost connectivity due to failure of large-scale nodes plays major role to degrade the system performance by generating unnecessary overhead or sometimes totally collapse the active network. There are many issues and challenges to restore the lost connectivity in an unattended scenario, i.e. how many recovery nodes will be sufficient and on which locations these recovery nodes have to be placed. A very few centralized and distributed approaches have been proposed till now. The centralized approaches are good for a scenario where information about the disjoint network, i.e. number of disjoint segments and their locations are well known in advance. However, for a scenario where such information is unknown due to the unattended harsh environment, a distributed approach is a better solution to restore the partitioned network. In this paper, we have proposed and implemented a semi-distributed approach called Relay node Placement using Fermat Point. The proposed approach is capable of restoring lost connectivity with small number of recovery relay nodes and it works for any number of disjoint segments. The simulation experiment results show effectiveness of our approach as compared to existing benchmark approaches.

Subjects: Algorithms & Complexity; Computation; Computer Engineering

Keywords: Spider Web-1C; recovery relay node placements; connectivity restoration; large-scale node failure; convex hull; Fermat point

ABOUT THE AUTHOR

Virender Ranga received his PhD degree in Computer Engineering from National Institute of Technology, Kurukshetra in 2016 and MTech in Computer Science and Engineering from Guru Jambeshwar Govt. Technical University Hissar in 2004 respectively. He has done his BTech in Electronics and Communications from Kurukshetra University. Currently, he is an assistant professor in the Computer Engineering Department, NIT Kurukshetra Haryana, India with more than 15 years of experience in academic and administrative affairs in the institute. He has published more than 50 research papers in various International/National referred journals and conferences like IEEE, Elsevier, Springer, T & F and ASP. He has guided more than 20 MTech. dissertations and currently guiding one MTech dissertation inside as well as outside the institute. His areas of interest are pervasive computing, wireless sensor networks, wireless networks, routing algorithms, and mobile clouds. He has chaired various sessions in the International and National Conferences.

PUBLIC INTEREST STATEMENT

The lost connectivity due to failure of large-scale nodes plays major role to degrade the system performance by generating unnecessary overhead or sometimes totally collapse the active network. A very few centralized and distributed approaches have been proposed till now. The centralized approaches are good for a scenario where information about the disjoint network, i.e. number of disjoint segments and their locations are well known in advance. However, for a scenario where such information is unknown due to the unattended harsh environment, a distributed approach is a better solution to restore the partitioned network. In this paper, we have proposed and implemented a semi-distributed approach called Relay node Placement using Fermat Point (RPFP). The proposed approach is capable of restoring lost connectivity with a small number of recovery relay nodes and it works for any number of disjoint segments. The simulation experiment results show the effectiveness of our approach as compared to existing benchmark approaches.

1. Introduction

The use of wireless sensor networks (WSNs) has become very common in the real life in recent years due to tremendous advancement in its wireless and sensing technologies. One type of applications such as combat field reconnaissance, border protection, space exploration, etc. operates in the harshest environments, where sensor nodes reduce the risk of the human life (Ranga, Dave, & Verma, 2013; Stojmenovic, Simplot-Ryl, & Nayak, 2011; Younis, Sentruk, Akkaya, Lee, & Senel, 2013). Since, a sensor node is typically constrained in its on-board energy, computational power and communication resources, a large scale of sensor nodes is involved to ensure critical area coverage and increase the fidelity of the collected data (Younis et al., 2013). Due to small form factor and limited on-board energy supply, a sensor is very much susceptible to its failure. Due to hostile environments in which the network operates sometime result in large-scale damage of the sensor nodes that causes network partitioning in the network and converts into multiple disjoint segments. Figure 1 shows the scenario of partitioned network consisting of multiple disjoint segments. For example, some sensor nodes may be damaged under snow or sand after the storm or in the battlefield, a part of the deployment area may be attacked by the enemy explosives and, thus a set of sensor nodes in the vicinity would be destroyed (it is assumed that terrain is not destroyed). Therefore, rehabilitation of this large-scale partitioned network is the current research topic of WSN researchers in recent years. The deployment of recovery relay nodes (RRNs) in the disconnected network is the one way to connect the large-scale partitioned network. A RRN is more robust and capable node with significantly higher energy reserve and longer communication range (R) than sensor nodes. Although, RRNs can, in principle, be equipped with sensor circuitry, they mainly perform valuable data aggregation and data forwarding. Unlike sensor nodes, a RRN may be mobile and has some navigation capabilities. Thus, RRNs are favored in the partitioned recovery process, because these are easily accurately placed relative to the sensor nodes, and their radio range (R) is even larger, which facilitates and expedites the connectivity restoration among the disjoint segments effectively and efficiently. Intuitively, RRNs are more expensive and thus, a small number of RRNs should to be used for the recovery of the partitioned network. However, a small number of RRNs for network partitioning recovery can be found out using Steiner Minimum Tree (SMT) with Minimum number of Steiner Points and Bounded Edge Length (SMT-MSPBEL), but it is shown to be a NP-hard problem (Senel, Younis, & Akkaya, 2011) for the large-scale WSNs. Therefore, a polynomial time-distributed algorithm is required to deploy a small number of RRNs in the partitioned network for efficient recovery.

Recently, two major RRNs placement heuristics are proposed and published in this research area. In the first approach, the authors have proposed bio-inspired heuristic and used a spider web-like RRNs placement technique known as Spider Web-1C approach (Senel et al., 2011) with the disjoint

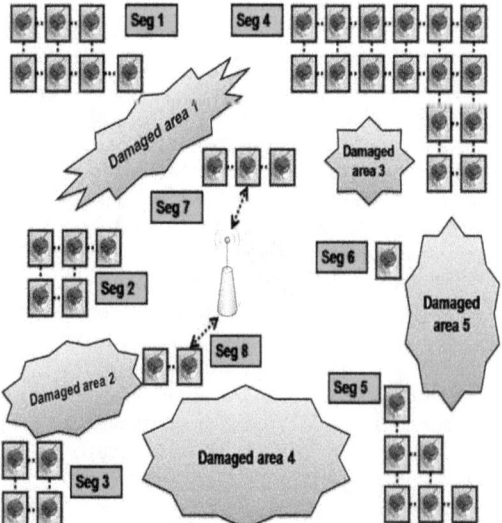

Figure 1. Articulation of segmented area due to large-scale failure of nodes (Ranga et al., 2015).

segments situated at the perimeter of the network. The proposed key idea is to form the stronger connectivity (i.e. 2-connectivity among the nodes), achieve better coverage and also enable balanced distribution of traffic load on the employed RRNs. One of the main advantages of the Spider Web-1C approach is that it connects the segmented network efficiently and effectively, but the major issue is the large number of deployed RRNs for the recovery of partitioned network.

The second approach is based on SMT called ORC-SMT (Lee & Younis, 2012). The key idea proposed by the authors is the use of the SMT by considering three outer disjoint segments that are formed in the grid structure after applying the convex hull algorithm recursively in the cyclic fashion. The points thus obtained are then applied recursively to find more Steiner Minimum Point (SMP) for the RRNs' placement. The multiple points that come in the radio range then become a single point for RRN's placement. Indeed, the procedure repeats itself till all the outer disjoint segments are not less than three segments for which the run is made. Then, RRNs are placed on these calculated points by applying Minimum Spanning Tree (MST) algorithm such as Kruskal or Prim algorithm. The main advantage of ORC-SMT that it connects various segments fastly and efficiently with small number of RRNs placements.

In this research paper, we consider the similar type of problem of large-scale nodes' failure with large number of partitions occurs in the network. The distinction of our proposed work as compared with the published research works is that in our proposed approach, a large-scale node failure issue is addressed and solved using global zero gradient point inside the triangle, (the point at which distance from all the vertices of the triangle is minimum called Fermat Point (FP) in the best case and center of triangle in the worst case) which is not yet seen in other published works. However, in Ghosh, Roy, and Das (2009), the authors have considered a global minima based geo-cast routing technique for data propagation to reduce data transmission distances among the nodes to enhance network lifetime and further reduce end-to-end delay. The main contribution of our proposed solution is shown below:

(1) Two naive approaches and two state-of-the-art heuristics are implemented along with our proposed approach Relay node Placement using Fermat Point (RPFP) to rehabilitate the lost connectivity of the partitioned network due to failure of large-scale nodes in WSNs.

(2) Our proposed approach can work perfectly for any number of disjoint segments, even for disjoint segments that do not form equilateral triangles which is a constraint in SMT-based approaches (i.e. SMT-ORC approach (Lee & Younis, 2012)).

(3) The proposed protocol RPFP is different from other published partitioning recovery approaches (i.e. ORC-SMT, Spider Web-1C) due to use of global zero gradient point inside the equilateral triangle in the best case or center of triangle in the worst case which is calculated using Equations 1–9 or 33–35, respectively.

(4) Finally, our proposed approach shows excellent results in terms of number of placed RRNs, recovery time (RT) and average path length (APL) as compared to benchmark approaches when number of disjoint segments is larger (which is more realistic scenario in real application).

The remainder of the paper is organized as follows: In the next section, related work is described. Sections 3 gives the problem statement of our proposed approach. In Section 4, the detail about our proposed novel approach, i.e. RPFP is given. In Section 5, detailed pseudo-code is depicted and explained. Section 6 shows various published state-of-the-art approaches for comparison. In Section 7, the performance evaluation of our proposed approach through simulation experiments is given and compared with traditional approaches to prove its effectiveness. In the next Section 8, the article is concluded with future scope.

2. Related works

Many approaches have been published till last five years to tolerate single-node failure in wireless sensor and actor networks (WSANs)/WSNs. A WSAN is an extension of WSN with more robust actor nodes for data communications. A very few large-scale node failure recovery approaches in WSNs have been proposed till last two years. The authors of Ranga et al. (2013) and Younis et al. (2013) proposed the comprehensive study of the network partitioning recovery approaches in WSANs based on the different criterion. All approaches are classified into two broad categories (Ranga et al., 2013): (a) centralized approaches, and (b) distributed or semi-distributed approaches. The classification is further divided into three different categories, i.e. proactive, reactive and hybrid approaches. For proactive schemes, many approaches have been pursued to tolerate node failure in this area. The similar type of method is applied to reactive and hybrid approaches. In all proposed approaches, controlled node mobility has been used to rehabilitate the lost network connectivity. For instance, in Kansal, Somasundara, Srivastava, and Estrin (2004), a small robot called Packbot has been used to serve as a mobile RRN. The use of small robot enables the recovery of partitioned network or break links. An algorithm is used to determine the trajectory of moving robot in the network. A similar type of work is presented by Wang, Srinivasan, and Chu (2005). They have used mobile RRNs within 2-hop of the sink in the network to restore the lost connectivity of the partitioned network. Unlike (Kansal et al., 2004), the idea is that the RRNs do not need to run the long distance in the network to save their energy for different work. However, the use of Packbot is inefficient due to unexpected delays in data delivery, even when multiple devices are used in delay tolerant applications. Another reason is the slow motion of these devices to cover every individual best point in the small-scale network. Moreover, the cost of these devices is more, consequently, it increases the application cost.

(Wang, Cao, Porta, and Zhang (2005) exploited the node controlled mobility in order to cover the coverage holes which are not covered by sensor nodes during their initial deployment. The idea behind their work is to identify some spare nodes from different parts of the network that can be relocated to coverage-hole places in the network. Since moving a node for longer distance can drain significant node power, a cascaded movement can be pursued if the sufficient number of spare sensor nodes is available on the way. Therefore, finding spare nodes in the network is another critical issue in this proposed approach.

Recently, some centralized/semi-centralized approaches have been proposed to handle large-scale node's failure in WSN using cascaded control mobility of the nodes. In Alfadhly, Baroudi, and Younis (2010), the recovery problem is formulated as an Integer Linear Program (ILP). The objective of ILP-based optimization model is to form a connected topology while minimizing the individual traveling distance of the nodes.

The authors of Sir, Senturk, Sisikoglu, and Akkaya (2011) strive to restore lost connectivity by using a Multi-Integer Linear Programming (MILP)-based transportation network flow model. The proposed idea is to rehabilitate the lost connectivity with a minimum traveling distance of the nodes with the assumption that every node should be able to go all destinations i.e. reaches all other node positions when lost network connectivity restoration is to be required. Due to centralized nature, this approach does not scale well.

Another approach is proposed by Senturk, Akkaya, and Senel (2012) to improve the scalability by reducing the number of candidate locations. A RRN placement algorithm is used to find the set of locations which can guarantee the connectivity if RRNs are to be deployed to these locations.

Vemulapalli and Akkaya (2010) described another distributed approach based on nodes' knowledge of full paths to sink. The pre-failure route information is used to determine the location of the failed nodes. The location of nodes is obtained when break paths are established. Thus, upon partitioning, nodes can attempt to re-establish the path towards sink node by moving to next hop location. However, many nodes do the same in the partition, therefore, recovery cost can be high. To limit the recovery cost, the recovery process elects only one node as a leader node based on its distance from failed node or sink. When the leader node moves towards the sink, a cascaded movement of nodes within that partition is also required in order to sustain intra-segment connectivity.

Another approach based on game theory is proposed by Senturk, Akkaya, and Yilmaz (2012) by assuming the complete knowledge of location of partitions, number of partitions, and failed nodes. Each partition is used as a player in the game. The payoff function is based on nodes' degree and elects a partition representative P_a. The elected P_a opts to maximize the payoff of its partition which motivates the partitions to move each other. Due to the centralized nature of this approach, each representative node must know the payoff function of the other partitions and eventually network reaches to Nash equilibrium when all partitions are moved to each other.

3. System model and problem statement

We assume a WSN in which a large number of sensor nodes are deployed throughout an area of interest and a sink node is located in the middle of deployment. Without losing the generality, this assumption ensures that there is a balanced traffic load in the network. Due to harsh environment of the application like sensor nodes deployed in a battlefield for field monitoring, where nodes could be destroyed by enemy explosives (assume that terrain is not destroyed), thus causing a large-scale node failure which leads to multiple disjoint partitions in the network. For e.g. Figure 1 shows the partitioned WSN with 8 disjoint segments having sink node is in the middle of the network. Thus, more robust RRNs are required to connect this disjoint network.

Our problem can be defined as follows: "N sensor nodes know their positions using some localizati algorithm are randomly deployed in an unattended area of interest (AOI). Let us assume that j disconnected sub-networks are formed as a result of failure of large-scale nodes in the network. Each sub-network G_j has n_j sensor nodes, where $0 < n_j \ll N$. Our goal is to implement a polynomial time algorithm that will rehabilitate the lost connectivity among the disconnected sub-networks G_j and heal the partitioned network by deploying minimum number of RRN's placement with their small deployment time, and thus, create a new temporary connected network."

4. Our proposed RPFP approach

Our proposed approach, unlike ORC-SMT, considers triangles of disjoint segments and finds a point P, where distance from each vertices of that Δ_i is minimum i.e. gradient of all vertices become zero inside Δ_i, instead of calculating individual SMT using three non-collinear segments (Lee & Younis, 2012). Our proposed approach exploits Fermat Point (*FP*) property of equilateral triangle to calculate zero gradient point F_p inside Δ_i for deploying RRNs towards the calculated point. If no equilateral triangle exists in the network, then the center of the triangle is taken as *FP*. There are few questions which need to be addressed to find the optimal solution for the recovery of lost connectivity due to failure of large-scale nodes in WSNs:

(1) How disjoint segments after the failure of large-scale sensor nodes in the network can discover each other to connect again?
(2) How RRNs should be placed on their proper locations?
(3) How many RRNs is to be required to connect the partitioned network?

To address the first question in the challenged environment, we use a small size robot-like Packbot initially to find the information about the disjoint segments and deliver this information to the sink node for further recovery action. To further improve the recovery action in the network, RPFP uses representative nodes (later explained) to deliver the information about its connected segment, instead of taking information from all the sensor nodes of the disjoint segments.

To address the second question, we use Fermat Point (*FP*) based technique or center of triangle to find the locations between the disjoint segments for placing RRNs.

The third question is addressed by placing RRNs by sink node without observing how many live sensor nodes are available in any disjoint segment. It is important to note here that the information of bigger segment is more crucial than smaller segment. Therefore, to give the priority to the bigger segments to connect first in the network, a convex hull algorithm is applied by each individual segment independently and calculates its representative nodes sits on the boundary. Further, each representative node calculates how many nodes (N_i) are attached in its segment by applying depth first search which is expressed as:

$$N_i = \sum_{i=1}^{S_n} n_{s_i}, \text{ where } S_n = \{s_1, s_2, s_3, ..., s_m\} \text{ are the disjoint segments in the network}$$

Based on N_i, a node density function (NDF) for each segment is computed as follows:

$$NDF = \frac{N_i}{\sum_{i=1}^{m} N_i}, \text{ where } m = \text{number of segments occurring in the network}$$

After finding NDF_i for each segment, these are sorted into ascending order. Now, zero gradient point i.e. FP is calculated by taking representative nodes (R_{p_s}) of first three disjoint segments at a time. The next FP is calculated by taking next three R_{p_s} of disjoint segments from the sorted list. In the first round, level first FP_s are computed using R_{p_s}. In the next round FP_s are calculated using previously calculated FP_s called level second Fermat Points and so on till network is connected. Figure 2 shows the actual methodology of calculation of FP_s in the network. It is assumed that the segments are sorted in ascending order i.e. $s_1, s_2, ..., s_n$ etc.

Definition 1   Let Δ_i be a triangle with vertices (x, y, z). The zero gradient point or Fermat Point (FP) is the point that minimizes the sum of Euclidean distance from the vertices of Δ_i to FP i.e. minimize $\left(d(x, FP) + d(y, FP) + d(z, FP)\right)$.

Definition 2   Let Δ_i be a triangle with vertices (x, y, z) and a arbitrary point k lies in+-side or on any vertex position of Δ_i. The number of recovery RRNs requires to connect the vertices to point k is computed by:

$$N_{RN_s}(\Delta_i, k) = (N_{RN_s}(x, w_1) + N_{RN_s}(y, w_1) + N_{RN_s}(z, w_1) + 1)$$
$$= \left(\frac{|d(x, w_1)|}{R} - 1\right) + \left(\frac{|d(y, w_2)|}{R} - 1\right) + \left(\frac{|d(z, w_3)|}{R} - 1\right)$$
$$= \left(\frac{|d(x, w_1)|}{R}\right) + \left(\frac{|d(y, w_2)|}{R}\right) + \left(\frac{|d(z, w_3)|}{R}\right) - 2$$

where w_1, w_2, w_3 are the weights along x, y, z vertices and R is the communication range of RRNs

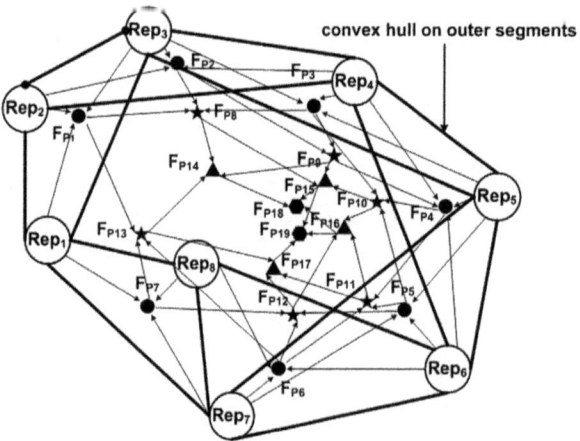

Figure 2. Example of calculation of chain of FP_s.

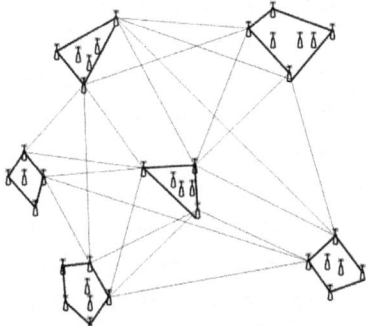

Figure 3. Illustrations of representative nodes R_{p_s} **(Ranga et al., 2015).**

In our system model, the following assumptions are taken in the simulation experiments without losing generality:

(1) All RRNs are under the direct control of sink node and also assume that these are sufficient in number for network partitioning recovery.

(2) The network is obstacle free for the movement of RRNs during the recovery process.

(3) The intermittent failure of RRN does not occur during the recovery process.

Our proposed approach RPFP contains four main steps for the recovery of the partitioned WSN network:

(1) Identification of failure of large-scale nodes in the partitioned network.

(2) Calculate the representative node $\left(R_{p_s} \right)$ of each disjoint segment in the construction of outer convex hull polygon.

(3) Identify global zero gradient point inside the triangle of disjoint segments for RRNs' placement.

(4) Deployment of RRNs to rehabilitate lost connectivity of the partitioned network.

4.1. Large-scale node failure identification

In the first step, our proposed approach senses large-scale nodes failures in the network. The detection of large-scale node failure is illustrated in procedure Failure_detection () in the pseudocode, where each node sited on the boundary detects the failure of its neighbor nodes in the network. When the large-scale failure of nodes occurs in the network, the boundary nodes as calculated by the convex hull algorithm send a small *Hello message* to their 1-hop neighbor nodes and, then wait for reply till duration T_w before judging that their neighbor nodes failed or not. The T_w is calculated and equal to the sum of the time period of sending and receiving messages plus the node processing time $\left((T_t + T_r) + T_p \right)$. In case the boundary node does not receive an answer in the stipulated period, then it considers the failure of its neighbor nodes and broadcasts *Failure message* for all the nodes connected to it. This process is repeated by all the different boundary nodes that are sited on the different disjoint segments as shown in Figure 3.

4.2. Calculation of R_{p_s}

Our second step is similar to that proposed in the approaches of (Ranga, Dave, & Verma, 2015) to find R_{p_s} of each disjoint segment. In this, our proposed approach finds out the point sets from each of the subnetworks by randomly selecting any point inside the disjoint segments and then determining its corresponding convex hull polygon. Indeed, the obtained convex hull polygons are smaller size polygons which consist of every point of its subnetworks. Hence, the nodes on the convex hull polygon are closer to other subnetworks than their corresponding convex hull polygon as illustrated in Figure 3. We considered these nodes as R_{p_s} in our proposed approach.

4.3. Calculation of FP inside the triangle (mathematical analysis)

To find the zero gradient point i.e. *FP* inside the triangle Δ, let us consider a point P_i which has coordinates (x_i, y_i), where $i = \{1, 2, \ldots, 3\}$ and another point P that has coordinates (x, y) inside that triangle. Let d_i be the distance between P_i and P, $\forall i \in [1 \ldots 3]$. Then, our problem is to minimize the function as given below (Ranga et al., 2015; Shen & Tolosa, 2008):

$$f(P) = min(f(x,y)) = w_1 d_1 + w_2 d_2 + w_3 d_3 = min \sum_{i=1}^{3} w_i d_i \tag{1}$$

It is a continuous function on 2-D plane $\mathbb{R}^2$ such that it must gain an absolute minimum value inside the closed Δ, i.e. $P_1, P_2, \cdot, P_n$, where w_1, w_2, w_3 are the weights assigned to the edges of Δ, connected to point P.

Let the distance between $P(x, y)$ and $\forall P_i$ is

$$d_i^2 = \left(x - x_i^2\right) + \left(y - y_i^2\right), \ \forall i \in [1 \ldots 3] \tag{2}$$

Then, gradient of $f(p)$ is given by:

$$g_d(P) = \frac{\partial}{\partial x}(d_i)^2 = 2(x - x_i) \tag{3}$$

Therefore, if $P \neq P_i$ then d_i it-self is differentiable i.e.

$$2d_i \frac{\partial}{\partial x} d_i = 2(x - x_i), \ if \ P \neq P_i, \tag{4}$$

$$\frac{\partial}{\partial x} d_i = \frac{(x - x_i)}{d_i}, \ if \ P \neq P_i \tag{5}$$

Similarly, we can obtain for y_i

$$\frac{\partial}{\partial x} d_i = \frac{(y - y_i)}{d_i} \ if \ P \neq P_i \tag{6}$$

Therefore, the gradient of $f(d_i)$ is given by

$$g_d(d_i) = \frac{1}{d_i}(x - x_i, y - y_i), \ if \ P \neq P_i, \ \forall i \in [1 \ldots 3] \tag{7}$$

Let $u_i = \frac{1}{d_i}\left(\vec{PP_i}\right)$

It is a unit vector defined for every $P \neq P_i, \forall i \in [1 \ldots 3]$. Therefore, we can conclude that $f(P)$ is differentiable on domain $\mathbb{R}^2$ i.e. $\Omega = \mathbb{R}^2 \backslash \{P_1 \ldots P_3\}$ and its gradient is equal to:

$$g_d(P) = w_1 u_1 + w_2 u_2 + w_3 u_3 = \sum_{i=1}^{3} w_i u_i \tag{8}$$

Since the function $f(x, y)$ has a minimum global value at this optimal point P, therefore, all the trajectories of system will

$$(x, y) = -g_d(x, y) \tag{9}$$

converge to the asymptotically stable equilibrium point P. It means that $G(\dot{x}, \dot{y}) = -\| g_d(x, y) \|^2 = 0$ is a global Lyapunov function for the system on $\mathbb{R}^2$ (proof is given in Appendix A). Moreover, the trajectories of Equation (9) are orthogonal and converged to a point called zero gradient point P. Figure 4 shows the situation when $\forall w_i$ converges to a point P. Furthermore, closed lines are the level curve of $f(x, y)$.

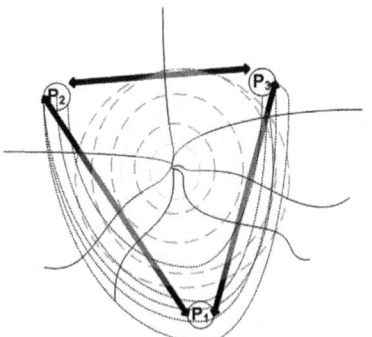

Figure 4. Example shows the orthogonal trajectories of $G(x, y)$

LEMMA 1   A necessary and sufficient condition for $g_d(P)$ to be zero at some point i.e. P on $\mathbb{R}^2$ i s

$$w_1 < w_2 + w_3 \tag{10}$$

$$w_2 < w_1 + w_3 \tag{11}$$

$$w_3 < w_1 + w_2 \tag{12}$$

Proof   Geometrically, we can construct a non-degenerate triangle with its sides w_1, w_2, w_3. Indeed, $g_d(P) = 0$ which is equivalent to $w_1 u_1 + w_2 u_2 + w_3 u_3 = 0$. Thus, it means that triangle curve with sides w_1, w_2, w_3 must be converged to point P (as proved in Equations 1 to 9). Therefore, a necessary and sufficient condition for $g_d(P)$ is zero at this point P.

LEMMA 2   If $g_d(P) = 0$ at some point $P \in \mathbb{R}^2$, then we have

$$u_1, u_2 = \left(\frac{w_3^2 - w_2^2 - w_1^2}{2w_1 w_2} \right) \tag{13}$$

$$u_2, u_3 = \left(\frac{w_1^2 - w_2^2 - w_3^2}{2w_2 w_3} \right) \tag{14}$$

$$u_3, u_1 = \left(\frac{w_2^2 - w_1^2 - w_3^2}{2w_3 w_1} \right) \tag{15}$$

Proof   Indeed, if $g_d(P) = 0$, then at P we have $w_1 u_1 + w_2 u_2 + w_3 u_3 = 0$. Let us take the dot multiplication of Equation $w_1 u_1 + w_2 u_2 + w_3 u_3 = 0$ successively by u_1, u_2 and u_3 with the fact that $\| u_i * u_i \| = 1$. Hence, we can get

$$w_1 u_1 u_1 + w_2 u_1 u_2 + w_3 u_1 u_3 = 0 \tag{16}$$

$$w_1 u_1^2 + w_2 u_1 u_2 + w_3 u_1 u_3 = 0 \tag{17}$$

$$w_1 + w_2 u_1 u_2 + w_3 u_1 u_3 = 0 \tag{18}$$

Similarly, we can obtain the Equations for u_2 and u_3

$$w_1 u_1 u_2 + w_2 + w_3 u_2 u_3 = 0 \tag{19}$$

$$w_1 u_1 u_3 + w_2 u_1 u_3 + w_3 = 0 \tag{20}$$

To simplify the Equations (18), (19), and (20), let us assume that

$$t_1 = u_2 u_3, \; t_2 = u_3 u_1, \; t_3 = u_1 u_2 \tag{21}$$

Therefore, Equations (18), (19), and (20) look like

$$w_1 + w_2 t_3 + w_3 t_2 = 0 \tag{22}$$

$$w_1 t_3 + w_2 + w_3 t_1 = 0 \tag{23}$$

$$w_1 t_2 + w_2 t_1 + w_3 = 0 \tag{24}$$

Let us multiply the Equation (22) by w_1, Equation (23) by w_2, and subtract Equation (23) from Equation (22). We get

$$w_1^2 - w_2^2 + w_1 w_3 t_2 - w_2 w_3 t_1 = 0 \tag{25}$$

Take Equation (24) after multiply by w_3 and subtract it from Equation (25). Therefore, the resultant Equation looks like

$$u_2 u_3 = t_1 = \frac{w_1^2 - w_2^2 - w_3^2}{2 w_2 w_3} \tag{26}$$

Similarly we can find the following resultant Equations

$$u_1 u_2 = t_3 = \frac{w_3^2 - w_1^2 - w_2^2}{2 w_1 w_2} \tag{27}$$

$$u_1 u_3 = t_2 = \frac{w_2^2 - w_1^2 - w_3^2}{2 w_1 w_3} \tag{28}$$

LEMMA 3   If a point P lies on one of the sides of Δ_i i.e. P_1, P_2, P_n, as shown in Figure 5 and also it does not lie on the triangle vertices, then $g_d(P) \neq 0$.

Proof   Let us assume that P lie on the side of $P_1 P_2$ as shown in Figure 5. Then unit vectors i.e. u_1 and u_2 are parallel. Therefore, $w_1 u_1 + w_2 u_2 + w_3 u_3$ are linearly independent and at least one is non-zero. Thus, $g_d(P) = w_1 u_1 + w_2 u_2 + w_3 u_3 = \sum_i^3 w_i u_i \neq 0$.

LEMMA 4   If point P lies on the outside of the triangle, then $g_d(P) \neq 0$.

Proof   Let us assume that the point P lies on the outside of Δ_i as shown in Figure 6. Then, it must lie on one half plane of the Δ_i whose boundary is the line joining between two vertices i.e. $P_1 P_2$ and it does not contain the remaining point i.e. P_3. Therefore, we draw the vectors $w_1 u_1, w_2 u_2, w_3 u_3$ terminate to common point P with the fact that all points lie on the same half plan with the boundary being parallel to $P_1 P_2$ through P. Since all the vectors are non zero, therefore their sum is $w_1 u_1 + w_2 u_2 + w_3 u_3 = g_d(P)$. Hence, it is contradicted with our assumption that P lies outside the triangle.

LEMMA 5   If a point P lies inside the triangle i.e. $P_1, P_2, \cdot P_n$, then $g_d(P)$ must gain its absolute minimum value in the interior of the triangle at exactly one point.

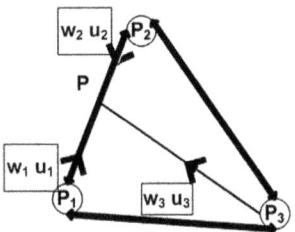

Figure 5. Example of a point lies on the edge of $\vec{P_1P_2}$

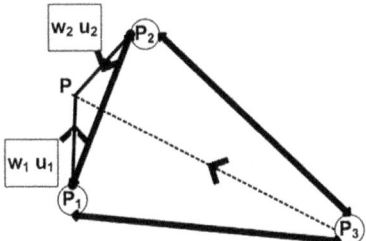

Figure 6. Example of point lies outside the edge of $\vec{P_1P_2}$.

Proof: we have already proved in Lemma 1 that the gradient $g_d(P)$ of all the points vanishes at some point P. Let us consider a contradiction assumption that the minimum value is achieved at some other point P' other than point P inside the triangle. Then point P' lies on one of the triangles $\angle P_1P'P_2$, $\angle P_2P'P_3$, $\angle P_3P'P_1$ as shown in Figure 7. Since we have both $g_d(P) = 0$ and $g_d\left(P'\right) = 0$, therefore we must have

$$u_1u_2 = u_1'u_2' = \frac{w_3^{2'} - w_2^{2'} - w_1^{2'}}{2w_1'w_2'} \tag{29}$$

On the other hand, from Figure 7, we have

$$u_1u_2 = cos\angle P_1PP_2 \tag{30}$$

$$u_1'u_2' = cos\angle P_1P'P_2 \tag{31}$$

But, $\angle P_4P'P_5$ is strictly bigger than $\angle P_1PP_2$, therefore, we must have $u_1'u_2' < u_1u_2$, a contradiction assumption.

4.4. Placement of RRNs to rehabilitate the lost connectivity of partitioned network
After the identification of a point P on which the gradient vanishes inside Δ_i, our proposed approach RPFP will deploy RRNs towards that point to restore lost connectivity. However, the number of nodes to connect the segmented subnetworks depends upon the distance of any vertex to point P. Let R be the range of a RRN node; therefore, our proposed approach deploys RRNs from each vertex towards P at a distance $\left(\frac{d_i}{R}\right)$. Since, our approach is distributed in nature; therefore, we use greedy strategy to deploy RRNs towards P. To accomplish RRNs deployment task, the following substeps are given below:

(1) The sink node executes our algorithm as given in Figure 8 on area of interest (AOI)to obtain a list of locations (i.e. L_i) towards P on which the RRNs have to be placed. After that the sink node then broadcasts these calculated locations to all RRNs (it is assumed that all RRNs are in the vicinity of the sink node).

(2) After receiving L_i by all RRNs, they will keep it and mark each calculated location (i.e. x_i, y_i) as unoccupied, where $i = \{1, \ldots, m\}$.

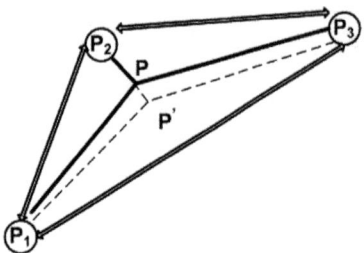

Figure 7. Illustrations of existence of another point P'.

(3) The nearby RRN chooses an unoccupied location from L_i as its target position. The choice of the position is dependent on our objective function as given in Equation (1).

(4) The selected RRN then moves to the calculated location (x_i, y_i) and marks this position as occupied location. After landing to the target position, RRN will periodically broadcast the status of L_i to sink for its connectivity. Moreover, while moving towards the calculated position, it is quite obvious that more than one RRN may move to same location, but these RRNs will compete with their cost (i.e. distance and their residual power). The cost function is calculated by each RRN:

$$cost = \frac{(Remaining\ residual\ power)}{Distance} \qquad (32)$$

Therefore, one with higher cost will win and keep moving towards the calculated position. Indeed, the nodes having lowest cost will reselect the new destination in the network after refresh their L_i. In case of tie-break node ID is used for the same.

(5) Once a RRN is placed to its marked location it becomes the part of ith segment. Now, by taking each relocated RRN as reference node, the next node is placed until the distance between reference RRN and next node is less than R. The same procedure is repeated for each disjoint segment according to the sorting order of node density function (NDF_i).

(6) Each RRN will repeat steps 2–5 until it reaches its calculated destination and marks its position as occupied.

In this way, the segmented subnetworks are contracted into a new connected network as shown in Figure 8. As aforementioned, our approach uses greedy strategy from all the disjoint segments to deploy RRNs, therefore, recovery time is lesser as compared with other state-of-the-art proposed approaches.

THEOREM 1   The worst case time complexity of RPFP is $O(m^3)$, where m is the number of disjoint segments that occurs after the large-scale node failure in the network and which is mapped on a given graph $G = (V, E)$.

Proof   We use depth first search (DFS) to find the connected components in our proposed RPFP (Ranga, Dave, & Verma, 2014). Therefore, DFS takes $O(m + e)$ time to find the connected components, where m is the number of segments in the network and e is the edges between the neighboring segments. The convex hull polygon can be found using convex hull algorithm (Graham, 1972) and it takes $O(m \log m)$ time complexity. Since we apply convex hull algorithm on m disjoint segments as explained in the first step of our implementation, therefore, the total worst case time complexity is $O(m^2 \log m)$. The minimum distance between two non-intersecting convex polygons can be found in $O(m^3)$ time, because there are at most $O(m^2)$ pairs of convex hull polygons in the configuration (Toussaint, 1984). The gradient point can be found in $O(m)$ by applying Equations 4 to 12. Thus, the total worst case time complexity of our proposed RPFP is given by $O(m + e) + O(m^2 \log m) + O(m^3) + O(m)$, which is equal to $O(m^3)$.

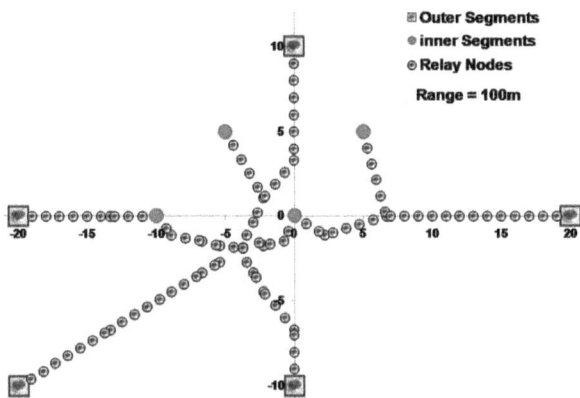

Figure 8. Illustrations of rehabilitation of lost connectivity using RPFP approach.

THEOREM 2   Our proposed approach RPFP connects the partitioned topology successfully and termi-nates guaranteed.

Proof   Since our proposed approach is distributed in nature; therefore, in step 4 of the RRNs' place-ment guarantees that a RRN will eventually occupy its position (x_i, y_i) if it wins the competition based on cost function. In case, RRN loses the competition, it will not move from its original position and reselect another position calculated by the sink node. Therefore, every time a selected RRN will move until it occupies its calculated location in the partitioned network. Thus, all calculated loca-tions will eventually be occupied by RRNs, if sufficient RRNs are available with sink node. Therefore, our algorithm restores the partitioned topology successfully and terminates guaranteed.

5. Pseudo-code of our proposed RPFP

This section describes the pseudo-code of our proposed approach RPFP to rehabilitate the lost con-nectivity due to failure of large-scale nodes in the network.

The pseudo-code for RPFP() is shown in Figure 9. Before start of actual deployment of RRNs in the partitioned network, our proposed approach forms a convex hull polygon of the outer disjoint seg-ments and computes R_{p_s} as shown in procedure Failure_detection(). Line 2 shows how to compute R_{p_s} sited on the boundary of the subnetworks. After detection of nodes' failure, then, zero gradient point (*P*) i.e. *FP* inside the triangle Δ_i is calculated based on these R_{p_s} and NDF_i in the procedure RPFP(). Line 3 to 13 in the same procedure is used to calculate *P* inside the triangle. Further, we draw the virtual lines (i.e. *L*) for the deployment of RRNs from each R_{p_s} to *P*. Line 19 is used in the procedure RPFP() to perform this operation. Line 10 to 13 is used to check that formed triangle is equilateral triangle or not. If it is the case, then *FP* is calculated otherwise center of Δ_i is taken as *FP* for conver-gence. Further line 15 to 19 is used to check the status of the path i.e. path is connected or not and compute the location for RRNs' placement. Our approach skips the virtual line if network is already connected by RRNs. Lines 1 to 3 is used to deploy the virtual lines from R_{p_s} to *L* as mentioned in the procedure deploy_virtualline(). Furthermore, the status of RRN's deployment is checked and listed in the procedure deploy_RRNs () from lines 1 to 7. After that, we compute the location of RRN's along the virtual line (*L*) from R_{p_s} to *P* and RRNs are added in the network based on their node radio range (i.e. R). Line 8 is used in the procedure RPFP() to perform this operation. We call our procedure RPFP() iteratively until all RRNs are not deployed up to *P*.

6. Various relay node placement state-of-the-art approaches

The following approaches are used to compare with our proposed novel approach RPFP:

1. Basic Deployment (BD): It is a very basic approach in which the isolated segments apply the Graham Scan i.e. convex hull algorithm in the partitioned network to form closed polygon. The outer segments then deploy the RRNs along the borders of the convex hull

```
Procedure Failure_detection()                    Procedure RPFP()
1.  Polygon ← Convex_hull(Terminals)             1.  P ← Zero_gradient_point(Triangle, R_{P_s})
2.  R_{P_s} ← Rpresentative_nodes(Polygon, Terminals)  2.  L_i ← Lines(R_{P_s}, P)
3.  T_w ← Wait period = (T_t + T_r) + T_p         3.  m ← Number of segments
4.  N_{eg_i} ← Neighbours' of i^{th} node         4.  compute NDF_i
5.  Send Hello message to ∀N_{eg_i}               5.  Sort segments(m) based on NDF_i
6.  Wait T_w                                       6.  for i ∈ {1...m} do
7.  If no reply by N_{eg_i}                        7.     while true do
8.  N_{eg_i} ← Fails                               8.     breakwhile ← true
9.  Broadcast Failure message                      9.     Take three R_{P_s} based on NDF_i
10. end if                                        10.    if equilateral triangle then
11. Wait T_w                                       11.       compute (P)
12. RPFP()                                         12.    else
                                                  13.       compute (centre of triangle)
Procedure deploy_RRNs()                           14.    end if
1.  R ← Relay communication range                 15.    for each p ∈ L_i do
2.  R_{P_i} ← i^{th}representative node            16.       if p.status = connected then
3.  R_{N_i} ← Relay node_i                         17.          deploy_RRNs(L_i,P)
4.  v ← Speed of R_{N_i}                           18.       else
5.  x_i ← x_i + (d_i)/R                            19.          deploy_virtualline(L_i,P,R_{P_s})
6.  y_i ← y_i + (d_i)/R                            20.       end if
7.  R_{N_i}.set_coordinates(x_i,y_i)              21.    end for
8.  L.deploy(R_{N_i},R,v)                          22.    end while
                                                  23. end for
Procedure deploy_virtualline()                    24. RPFP()
1.  d_i ← √((x − x_i^2) + (y − y_i^2)), ∀i ∈ [1...m]
2.  g_d(d_i) ← (1/d_i)(x − x_i, y − y_i) = Σ_{i=1}^{3} w_i d_i, if P ≠ P_i, ∀i ∈ [1...m]
3.  deploy_line(L_i,P,R_{P_s})
```

Figure 9. Pseudo code of our proposed approach RPFP.

in the circular fashion. Similarly, the inner segments deploy the RRNs towards the nearest placed RRN as shown in Figure 10. In this approach, it is assumed that all nodes know the complete topology of the network before the partition occurs in the network. The main issue of this proposed approach is the number of required RRNs for healing the disjoint network.

2. Center Deployment with Convex Hull (CDCH): In this approach, first we calculate the out segment nodes like RPFP. The obtained outer segments then calculate representative nodes R_{p_s} and compute the center of deployment (CoD) for RRN's deployment. Then, all R_{p_s} apply the convex hull algorithm to form closed polygon of the outer segments. Further, each representative node of the outer segment which is closer to CoD deploys the RRNs towards CoD. Moreover, the inner representative node deploys the RRNs towards the nearest deployed RRNs as shown in Figure 11. The main advantage of CDCH is that it requires small number of RRN placements as compared with the BD approach, although CDCH is also a centralized approach. The main problem in this approach is the scalability issue for large-scale network. The CoD can be computed as given below:

$$Area(A) = \frac{1}{2} \sum_{i=0}^{n-1} \left(x_i y_{i+1} - x_{i+1} y_i \right) \tag{33}$$

$$X = \frac{1}{mA} \sum_{i=0}^{m} \left\{ \left(x_i + x_{i+1} \right) \left(x_i y_{i+1} - x_{i+1} y_i \right) \right\} \tag{34}$$

$$Y = \frac{1}{mA} \sum_{i=0}^{m} \left\{ \left(y_i + y_{i+1} \right) \left(y_i x_{i+1} - y_{i+1} x_i \right) \right\} \tag{35}$$

where X and Y are the coordinates of the CoD and m is the number of disjoint segments occurs in the network.

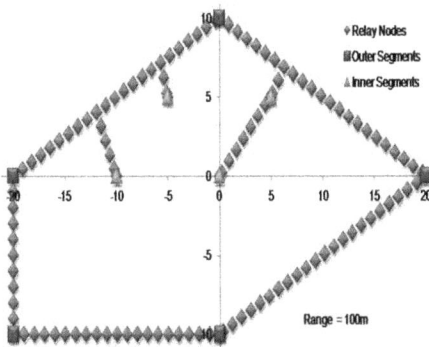

Figure 10. RRNs placements using BD approach (Ranga et al., 2015).

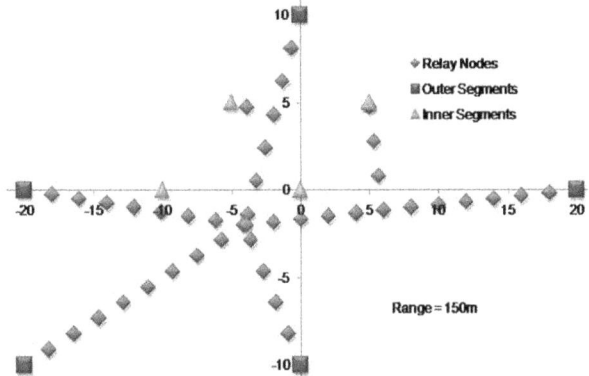

Figure 11. Illustration of repairing of network using CDCH approach (Ranga et al., 2015).

3. Spider Web-1C heuristic: The key idea behind Spider Web-1C deployment strategy as explained by the authors (Senel et al., 2011) is to place the RRNs inward of the damaged area to yield better network connectivity and coverage. To balance the inter-segment path length in terms of the number of hops, RRNs are placed toward the estimated center of mass (CoM) of the segments. Basically, from each partition to CoM, Spider Web-1C gradually deploys nodes until all the partitions are connected effectively. In this way, Spider Web-1C not only increases the total coverage of the network, but also reduces the possible number of cut vertex nodes in the network as well. Before the placement of RRNs in the partitioned network, Spider Web-1C first needs to identify the outer segments in *AOI*. To do this, it randomly picks R_{p_s} from each partition and runs a convex hull algorithm. The convex hull algorithm returns a subset of R_{p_s} that are situated on the corner of a convex hull polygon. After identifying the convex hull polygon, it determines the CoM of the polygon as calculated in CDCH. Then, RRNs are deployed along the line between a segment and CoM. Obviously, the RRNs around the CoM will be in the communication range of each other, and all disjoint segments become connected. Figure 12 shows the pictorial representation of connected network with Spider Web-1C heuristic approach. The main advantage of this approach is that it requires small number of RRNs' placement to rehabilitate lost connectivity in the partitioned WSN network as compared with BD and CDCH approaches.

4. Optimal Relay Node Placement Algorithm using Steiner Minimum Tree (SMT) on Convex Hull (ORC-SMT): ORC-SMT (Lee & Younis, 2012) pursues greedy heuristic that has two main phases: (1) To identify the Steiner Points (SP_s) at which RRNs would be placed with the objective of minimum number of deployed RRNs to connect the segments, and (2) add additional RRNs in order to form a fully connected inner SP_s topology while taking the communication range (*r*) of a RRN into consideration. The first phase contains further two main substeps that are applied repeatedly till the required SP_s are not calculated. In the first

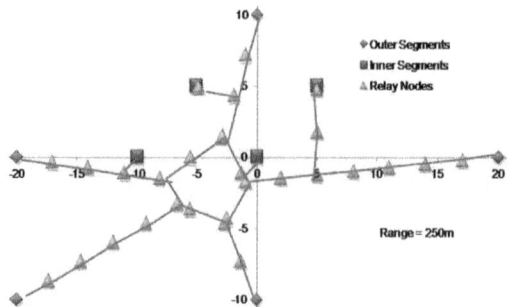

Figure 12. RRNs deployment in Spider Web-1C approach using left and right RRN placement (Ranga et al., 2015).

substep, ORC calculates the convex hull using convex hull algorithm to identify the boundary disjoint segments. Then, SP_s that connect every three non-collinear neighboring boundary disjoint segments are identified. These SP_s are defined as first-tier SP_s. Furthermore, for the unengaged segments, the convex hull is again computed to identify boundary terminals (i.e. disjoint segments or first tier SP_s) that are used in the second round and then second tier SP_s are found. Indeed, third-tier SPs will be identified based on the second-tier SP_s and so on. In other words, two substeps are applied recursively for m rounds until the number of points considered for computing a convex hull is less than three or they form a complete graph in terms of R of a RRN. ORC-SMT then moves to the second phase in which the identified SPs and disjoint segments are bound together. Basically, every segment Seg_i identifies the closest SP and then RRNs get placed on the line from Seg_i to such SP. The same procedure applies for the first-tier SP to connect them to the second tier and so on. As mentioned above, in the first phase, ORC operates in rounds. In the first round ($m = 0$), ORC identifies a set of disjoint segments in the damaged area, which forms the smallest polygon that contains the other segments. Considering the segments as terminals, the convex hull of all segments is used to identify the boundary segments. The authors assume that there exist at least three non-collinear segments such that the convex hull ch_0 found in the first round forms a closed polygon. To find a convex hull, the authors use the Graham Scan algorithm. The main advantage of this approach is that it deploys small number of RRNs to connect the large damaged area. Figure 13 illustrates the connected topology of the partitioned network after the execution of ORC-SMT.

7. Simulation results and discussion

This section evaluates the performance of our proposed approach RPFP through simulation experiments. The purpose of simulation experiments acts as a proof of concept for the designed protocol. Using simulation experiments, it can be determined that whether the designed protocol adheres to the design requirements. The goal of simulation is also used to observe that the purposed approach RPFP outperforms other proposed approaches like ORC-SMT, CDCH, and Spider Web-1C. Our proposed approach is implemented and validated in C++ environment on (NS2.34, 2013). In the simulation, we also consider a linear energy model where energy consumption due to the movement of the RRNs is equal to 27.96 J/m (Ranga et al., 2015). Table 1 shows the simulation parameters used in the simulation.

The following parameters are considered in our experiments for simulation and comparison:

(1) Number of segments (N_s).

(2) Communication range (R) of an RRN.

(3) Number of placed RRNs.

(4) Recovery time (T)

(5) Average path length (APL)

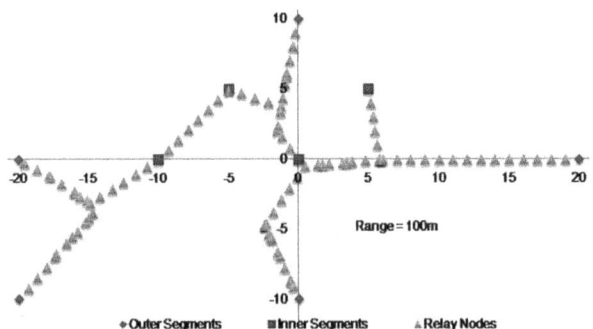

Figure 13. Connected topology using ORC-SMT approach.

In the simulation experiments, we have taken different topologies with the number of outer segments varies from 4 to 8 and inner segments varies from 2 to 5 i.e. total disjoint segments varies from 6 to 13 that are randomly located in an area of interest (i.e. 3000 m × 3000 m). While study the impact of R on the performance of the proposed approaches, it varies between 50 and 200 m in the simulation experiments. The results of the individual experiments are averaged over 40 trials of different topologies. We have also observed that with 95% confidence level, the simulation results stay within 6–10% of the sample mean. We also consider the number of placed RRNs, recovery time (sec), and APL for evaluating the performance of our proposed approach and compare with the existing approaches.

7.1. Number of placed RRNs

This metric reports the total number of required RRNs to rehabilitate the lost connectivity in the partitioned network. As aforementioned, RRNs are usually more expensive than sensor nodes. Thus, this metric reflects the total cost of repairing of partitioned network. Figure 14(a and b) shows the required number of RRNs placement while varying node radio range in the configuration. It is clear from the simulation graphs that the proposed ORC-SMT performs better than our proposed approach RPFP only when the number of partitions in the network is less than 5. However, our proposed approach performs well for any number of disjoint segments. Moreover, BD approach shows the large number of RRNs placement for the repairing of partitioned network due to deployment of nodes along the border of the convex hull in the circular fashion as explained earlier. Furthermore, Spider Web-1C shows similar result like our proposed approach RPFP as the node radio range increases due to observe the large size web-like structure made by Spider Web-1C approach for the placement of RRNs' towards CoM.

In a nutshell, it is observed that ORC-SMT fails when the number of outer disjoint segments is more than 5 as shown in Figures 15 and 16. The reason is that in the randomly deployed topologies, when number of outer disjoint segments increases, more than one of the angles of the Steiner Triangle of SMT comes out to be greater than 120° (obviously some angles are less than equal to 120°), therefore, the calculated SP_s comes out to be on the segment itself (on the segment whose edge angle is greater than 120°) as it is the property of the FP (i.e. SMT with three points behave like a Fermat Point). This raises the question of convergence ability of ORC-SMT approach towards the center for which the authors have claimed in their approach (Ranga et al., 2015). The situation becomes more intensive and critical when the number of outer segments grows critically which is a more common scenario in a harsh environment and thus, ORC-SMT fails in the simulations as observed in our experiments. In a nutshell, we can say that ORC-SMT behaves well when it serves with the small number of disjoint segments (i.e. less than 5), as we have verified in the simulation as shown in Figure 14(a and b). Furthermore, the Spider Web-1C heuristic runs almost parallel to the CDCH when the node radio range is larger. This is because the web formed by Spider Web-1C would be much earlier from the CoM; therefore, the small number of nodes is required for the repairing of the lost connectivity. The RPFP shows excellent results as compared with ORC-SMT, Spider Web-1C, CDCH, and BD as the number of outer disjoint segments increases or as a node radio range is larger. The reason is the

Table 1. Simulation parameters (Ranga et al., 2015)	
Parameter	**Value**
Simulation area	2,000 m × 2,000 m
Sensor nodes (n)	250
Radio model	Path loss model
MAC layer	IEEE 802.15.4
Communication range (R)	50–200 m
Node initial energy (E_i) (AA battery)	16,200 J
Total number of partitions observed	6-13
Channel frequency	2.4 GHz
Packet size	1 byte
Antenna model	Omni-directional
Failure model	Random
Data transmission rate	1 packet/s
Simulation time	100 s

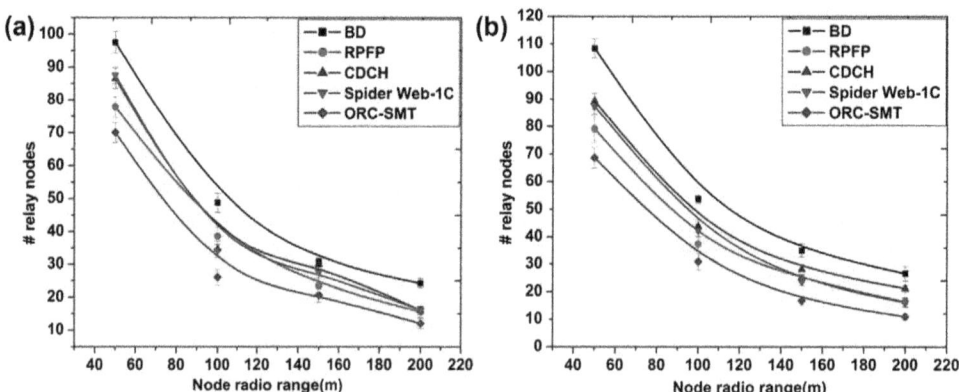

Figure 14. Number of relay nodes (a) vs. node radio range when outer segments are 4 and inner segments varies from 2 to 8, (b) vs. node radio range when outer segments are 5 and inner segments varies from 2 to 8.

deployment of a small number of RRNs from all the segments towards zero gradient point *FP* as explained earlier. Moreover, Figures 15 and 16 confirm the effectiveness of our proposed approach.

7.2. Recovery time of the network (RT)

It defines the total time taken by any approach to rehabilitate lost connectivity due to failure of large-scale nodes in the network. It is always expressed in CPU time (i.e. in sec). Figure 17(a) shows the effectiveness of our proposed RPFP over compared approaches. The recovery time of BD and CDCH is more due to their centralized nature. Although, CDCH performs better than BD due to node deployment with this approach towards CoD rather than on the edges of convex hull polygon. It means CDCH takes less time to rehabilitate the network partitioning as we observed in Figure 16(a). The ORC-SMT behaves well because of its distributed in nature when number of segments are up to 5. Moreover, our proposed approach RPFP also shows excellent results as the node radio range is larger in the network. However, Spider Web-1C shows good results as the node radio range is larger, because the network connects quickly due to large size of web made by the proposed solution before reaching to CoD. Figure 17(b) shows the recovery time varying with the number of outer disjoint segments. Proposed solution shows excellent results due to deployment of RRNs towards zero gradient point inside the triangle and can work for any number of disjoint segments. Moreover, RPFP shows small variation in its plot due to the least change in zero gradient point position in the triangle for a large number of segments.

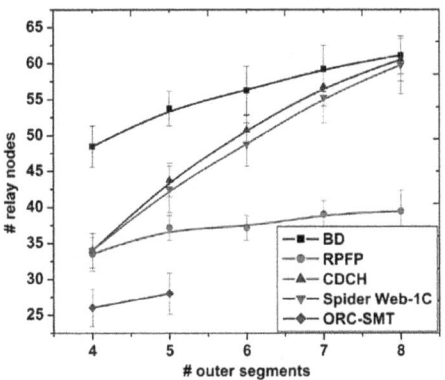

Figure 15. Number of relay nodes vs. number of outer segments with node radio range is 100 m.

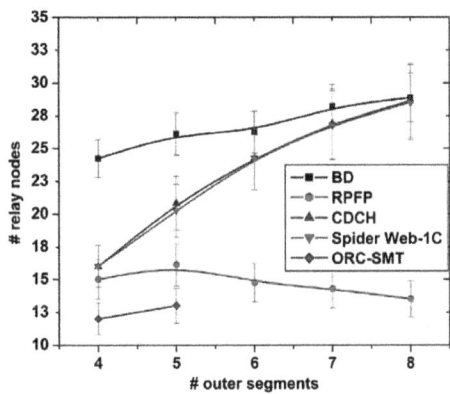

Figure 16. Number of relay nodes vs. number of outer segments with node radio range is 200 m.

7.3. APL

This metric depicts the expected path length between the partitions after the recovery has been done. A small APL is desirable as explained in various state-of-the-the-art approaches, because it will reduce the data latency between the various partitions when network partitioning is rehabilitated between various disjoint segments. Figure 18(a), (b) show APL as the function of number of outer segments and node radio range, respectively. It has been clearly seen that ORC-SMT shows excellent results only when the number of disjoint segments is smaller, but our proposed approach RPFP shows excellent results for any number of disjoint segments. Moreover, the accuracy of the calculated zero gradient point and the diameter of the convex hull polygon also affects the APL. Thus, Spider Web-1C shows excellent results compared with BD and CDCH approaches because of

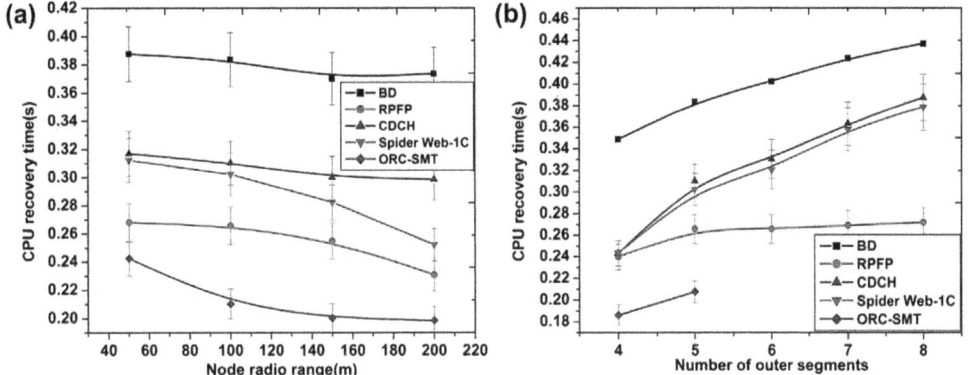

Figure 17. CPU recovery time (a) vs. node radio range when outer segments are 5 (b) vs. number of segments with node radio range is 100 m.

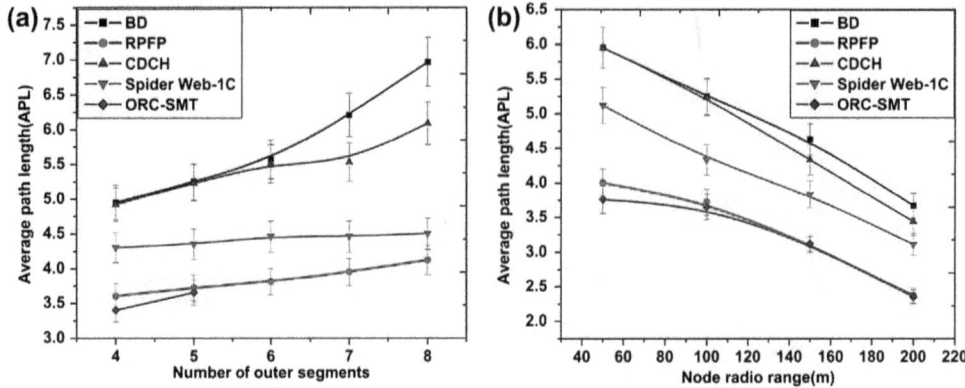

Figure 18. APL (a) vs. number of outer segments when node radio range is 100 m (b) vs. node radio range when outer segments are 5.

big size web-like structure maintained by this approach as node radio range increases. Furthermore, ORC-SMT and our proposed approaches show similar results as the node radio range is higher and when number of outer disjoint segments are 5, because of accuracy of zero gradient point (i.e. like a center point of a circle) inside the convex hull polygon as observed in Figure 18(b).

8. Conclusion and future scope

The performance of unattended WSNs depends upon the connectivity among the backbone connected dominating set (CDS) of sensor nodes. There are many reasons which can disrupt network connectivity, permanently such as low battery level of CDS nodes, physical damage of large-scale sensor nodes due to hostile natural incidents like natural disasters such as a sandstorm, earthquake, fire storm, explosive attack of an enemy, etc. In this paper, we have proposed a new approach based on the Fermat Point called RPFP for RRNs' placement in the large-scale partitioned WSN. The main strength of our proposed approach is that it requires a small number of RRN placements and also works for any number of disjoint segments as compared with existing benchmark approaches. The simulation results also confirm the goodness of our proposed approach. In the future, our study can focus on testing of our proposed approach with routing protocol in the presence of obstacles to evaluate the actual network performance parameters like throughput, end-to-end delay, packet loss, delivery ratio, etc.

Funding
The authors received no direct funding for this research.

Author details
Virender Ranga[1]
E-mail: virendersinghmtech@gmail.com
ORCID ID: http://orcid.org/0000-0002-2046-8642
Mayank Dave[1]
E-mail: m.dave@ieee.org
Anil Kumar Verma[2]
E-mail: akverma@thapar.edu
[1] Department of Computer Engineering, National Institute of Technology, Kurukshetra, Haryana, India.
[2] Department of Computer Science and Engineering, Thapar University, Patiala, Punjab, India.

References
Alfadhly, A., Baroudi, U., & Younis, M. (2010). Optimal node repositioning for tolerating node failure in wireless sensor actor network. *Proceeding of the 25th Biennial Symposium on Communication(QBSC'10)* (pp.67–71). Kingston: IEEE.
Ghosh, K., Roy, S., & Das, P. K. (2009). An alternative approach to find Fermat point of a polygon geographic region for energy efficient geo-cast routing protocols: Global minima scheme. *Proceeding of First IEEE International Conference on Networks and Communications (NetCom'09)* (pp. 332–337). Chennai: IEEE.
Graham, R. L. (1972). An efficient algorithm for determining the convex hull of a finite planar set. *Information Processing Letters, 1*, 132–133. http://dx.doi.org/10.1016/0020-0190(72)90045-2
Kansal, A., Somasundara, A., Srivastava, D. J. M., & Estrin, D. (2004). Intelligent fluid infrastructure for embedded networks. *Proceeding of the 2nd International Conference on Mobile Systems, Applications and Services (MobiSys'04)* (pp. 1–14). Boston, MA: ACM.
Lee, S., & Younis, M. (2012). Optimized relay node placement for connecting disjoint wireless sensor networks. *Computer Networks, 56*, 2788–2804. http://dx.doi.org/10.1016/j.comnet.2012.04.019
NS2.34. (21 October 2013). *Network simulator for wireless ad hoc and sensor network.* Retrieved from http://sourceforge.net/projects/nsnam/files/allinone/ns-allinone-2.34/
Ranga, V., Dave, M., & Verma, A. K. (2013). Network partitioning recovery mechanisms in WSANS: A survey. *Wireless*

Personal Communications, 72, 857–917.
http://dx.doi.org/10.1007/s11277-013-1046-7

Ranga, V., Dave, M., & Verma, A. K. (February 2014). A hybrid timer based single node failure recovery approach for WSANs. Wireless Personal Communications (Springer) (pp. 1–28). doi:10.1007/s11277-014-1631-4

Ranga, V., Dave, M., & Verma, A. K. (October, 2015). Relay node placement to heal partitioned wireless sensor networks. Computers and Electrical Engineering, 1–18. doi:10.1016/j.compeleceng.2015.09.014

Senel, F., Younis, M. F., & Akkaya, K. (May 2011). Bio-inspired relay node placement heuristics for repairing damaged wireless sensor networks. IEEE Transactions on Vehicular Technology, 60, 1835–1848.
http://dx.doi.org/10.1109/TVT.2011.2131158

Senturk, I. F., Akkaya, K., & Senel, F. (2012). An effective and scalable connectivity restoration heuristic for mobile sensor/actor networks. Proceeding of the IEEE Global Communications Conference (GLOBECOM'12) (pp. 518–523). Anaheim, CA: IEEE.

Senturk, I. F., Akkaya, K., & Yilmaz, S. (June 2012). A game-theoretic approach to connectivity restoration in wireless sensor and actor networks. Proceeding of IEEE International Conference on Communications (pp. 7110–7114). Ottawa: IEEE.

Shen, Y., & Tolosa, J. (2008). The weighted Fermat triangle problem. International Journal of Mathematics and Mathematical Sciences, 1–16.
http://dx.doi.org/10.1155/2008/283846

Sir, M., Senturk, I., Sisikoglu, F., & Akkaya, K. (2011). An optimization-based approach for connecting partitioned mobile sensor/actuator networks. Proceeding of 3rd International Workshop on Wireless Sensor, Actuator and Robot Networks (WiSARN), in Conjunction with IEEE INFOCOM'11 (pp.525–530). Shanghai: IEEE.

Stojmenovic, I., Simplot-Ryl, D., & Nayak, A. (2011). Toward scalable cut vertex and link detection with applications in wireless ad hoc networks. IEEE Network, 25, 44–48.
http://dx.doi.org/10.1109/MNET.2011.5687952

Toussaint, G. T. (1984). An optimal algorithm for computing the minimum vertex distance between two crossing convex polygons. Computing, 32, 357–364.
http://dx.doi.org/10.1007/BF02243778

Vemulapalli, S., & Akkaya, K. (October 2010). Mobility-based self route recovery from multiple node failures in mobile sensor networks. Proceeding of IEEE International Workshop on Wireless Local Networks (WLN'10) (pp. 699–706). Denver, CO: IEEE.

Wang, W., Srinivasan, V., & Chu, K. (2005). Using mobile relays to prolong the lifetime of WSNs. Proceeding of the 11th Annual International Conference on Mobile Computing and Networking (Mobicom'05) (pp. 270–283). Cologne: ACM.

Wang, G., Cao, G., Porta, T. L., & Zhang, W. (2005). Sensor relocation in mobile sensor networks. Proceeding of the 24th International Annual Joint Conference of IEEE Computer and Communication Societies (INFOCOM'05) (pp. 2302–2312). Miami, FL: IEEE.

Younis, M., Sentruk, I. F., Akkaya, K., Lee, S., & Senel, F. (2013). Topology management techniques for tolerating node failures in WSNS: A survey. Computer Networks (Elsevier) (pp. 1–30). doi:10.1016/j.comnet.2013.08.021

Appendix A

(Proof of $\| g_d(x, y) \|^2 = 0$):

Proof   We know that $w_1 u_1 + w_2 u_2 + w_3 u_3 = \sum_{i=1}^{3} w_i u_i = 0$ such that $g_d(P) = 0$. Therefore, we have

$$g_d(P) = w_1 u_1 + w_2 u_2 + w_3 u_3 \tag{36}$$

Take square of Equation (36) i.e.

$$\| g_d(P) \|^2 = \left(w_1 u_1 + w_2 u_2 + w_3 u_3\right)\left(w_1 u_1 + w_2 u_2 + w_3 u_3\right) \tag{37}$$

$$= \left(w_1^2 + w_2^2 + w_3^2 + 2w_1 w_2 u_1 u_2 + 2w_1 w_3 u_1 u_3 + 2w_2 w_3 u_2 u_3\right)$$

We know that according to cosine law

$$w_1 w_2 = \cos\left(\Pi - \Theta_3\right), \ w_2 w_3 = \cos\left(\Pi - \Theta_1\right), \ w_3 w_1 = \cos\left(\Pi - \Theta_2\right)$$

Replace these values in Equation (38), and then we get following Equations

$$\| g_d(P) \|^2 = \left(w_1^2 + w_2^2 + w_3^2 + 2w_1 w_2\left[\cos\left(\Pi - \Theta_3\right)\right] + 2w_1 w_3\left[\cos\left(\Pi - \Theta_2\right)\right] + 2w_2 w_3\left[\cos\left(\Pi - \Theta_1\right)\right]\right) \tag{38}$$

$$\| g_d(P) \|^2 = \left(w_1^2 + w_2^2 + w_3^2 - 2w_1 w_2 \cos\Theta_3 - 2w_1 w_3 \cos\Theta_2 - 2w_2 w_3 \cos\Theta_1\right) \tag{39}$$

Again, according to cosine law

$$w_1^2 + w_2^2 - 2w_1 w_2 \cos\Theta_3 = w_3^2$$

Putting this value to Equation (39) for further simplification

$$\| g_d(P) \|^2 = \left(w_3^2 + w_3^2 - 2w_1w_3 \cos \Theta_2 - 2w_2w_3 \cos \Theta_1 \right) \qquad (40)$$

Add and subtract w_1^2 to Equation (40) for further simplification

$$\| g_d(P) \|^2 = \left(w_1^2 + w_3^2 - 2w_1w_3 \cos \Theta_2 + w_3^2 - 2w_2w_3 \cos \Theta_1 - w_1^2 \right) \qquad (41)$$

$$\| g_d(P) \|^2 = \left(w_2^2 + w_3^2 - 2w_2w_3 \cos \Theta_1 - w_1^2 \right) \qquad (42)$$

$$\| g_d(P) \|^2 = \left(w_1^2 - w_1^2 \right) = 0 \qquad (43)$$

Hence proved.

8

Modeling friction factor in pipeline flow using a GMDH-type neural network

Saeb M. Besarati[1], Philip D. Myers[1*], David C. Covey[2] and Ali Jamali[3]

*Corresponding author: Philip D. Myers, Department of Chemical and Biomedical Engineering, University of South Florida, 4202 E Fowler Ave, ENB118, Tampa, FL, USA

E-mail: PhilipMyers@mail.usf.edu

Reviewing editor: Jenhui Chen, Chang Gung University, Taiwan

Abstract: The standard methods of calculating the fluid friction factor, the Colebrook–White and Haaland equations, require iterative solution of an implicit, transcendental function which entails high computational costs for large-scale piping networks while introducing as much as 15% error. This study applies the group method of data handling to the development of an artificial neural network optimized by multi-objective genetic algorithms to find an explicit polynomial model for friction factor. We developed a relatively simple and explicit model for friction factor that performs well over the entire range of applicability of the Colebrook–White equation: Reynolds number from 4,000 to 10^8 with relative roughness ranging from 5×10^{-6} to 0.05. For a network with only two hidden layers and a total of five neurons, this model was found to have a mean relative error of only 3.4% in comparison with the Colebrook–White equation; a determination coefficient (R^2) over the range of input data was calculated to be 0.9954. The accuracy and simplicity of this model may make it preferable to traditional, transcendental representations of fluid friction factor. Further, this method of model development can be applied to any pertinent data-set—that is to say, the model can be tuned to the physical situation and input data range of interest.

Subjects: Fluid Mechanics; Mathematical Modeling; Neural Networks

Keywords: friction factor; Colebrook–White equation; artificial neural networks; genetic algorithms

ABOUT THE AUTHOR

Saeb M. Besarati earned his bachelor and master's degrees in mechanical engineering from University of Guilan, Iran. He earned his PhD in chemical engineering from the University of South Florida (USF) in 2014. The focus of Dr. Besarati's work has been the use of advanced numerical techniques to solve complex engineering problems in the field of clean energy research. He conducted his doctoral studies at the USF Clean Energy Research Center under the guidance of Dr. Yogi Goswami. His doctoral research concerned the analysis of supercritical carbon dioxide power cycles for concentrated solar power applications. During his PhD study, he contributed in writing two book chapters and ten technical papers. He has been a lecturer for courses in the Department of Mechanical Engineering at the Azad University of Takestan and the Department of Chemical Engineering at USF. He is currently an engineering analyst with the firm eSolar.

PUBLIC INTEREST STATEMENT

In this paper, we analyze a classical engineering problem—that of friction in pipeline flow—using the comparatively modern techniques of artificial neural networks and genetic algorithms. In the process, we obtain a set of simple (i.e. non-transcendental) equations that give excellent agreement with the Colebrook–White equation. The method can also be tailored to experimental data for more specific applications.

1. Introduction

The flow of real fluids (e.g. through pipes, ducts, etc.) involves the loss of mechanical energy through the friction that accompanies flow-induced shear stresses. The magnitude of this loss depends on the viscosity of the fluid(s) in question as well as the size of the fluid flow system. Often, this loss can be quite severe, and calculations to determine the degree of viscous friction become a necessary part of the design, implementation, and control of engineered applications of fluid flow. In process control especially, such calculations must be repeated continually, and for systems of substantial size (e.g. large-scale piping networks) they constitute a high computational cost.

1.1. Colebrook–White equation

A common and comparatively simple context for these fluid flow analyses is fully-developed Newtonian flow in pipes or ducts. Through dimensional analysis, it is possible to express the viscous losses as a function of a dimensionless friction factor—as a matter of convention, fluid mechanics texts typically choose the Darcy friction factor, f, which is a function of Reynolds number, Re, and the relative roughness of the pipe, ϵ/D. In such a way, the loss of mechanical energy, or head loss, h_f, as it is termed when expressed as an equivalent height of fluid, can be calculated with the Darcy–Weisbach equation (White, 1998).

$$h_f = f \frac{L}{D} \frac{V^2}{2g} \tag{1}$$

Here, L represents the length of the pipe or duct, D is the hydraulic diameter, V is the average flow velocity, and g is the acceleration due to gravity. It should be noted that this equation is valid for any flow regime or pipe/duct geometry, provided the hydraulic diameter and the Darcy friction factor are appropriately derived.

The straightforward nature of the calculation of head loss for a given friction factor (i.e. Equation 1) belies the complexity of the calculation of the friction factor itself. While, in the laminar case ($Re < 2,000$), the friction factor becomes a rather simple function of Reynolds number (White, 1998), turbulent flow requires more complicated, typically transcendental functions to capture the variation of the friction factor with respect Reynolds number and relative roughness. The most broadly applicable function for determining the friction factor in turbulent flow regimes is the Colebrook–White equation, developed by the eponymous researcher, Colebrook (1939).

$$\frac{1}{f^{1/2}} = -2.0 \log \left(\frac{\frac{\epsilon}{D}}{3.7} + \frac{2.51}{Re f^{\frac{1}{2}}} \right) \tag{2}$$

This expression is known to apply over a range in Reynolds number of approximately 4,000–10^8 (White, 1998).

It is clear that, owing to the implicit nature of the friction factor in Equation 2, iterative methods are required to calculate the friction factor for a given Reynolds number and relative roughness. Although approximations of the Colebrook–White equation that are explicit in Darcy friction factor f have been formulated, they tend to apply to specific flow scenarios and/or pipe geometries, and they introduce additional error. The Haaland equation (Equation 3), for example, assumes the same basic form of the Colebrook–White, but is explicit in terms of the friction factor; it is among the more accurate approximations, varying less than 2% from the behavior of Equation 2 (Haaland, 1983; White, 1998).

$$\frac{1}{f^{1/2}} = -1.8 \log \left[\left(\frac{\frac{\epsilon}{D}}{3.7} \right)^{1.11} + \frac{6.9}{Re} \right] \tag{3}$$

It should be noted that the Colebrook–White equation itself is known to introduce a degree of error, perhaps as high as 15%, over its range of applicability (White, 1998). Of course, this error applies with respect to the real (i.e. experimentally quantified) behavior of fluids. The error in the Haaland equation, on the other hand, applies with respect to the performance of the Colebrook–White equation, thereby compounding the overall error in design calculation, potentially to a degree greater than 15% of the real value.

1.2. Calculation of friction factor via neural networks

For calculations concerning smaller data-sets, the iteratively solved Colebrook–White equation will generally suffice. However, a review of recent literature demonstrates the need for more efficient methods of computation, especially for larger, more complex piping networks, such as large-scale micro-irrigation systems (Shayya & Sablani, 1998), combined sewer systems (Haaland, 1983), etc. In particular, much work has been done to employ artificial neural networks (ANNs) and evolutionary algorithms (EAs) to calculate pipeflow friction factors. Indeed, such numerical techniques proved to be a powerful tool in solving non-linear, transcendental, or otherwise complex mathematical relations such as the Colebrook–White equation, as they allow for the modeling of perhaps mathematically intractable phenomena with little or no *a priori* knowledge of the mathematical characteristics of the physical processes that inhere therein.

An ANN is typically structured in three distinct parts: the input layer, an output layer, and any number of hidden layers between the input and output. Each of these layers is made up of neurons, and each neuron is interconnected through adjacent layers. An ANN is developed via "training" with a data-set, allowing the network to adjust the relative weights of the connections between each neuron such that an output of acceptable error is produced (Fausett, 1993). In the case of the Colebrook–White equation considered in this study, the network is made up of two input neurons, corresponding to each input (Reynolds number and relative roughness), an undetermined number of neurons in the hidden layers to operate on the input data, and one output neuron (the desired calculable quantity, the friction factor). The input or output data used to train the network may be transformed in any number of ways to improve the performance of the resultant model—for example, the base-ten logarithm of the Reynolds number may be chosen as an input neuron in lieu of the Reynolds number itself, as described in the methodology section. Of course, additional input neurons may be introduced by considering the individual parameters that constitute the Reynolds number (i.e. fluid velocity, effective diameter, and kinematic viscosity) (Mittal & Zhang, 2007), though such a complication was deemed unnecessary for the purposes of this study.

1.3. Literature review

A significant amount of effort has been expended on the application of ANNs to the problem of fluid flow friction factor determination in both Newtonian (Bilgil & Altun, 2008; Fadare & Ofidhe, 2009; Mittal & Zhang, 2007; Özger & Yildirim, 2009; Shayya & Sablani, 1998; Yazdi & Bardi, 2011; Yuhong & Wenxin, 2009) and non-Newtonian (Mittal & Zhang, 2007; Sablani & Shayya, 2003; Sablani, Shayya, & Kacimov, 2003; Shayya, Sablani, & Campo, 2005) flows. For reference, a summary of these studies in included here as Table 1. Inasmuch as the Colebrook–White equation assumes Newtonian flow, this study will focus primarily on the work dealing with such flow behavior. While in some cases, the data range for Reynolds number employed in ANN development was outside the acceptable range for the Colebrook White equation (Fadare & Ofidhe, 2009; Shayya & Sablani, 1998), very close agreement was obtained for sufficiently large networks and appropriate transformation of input and/or output parameters. In one particular study, an attempt was made to fit the friction factor behavior in both the laminar and turbulent flow regimes, though the inclusion of points in the highly indeterminate transition region introduces some uncertainty as to the reliability of the model and its ostensibly low error (Mittal & Zhang, 2007). Another study performed a model fit of the Haaland equation (Equation 3) with very high accuracy, although, here again, points were included in the training of the network that fall outside the realm of acceptability for such empirical relations (Yazdi & Bardi, 2011). The work performed in this field demonstrated that rather complex ANNs achieve a high degree of accuracy in modeling experimental data (Yuhong & Wenxin, 2009), the Colebrook–White equation (Fadare & Ofidhe, 2009; Mittal & Zhang, 2007; Shayya & Sablani, 1998), and other empiricisms of Newtonian flow (Bilgil & Altun, 2008; Mittal & Zhang, 2007; Yazdi & Bardi, 2011; Yuhong & Wenxin, 2009). No explicit relations for the friction factor were put forth in these works.

Table 1. Literature review summary

References	Description	Method	Data-set	Source for data-set	Range—ϵ/D	Range—Re
Shayya et al. (2005)	Authors developed ANN to find Fanning friction factor for Herschel–Bulkley fluids in closed pipes. Input parameters were Re and He.	Feed-forward ANN	1,991 (training), 29,507 (validation)	Regula-Falsi iterative method to solve an implicit functions based on mechanical energy balance, laminar flow function, pressure gradient and friction factor. Solutions apply for laminar, transition and turbulent flows.	n/a	2–1E8
Sablani et al. (2003)	Authors develop an ANN to find Fanning friction factor for flow of Bingham plastic fluids ir closed pipes. Input parameters were Re and He.	Feed-forward ANN	1,177 (training), 32,141 (validation)	Regula-Falsi iterative method was used to solve for f given Re and He in laminar and turbulent conditions.	n/a	2–1E8
Sablani and Shayya (2003)	Authors developed an ANN to find the Fanning friction factor for power law (shear thinning) fluids ir closed pipes.	Feed-forward ANN	7,420 (training), 72,400 (validation)	Regula-Falsi iterative method was used to solve an equation the authors developed based on the von Karman equation, which is a function of Re and n, where n is the flow behavior index.	n/a	2E3–1E8
Shayya and Sablani (1998)	Authors developed an ANN to find the Darcy friction factor for flow of Newtonian fluids in closed pipes.	Feed-forward ANN	1,720 (training), 82,100 (validation)	Regula-Falsi iterative method was used to solve the Colebrook–White equation for specified ranges of relative roughness and Reynolds number.	1E-6 to 5E-2	2E3–1E8
Tufail and Ormsbee (2006)	Authors develop a FFSGA based on genetic algorithms and least squares optimization to find Darcy friction factor. The method combin es numerical coefficients, functions of decision variables, and mathematical operators.	Fixed functional set genetic algorithm (FFSGA)	100	Authors used the Swamee-Jain equation (explicit version of Colebrook-White equation, limited to full flow circular pipe) to generate data-sets, with specified ranges of relative roughness and Re.	0.001–0.01	1E5–1E6
Mittal and Zhang (2007)	Authors created 4 ANNs to find friction factor for Newtonian, Bingham plastic, Power law, and Herschel–Bulkely fluids. Inputs were mean velocity, viscosity, density, and pipe diameter.	Back-propogation ANN	45,747 (training), 6,862 (validation)	Authors used an iterative solution to yield friction factor from the von Karman correlation.	n/a	n/a
Bilgil and Altun (2008)	Authors develop an ANN to predict friction factor in open channel flow for a Newtonian fluid in comparison with prediction of the Manning equation, given experimental data.	Feed-forward ANN	n/a	Authors created an experimental setup with an adjustable-slope open channel and varied the W/h ratio of the channel and water discharge. They compared their experimental results to their ANN as well as the Manning equation.	n/a	8,291–217,791

(Continued)

Table 1. (Continued)

References	Description	Method	Data-set	Source for data-set	Range—ϵ/D	Range—Re
Özger and Yildirim (2009)	Authors used a set of 9 "fuzzy" rules (IF THEN statements) relating Re, relative roughness and f, whereby the rules are structured similar to an ANN to predict f.	Adaptive neuro-fuzzy inference system (ANFIS)	1,042 (training), 700 (validation)	Authors used the graph reading software *Techdig 2.0* to sensitively read data from the Moody diagram.	1E-6–5E-2	4E3–1E8
Yazdi and Bardi (2011)	Authors developed an ANN to predict Darcy friction factor, given Re and relative roughness as inputs. They also compared predictions of f depending on the training algorithm used.	Feed-forward ANN	1,600 (training), 400 (validation)	Authors generated a data-set from the Haaland equation, which is explicit in f, given specified ranges of relative roughness and Re.	n/a	3E3–1E8
Fadare and Ofidhe (2009)	Authors developed an ANN to predict Darcy friction factor, given Re and relative roughness as inputs. They also compared predictions of f depending on the training algorithm used.	Feed-forward ANN	1,920 (training), 640 (validation)	Authors generated a data-set from the Haaland equation, which is explicit in f, given specified ranges of relative roughness and Re.	5E-6–7E-2	2.5E3–1E8

Acronyms: MRE = Mean relative error; MSE = Mean square error; MAPE = Mean absolute percentage error; SSE = Sum of square error; R = Correlation coefficient; R^2 = Coefficient of determination; STD = Standard deviation.

MAE, STD (of MAE), MRE, STD (of MRE), R^2.

MAE, STD (of MAE), MRE, STD (of MRE), R^2.

MAE, STD (of MAE), MRE, STD (of MRE), R^2.

MAE, STD (of MAE), MRE, STD (of MRE), R^2.

MSE, Max absolute error.

Avg. Absolute error, R.

R^2.

MSE, R, Max % Error, Time, Iterations.

MSE, MAPE (%), SSE, R.

There is a tendency in ANN-based modeling to develop the network model as a "black-box" (Tufail & Ormsbee, 2006)—a complex, abstruse system of functions that convert input data to desired results, oftentimes quite accurately, yet with little innate understanding of the mathematical machinery of the model. For the problem considered in this paper, it is clear that such a complex model defeats the purpose of approximating the Colebrook–White equation in the first place. Equation 3 is acceptable in terms of approximating the Colebrook–White equation, although its transcendental nature makes it less desirable, in terms of computational effort, than a simple polynomial (Davidson, Savic, & Walters, 1999). However, certainly a simply stated transcendental function is more tractable than a complex system of intermarried polynomial functions, such as those often output by proprietary neural network software packages. The maxim of model-parsimony may suggest the choice of the simpler and slightly less accurate over the more accurate and more unwieldy, a balancing act described in the non-Newtonian flow ANN modeling of Sablani, Shayya, et al. (Sablani & Shayya, 2003; Sablani et al., 2003; Shayya et al., 2005). For more information on the black box method employing software packages for ANN development, the reader is encouraged to peruse the pertinent references (Fadare & Ofidhe, 2009; Mittal & Zhang, 2007; Shayya & Sablani, 1998; Yazdi & Bardi, 2011).

Also of unique interest in this field is the combination of fuzzy logic with ANNs in model development. An adaptive neuro-fuzzy inference modeling system involves the use of stochastic membership functions and conditional statements with associated model functions to fit real values of interest from pseudo-qualitative assessment of input data (e.g. low, medium, and high). Such a system was shown to have near perfect agreement with the Colebrook–White equation over the Reynolds number range of interest, $4,000–10^8$ (Özger & Yildirim, 2009). Unfortunately, the multitude of fuzzy rules and attendant modeling functions render this method a black box, as well.

EAs present a potential improvement when wedded with conventional ANN techniques (Onwubolu, 2009). The idea behind the use of such genetic algorithms in this context is that models or functional interactions that produce the best fit to the training data have the best chance of reproducing and therefore shaping the final model system. Already, genetic algorithms, without the use of neural networks, have been employed to fit the Colebrook–White equation. In one study, standalone polynomial functions of varying complexity were developed with such a technique, and most were shown to yield a good fit (Davidson et al., 1999). This work was extended in a subsequent study that utilized a fixed function set genetic algorithm that considered a wider variety of functional forms in its model development (Tufail & Ormsbee, 2006). Explicit functions for the Colebrook–White equation were presented in both cases; however, the models developed applied only over a relatively narrow range of Reynolds number and relative roughness ($10^5 \leq Re \leq 10^6$; $0.001 \leq \epsilon/D \leq 0.01$). A wider range of Reynolds number and relative roughness ($4 \times 10^4 \leq Re \leq 10^8$; $10^{-6} \leq \epsilon/D \leq 0.05$) was considered in the gene expression programming (GEP) analysis of Samadianfard (Samadianfard, 2012). The explicit expression obtained in that study compared well with the various approximations described therein; however, a separate study highlighted the potentially high errors obtained with its use and also suggested similar expressions with improved accuracy (Vatankhah, 2014). It should be noted that the GEP techniques referenced here, while generally related to genetic algorithms, make no use of ANNs.

1.4. Investigation objectives

The main goal of this study is to apply the group method of data handling (GMDH) ANN, optimized by multi-objective genetic algorithms, to find an explicit model for friction factor. This methodology has been proven effective in the modeling and prediction of complex and non-linear processes such as explosive cutting, a variable valve-timing spark-ignition engine, and others (Atashkari, Nariman-Zadeh, Gölcü, Khalkhali, & Jamali, 2007; Onwubolu, 2009). The quasi-Monte Carlo method of Hammersley (Press, Teukolsky, Vetterling, & Flannery, 2007) will be used to generate an input dataset of random yet uniformly spaced points over the entire range of applicability of the Colebrook–White equation: Reynolds number from 4,000 to 10^8 and relative roughness from 5×10^{-6} to 0.05. The Colebrook–White equation shall be solved with non-linear solution methods to obtain the friction factor values for use in training and testing the neural network. Ultimately, the development of this GMDH-type ANN shall yield an explicit polynomial model for friction factor to be presented herein.

2. Methodology

2.1. Construction of the neural network

By means of the GMDH algorithm, a model can be represented as a set of neurons in which different neuron pairs in each layer are connected through a quadratic polynomial and thus produce new neurons in subsequent layers. Such representation can be used in modeling to map inputs to outputs. The formal definition of the identification problem is to develop a function, $\hat{f}$, that approximates the actual function, f, to a sufficient accuracy to predict the actual output y for a given input vector $X = (x_1, x_2, \ldots, x_n)$ as $\hat{y}$. Therefore, given M observations of multi-input, single output data pairs, we define the system in the following manner.

$$y_i = f(x_{i1}, x_{i2}, \ldots, x_{in}), \text{ for } i = 1, 2, \ldots M \tag{4}$$

It is possible to train a GMDH-type neural network to predict the output values for any given input vector, as illustrated in Equation 5.

$$\hat{y}_i = \hat{f}(x_{i1}, x_{i2}, \ldots, x_{in}), \text{ for } i = 1, 2, \ldots M \tag{5}$$

The problem is now to determine a GMDH-type network so that the square of the differences between the actual output and the predicted one is minimized, that is:

$$\sum_{i=1}^{M} [\hat{y}_i - y_i]^2 \to \min \tag{6}$$

The general connection between the inputs and the output variables can be expressed by a discrete form of the Volterra functional series, as follows.

$$y = a_0 + \sum_{i=1}^{n} a_i x_i + \sum_{i=1}^{n} \sum_{j=1}^{n} a_{ij} x_i x_j + \ldots \sum_{i=1}^{n} \sum_{j=1}^{n} \sum_{k=1}^{n} a_{ijk} x_i x_j x_k + \cdots$$

This form of the series is known as the Kolmogorov–Gabor polynomial (Farlow, 1984). This full form of mathematical description can be represented by a system of partial quadratic polynomials consisting of only two input variables (neurons), in the following form.

$$\hat{y} = G(x_i, x_j) = a_0 + a_1 x_i + a_2 x_j + a_3 x_i x_j + a_4 x_i^2 + a_5 x_j^2 \tag{7}$$

Such partial quadratic description is recursively used in a network of connected neurons to build the general mathematical relation of the inputs and output variables. The coefficients a_i in Equation 7 are calculated using regression techniques (Farlow, 1984; Iba, DeGaris, & Sato, 1996; Ivakhnenko, 1971), so that the difference between the actual output, y, and the calculated one, $\hat{y}$ for each pair of x_i, x_j as input variables is minimized. It can be seen that a tree of polynomials is constructed using the quadratic form, Equation 7, whose coefficients are regressed in a least-squares sense. In this way, the coefficients of each quadratic function G_i are obtained to fit optimally the output in the whole set of input/output data pairs.

In the basic form of the GMDH algorithm, all the possibilities of two independent variables out of the total n input variables are taken in order to construct the regression polynomial (Equation 7) that best fits the dependent observations (Jamali, Nariman-zadeh, Darvizeh, Masoumi, & Hamrang, 2009; Nariman-Zadeh, Darvizeh, & Ahmad-Zadeh, 2003; Nariman-Zadeh, Darvizeh, Jamali, & Moeini, 2005). In this paper, the general structure of GMDH-type neural network (GS-GMDH) (Jamali et al., 2009; Nariman-Zadeh et al., 2005) is used for modeling and prediction of the friction factor. In the GS-GMDH ANN, neuron connections can occur between different layers that are not necessarily immediately adjacent, unlike the conventional structure GMDH (CS-GMDH) neural networks in which such connections only occur between adjacent layers. Consequently, this generalization of the network's structure can extend the performance of GS-GMDH neural networks in modeling of real-world complex processes.

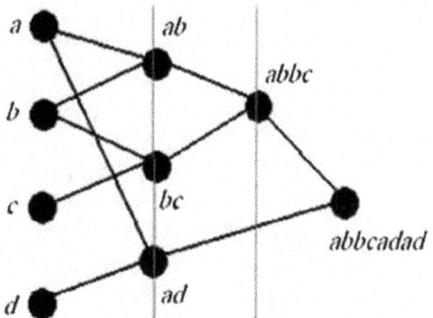

Figure 1. Example GMDH ANN.

Genetic algorithms can be used to derive the optimal connectivity configurations of such GMDH networks. The genome or chromosome representation, which depicts the topology of a GMDH-type neural network, consists of a symbolic string composed of alphabetic representation of input variables. In this coding scheme, each input variable is assigned an alphabetic name and the chromosome is a string consisting of the concatenated sub-strings of these names. In other words, for a given input vector $X = (x_1, x_2, \ldots, x_n)$, a chromosome can be represented as a string of the concatenated symbols of $\alpha_i \in \{a, b, c, d, \ldots\}$ in the form of $choromosome = (\alpha_1, \alpha_2, \ldots, \alpha_i, \ldots)$, where "a," "b," "c," etc., stand for alphabetical name of inputs x_1, x_2, x_3, etc., respectively.

The same procedure for defining chromosomes described by Nariman-Zadeh et al. (2005) can now be readily modified to apply to GS-GMDH networks. This modification is accomplished by repeating the name of the neuron which directly passes the next layers. For example, a network structure, as depicted in Figure 1, exhibits such a connection between neuron "ad" and the output layer. It is clear that neuron "ad" in the first hidden layer is connected to the output layer by directly bypassing the second hidden layer. Therefore, the name of the output neuron includes "ad" twice as "abbcadad." Essentially, a virtual neuron named "adad" has been constructed in the second hidden layer and used with "abbc" in the same layer to make the output neuron "abbcadad." It should be noted that in this coding method such repetition occurs whenever a neuron passes adjacent hidden layers and connects to a neuron in subsequent layers. The number of repetitions of that neuron's signifier depends on the number of passed hidden layers, $\tilde{n}$, and is calculated as $2^{\tilde{n}}$. It is evident that a chromosome such as "abab bcbc," unlike chromosome "abab acbc," is not valid in GS-GMDH networks, and therefore it should be rewritten as "abbc."

2.2. Application of the network to the Colebrook–White equation

For the purposes of finding an explicit form of the Colebrook–White equation, it is sufficient to consider two inputs—the Reynolds number and relative roughness—and one output—the friction factor. As suggested by multiple prior studies (Sablani & Shayya, 2003; Sablani et al., 2003; Shayya et al., 2005) and independently verified by this study, transforming the inputs with a base-ten logarithm greatly improves the accuracy of the resultant ANN model. As such, the two inputs used in developing this ANN model were the base-ten logarithms of Reynolds number and relative roughness—i.e. $\log_{10} Re$ and $\log_{10}(\epsilon/D)$. Also, a variety of transforms for the friction factor output is essayed, including a base-ten logarithm and several negative rational exponents between zero and one. It was determined through analysis of the resultant models' coefficients of determination (compared to the Colebrook–White equation) that the most accurate networks were obtained when the friction factor output was transformed by raising it to the power of negative one-half. As such, the output used to train and test the network was the inverse of the square root of the friction factor, $1/\sqrt{f}$. These inputs and outputs are not unexpected, as they mimic the form of the Colebrook–White and Haaland equations (Equations 2 and 3).

In addition to strategic transformation of the input and output data, a sufficiently large and appropriately spaced sampling set of input variables is necessary to ensure that the training and testing of

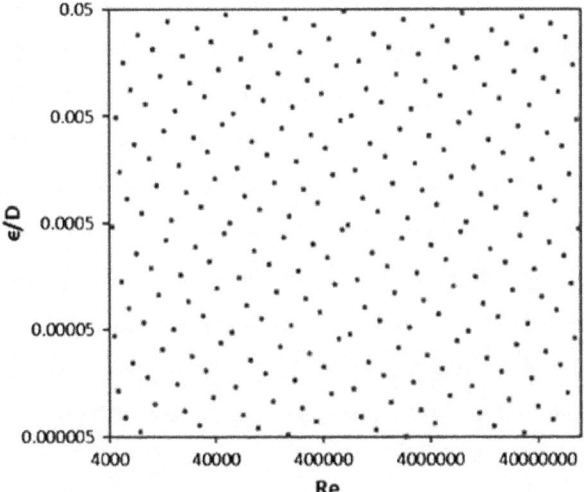

Figure 2. Distribution of samples over the range of Reynolds number and relative roughness.

the neural network results in an accurate model. To achieve adequate distribution over the range of input variables, Hammersley sequence sampling (Press et al., 2007) was employed to generate 250 sample points between 0 and 1 in two dimensions, and these fractional values were applied over the individual variable ranges to create the input data sampling set. The range of inputs considered, prior to logarithmic transform, was as follows: Reynolds number from 4,000 to 10^8 and relative roughness from 5×10^{-6} to 0.05. It was determined that using such a sampling method will allow for greater accuracy with fewer training/testing points. The sampling set is shown in Figure 2.

The output data for training and testing the network were obtained by non-linear solution of the Colebrook–White equation for each of the 250 data points generated by the Hammersley sampling algorithm. A variant of the Powell dogleg method was used to solve the non-linear, transcendental equations at each data point; thereafter, the friction factor data was transformed into the appropriate ANN output, as described previously. To train the network, a total of 125 points of the sampling set were used—that is, an equal number of points were used to train and then test the network. To prevent either the training or testing sets from becoming biased to any particular region of the input data range, the 250-point Hammersley sampling set was randomized prior to equal separation into training and testing sampling sets. In the next step, genetic algorithms were used to find an optimal structure of the GMDH-type neural network to yield an explicit equation for friction factor. Two hidden layers were ultimately settled upon for the general structure of the network: while three hidden layers provided some improved accuracy, the reduction in error in that case was deemed too slight to justify the additional complexity of the model.

2.3. Error analysis
In comparison with the Colebrook–White equation and other efforts made in this field of study, the following error analysis metrics were used.

Coefficient of Determination

$$R^2 = 1 - \frac{\Sigma \left(f_p - f_d\right)^2}{\Sigma \left(f_d\right)^2} \tag{8}$$

Mean Relative Error

$$\text{MRE} = \frac{1}{n} \sum_{i=1}^{n} \left| \frac{f_p - f_d}{f_d} \right| \tag{9}$$

Mean Absolute Error

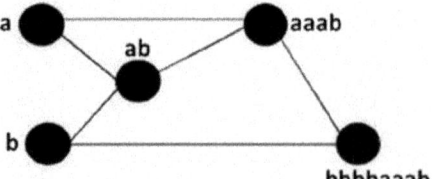

Figure 3. Optimal structure of GS-GMDH network for modeling of friction factor.

$$MAE = \frac{1}{n} \sum_{i=1}^{n} \left| f_p - f_d \right| \tag{10}$$

Here, f_p is the predicted value from the ANN, f_d is the desired value from the iterative solution of the Colebrook–White equation, and n is the total number of data points—in this case, 250. R^2 is especially important here, as it measures the accuracy of the overall fit of the predicted data to the desired outputs. A value of unity indicates perfect correlation. For the mean-relative and mean-absolute errors (MRE, MAE), the greater the quantity, the greater the disagreement between the predicted and desired values. The MRE, incidentally, provides a more objective quantification of error than the MAE, as it normalizes the measured error to the mean value of the dataset in question.

3. Results and discussion

The input–output data-set was used to train a GMDH-type neural network to find a polynomial model of friction factor in terms of the input variables. In order to genetically refine this GMDH-type ANN, a population of 40 individuals in 120 generations with a crossover probability of 0.95 and a mutation probability of 0.01 was used; no additional improvement was observed for larger population sizes. The objective functions to be minimized simultaneously were the prediction and test error functions; the final trade-off structure of GMDH-type neural network was optimally selected by a genetic algorithm that minimized these two objective functions. The resultant ANN structure is shown in Figure 3, where "a" and "b" represent $\log_{10}(Re)$ and $\log_{10}(\epsilon/D)$, respectively.

The corresponding polynomial representation of the model is as follows.

$$y_1 = -0.434566150456166 + 1.198691961744151a - 0.260419382502325b$$
$$- 0.176284322797722a^2 - 0.246506318905692b^2 - 0.452913784505939ab$$

$$y_2 = -0.264590878809085 + 0.104548473076918a + 0.991211881271789y_1$$
$$+ 0.027044863177819a^2 + 0.036354915327913y_1^2 - 0.075133478936023ay_1$$

$$y_3 = 0.049539595715222 - 0.574835644104601b + 0.741634220598117y_2$$
$$- 0.096991484123168b^2 + 0.016506184006448y_2^2 - 0.006996298079579by_2$$

$$f = \frac{1}{y_3^2}$$

Figure 4 shows the ability of the polynomial function to predict friction factor with a high level of accuracy. In Figure 4(a), we see the model function's behavior relative to that of the Colebrook–White equation over the entire 250-point data-set, with most deviation observed for higher values of the friction factor. In Figure 4(b), selected constant values for relative roughness were used to reproduce a simplified version of the classical Moody diagram: the performance of the ANN model is shown in solid and dashed lines with data points from the Colebrook–White equation overlain. Again, we see greater deviation at

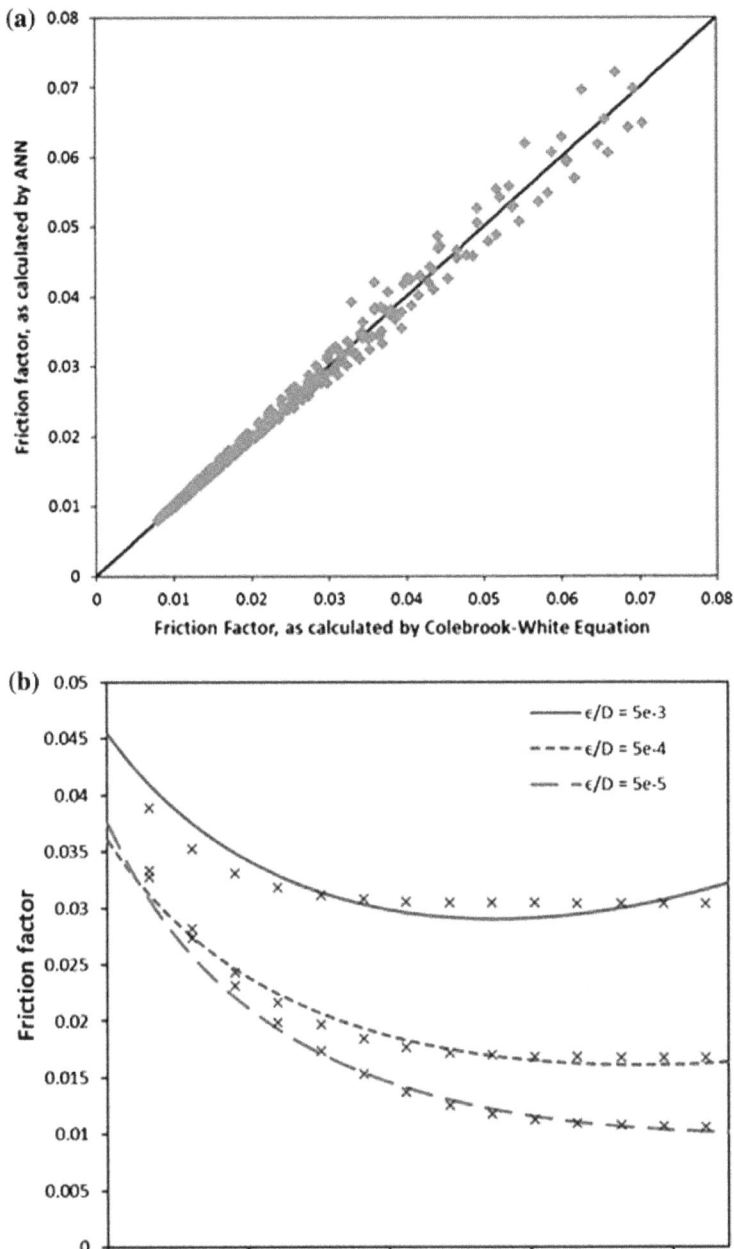

Figure 4. (a) Correlation plot of the model versus the Colebrook–White equation for the entire dataset (b) A simplified reproduction of the classical Moody diagram using the ANN model (solid and dashed lines) with Colebrook–White data points (X) overlain.

higher friction factor values. Also, it seems the model is more accurate (compared to the Colebrook–White equation) for lower relative roughness values and higher Reynolds number values.

In the review of previous work on this topic, the authors noted several statistical measurements that were common to many of the publications. Three of these statistical tools were selected to compare the ANN model developed herein to previously developed ANNs. Table 2 shows the error measurements and complexity of the various neural networks. It is clear from this table that the model developed in this study has the simplest structure among those considered, yet it maintains a high degree of accuracy.

Table 2. Comparison of error and network complexity between this paper and other investigations

References	Structure	No. of neurons	R^2	MRE	MAE
This study	2-1-1-1	5	0.9954	0.0344	0.0011
Shayya et al. (2005)	2-12-12-12-1	39	0.9899	0.0173	0.00013
Sablani et al. (2003)	2-8-8-1	19	0.9870	0.0201	0.000079
Sablani et al. (2003)	2-4-1	7	0.972	0.0316	0.00105
Sablani and Shayya (2003)	2-12-12-1	27	0.9999	0.0019	2.0E-7
Shayya and Sablani (1998)	2-14-14-14-1	45	0.9996	0.0122	3.0E-6
Bilgil and Altun (2008)	6-7-15-1	29	0.9926	–	–
Özger and Yildirim (2009)	2-6-9-9-1-1	28	–	0.0068	–

Only one other study produced a polynomial equation as an approximation for friction factor. Using a related method of genetic programming, Davidson et al. produced a 14-term polynomial in order to explicitly determine f (Davidson et al., 1999). Further, they found that this polynomial performed 33% better than the explicit Haaland equation; in terms of computational cost, it was simpler for computers as such a model requires no transcendental functions, unlike Haaland or any other explicit approximation of the Colebrook–White equation (Davidson et al., 1999). However, Davidson's polynomial applies to a much narrower range of both Reynolds number and relative roughness, 10^5–10^6 and 0.001–0.01, respectively.

This study considered the entire range of applicability of the Colebrook–White equation: 4,000–10^8 for Reynolds number; 5×10^{-6}–0.05 for relative roughness. The GS-GMDH offers a compromise on both fronts, whereby a polynomial can be given that applies to a realistic, applicable range for input variables, while still avoiding transcendental, large ANNs, and complex computations. Further, as is evident from Table 2, a good fit is obtained with acceptable error for a very simple network and system of model equations.

4. Conclusions

A GMDH-type neural network model was designed to predict friction factor from Reynolds number and relative roughness. The minimum error was achieved by using base-ten logarithms of the inputs, Reynolds number and relative roughness, and the inverse square root of the output, friction factor, as the input and output, respectively, used to train and test the neural network. Using Hammersley sequence sampling method decreased the quantity of input data to only 250 points, from which 125 were used for training and 125 were used for testing the neural network. A genetic algorithm was used to refine the model based on the minimization of two objective functions, the training and testing error. The regressed polynomial representation of friction factor showed a low percentage of error despite its simplicity. The value of the numerical methods used in the development of this model lay in their ability to derive a relatively simple system of equations with relatively low computational cost—lower volume of training/testing data, smaller population sizes and fewer generations in the EA, etc.

The simplicity of the ANN model developed here is one of its primary strengths. Transcendental functions, such as those seen in the Colebrook–White equation and many of its approximations, carry a high computational cost. For applications such as large-scale piping networks, which involve high volume of computation by their very nature, or for continuous computation applications, such as process system controls, the use of a model such as that presented here would improve the speed of the computations involved in calculation of the friction factor (e.g. for real-time determination or estimation of pressure drop in pipe flow).

Another strength of this method is its inherent tunability. Note that while this model showed a 3.4% relative error to the data with which it was trained and tested, the Colebrook–White equation itself can vary by as much as 15% from real fluid flow behavior. This model, unlike the Colebrook–White equation, can be tuned to represent a real system through use of experimental data. It is believed that the accuracy and simplicity of this method, as well as its simplicity in development, may make it preferable to traditional, transcendental representations of fluid friction factor.

Funding
The authors received no direct funding for this research.

Author details
Saeb M. Besarati[1]
E-mail: sbesarati@mail.usf.edu
Philip D. Myers[1]
E-mail: PhilipMyers@mail.usf.edu
ORCID ID: http://orcid.org/0000-0002-4591-3319
David C. Covey[2]
E-mail: coveydc@gmail.com
Ali Jamali[3]
E-mail: Ali.jamali@guilan.ac.ir
[1] Department of Chemical and Biomedical Engineering, University of South Florida, 4202 E Fowler Ave, ENB118, Tampa, FL, USA.
[2] Department of Mechanical Engineering, University of South Florida, 4202 E Fowler Ave, ENB118, Tampa, FL, USA.
[3] Department of Mechanical Engineering, Engineering Faculty, The University of Guilan, P.O. Box 3756, Rasht, Iran.

References
Atashkari, K., Nariman-Zadeh, N., Gölcü, M., Khalkhali, A., & Jamali, A. (2007). Modelling and multi-objective optimization of a variable valve-timing spark-ignition engine using polynomial neural networks and evolutionary algorithms. *Energy Conversion and Management, 48*, 1029–1041. http://dx.doi.org/10.1016/j.enconman.2006.07.007

Bilgil, A., & Altun, H. (2008). Investigation of flow resistance in smooth open channels using artificial neural networks. *Flow Measurement and Instrumentation, 19*, 404–408. http://dx.doi.org/10.1016/j.flowmeasinst.2008.07.001

Colebrook, C. F. (1939). Turbulent flow in pipes, with particular reference to the transition region between the smooth and rough pipe laws. *Journal of the ICE, 11*, 133–156. http://dx.doi.org/10.1680/ijoti.1939.13150

Davidson, J. W., Savic, D., & Walters, G. A. (1999). Method for the identification of explicit polynomial formulae for the friction in turbulent pipe flow. *Journal of Hydroinformatics, 1*, 115–126.

Fadare, D. A., & Ofidhe, U. I. (2009). Artificial neural network model for prediction of friction factor in pipe flow. *Journal of Applied Sciences, 5*, 662–670.

Farlow, S. J. (1984). *Self-organizing method in modeling: GMDH type algorithm.* New York, NY: Marcel Dekker.

Fausett, L. (1993). *Fundamentals of neural networks.* Upper Saddle River, NJ: Prentice Hall.

Haaland, S. E. (1983). Simple and explicit formulas for the friction factor in turbulent pipe flow. *Journal of Fluids Engineering, 105*, 89–90. http://dx.doi.org/10.1115/1.3240948

Iba, H., DeGaris, H., & Sato, T. (1996). A numerical approach to genetic programming for system identification. *Evolutionary Computation, 3*, 417–452.

Ivakhnenko, A. G. (1971). Polynomial theory of complex systems. *IEEE Transactions on Systems, Man, and Cybernetics, 1*, 364–378.

http://dx.doi.org/10.1109/TSMC.1971.4308320

Jamali, A., Nariman-zadeh, N., Darvizeh, A., Masoumi, A., & Hamrang, S. (2009). Multi-objective evolutionary optimization of polynomial neural networks for modelling and prediction of explosive cutting process. *Engineering Applications of Artificial Intelligence, 22*, 676–687. http://dx.doi.org/10.1016/j.engappai.2008.11.005

Mittal, G. S., & Zhang, J. (2007). Friction factor prediction for Newtonian and non-Newtonian fluids in pipe flows using neural networks. *International Journal of Food Engineering, 3*(1), 1–18.

Nariman-Zadeh, N., Darvizeh, A., & Ahmad-Zadeh, G. R. (2003). Hybrid genetic design of GMDH-type neural networks using singular value decomposition for modelling and prediction of the explosive cutting process. *Proceedings of the Institution of Mechanical Engineers Part B: Journal of Engineering Manufacture, 217*, 779–790. http://dx.doi.org/10.1243/09544050360673161

Nariman-Zadeh, N., Darvizeh, A., Jamali, A., & Moeini, A. (2005). Evolutionary design of generalized polynomial neural networks for modelling and prediction of explosive forming process. *Journal of Materials Processing Technology, 164–165*, 1561–1571. http://dx.doi.org/10.1016/j.jmatprotec.2005.02.020

Onwubolu, G. C. (2009). *Hybrid self-organizing modeling systems.* Berlin-Heidelberg: Springer-Verlag. http://dx.doi.org/10.1007/978-3-642-01530-4

Özger, M., & Yildirim, G. (2009). Determining turbulent flow friction coefficient using adaptive neuro-fuzzy computing techniques. *Advances in Engineering Software, 40*, 281–287.

Press, W. H., Teukolsky, S. A., Vetterling, W. T., & Flannery, B. P. (2007). *Numerical recipes: The art of scientific computing* (3rd ed.). Cambridge: Cambridge University Press.

Sablani, S. S., & Shayya, W. H. (2003). Neural network based non-iterative calculation of the friction factor for power law fluids. *Journal of Food Engineering, 57*, 327–335. http://dx.doi.org/10.1016/S0260-8774(02)00347-3

Sablani, S. S., Shayya, W. H., & Kacimov, A. (2003). Explicit calculation of the friction factor in pipeline flow of Bingham plastic fluids: A neural network approach. *Chemical Engineering Science, 58*, 99–106. http://dx.doi.org/10.1016/S0009-2509(02)00440-2

Samadianfard, S. (2012). Gene expression programming analysis of implicit Colebrook–White equation in turbulent flow friction factor calculation. *Journal of Petroleum Science and Engineering, 92–93*, 48–55. http://dx.doi.org/10.1016/j.petrol.2012.06.005

Shayya, W. H., & Sablani, S. S. (1998). An artificial neural network for non-iterative calculation of the friction factor in pipeline flow. *Computers and Electronics in Agriculture, 21*, 219–228. http://dx.doi.org/10.1016/S0168-1699(98)00032-5

Shayya, W. H., Sablani, S. S., & Campo, A. (2005). Explicit calculation of the friction factor for non-Newtonian fluids using artificial neural networks. *Developments in Chemical Engineering and Mineral Processing, 13*, 5–20.

Tufail, M., & Ormsbee, L. E. (2006). A fixed function set genetic algorithm (FFSGA) approach for function approximation. *Journal of Hydroinformatics, 8*, 193–206.

Vatankhah, A. R. (2014). Comment on "Gene expression programming analysis of implicit Colebrook–White equation in turbulent flow friction factor calculation". *Journal of Petroleum Science and Engineering, 124*, 402–405. http://dx.doi.org/10.1016/j.petrol.2013.12.001

White, F. M. (1998). *Fluid mechanics* (4th ed.). Boston, MA: McGraw-Hill.

Yazdi, M., & Bardi, A. (2011). Estimation of friction factor in pipe flow using artificial neural networks. *Canadian Journal on Automation, Control and Intelligent Systems, 2,* 52–56.

Yuhong, Z., & Wenxin, H. (2009). Application of artificial neural network to predict the friction factor of open channel flow. *Communications in Nonlinear Science and Numerical Simulation, 14,* 2373–2378. http://dx.doi.org/10.1016/j.cnsns.2008.06.020

9

The performance of immune-based neural network with financial time series prediction

Dhiya Al-Jumeily[1]* and Abir J. Hussain[1]

*Corresponding author: Dhiya Al-Jumeily, Faculty of Engineering and Technology, Applied Computing Research Group, Liverpool John Moores University, Byrom Street, Liverpool L3 3AF, UK

E-mail: d.aljumeily@ljmu.ac.uk

Reviewing editor: Duc Pham, University of Birmingham, UK

Abstract: This paper presents the use of immune-based neural networks that include multilayer perceptron (MLP) and functional neural network for the prediction of financial time series signals. Extensive simulations for the prediction of one-and five-steps-ahead of stationary and non-stationary time series were performed which indicate that immune-based neural networks in most cases demonstrated advantages in capturing chaotic movement in the financial signals with an improvement in the profit return and rapid convergence over MLPs.

Subjects: Artificial Intelligence; Computation; Software Engineering & Systems Development; Technology

Keywords: financial signals; immune-based neural network; time series prediction

1. Introduction

Neural networks have been shown to be a promising tool for forecasting financial times series. Numerous research and application of neural networks for business applications have proven their advantage in relation to classical methods that do not include artificial intelligence. What makes this particular use of neural networks so attractive to financial analysts and traders is the fact that government sectors and companies have used this technique to make decisions on investment and trading. However, when the number of inputs to the model and the number of training examples becomes extremely large, the training procedure for ordinary neural network architectures becomes

ABOUT THE AUTHOR

Dhiya Al-Jumeily is a principal lecturer in applied computing and leads the applied computing research group at the faculty of Engineering and Technology. He is also the Head of Enterprise for the faculty and he has already developed fully the first online MSc and BSc Courses for Liverpool John Moores University. He has published numerous referred research papers in multidisciplinary research areas including: Applied Artificial Intelligence, Neural Networks, Signal Prediction, Telecommunication Fraud Detection, Health Informatics, Personalised Health Care, Image Compression and Technology Enhanced Learning. He is a PhD supervisor and an external examiner for the degree of PhD. He has been actively involved as a member of editorial board and review committee for a number of peer-reviewed international journals, and is on program committee or as a general chair for a number of international conferences.

PUBLIC INTEREST STATEMENT

As businesses grow in size and scale it becomes increasingly difficult to predict how its' stocks and revenue will fluctuate. This can be sorted by using artificial neural networks, data processes that monitor and react to data according to how they were trained, it allows them to not only recognise patterns but also, in certain types of artificial neural network, teach itself to react differently to that pattern. The major limitation of artificial neural networks is the time it takes to train them, which increases exponentially as you increase the amount of data they must process. The purpose of this study is to compare a new form of artificial neural network against the current forms and evaluate the outcome of the tests, in hopes of seeing an improvement in performance for the new version over the old.

tremendously slow and unduly tedious. To overcome such time-consuming operations, this research work proposes the use of immune-based neural network to improve the recognition and generalisation capability of the backpropagation neural networks.

The efficient market hypothesis states that a stock price, at any given time, reflects the state of the environment for that stock at that time. That is, the stock price is dependent on different variables, such as news events, other stock prices and exchange rates. The hypothesis suggests that future trends are completely unpredictable and subject to random occurrences. Thus making it infeasible, to use historical data or financial information, to produce above average returns. However, in reality, market responses are not always instantaneous. Markets may be slow to react due to poor human reaction time or other psychological factors associated with the human actors in the system. Therefore, in these circumstances, it is possible to predict financial data, based on previous results (Jensen, 1978). There is a significant body of evidence showing that markets do not work in a totally efficient manner. Much of the research shows that stock market returns are predictable by various methods such as; time series data analysis on financial and economic variables (Fama & French, 1989; Fama & Schwert, 1977; Ferson, 1989).

Various studies have been carried out on the use of neural networks for financial time series prediction; these include the forecasting behaviour of the financial market using neural networks. Multiple decisions, each of which affects the performance of the neural networks forecasting model, must be made, including; which data to use, the size and the architecture of the neural network systems (Zhang, 2003). The following are some of the difficulties of using neural networks in financial time series applications:

- There are infinitely many models which fit the training data well, but few of them generalise well. Supplementary degrees of freedom may lead to a better fitting of the model during the training of the network, but to worse generalisation ability on the out-of-sample data (Lendasse, de Bodt, Wertz, & Verleysen, 2000).
- In order to form a more accurate model, it is desirable to use as large training set as possible. However, for the case of highly non-stationary data, increasing the size of training set results in more data with statistics that are less relevant to the task at hand being used in the creation of the model.
- The high noise and too many parameters (compared to the number of data available) make the models prone to overfitting (Dorffner, 1996; Lendasse et al., 2000).
- The requirement of large number of sample data, due to their large number of free parameters (Dorffner, 1996). The limitation exists for the fact that some new founded companies do not have much of the previous data.

To improve the recognition and generalisation capability of the backpropagation neural networks, Widyanto, Nobuhara, Kawamoto, Hirota, and Kusumoputro (2005) used a hidden layer inspired by immune algorithm (SMIA) for the prediction of sinusoidal signal and time temperature-based quality food data. Their simulations indicated that the prediction of sinusoidal signal showed an improvement of 1/17 in the approximation error in comparison to the backpropagation and 18% improvement in the recognition capability for the prediction of time temperature-based quality food data.

In this paper, we propose the use of a multilayer perceptron (MLP), the functional link networks and the self-organised neural network inspired by the SMIA for single and multi-step ahead prediction of financial time series. Furthermore, a novel application of the regularisation technique is used with the self-organised MLPs network that is inspired by the immune algorithm (R_SMIA). The aim is to increase the generalisation ability of the SMIA network for financial time series prediction and to avoid the problem of overfitting for the purpose of improving the prediction ability of the self-organised multilayer neural network which is inspired by SMIA.

Ten financial time series are used to test the performance of the various networks such as the exchange rates time series and the oil price. In these extensive experiments, our primary interest is to concentrate on the profitable value contained in the predictions for all neural network models and hence during generalisation. The work focuses more on how the network generates the profits. For this reason, the neural networks structure, which provides the highest percentage of annualised return (AR) on out-of-sample data, is considered to be the best. A new training algorithm was utilised with the self-organised neural network that is inspired by the SMIA using weight decay; the simulation results indicated significant improvement of the proposed training algorithm over the standard network.

2. Financial time series forecasting

Time series forecasting is the process of predicting future values using current values. Forecasting the behaviour of the financial market is a non-trivial task due to its non-linear and non-stationary behaviour, furthermore it has been suggested that some financial time series are not predictable (Thimm, 1995).

Dunis and Wiliams (2002) implemented Neural Network Regression to forecast foreign exchange rates on UER/USD time series data. The study was benchmarked against several traditional forecasting techniques including Naïve Strategy, MACD Strategy, ARMA Methodology and Logit Estimation. Their observations have confirmed the applicability of neural network for financial forecasting.

Yao and Tan (2000) examined the forecasting performance of neural network on the exchange rates between American Dollar and five other major currencies; Japanese Yen, Deutsch Mark, British Pound, Swiss Franc and Australian Dollar. The results showed that without the use of extensive market data or knowledge, useful prediction can be made and significant paper profits can be achieved for out-of-sample data. They also concluded that a backpropagation network used in their study has proved to be adequate for forecasting and simple technical indicators such as moving average (MA) are enough.

Another approach for time series forecasting can be found in (Lawrence & Giles, 2000) which analysed the predictability of major world stock markets such as Canada, France, Germany, Japan, United Kingdom (UK) the United States (US), and the world excluding US (World) using MLP models. They found that MLP models with logistic activation functions predict daily stock returns better than the traditional ordinary least squares and general linear regression models. Neural networks are promising tool for forecasting financial times series. They have been widely used to model the behaviour of financial time series and to forecast future values (Yao & Tan, 2000).

3. Traditional approaches to time series prediction

The standard method for time series prediction is the statistical linear approach. In this approach, the signal S_n is considered the output of a system with unknown input u_n and its value is determined by the linear combinations of previous outputs and inputs according to the following equation (Makhoul, 1975):

$$S_n = \sum_{k=1}^{P} a_k S_{n-k} + G \sum_{m=0}^{q} b_m u_{n-m}, \quad b_0 = 1 \tag{1}$$

where a_k, b_m and G are the model parameters. Usually, the input u_n is modelled by a zero mean Gaussian noise source. The above equation can be specified in the frequency domain by taking the Z transform of both sides of the equation. Let $H(Z)$ represent the transfer function of the system in the Z domain, then:

$$H(Z) = \frac{S(Z)}{U(Z)} = G \frac{1 + \sum_{m=1}^{q} b_m z^m}{1 + \sum_{k=1}^{p} a_k z^k} \tag{2}$$

And the Z transform of the signal is:

$$S(Z) = \sum_{n=\infty}^{\infty} s_n z^n \tag{3}$$

In this case, the roots of the numerator and the denominator of the transfer function $H(Z)$ are the zeros and the poles of the model, respectively. When $a_k = 0$, the model is considered as all zeros and called the Moving Average (MA) model, when $b_m = 0$, the model is considered as all poles and known as Autoregressive (AR) model, while a model that has pole sand zeros values is referred to as an autoregressive moving average (ARMA) model.

For the non-linear model, we have:

$$g(S_n, S_{n-1}, S_{n-2}, \ldots) = u_n \tag{4}$$

In this case, u_n is a zero mean white noise. The function g is a highly non-linear and very complicated. Non-linear prediction can be determined using either the Volterra or the bilinear models, where the process is assumed to be inevitable, i.e. u_n can be approximated using a finite number of terms (Manikopoulos, 1992) and in which:

$$S_n = \sum_i a_i u_n + \sum_i \sum_j a_{ij} u_{ni} u_{nj} + \sum_i \sum_j \sum_k a_{ijk} u_{ni} u_{nj} u_{nk} + \ldots \tag{5}$$

Using the discrete Volterra series expansion. Where $\{u_i\}$, $\{u_{ij}\}$, $\{u_{ijk}\}$ are Gaussian random variables and $\{a_i\}$, $\{a_{ij}\}$, $\{a_{ijk}\}$ are sets of constant coefficients.

Using the bilinear model, we can determine S_n as follows:

$$S_n = \sum_{i=1}^{P} a_i S_{ni} + \sum_{j=1}^{q} a_j u_{nj} + \sum_{l=1}^{P} \sum_{m=1}^{q} b_{lm} S_{nl} u_{nm} \tag{6}$$

where $c_0 = 0$, and u_n is a white noise process.

To solve the non-linear model, it is required to determine the unknown parameters, which are usually very difficult to determine using traditional methods. Neural networks can be used to solve this problem in which the parameters (weights and biases) are determined implicitly using suitable training algorithms.

4. The networks
Although most neural network models share a common goal in performing functional mapping, different network architectures may vary significantly in their ability to handle different types of problems. For some tasks, higher order combinations of some of the inputs or activations may be appropriate to help form good representation for solving the problems.

This section is concerned with introducing Functional link neural network, and the Immune-based neural networks.

4.1. Functional link neural network (FLNN)
FLNN was first introduced by Giles and Maxwell (1987). It naturally extends the family of theoretical feedforward network structure by introducing non-linearities in inputs patterns enhancements (Durbin & Rumelhart, 1989). These enhancement nodes act as supplementary inputs to the network. FLNN calculates the product of the network inputs at the input layer, while at the output layer the summations of the weighted inputs are calculated.

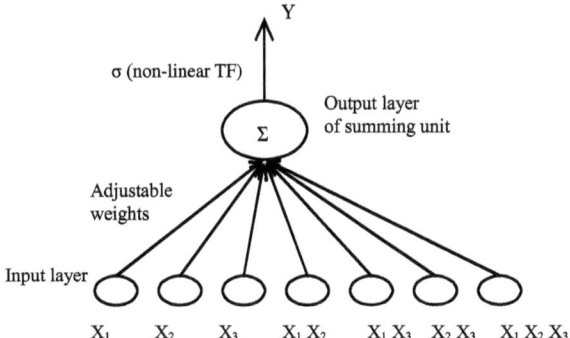

Figure 1. Functional link neural network.

FLNN can use higher order correlations of the input components to perform non-linear mappings using only a single layer of units. Since the architecture is simpler, it is suppose to reduce computational cost in the training stage, whilst maintaining good approximation performance (Mirea & Marcu, 2002). A single node in FLNN model could receive information from more than one node by one weighted link. The higher order weights, which connect the high order terms of the input products to the upper nodes, have simulated the interaction among several weighted links. For that reason, FLNN could greatly enhance the information capacity and complex data could be learnt (Cass & Radl, 1996; Giles & Maxwell, 1987; Mirea & Marcu, 2002).

Fei and Yu (1994) showed that FLNN has a powerful approximation capability than conventional Backpropagation network, and it is a good model for system identification (Mirea & Marcu, 2002). Cass and Radl (1996) used FLNN in the optimisation process and found that FLNN can be trained much faster than MLP network without scarifying computational capability. FLNN has the properties of invariant under geometric transformations (Durbin & Rumelhart, 1989). The model has the advantage of inherent invariance, and only learns the desired signal. Figure 1 shows an example of third-order FLNN with three external inputs X_1, X_2 and X_3, and four high order inputs which act as supplementary inputs to the network.

The output of FLNN is determined as follows:

$$Y = \sigma \left(W_0 + \sum_j W_j X_j + \sum_{j,k} W_{jk} X_j X_k + \sum_{j,k,l} W_{jkl} X_j X_k X_l + \ldots \right) \tag{7}$$

where σ is a non-linear transfer function, and W_0 is the adjustable threshold. Unfortunately, FLNN suffers from the explosion of weights which increase exponentially with the number of inputs. As a result, second- or third-order functional link networks are considered in practice (Kaita, Tomita, & Yamanaka, 2002; Thimm, 1995).

4.2. The self-organised network inspired by the SMIA

The SMIA which was first introduced by Timmis (2001) has attracted many interests. Widyanto et al. (2005) introduced a method to improve recognition as well as generalisation capability of the backpropagation by suggesting a self-organisation hidden layer inspired by SMIA network. The input vector and hidden layer of SMIA network are considered as antigen and recognition ball, respectively. The recognition ball which is the generation of the immune system is used for hidden unit creation.

In time series prediction, the recognition balls are used to solve overfitting problem. In the immune system, the recognition ball has a single epitope and many paratopes. In which, the epitope is attached to B cell and paratopes are attached to antigen, where there is a single B cell that represents several antigens.

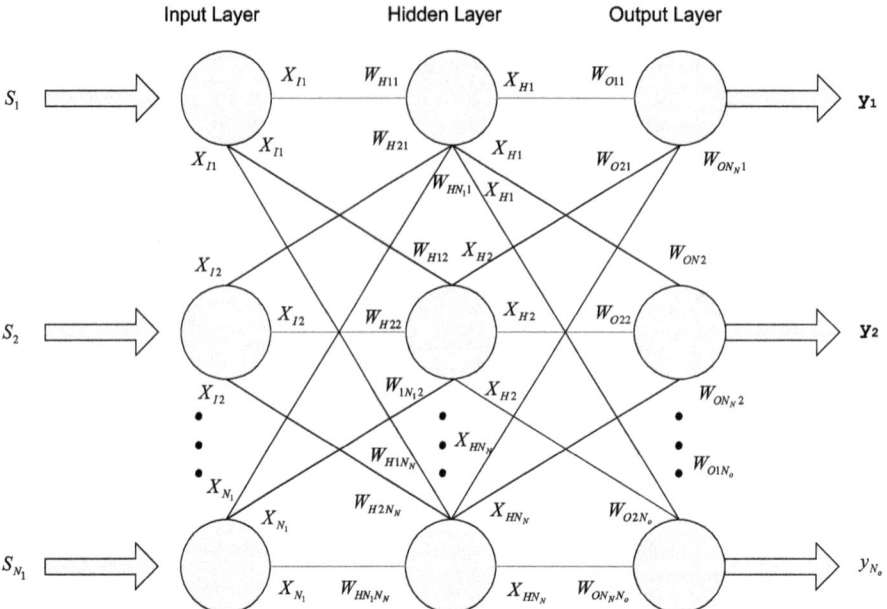

Figure 2. The structure of the SMIA network (Widyanto et al., 2005).

For SMIA network, each hidden unit has a centre that represents the number of connections of the input vectors that are attached to it. To avoid the overfitting problem, each centre has a value which represents the strength of the connections between input units and their corresponding hidden units. The SMIA network consists of three layers which are input, self-organised and output layers as shown in Figure 2.

In what follows the dynamic equations of SMIA network are considered. The ith input unit receives normalised external input S_i where $i = 1, ..., N_I$ and N_I represents the number of inputs. The output of the hidden units is determined by the Euclidean distance between the outputs of input units and the connection strength of input units and the jth hidden unit. The use of the Euclidian distance enables the SMIA network to exploit locality information of input data. This can lead to improve the recognition capability. The output of the jth hidden unit is determined as follows:

$$X_{Hj} = f\left(\sqrt{\sum_{i=1}^{N_I}\left(W_{Hij} - X_{Ii}\right)^2}\right)$$
$$j = 1, ... , N_H$$

(8)

where W_{Hij} represents the strength of the connection from the ith input unit to the jth hidden unit, and f is a non-linear transfer function.

The outputs of the hidden units represent the inputs to the output layer. The network output can be determined as follows:

$$y_k = g\left(\sum_{j=1}^{N_H} W_{ojk}X_{Hj} + b_{ok}\right)$$
$$k = 1, ... , N_o$$

(9)

where W_{ojk} represents the strength of the connection from the jth hidden unit to the kth output unit and b_{ok} is the bias associated with the kth output unit, while g is the non-linear transfer function.

4.3. Training the SMIA network

In this subsection, the training algorithm of the SMIA network will be shown. Furthermore, a B cell construction-based hidden unit creation will be described.

For the SMIA, inside the recognition ball, there is a single B cell which represents several antigens. In this case, the hidden unit is considered as the recognition ball of SMIA. Let $d(t + 1)$ represents the desired response of the network at time $t + 1$. The error of the network at time $t + 1$ is defined as:

$$e(t+1)=d(t+1)-y(t+1) \tag{10}$$

The cost function of the network is the squared error between the original and the predicted value, that is:

$$J(t+1) = \frac{1}{2}[e(t+1)]^2 \tag{11}$$

The aim of the learning algorithm is to minimise the squared error by a gradient descent procedure. Therefore, the change for any specified element W_{oij} of the weights matrix is determined according to the following equation:

$$\Delta W_{oij}(t+1)=-\eta\frac{\partial J(t+1)}{\partial W_{oij}} \tag{12}$$

where $(i = 1, ..., N_H, j = 1, ..., N_o)$ and η is a positive real number representing the learning rate.

The change for any specified element b_{ok} of the bias matrix can is determined as follows:

$$\Delta b_{oj}(t+1)=-\eta\frac{\partial J(t+1)}{\partial b_{oj}} \tag{13}$$

where $(j = 1, ..., N_o)$. The initial values of W_{oij} are set to zero and the initial values of b_{oj} are given randomly.

4.4. Regularised SMIA network (R_SMIA)

In this section, the regularisation technique has been introduced in order to improve the performance of the SMIA network. Regularisation is the technique of adding a penalty term Ω to the error function which can help obtaining a smoother network mappings. It is given by:

$$\tilde{A}=E+\lambda\Omega \tag{14}$$

where E represents one of the standard error functions such as the sum-of-squares error and the parameter λ controls the range of the penalty term Ω in which it can influence the form of the solution.

The network training should be implemented by minimising the total error function $\tilde{A}$ (Bishop, 1995). One form of regularisation is called weight decay. This form is based on the sum of the squares of the adaptive parameter in the network.

$$\Omega = \frac{1}{2}\sum_i W_i^2 \tag{15}$$

Although the use of weight decay in some cases leads to degraded performance of the network, it has been proven in most cases that it can avoid the overfitting problem and as a result enhance the network performance (Duda, Hart, & Stork, 2000).

The reason behind the popularity of weight decay approach is the simplicity of using this method. The idea is that every weight once updated, is simply decayed or shrunk as follows:

$$W^{new} = W^{old}(1-\lambda) \tag{16}$$

where $0 < \lambda < 1$. The weight decay is performed by adding a bias term to the original objective function E, thus the weight decay cost function is determined as follows (Bishop, 1995):

$$Ewd = E + (\lambda/2)B \tag{17}$$

where λ is the weight decay rate, B represents the penalty term.

The simplest form of calculating the penalty term B is:

$$B = \sum W_{ij}^2 \tag{18}$$

where W_{ij} is the weight connections between the ith units and jth nodes in the next layer. In R_SMIA network, the weight decay was used to adjust the weights between the hidden nodes and output units. The change of weights using weight decay method could be calculated as follows:

$$\Delta W_{ojk} = -\eta \frac{\partial E}{\partial W_{ojk}} = -\eta \frac{\partial}{\partial W_{ojk}} \left(E_{std} + \frac{\lambda}{2} \sum W_{ojk}^2 \right) \tag{19}$$

$$\Delta W_{ojk} = \eta \left(\sum e\hat{f}_{ot} f_{ot} - \lambda \sum W_{ojk} \right) \tag{20}$$

where ΔW_{ojk} is the updated weights between hidden units and output unit. The R_SMIA network is used to examine the effect of the regularisation technique and to enhance the performance of the SMIA network in the prediction.

5. Prediction of financial signals

Ten noisy financial time series signals are considered as shown in Table 1. All the signals were obtained from a historical database provided by Datastream®, forepart from the IBM common stock closing price time series, which was taken from the Time Series Data Library (Datastream, 2005). The networks are tested for the prediction of one- and five-steps-ahead predictions of financial time series in which two methods are utilised; in the first method, the data are passed directly to the neural network as non-stationary signals; while in the second method, the financial data are transformed into stationary signals.

For non-stationary signals, the data are presented to the networks directly without any transformation. The data are scaled between the upper and lower bounds of the transfer function. On the other hand, the stationary version of the signals needs some series of transformations before passing them to the networks. For the stationary signals, we systematically investigate a method of pre-processing the financial signals in order to reduce the influence of their trends. To smooth out

No	Time series data	Total
Table 1. Financial time series data used		
1	US Dollar to EURO exchange rate (USD/EUR) 01/07/2002–13/11/2008	1607
2	US Dollar to UK Pound exchange rate (USD/UKP) 01/07/2002–13/11/2008	1607
3	Japanese Yen to US Dollar exchange rate (JPY/USD) 01/07/2002–13/11/2008	1607
4	Dow Jones Ind. Average stock opening price (DJIAO) 01/07/2000–11/11/2008	1605
5	Dow Jones Industrial Average stock closing price (DJIAC) 01/07/2000–11/11/2008	1605
6	Dow Jones Utility Average stock opening price (DJUAO) 01/07/2000–11/11/2008	1605
7	Dow Jones Utility Average stock closing price (DJUAC) 01/07/2000–11/11/2008	1605
8	NASDAQ composite stock opening price (NASDAQO) 01/07/2000–12/11/2008	1606
9	NASDAQ composite stock closing price (NASDAQC) 01/07/2000–12/11/2008	1606
10	Oil price of West Texas Intermediate crude (OIL) 01/01/1985–01/11/2008	389

Table 2. Calculations for input and output variables		
	Indicator	**Calculations**
Input variables	EMA15	$P(i) - \overline{EMA_{15}(i)}$
	RDP-5	$(p(i) - p(i-5))/p(i-5) \times 100$
	RDP-10	$(p(i) - p(i-10))/p(i-10) \times 100$
	RDP-15	$(p(i) - p(i-15))/p(i-15) \times 100$
	RDP-20	$(p(i) - p(i-20))/p(i-20) \times 100$
Output variables	RDP+5	$(\overline{p(i+5)} - \overline{p(i)})/\overline{p(i)} \times 100$
		$\overline{p(i)} = \overline{EMA_3(i)}$

Notes: $EMA_n(i)$ is the n-day exponential moving average of the ith day.
$p(i)$ is the closing price of the ith day.

the noise and to reduce the trend, the original raw data was pre-processed into a stationary series by transforming them into measurements of relative difference in percentage of price (RDP) (Thomason, 1999). The calculations for the transformation of input and output variables are presented in Table 2. Subsequent to transformation, all the input and output variables in Table 2 were scaled between the upper and lower bounds of the transfer function in order to avoid computational problems and to meet algorithm requirements.

6. Training the networks
The performances of the SMIA and the R_SMIA are benchmarked against the performance of MLP, the regularised MLP (R_MLP) and the FLNN network. Early stopping was utilised and each signal was divided into three data-sets which are the training, validation and the out-of-sample data which represent 25, 25 and 50% of the entire data-set, respectively. For FLNN, the higher order terms were empirically selected between two and five. The MLP were trained with hidden units varies from three to eight. The prediction performance of all networks was evaluated using three financial metric (Dunis & Wiliams, 2002), where the objective was to use the networks predictions for profit purpose, and three statistical metrics (Cao & Tay, 2003) which provide accurate tracking of the signals, as shown in Table 3.

7. Simulation results
As we are concerned with financial time series prediction, in these extensive experiments, our primary interest is to concentrate on the profitable value contained in the predictions for all neural network models. For this reason, the neural networks structure, which provides the highest percentage of the AR on out-of-sample data, is considered to be the best model. Tables 4–7 summarise the average results of 50 simulations obtained on out-of-sample data for the prediction of both stationary and non-stationary signal, when used to predict one- and five-steps-ahead predictions.

7.1. One-step-ahead prediction (stationary)
For the AR, the simulation results indicated that the R_SMIA network has outperformed the MLP and R_MLP prediction for all the ten stationary signals. Conversely, the R_SMIA set of results shows lowest profits when compared with FLNN. While the R_SMIA network outperformed the SMIA network for forecasting all the signals apart from the JPY/USD exchange rate and the DJIAO stock opining.

Although using the regularisation technique with the standard MLP network results in an improvement in the performance of the R_MLP, the SMIA network has shown the highest profit in all 10 series data than the R_MLP network except for the USD/EUR.

It could be observed that the results of the maximum drawdown demonstrate higher values were obtained using the R_SMIA network when used to predict the USD/UKP, NASDAQO, NASDAQC and OIL time series. The FLNN produced better results in comparison to multilayer networks for the remaining time series.

Table 3. Performance metrics and their calculations	
Annualised return (%AR)	**Normalised mean squared error (NMSE)**
$AR = \frac{Profit}{All\,profit} \times 100$ $Profit = \frac{252}{n} \times CR, \quad CR = \sum_{i=1}^{n} R_i$ $R_i = \begin{cases} +\lvert y_i\rvert & \text{if } (y_i)(\hat{y}_i) \geq 0, \\ -\lvert y_i\rvert & \text{otherwise} \end{cases}$ $All\,profit = \frac{252}{n} \times \sum_{i=1}^{n} abs(R_i)$	$NMSE = \frac{1}{\sigma^2 n} \sum_{i=1}^{n} (y_i - \hat{y}_i)^2$ $\sigma^2 = \frac{1}{n-1} \sum_{i=1}^{n} (y_i - \bar{y})^2$ $\bar{y} = \sum_{i=1}^{n} y_i$
Maximum drawdown (MD)	Signal to noise ratio (SNR)
$MD = \min\left(\sum_{t=1}^{n} \left(CR_t - \max\left(CR_1, \ldots, CR_t \right) \right) \right)$ $CR_t = \sum_{i=1}^{t} R_i, t = 1, \ldots, n$ $R_i = \begin{cases} +\lvert y_i\rvert & \text{if } (y_i)(\hat{y}_i) \geq 0, \\ -\lvert y_i\rvert & \text{otherwise} \end{cases}$	$SNR = 10 \times \log_{10}(\sigma)$ $\sigma = \frac{m^2 \times n}{SSE}$ $SSE = \sum_{i=1}^{n} (y_i - \hat{y}_i)^2$ $m = \max(y_i)$
Annualised volatility (VOL)	Correct directional change (CDC)
$VOL = \sqrt{252} \times \sqrt{\frac{1}{n-1} \sum_{i=1}^{n} (R_i - \bar{R})^2}$	$CDC = \frac{1}{n} \sum_{i=1}^{n} d_i$ $d_i = \begin{cases} 1 & \text{if } (y_i - y_{i-1})(\hat{y}_i - \hat{y}_{i-1}) \geq 0, \\ 0 & \text{otherwise} \end{cases}$

Notes: n is the total number of data patterns.

y and $\hat{y}$ represent the actual and predicted output value, respectively.

Nevertheless, the R_SMIA networks outperformed all multilayer networks in most of the time series. For the volatility, the comparison between the multilayer networks clearly represents that the R_SMIA has the lower values than the other networks except for the prediction of the JPY/USD and DJIAO time series as the values slightly rising. However, the FLNN produces lower volatility than all other networks for predicting all the 10 signals.

When evaluating the Sharpe Ratio (SR) measure, it can be noticed that higher value is preferable. Table 5 indicated that the FLNN provides the best SR.

Figure 3 shows the value of the AR which has been forecasted by all networks used in this research.

In order to compare the rate of the weight decay (decay rate), that were utilised in the prediction of the R_MLP and R_SMIA networks, Figure 4 represents the best decay rate used in this experimental work.

7.2. Five-step-ahead prediction (stationary)
The simulation results indicated that using eight hidden nodes in the MLP and R_MLP network can produce the best average of profits. While four order FLNN model can obtain the highest profits. The simulation results for the prediction of the exchange rate time series using the percentage of AR indicated that the SMIA network outperforms the MLP and the FLNN models by 0.38–10.47%, respectively. These results show that the SMIA network made the best profits on average for all exchange rate data signals when compared to MLP and FLNN networks.

Table 4. Average results on stationary signals for the prediction of one-step ahead

Performance measures	Neural networks	US/UK	JP/US	US/EU	NASDAQO	NASDAQC	DJIAO	DJIAC	DJUAO	DJUAC	OIL
AR (%)	MLP	65.14634	64.72067	69.91986	60.5218	62.32483	59.49555	58.85693	52.97216	52.01663	51.19201
	FLNN	78.18972	77.67146	78.58212	67.91466	67.16377	74.08653	73.57757	72.81365	70.84033	73.64221
	SMIA	73.15769	76.19371	71.00268	62.66176	63.35985	63.71905	62.29099	67.01270	68.02663	72.16195
	R_MLP	69.87597	69.11974	72.43294	61.31236	63.32054	60.396	57.27957	53.52269	56.41693	54.96625
	R_SMIA	73.63894	75.08265	74.79281	63.4887	66.11718	62.14083	63.69784	69.75802	69.74614	73.578
MD	MLP	-1.4304	-1.5806	-1.7923	-4.8447	-4.8762	-4.4906	-2.9165	-6.1459	-5.6157	-19.024
	FLNN	-1.14585	-1.03966	-0.98186	-8.37879	-5.31515	-1.87348	-1.88483	-2.51275	-2.974	-8.70562
	SMIA	-1.51535	-1.24388	-2.69518	-8.84982	-8.32449	-6.60512	-7.99077	-3.55542	-4.17998	-8.32751
	R_MLP	-1.14692	-1.38279	-1.3342	-4.58009	-5.12025	-2.82338	-2.98009	-3.85035	-3.54951	-17.3305
	R_SMIA	-1.14585	-1.37047	-1.24481	-4.19713	-4.14573	-3.10446	-5.62573	-3.29048	-3.3862	-6.76682
AV	MLP	4.526048	5.717462	4.666936	13.27316	12.58836	11.18889	11.27457	12.48506	12.56166	67.3681
	FLNN	4.204148	5.379993	4.428998	12.92789	12.31514	10.48708	10.56609	11.63671	11.78889	59.43905
	SMIA	4.346859	5.424529	4.63746	13.20117	12.53349	11.00119	11.12426	11.93661	11.94297	60.15546
	R_MLP	4.434009	5.621507	4.604267	13.23235	12.53594	11.1544	11.34621	12.51297	12.45137	65.8069
	R_SMIA	4.334805	5.457777	4.539692	13.15954	12.37758	11.07906	11.06588	11.79905	11.84642	59.63936
SR	MLP	14.50009	11.36989	15.00254	4.575426	4.955069	5.322315	5.22938	4.267582	4.169173	0.766643
	FLNN	18.59827	14.43758	17.74275	5.253586	5.453892	7.064812	6.963861	6.257906	6.010538	1.246236
	SMIA	16.83866	14.04827	15.34295	4.742449	5.057593	5.800506	5.610039	5.614729	5.678424	1.20381
	R_MLP	15.76153	12.30291	15.73393	4.649596	5.053141	5.416199	5.051273	4.28039	4.531404	0.857579
	R_SMIA	16.98832	13.75739	16.47533	4.82642	5.341885	5.610178	5.760461	5.912536	5.888317	1.234447
SNR (dB)	MLP	20.35	21.75	22.29	23.7	22.83	24.45	23.26	23.84	23.9	21.03
	FLNN	22.95	23.99	24.26	25.07	23.51	24.99	24.99	25.06	25.15	23.13
	SMIA	21.93	23.41	23.04	24.14	22.75	23.61	23.53	25.02	25.03	22.2
	R_MLP	21.64	22.5	23.38	23.68	23.22	22.98	23	24.27	24.5	21.46
	R_SMIA	22.28	23.4	23.42	24.59	23.18	23.97	23.95	25.13	25.12	23.23
CDC	MLP	67.97	62.59	62.95	65.87	64.53	63.36	64.88	63.34	64.61	61.36
	FLNN	66.46	63.05	62.14	66.94	63.39	63.51	64.44	59.56	60.08	58.88
	SMIA	66.09	62.35	63.07	66.82	62.39	61.92	62.98	60.48	59.95	62.76
	R_MLP	68.42	63.74	62.78	67.07	65.07	56.24	66.01	64.33	64.67	61.33
	R_SMIA	66.74	62.46	61.54	68.73	62.7	63.6	63.84	60.7	61.1	61.73

Table 5. Average results on stationary signals for the prediction of five-step ahead

Performance measures	Neural networks	US/UK	JP/US	US/EU	NASDAQO	NASDAQC	DJIAO	DJIAC	DJUAO	DJUAC	OIL
AR (%)	MLP	84.72936	81.19235	91.46321	77.57114	83.09106	74.77388	65.96346	74.07559	68.93831	75.89575
	FLNN	77.68125	86.30544	86.37381	85.91437	85.81948	88.28172	88.31142	87.44099	86.69399	93.69838
	SMIA	88.15049	87.17208	91.84363	85.16167	85.02744	85.3598	84.89345	81.28562	86.66031	91.82156
	R_MLP	87.1223	83.74337	90.66374	77.94086	84.49206	74.35885	69.99318	76.14721	75.9389	81.74823
	R_SMIA	90.07944	86.87133	91.62076	85.4554	86.29109	83.8411	85.13061	86.84489	86.55567	91.28559
MD	MLP	-3.15533	-3.54864	-1.78913	-10.1308	-7.34318	-8.24405	-13.0605	-11.1968	-20.4777	-8.03638
	FLNN	-5.87622	-2.72277	-5.14140	-6.84715	-7.08089	-3.82649	-3.72506	-3.25588	-5.36821	-8.75378
	SMIA	-3.2779	-2.72278	-1.39054	-6.19597	-7.36317	-8.41446	-8.37277	-7.78359	-3.70212	-12.60818
	R_MLP	-2.45425	-2.72277	-2.555499	-9.173755	-7.024514	-8.166544	-10.711946	-12.706323	-13.174437	-57.254185
	R_SMIA	-1.77722	-2.72277	-1.35824	-6.3989	-7.08089	-7.00081	-6.72123	-3.4824	-4.75658	-13.3041
AV	MLP	16.24499	17.56791	15.69251	37.68809	36.53018	33.66308	35.11867	38.27525	39.02029	194.2871
	FLNN	17.04838	16.88852	16.39043	35.7455	35.85963	30.99444	31.03799	35.79927	36.26686	152.054
	SMIA	15.87492	16.76482	15.6362	35.93796	36.06489	31.63171	31.78481	37.03390	36.27336	157.372
	R_MLP	16.01374	17.240726	15.812136	37.578259	36.195788	33.752804	34.536964	37.978064	38.347615	180.79057
	R_SMIA	15.64255	16.80812	15.67015	35.86336	35.73558	31.95809	31.74464	35.92529	36.2965	158.8773
SR	MLP	5.246373	4.62544	5.829595	2.063196	2.278035	2.225729	1.888711	1.941499	1.786946	0.390889
	FLNN	4.569979	5.110325	5.289899	2.403571	2.393323	2.848333	2.845357	2.442637	2.390524	0.61651
	SMIA	5.561351	5.199892	5.873841	2.369793	2.357881	2.633558	2.672691	2.564821	2.389255	0.584465
	R_MLP	5.441671	4.857615	5.735123	2.079828	2.335423	2.20523	2.032267	2.005844	1.98104	0.46131
	R_SMIA	5.758673	5.168465	5.846852	2.382872	2.414784	2.623515	2.681791	2.417534	2.384731	0.575535
SNR (dB)	MLP	23.14	22.56	26.71	24.46	24.93	23.73	23.09	24.53	24.21	20.24
	FLNN	24.14	22.61	24.37	26.5	25.9	27.1	27.15	27.55	27.39	25.31
	SMIA	24.98	23.02	23.41	25.22	24.33	24.81	24.68	26.28	27.27	25.37
	R_MLP	26.59	23.46	25.87	25.27	25.5	24.04	23.77	25.07	24.94	22.02
	R_SMIA	25.68	23.5	23.61	23.82	24.67	24.99	24.99	27.42	27.03	25.36
CDC	MLP	63.7	62.18	64.65	61.47	59.92	61.92	61.45	60.86	59.66	56.88
	FLNN	63.47	64.44	63.17	61.23	60.72	63.48	63.84	62.61	63.09	56
	SMIA	65.49	63.16	65.09	62.49	59.48	62.91	62.99	61.72	62.97	60.06
	R_MLP	66.02	63.58	64.57	61.52	60.69	62.12	62.3	62.05	61.1	54.7
	R_SMIA	66.16	64.07	65.02	61.59	59.75	62.31	62.86	62.59	61.98	60.03

Table 6. Average results on non-stationary signals for the prediction of one-step ahead

Performance measures	Neural networks	US/UK	JP/US	US/EU	NASDAQO	NASDAQC	DJIAO	DJIAC	DJUAO	DJUAC	OIL
AR (%)	MLP	6.669613	-0.473902	7.703251	-6.27845	-10.20173	-9.977635	-12.48747	-7.6654061	-6.666097	4.151457
	FLNN	1.993203	-0.905553	9.82592	-3.3082592	-5.49312	-6.546531	-9.72016	-6.254837	-6.376194	-6.630352
	SMIA	2.073759	-8.271959	2.414358	-3.619703	3.531254	-15.34971	-15.34804	-5.068463	-5.201504	24.689167
	R_MLP	0.470592	-1.08558	13.39764	-5.15092	-2.75681	-2.12597	-5.46303	-7.75481	-8.15845	9.532212
	R_SMIA	13.222424	0.109788	10.548035	5.048035	-1929973	-1.448578	-3.431984	-7.377525	-0.69999	24.824701
MD	MLP	-14.957188	-22.500975	-11.293929	-15.470936	-70.907413	-63.928973	-73.355125	-67.988187	-67160675	-13.563781
	FLNN	-18.341226	-21.509273	-10.26734	-46.467443	-51.820357	-49.59282	-66.6875	-51.65052	-51.482152	-100.89227
	SMIA	-19.83157	-32.49779	-13.49779	-64.55476	-49.69712	-88.91595	-92.87567	40.012786	-45.16187	-50.27416
	R_MLP	-22.729432	-20.852478	-8.21238	-49.749368	46.533708	-36.2518	-48.166501	-52.472487	-55.995268	-70.085349
	R_SMIA	-11.377406	-15.434371	-9.23998	-30.243216	-40.470801	-31.948202	-14.144426	-51.271605	-44.666601	-51.651684
AV	MLP	11.403352	12.802219	10.106966	30.732116	30.476655	27.480595	27.88965	29.921184	30.590123	33.256952
	FLNN	11.410718	12.802582	10.095021	30.780716	30.565166	27.535189	23.240831	29.992717	30.660917	131.37748
	SMIA	11.399141	12.77795	10.105815	30.733801	30.472487	27.361664	27.773873	29.9737	30.642176	128.19774
	R_MLP	11.418611	12.804681	10.077155	30.774937	30.59627	27.56866	27.96083	29.985878	30.625883	130.31572
	R_SMIA	11.370933	12.807689	10.084079	30.777562	30.597727	27.580758	27.984762	29.992723	30.664225	126.72161
SR	MLP	0.585399	-0.037	-0.762452	-0.20439	-0.3351	-0.36342	-0.44844	-0.25648	-0.21824	-0.000123
	FLNN	0.175035	-0.07084	0.974008	0.107544	-0.17996	-0.23811	-0.41859	-0.20877	-0.20809	-0.05142
	SMIA	0.182488	-0.64743	0.239181	-0.1177	0.115987	-0.56231	-0.55418	-0.16912	-0.16979	0.193607
	R_MLP	0.041302	-0.084872	1.329773	-0.16743	-0.090141	-0.077248	-0.195888	-0.258771	-0.266283	0.074606
	R_SMIA	1.163817	0.00857	1.046945	0.164053	-0.6314	-0.05255	-0.12285	-0.24607	-0.02314	0.196018
SNR (dB)	MLP	16.3	17.68	13.41	17.74	19.38	12.7	13.07	14.19	14.94	19.08
	FLNN	29.26	25.72	30.06	31.13	30.84	29.4	24.76	32.86	32.53	9.04
	SMIA	20.5	27.04	13.97	19.83	16.05	16.97	18.51	16.51	16.88	11.44
	R_MLP	15.04	19.38	16.23	20.86	21.62	13.56	13.77	17.44	17.81	10.88
	R_SMIA	16.4	20.34	11.51	15.17	17.07	16.88	15.65	14.3	13.91	11.09
CDC	MLP	52.78	47.7	52.34	47.6	48.06	48.41	47.66	49.04	48.58	51.34
	FLNN	51.31	46.63	52.13	47.54	48.64	49.22	48.47	48.25	47.28	46.29
	SMIA	50.31	45.45	52.79	47.77	50.55	46.1	45.56	48.16	47.63	57.1
	R_MLP	50.48	46.06	53.37	47.42	49.8	50.6	49.58	47.64	46.55	52.29
	R_SMIA	53.43	47.92	52.33	51.45	50.55	50.25	49.62	47.28	51.48	65

Table 7. Average results on non-stationary signals for the prediction of five-step ahead

Performance measures	Neural networks	US/UK	JP/US	US/EU	NASDAQO	NASDAQC	DJIAO	DJIAC	DJUAO	DJUAC	OIL
AR (%)	MLP	-0.559585	-3.59391	1.117382	-2.40269	1.65726	-0.321544	-0.555403	-3.439273	-3.523605	0.01561
	FLNN	-1.2738	-5.9573	-0.1571	-3.8363	-0.915	-1.3329	-4.0139	-2.9823	-2.9541	-6.3419
	SMIA	-1.48508	2.839703	2.819774	-5.12982	-1.00699	2.440176	1.880855	2.857381	1.735058	-6.13704
	R_MLP	-3.09729	-3.309134	3.733809	-4.589262	-1.772365	-4.65767	-4.517743	-3.079075	-3.133686	0.113113
	R_SMIA	1.79951	2.034985	3.813749	-1.92625	-3.73281	-1.96245	-1.52512	0.054411	2.001813	-1.24209
MD	MLP	-14.8441	-20.2364	-11.8548	-37.1925	-34.1537	-37.7277	-40.42709	-49.0705	-51.062871	-88.71052
	FLNN	-16.0545	-20.2988	-12.3168	-38.3696	-40.0468	-39.5673	-47.5507	-50.6108	-15.8044	-94.3542
	SMIA	-17.776	-19.8414	-8.63958	-38.6083	-32.3624	-20.558	-22.1424	-35.7076	-34.5416	-90.0799
	R_MLP	-16.877584	-19.066487	-8.871813	-39.692504	-39.37541	-42.126048	-14.89301	-49.765621	-25.975362	-82.687761
	R_SMIA	-15.08815	-14.67284	-11.57839	-39.49456	-40.71476	-40.93965	-37.91129	-48.78379	-44.45037	-76.71338
AV	MLP	11.42579	12.8158	10.1309	30.8166	30.5985	27.5912	27.5927	29.9932	30.70504	131.6793
	FLNN	11.4246	12.8066	10.1311	30.8154	30.6204	27.5939	23.288	30.0396	30.7071	131.135
	SMIA	11.41287	12.7995	10.11326	30.77346	30.59728	27.58149	28.00402	29.9849	30.67759	130.3251
	R_MLP	11.43124	12.807072	10.130352	30.813032	30.635332	27.587913	28.014315	30.050515	30.717461	131.81674
	R_SMIA	11.42942	12.8153	10.13094	30.82329	30.62114	27.59616	28.01929	30.06198	30.72487	132.1194
SR	MLP	-0.049097	-0.28073	0.11028	-0.07803	0.054188	-0.011719	-0.020069	-0.11477	-0.114946	-0.000611
	FLNN	-0.1116	-0.4654	-0.0155	-0.1245	-0.0299	-0.0483	-0.1725	-0.0993	-0.0962	-0.0484
	SMIA	-0.13091	-0.22183	0.378768	-0.16675	-0.1253	0.088481	0.067178	0.095616	0.056716	-0.04803
	R_MLP	-0.271036	-0.258545	0.368653	-0.148991	-0.057879	-0.168913	-0.161395	-0.102547	-0.10209	0.000935
	R_SMIA	0.157756	0.159264	0.376467	0.062527	-0.1219	-0.07122	-0.05443	-0.001792	-0.065155	-0.00939
SNR (dB)	MLP	14.7	16.34	13.22	16.54	17	12.39	12.42	14.07	15.49	10.6
	FLNN	15.3	16.51	14.02	23.88	27.7	26.59	22.23	29.39	29.51	9.59
	SMIA	16.83	21.66	13.32	19.94	17.1	16.83	17.14	13.38	14.88	10.92
	R_MLP	15.85	16.15	13.41	20.5	20.61	13.31	13.41	17.32	17.63	10.82
	R_SMIA	14.11	16.19	11.37	16.13	16.56	14.9	12.47	17.15	16.52	10.99
CDC	MLP	52.27	47.95	50.79	48.44	49.79	52.28	51.27	49.57	49.44	49.42
	FLNN	52.52	46.98	50.91	48.04	50.99	52.62	49.44	49.3	49.27	48.58
	SMIA	53.2	50.98	51.89	48.05	48.41	52.54	52.36	50.15	49.83	49.03
	R_MLP	54.27	48.69	51.38	48.22	51.01	51.87	51.09	49.58	49.05	49.71
	R_SMIA	51.4	46.34	51.93	47.64	51.41	51.19	51.91	49.74	49.67	52.61

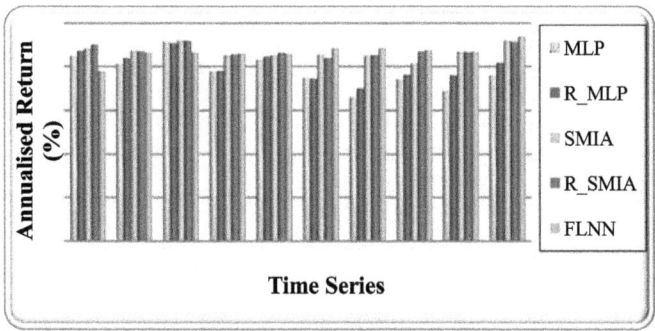

Figure 3. The average of AR predicted from all networks.

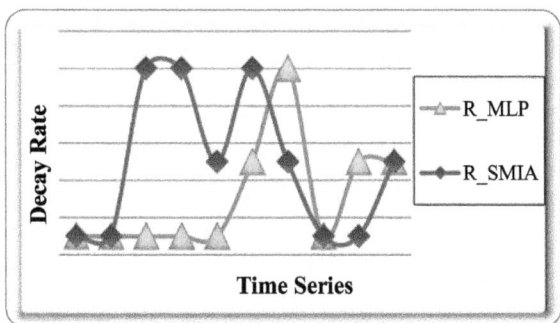

Figure 4. Best decay rate used in prediction of all financial signals.

The comparison between the performance of the SMIA network and the R_SMIA network based on the percentage of AR detect an increasing on profits obtained with R_SMIA network. The R_SMIA successfully reaches the highest profits than SMIA network when forecasting the following five financial time series: USD/UKP, NASDAQO, NASDAQC, DJIAC and DJUAO.

The overall performances of the five networks which are utilised in forecasting the various signals using the AR is depicted in Figure 5. The five-steps-ahead prediction for all networks indicated that the SMIA and R_SMIA networks produce better percentage of AR than the other multilayer networks. Meanwhile, it complements the FLNN in some stock prices data.

For the value of the decay rate, it can be noticed from Figure 6 that the signals can reach the best ratio of profits by using small values of decay rate (which is 0.0001) when predicting the five-step-ahead prediction for R_MLP and R_SMIA networks.

7.3. One-step-ahead prediction using non-stationary signals
The number of hidden units or network order used to obtain the best prediction showed that the performance of MLP network produces the best results of profits using six or eight hidden nodes

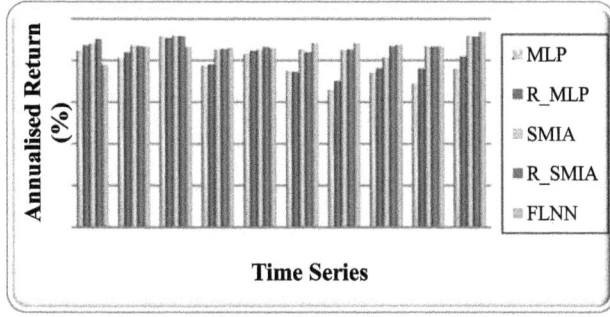

Figure 5. The average of AR predicted from all networks.

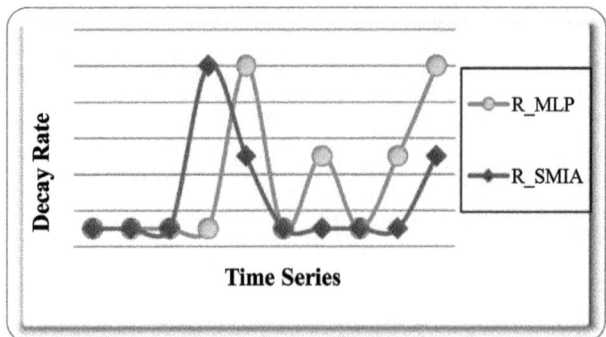

Figure 6. Best decay rate used in the prediction of all financial signals (five-steps ahead).

while the R_MLP network gives better profits using seven or eight hidden nodes. Furthermore, the SMIA and R_SMIA networks could reach high values of profits using seven or eight hidden units and above. The FLNN reaches the best performance when using only the third order in most cases.

For the AR, the R_SMIA shows higher values than all other network for the USD/UKP, JPY/USD, NASDAQO, DJIAO, DJIAC, DJUAC and OIL time series. The SMIA network achieved the highest profit on two signals the NASDAQC and the DJUAO signals. Meanwhile the R_MLP can obtain the best average of profit only when it is used to forecast the USD/EUR signal. Figure 7 illustrates the performance of the AR for the forecast of the five network models that are used in this research work, while Figure 8 shows the rate decay values which were used for the prediction of all data signals.

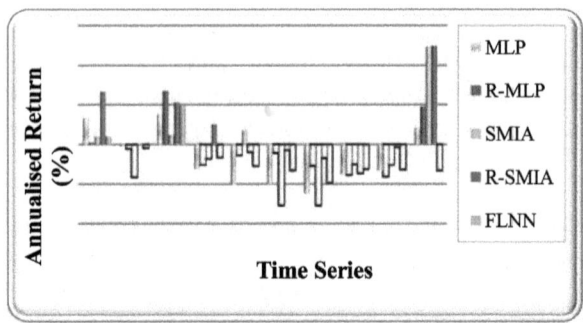

Figure 7. The best average of AR predicted from all networks.

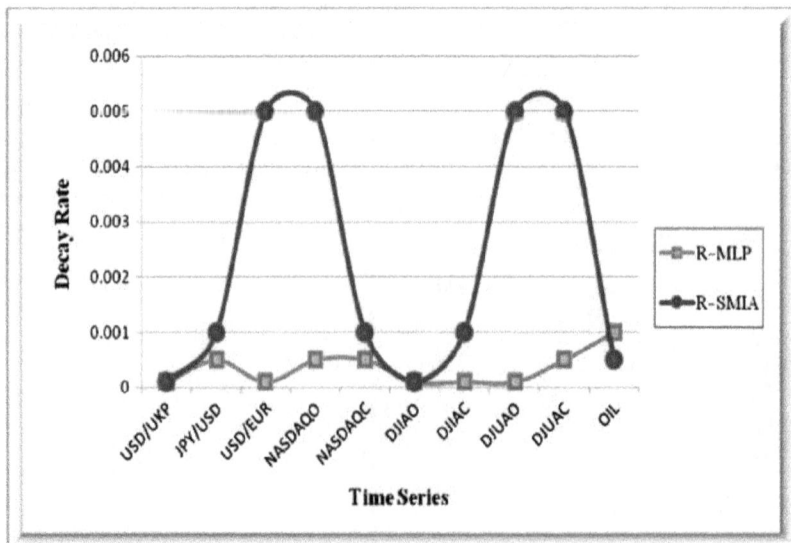

Figure 8. Best decay rate used in prediction of all financial signals.

7.4. Five-step-ahead prediction using non-stationary signals

Although the prediction for the non-stationary signals usually give inconsistent results, the extensive experiments of this research proved that the proposed application of the SMIA and R_SMIA for the prediction of financial time series showed the best profit values when compared to other neural networks.

The MLP and R_MLP networks can produce the best average results of profits with seven or eight hidden nodes. The SMIA network gives the best results using only five or seven hidden units. However, the R_SMIA network attains the highest percentage of AR with four hidden nodes and above. For the FLNN most prediction results indicated that the best profits can be achieved using two or three network order.

The comparison between all networks demonstrated that the high ratio of the AR is achieved using the SMIA and R_SMIA networks. Meanwhile, for the MLP and R_MLP networks, each network can attain higher profit value for only one signal namely NASDAQC and OIL signals, respectively. Furthermore, the FLNN produced the worst profits in comparison to the multilayer networks.

Figure 9 shows the values of the AR for the prediction of the various networks. The simulation results indicated that the SMIA and R_SMIA networks produced better percentage of AR than the other networks in most cases. Figure 10 represents the best decay rate values that are used for the R_SMIA and R_MLP neural networks.

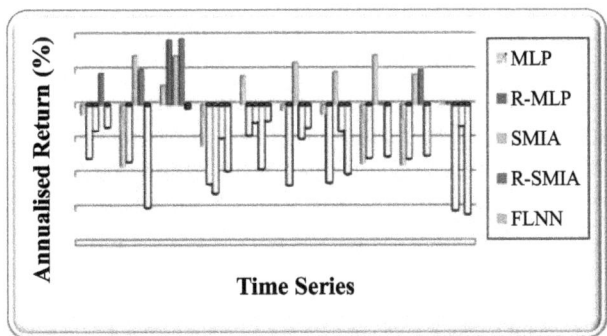

Figure 9. The average of AR predicted from all networks.

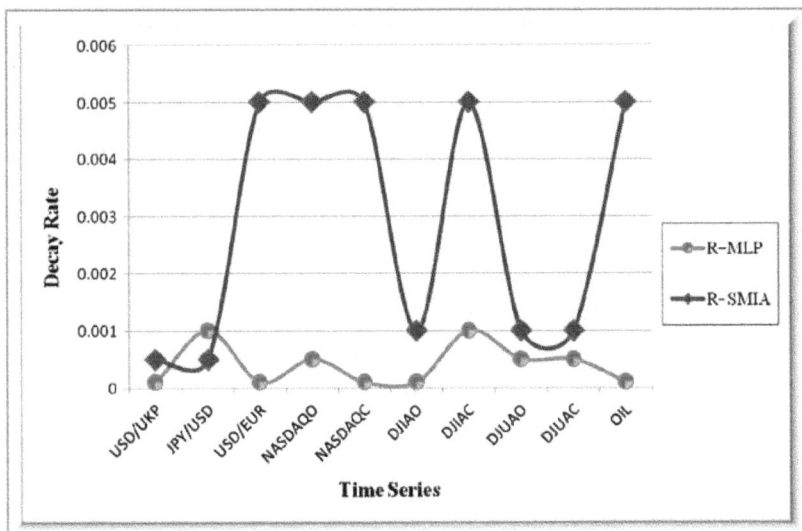

Figure 10. Best decay rate used in prediction of all financial signals.

Table 8. The standard deviation for the exchange rate between the UK/US Dollar time series over 50 simulations with respect to the profit value

Network	One-step-ahead prediction using stationary data	Five-steps-ahead prediction using stationary data	One-step-ahead prediction using non-stationary data	Five-steps-ahead prediction using non-stationary data
SMIA	0.4709	0.3538	6.5302	7.1744
R_SMIA	0.1795	0.2654	5.9049	6.4938
MLP	13.7166	6.9672	7.4127	7.7695
R_MLP	1.1148	2.6221	3.2671	4.0839

8. Discussion

Simulation results demonstrate that all the neural networks models used in this research work were potentially profitable, the non-stationary financial signals are very difficult to predict due to its instability behaviour. The non-stationary signals are highly volatile and noisy and that is why they often change their behaviour and fall sharply at some point during the training. The networks are trying to learn the price values of the non-stationary signals during the training phase where they are unable to respond well, since the prices values include high-frequency components. Therefore, the networks generate unpromising prediction using the AR measure.

For the stationary signals, the networks predicted high percentage of profits. The non-stationary signals are smoothed and transferred into Relative Different in Price (RDP) and the neural networks generate better forecasting and profit. Consequently, neural networks can attain stable prediction and higher profits for stationary signals than the non-stationary signals.

In this research study, six stock opining prices and stock closing prices time series data have been used which includes NASDAQO, NASDAQC, DJIAO, DJIAC, DJUAO and DJUAC. Three of these time series are stock opening prices and the others are stock closing prices. The aim of these signals is to investigate the differences between the predictions of the opening stock price and closing stock results.

For stationary signals, the simulation results showed that for all networks used in this work, there is a slightly differences in the results when using these signals in one-step-ahead prediction. While the prediction results for five-steps-ahead illustrate variances between these series.

The non-stationary signals show that in most cases the prediction results for one-step-ahead and five-steps-ahead have small difference between the opening and closing stock prices for all networks which have been utilised in the current work.

It is worth to notice that these differences related to the raw data, since the data are affected by several factors such as the threats of war, good or bad economic climate, announcements of company earning and the advertisements of economic statistics.

As it can be noticed from Table 8, the simulation results indicated for the prediction of the US/UK exchange rate time series that the standard deviations for the SMIA, R_SMIA, MLP and the R_MLP have significantly different values which indicate that the results achieved by each network is strategically different.

9. Conclusion

This research work underlines an important contribution of a new application of the self-organised multilayer neural network inspired by the SMIA for the prediction of the financial time series; namely, its elegant ability to approximate non-linear financial time series. The network has shown its advantages in forecasting both stationary and non-stationary signals. A considerable profitable value does exist in the proposed network when compared to other networks and the network demonstrated a vast speed in convergence time. Hence, it is anticipated that the self-organised multilayer neural network inspired by the SMIA can be used as an alternative method for predicting financial variables and thus justified the potential use of this model by practitioners. The superior property hold by the network could promise more powerful applications in many other real world problems.

Funding
The authors received no direct funding for this research.

Author details
Dhiya Al-Jumeily[1]
E-mail: d.aljumeily@ljmu.ac.uk
Abir J. Hussain[1]
E-mail: a.hussain@ljmu.ac.uk
[1] Faculty of Engineering and Technology, Applied Computing Research Group, Liverpool John Moores University, Byrom Street, Liverpool L3 3AF, UK.

References
Bishop, C. M. (1995). *Neural networks for pattern recognition.* Oxford: Clarendon Press.

Cass, R., & Radl, B. (1996). Adaptive process optimization using functional-link networks and evolutionary optimization. *Control Engineering Practice, 4,* 1579–1584. http://dx.doi.org/10.1016/0967-0661(96)00173-6

Cao, L. J., & Tay, F. E. H. (2003). Support vector machine with adaptive parameters in financial time series forecasting. *IEEE Transactions on Neural Networks, 14,* 1506–1518. http://dx.doi.org/10.1109/TNN.2003.820556

Datastream International Limited all rights reserved/ Datastream database, [machine-readable data]. (2005). London: Thompson Financial Limited [Producer and Distributor]. Retrieved November 14, 2005 from http://financial.thomsonreuters.com/en.html

Dorffner, G. (1996). Neural networks for time series processing. *Neural Network World, 6,* 447–468.

Duda, R. O., Hart, P. E., & Stork, D. G. (2000). *Pattern classification* (2nd ed.). New York, NY: Wiley-Interscience.

Durbin, R., & Rumelhart, D. E. (1989). Product units: A computationally powerful and biologically plausible extension to backpropagation networks. *Neural Computation, 1,* 133–142. http://dx.doi.org/10.1162/neco.1989.1.1.133

Dunis, C. L., & Wiliams, M. (2002). Modeling and trading the UER/USD exchange rate: Do neural network models perform better? *Derivatives Use, Trading and Regulation, 8,* 211–239.

Fama, E. F., & French, K. R. (1989). Business conditions and expected returns on stocks and bonds. *Journal of Financial Economics, 25,* 23–49. http://dx.doi.org/10.1016/0304-405X(89)90095-0

Fama, E. F., & Schwert, G.W. (1977). Asset returns and inflation. *Journal of Financial Economics, 5,* 115–146. http://dx.doi.org/10.1016/0304-405X(77)90014-9

Fei, G., & Yu, Y. L. (1994). A modified sigma-pi BP network with self-feedback and its application in time series analysis. *Proceedings of the 5th International Conference, 2243,* 508–515.

Ferson, W. (1989). Changes in expected security returns, risk, and the level of interest rates. *The Journal of Finance, 44,* 1191–1217. http://dx.doi.org/10.1111/j.1540-6261.1989.tb02650.x

Giles, C. L., & Maxwell, T. (1987, December). Learning, invariance and generalisation in high-order neural networks. *Applied Optics, 26,* 4972–4978.

Jensen, M. (1978). Some anomalous evidence regarding market efficiency. *Journal of Financial Economics, 6,* 95–101. http://dx.doi.org/10.1016/0304-405X(78)90025-9

Kaita, T., Tomita, S., & Yamanaka, J. (2002). On a higher-order neural network for distortion invariant pattern recognition. *Pattern Recognition Letters, 23,* 977–984. http://dx.doi.org/10.1016/S0167-8655(02)00028-4

Lawrence, S., & Giles, C. L. (2000). Overfitting and neural networks: Conjugate gradient and backpropagation. In *International Joint Conference on Neural Network, Italy* (pp. 114–119). Los Alamitos, CA: IEEE Computer Society.

Lendasse, A., de Bodt, E., Wertz, V., & Verleysen, M. (2000). Non-linear financial time series forecasting—Application to the Bel 20 stock market index. *European Journal of Economic and Social Systems, 14,* 81–91. http://dx.doi.org/10.1051/ejess:2000110

Makhoul, J. (1975). Linear prediction: A tutorial review. *Proceedings of the IEEE, 63,* 561–580. http://dx.doi.org/10.1109/PROC.1975.9792

Manikopoulos, C. N. (1992). Neural network approach to DPCM system design for image coding. *IEE Proceedings-I, 139,* 501–507.

Mirea, L., & Marcu, T. (2002). System identification using functional-link neural networks with dynamic structure. In *15th Triennial World Congress,* Barcelona, Spain.

Thimm, G. (1995). *Optimisation of high order perceptron.* Lausanne: Swiss federal Institute of Technology (EPFL).

Thomason, M. (1999). The practitioner method and tools. *Journal of Computational Intelligence in Finance, 7,* 36–45.

Timmis, J. I. (2001). *Ariticial immune systems: A novel data analysis technique inspired by the immune network theory.* Aberystwyth: University of Wales.

Widyanto, M. R., Nobuhara, H., Kawamoto, K., Hirota, K., & Kusumoputro, B. (2005). Improving recognition and generalization capability of back-propagation NN using a self-organized network inspired by immune algorithm (SONIA). *Applied Soft Computing, 6,* 72–84. http://dx.doi.org/10.1016/j.asoc.2004.10.008

Yao, J., & Tan, C. L. (2000). A case study on using neural networks to perform technical forecasting of forex. *Neurocomputing, 34,* 79–98. http://dx.doi.org/10.1016/S0925-2312(00)00300-3

Zhang, G. P. (2003). *Neural networks in business forecasting.* Hershey, PA: Idea. http://dx.doi.org/10.4018/978-1-59140-176-6

10

Efficient constraint-based Sequential Pattern Mining (SPM) algorithm to understand customers' buying behaviour from time stamp-based sequence dataset

Niti Ashish Kumar Desai[1]* and Amit Ganatra[2]

*Corresponding author: Niti Ashish Kumar Desai, Department of Computer Engineering, Uka Tarsadia University, Bardoli, Surat, Gujarat, India

E-mail: nitiadesai@gmail.com

Reviewing editor: Hsien-Tsung Chang, Chang Gung University, Taiwan

Abstract: Business Strategies are formulated based on an understanding of customer needs. This requires development of a strategy to understand customer behaviour and buying patterns, both current and future. This involves understanding, first how an organization currently understands customer needs and second predicting future trends to drive growth. This article focuses on purchase trend of customer, where timing of purchase is more important than association of item to be purchased, and which can be found out with Sequential Pattern Mining (SPM) methods. Conventional SPM algorithms worked purely on frequency identifying patterns that were more frequent but suffering from challenges like generation of huge number of uninteresting patterns, lack of user's interested patterns, rare item problem, etc. Article attempts a solution through development of a SPM algorithm based on various constraints like Gap, Compactness, Item, Recency, Profitability and Length along with Frequency constraint. Incorporation of six additional constraints is as well to ensure that all patterns are recently active (Recency), active for certain time span (Compactness), profitable and indicative of next timeline for purchase (Length—Item—Gap). The article also attempts to throw light on how proposed

ABOUT THE AUTHORS

Niti Ashish Kumar Desai has received her BE in Computer Engineering from SGU, Gujarat, India in 2003 and ME from Dharmsinh Desai University, Gujarat, India in 2005. She has joined her PhD in the area of Data Mining at Uka Tarsadia University, Bardoli, Gujarat in June 2012. Her areas of interest include Database and Data Mining. During her 8+ years of academic journey she has published more than 10 papers in various National and International Journals.

Dr. Amit Ganatra has received his BE and M.E. in 2000 and 2004 from DDIT-Nadiad, Gujarat. He has completed Ph.D. in Information Fusion Techniques in Data Mining from KSV University, Gandhinagar, Gujarat. He is a member of IEEE and CSI. He has 15+ years of teaching and research experience. He has published and contributed over 100+ papers. He is concurrently holding Professor, headship in computer Department and Deanship in Faculty of Technology-CHARUSAT, Gujarat.

PUBLIC INTEREST STATEMENT

The main objective of a business economic activity is to satisfy needs and wants of customers. Hence management of any business aims at identifying and predicting purchase tendency of customers with a view to plan its business strategy including product development and marketing sub-strategies. This requires data mining tools including sequential pattern mining (SPM) techniques that help in achieving aforesaid objective. Most of the existing SPM approaches work purely on frequency, which fail to extract sequential patterns of users' interest. Incorporation of constraints in SPM is able to address such shortcomings. Proposed framework might be useful for decision-maker to understand business, to identify past, current as well future buying pattern of customers. Further Emerging Patterns (EPs) that can help in predicting future buying behaviour can also be identified with the proposed framework. Paper also highlights obsolete, new and forming stage patterns that will be relevant for business managements.

Constraint-based Prefix Span algorithm is helpful to understand buying behaviour of customer which is in formative stage.

Subjects: Computer Engineering; Data Preparation & Mining; I.T. Research

Keywords: constraints; sequential pattern mining; constraint-based Prefix Span

1. Literature survey

To mine important information and mould it into proper knowledge is important task from past few decades, known as data mining. (Chen, Han, & Philip, 1996). Data mining uses to extract knowledge from huge extent of data (Mary & Iyengar, 2010; Raza, 2010). There are certain activity which is necessary to happen in sequence to mine such sequence are important data mining activity known as sequential pattern Mining (SPM), was introduced in (Agrawal & Srikant, 1995; Srikant & Agrawal, 1996). It is useful in various data mining applications, to discover useful customer and market information from the data, such as product recommendation (Lawrence et al., 2001), e-retailing, customer profiling (Hu & Chen, 2008; Mahdavi, Cho, Shirazi, & Sahebjamnia, 2008). Current SPM techniques are mainly differentiate by *a priori* based (Agrawal & Srikant, 1994) and FP-Growth-based (Han, Pei, & Yin, 2000) techniques. Both *a priori*-based GSP (Srikant & Agrawal, 1996), SPADE (Zaki, 2001), SPAM (Ayres, Flannick, Gehrke, & Yiu, 2002), SPIRIT (Garofalakis, Rastogi, & Shim, 1999) and FP-Growth-based Freespan (Han, Dong et al., 2000), Prefix span (Pei, Han, Mortazavi, & Pino, 2001) are purely worked on sole parameter frequency, known as support threshold. Conventional SPM techniques often take substantial computational time and space for mining the complete set of sequential patterns in a large sequence database. Introduction of constraint may open a new opportunity for performance improvement: "Can we improve the efficiency of sequential pattern mining by focusing only on interesting patterns?" Constraint-based mining may improve or overcome both the difficulties: efficiency and effectiveness. Conventional SPM techniques are not successful to extract those patterns which are having more potential in terms of Monitory value and Recency. (Chen, Kuo, Wu, & Tang, 2009) has taken care of these parameters by introducing Recency, Frequency and Monitory (RFM) parameters in SPM.

The algorithm RFM-*A priori* is helpful to users for identification of those patterns which are more frequent, active recently and have high monetary value (Chen et al., 2009). RFM is used in many data mining activities likes, association rule mining, clustering, classification, etc. (Chen, Wu, & Chen, 2005; Mohammad, Hosseini, Maleki, & Mohammad, 2009; Qiasi, Dehnavi, Minaei-Bidgoli, & Amooee, 2012). (Goodman, 1992) has applied RFM model to find valuable customers. RFM is used to specify loyal and profitable customers on based of clustering. Classification algorithms are useful to obtain rules for implementing effective customer relationship management. Combinations of behavioural and demographical characteristics are used to estimate loyalty (Qiasi et al., 2012). Extended RFM model called Weighted RFM (WRFM) and K-means algorithm applied classify customer product loyalty in under B2B concept. Customer loyalty is used in marketing strategy (Mohammad et al., 2009). In most of the researches, two methods are common for identifying loyal customers, one of them is in terms of demographic variables (such as age, gender, etc.) and the other is in terms of interactive behaviours of customers that are expressed with the so-called RFM. RFM model is proposed by (Hughes, 1994) and has been used in direct marketing for several decades (Chen et al., 2005). (Chen et al., 2009) focused on effective discovery of current spending pattern of customers and trends of behavioural change using classification-based clustering on bases of RFM model to identify high-profit, gold customers. It helps to identifies customer preference, and provide desired service according to customer need which prevent customer attrition (Chen et al., 2005). (Shaw, Subramaniam, Tan, & Welge, 2001) mainly describes how to incorporate data mining into the framework of marketing knowledge management. (Song, Kim, & Kim, 2001) depicts a method to detect changes of customer behaviour at different time snapshots from customer profiles and sales data. (Shen & Chuang, 2009) used RFM model-based cluster analysis for customers, which can evaluate high value customers in terms of high loyalty, high interest, and a high amount of purchase. On bases of results company can apply appropriate target marketing to enhance customers' lifetime value (CLV) (Shen & Chuang, 2009). The problem of sequential pattern mining in B2C (Business to customer) environment and in B2B (Business to Business) environment has been investigated by Chen.[1] Importance of Compact, Frequent, and Recent sequential patterns (CFR-patterns) in (Business to customer) B2C environment and Compact, Frequent, Recent, and Repeated sequential patterns (CFR^2-patterns) in B2B (Business to Business) environment has been described (see Note 1). The algorithm CFM-PREFIX SPAN has incorporated compactness and Monitory constraint in pattern growth-based Prefix Span which give precise patterns in context of high-valued patterns and pattern active during precise time span (Mallick, Garg, & Grover, 2012). The Algorithm C-Prefix Span has incorporated Gap, Compactness, Recency along with conventional Frequency (Bhensdadia & Kosta, 2012). Following advantages can be achieved by constraint-based sequential mining:

(i) Enhance performance of algorithm by reducing computation cost of uninteresting patterns.

(ii) Along with frequency other important parameter are focused.

(iii) User can focused on only those patterns which are really of his/her interest.

(iv) User can get goal or application-oriented result.

1.1. Major research findings and basic outline of proposed research

(I) Most of the existing SPM methods work purely on frequency parameter, formally known as *support threshold*. Support is important to distinguish if patterns appear repeatedly or not. On the other hand, the proposed *Constraint-based Prefix Span* algorithm would be concerned about decision maker's perception. Proposed algorithm through use of Recency constraint determines current buying patterns and through use of profit constraint determines the more profitable buying patterns. Further compactness constraint can be used to identify buying behaviour of customer during specific time span including seasonal patterns. Item and length constraint will help to give detailed buying behaviour of customer. Further length constraint in the algorithm can be used to understand customers' buying preferences for identifying influential items of purchase leading or indicating higher probability for next purchase.

(II) Almost all the existing SPM methods are focused on the current scenario. There are some patterns which have potential to become strong in future, but are suffering from slightly less support. Minor reduction in support values may bring such patterns into focus, which can be potential buying patterns for future. Our research highlights such potential patterns using *Boundary value reduction* and *Recency*-based Emerging Patterns (EPs) algorithm.

(III) Extraction of sequential patterns works on objective measures like support and confidence. SPM with subjective measures is an unchartered area that needs to be explored. Our research includes subjective analysis for purchase such as *profitability, loyalty* and *influential purchase* using amalgamation of various constraints. Customers who are frequent, profitable and recent are identified as *loyal customers*. Segmentation of customers based on such subjective survey criteria can be done using the proposed method.

(IV) Our research provides an algorithm to study customers' current buying behaviour and identification of patterns that are likely to become obsolete in future and those that are at their formative stage.

2. System framework

Theoretical physicist Albert Einstein once said: *"Everything that can be counted does not necessarily count; everything that counts cannot necessarily be counted."* Since marketers can't measure everything, the challenge is to focus on those parameters that truly matter to enhance business performance.[2] Article has adopted this philosophy. Article focused on those constraints which are useful to track customer's present as well future buying behaviour. Future buying trend of purchase can be discovered by following:

(i) Emerging Patterns (to highlight buying habits of customers which will useful for future).

(ii) High-influenced item (on bases of customer buying preferences).

(iii) Buying habit of customer on forming stage.

(iv) Seasonal buying habit of customer.

Customers' behavioural study provides current as well future buying snapshot which will be useful for expansion of business.

2.1. Analysis on customers' buying behaviour based on constraints

2.1.1. Emerging patterns (EPs)

Almost all the existing SPM techniques are concentrated on the present buying behaviour of customer but there are some patterns which are having sufficient potential to become strong in future, which are suffering from slightly less support. Slight reduction in support boundary can laid such pattern in consideration, which can be emerging purchase patterns for tomorrow. Such *Emerging Patterns (EPs)* are considered in proposed approach here.

In Equation 1, SD is Sequential Database with timestamp. FP is Frequent Patterns, which are generated for support values. x is support value which generates frequent patterns (FP) $_{Support=x\%}$. support y is generated by reduction of 2% in support value x. (FP) $_{Support=y\%}$ is frequent patterns generated by slight reduction of support value which high lights those patterns which are facing problem of little low frequency. SEQ $_{EP1}$ is emerging patterns generated by reduced boundary value, recent patterns from those patterns might be potential patterns of tomorrow.

$$
\begin{aligned}
(SD)_{Support=x\%} &\rightarrow (FP)_{Support=x\%} \\
(support = y\%) = (support = x\%) &- (0.002 - (support = x\%)) \\
(SD)_{Support=y\%} &\rightarrow (FP)_{Support=y\%} \\
SEQ_{EP1} = (FP)_{Support=x\%} &- (FP)_{Support=y\%}
\end{aligned}
\tag{1}
$$

Where, |Y-X | = Boundary value > 0, SD = Sequential Database, FP = frequent pattern, SEQ $_{EP1}$ = Sequential Pattern for reduced boundary value; X,Y > 0 (refer Equation 2)

$$
\begin{aligned}
SEQ_{recency\_EP} &= SEQ_{EP1} \text{ satisfied } C_{recency} \\
EP &= SEQ_{recency\_EP}
\end{aligned}
\tag{2}
$$

Where, $C_{recency}$ is recency timestamp constraint. $SEQ_{recency\_EP}$ is emerging sequential patterns generated by recency constraint and EP is Emerging Patterns which are recent. Generated patterns are suffering from low support but not old. Old patterns are eliminated by inclusion of recency constraint. For example, <(Computer) (Floppy)> was earlier famous buying pattern. Suppose, it's having 18% support value. It was rejected for support value 20%. Reduction of boundary value high lights this pattern though it is old (SEQ $_{EP1}$ = (FP) $_{Support=x\%}$ — (FP) $_{Support=y\%}$). Another buying pattern <(laptop)(blue ray disk) > is recent but not too frequent as compared to complete transactional database. Because of less little value of support, it is rejected. Pattern <(Laptop)(Blue ray disk)> is selected by slight reduction of boundary. The patterns which are on its forming stage can be easily detected.

2.1.2. Profitable pattern

It is important for any business to understand profitable purchase. Profit is indirectly derived from Monitory constraint. Profit is depends upon two valuable parameters: purchase price and sold price. Profitability is one of the important parameter of customer segregation and retention. The Profitable constraint define item in a sequence must be more than the defined threshold value. The Profitable constraint is formally represented as following:

$$
C_{Profit} \equiv Sold - Purchase(\alpha) \, \omega \, \Delta T
\tag{3}
$$

Where, $\omega \in \{\geq\}$, ΔT integer value/ Profitable threshold. α is sequence.

A sequence S_s = <(q_1(qty$_1$), t_1, M_Sold$_1$, M_Pur$_1$), (q_2(qty$_2$), M_Sold$_2$, M_Pur$_2$), ... , (q_m(qty$_m$), M_Sold$_m$, M_Pur$_m$) > is said to be a subsequence of S only if, (1) item set S_s is a subsequence of S, $S_s \in S$ and (2) the number of items in S should satisfied (refer Equations 3 and 4)

$$\left[\frac{\sum_{i=1}^{m}(M\_Sold - M\_Pur)i}{m}\right] \geq T_{Profit} \tag{4}$$

2.1.3. Influential item
It is important for decision maker to understand purchase of which item leads to another purchase(s) after some time period. For example, TV→DVD→(CD,CD Box). TV is highly influenced item which leads to second or third purchase(s). High association of such chain purchase leads to loyal customer, with the help of length constraint such chain purchase can be identified. Amalgamation of length and profitability can highlight those patterns which are building strong relationship with customer and lead to sequence purchase.

2.1.4. Seasonal buying patterns
Most of the customer moving for purchase during festival seasons like Diwali and Christmas. Purchase of garment and house hold is drastically increased during these time span. In India, purchase of gold and diamond are increased during Akshay Tritya, Lakshmi Pujan and Pushya Nakshtra every year.[3] Compactness constraint which used to represent duration is helpful parameter to understand active purchase during particular time span. Patterns which are highly purchased can be extracted by compactness constraint; business maker can change sale value of such items which leads to profitability (Pei, Han, & Wang, 2007). (Refer Equation 5)

$$C_{Comp} \equiv Comp(\alpha)\, \theta\, \Delta t \tag{5}$$

2.2. Constraints to understand proposed algorithm
Traditional sequential pattern mining only is distinguishes whether a pattern appears or not (Ayres et al., 2002; Garofalakis et al., 1999; Zaki, 2001). The original Prefix span algorithm only worked on frequency constraint to discover sequential patterns from sequence database (Pei et al., 2001). RFM pattern mining approach not only determines the existence of a pattern but also checks whether it satisfies the recency and the monetary constraints (Chen et al., 2009). Proposed approach worked on seven constraints—Frequency constraint, Item constraint, Length constraint, Gap constraint, Compactness constraint, Recency constraint, Quantity constraint and profitable constraint. Above constraints are incorporated in original Prefix span algorithm. Following key concepts are required to understand the proposed algorithm:

2.2.1. Frequency constraint
The frequency constraint is defined as each discovered pattern must satisfy minimum support That is, the support of an item is the percentage of transaction in which that items occurs (Refer Equation 6).

$$C_{Freq} \equiv P(\alpha) = (\alpha)/N\, \omega\, \Delta T \tag{6}$$

Where, $\omega \in \{\geq\}$, ΔT integer value/ Frequency threshold. α is sequence. N Number of transaction of Sequence Database SDB (Pei et al., 2007).

2.2.2. Recency constraint
Recency constraint is specified by giving a recency minimum support (r_minsup). In time stamped-based dataset minimum Recency time stamp is given. The patterns having more time stamp can be selected. For example, ((a)<1>(b,c)<2>) and ((a,b)<3>(b,c)<5>) are frequent patterns. Suppose, r_minsup = 3 than only ((a,b)<2>(b,c)<5>) is selected because pattern is generated at later time stamped value, which are considered as recent pattern.

"after buying item a and b, the customer moves to buy item b and item c." Then, the transaction in the sequence that buys item b and item c must satisfy recency constraint. Time stamp of last buying item (b, c) should $\geq$ r_minsup = 3. Formally, Recency constraint is define in Equation 7 (Pei et al., 2007).

$$C_{recency} \equiv recency(\alpha) \; \theta \; \Delta t \tag{7}$$

where $\theta \in \{\leq, \geq\}$ and Δt is a given integer. A sequence α satisfies the constraint if $|\{ \beta \in SDB | \exists 1 \leq i_1 < \cdots <i_{len(\alpha)} \leq len(\beta)$ s.t. $\alpha[1] \sqsubseteq \beta[i_1], \dots ,\alpha[len(\alpha)] \sqsubseteq \beta[i_{len}(\alpha)]$, and $(\beta[i_{len}(\alpha)]$. time $\theta \; \Delta t \;| \geq min\_sup$

2.2.3. Gap constraint
Gap constraint is specified by giving gap range (min_gap and max_gap). In sequence databases each transaction in every sequence has a timestamp. The time-stamp difference (difference of days) between every two adjacent transactions in a discovered sequential pattern must not be greater than given range of gap. min_gap and max_gap time-stamp by 2 and 4 means (4 − 2 = 2). so, pattern <t2:(a), t4:(bc), t7:(ac)> can't be discovered because of more time gap occur at <t4:(bc), t7:(ac)>, (7 − 4 = 3) though time-stamp (4 − 2 = 2) is satisfied for sub-pattern <t1:(a), t4:(bc)>. Formally, a gap constraint is in the form of (Refer Equation 8), (Pei et al., 2007).

$$C_{gap} \equiv Gap(\alpha) \; \theta \; \Delta t \tag{8}$$

where $\theta \in \{\leq, \geq\}$ and Δt is a given integer. A sequence α satisfies the constraint if and only if

$|\{ \beta \in SDB | \exists 1 \leq i1 < \cdots <ilen(\alpha) \leq len(\beta)$ s.t. $\alpha[1] \sqsubseteq \beta[i1], \dots , \alpha[len(\alpha)] \sqsubseteq \beta[ilen(\alpha)]$, and for all $1 < j \leq len(\alpha)$, $(\beta[ij]$ .time - $\beta[ij-1]$ .time) $\theta \; \Delta t\} \; | \geq min\_sup$.

2.2.4. Compactness constraint
Compactness constraint is specified by giving compactness range (min_compactness, max_compactness). In sequence databases each transaction in every sequence has a timestamp. The time-stamp difference (difference of days) between the first and the last transactions in a discovered sequential pattern must not be greater than given period. (Refer Equation 9) (Pei et al., 2007).

$$C_{Comp} \equiv Comp(\alpha) \; \theta \; \Delta t, \tag{9}$$

where $\theta \in \{\leq, \geq\}$ and Δt is a given integer. A sequence α satisfies the constraint if and only if

$|\{ \beta \in SDB | \exists 1 \leq i1 < \cdots <icomp(\alpha) \leq comp(\beta)$ s.t. $\alpha[1] \sqsubseteq \beta[i1],\dots, \alpha[comp(\alpha)] \sqsubseteq \beta[icomp(\alpha)]$, and for all $1 < j \leq comp(\alpha)$, $(\beta[ij]$ .time - $\beta[ij-1]$ .time) $\theta \; \Delta t\} \; | \geq min\_sup$.

2.2.5. Quantity constraint
Quantity constraint is specified by giving minimum quantity support (q_minsup). Total quantity value of the discovered pattern must be greater than q_minsup. Suppose the pattern is <(a(10)),(b(5) c(2))> and m_minsup =15. The sequence contains total quantity value = 10 + 5 + 2 =17 $\geq$ 15, which satisfied quantity constraint.

A sequence $S_s = < (q_1(qty_1)), (q_2(qty_2)), \dots , (q_m(qty_m)) >$ is said to be a subsequence of S only if, (1) itemset S_s is a subsequence of S, $S_s \in S$ and (2) the number of items in S should satisfied $\sum_{i=1}^{m}(qty) \geq T_{qty}$ Where, T_{Qty} is quantity constraint.

2.2.6. Monitory constraint
Monetary constraint is specified by giving minimum monitory support (m_minsup). Total monetary value of the discovered pattern must be greater than m_minsup. Suppose the pattern is <(a(100)), (b(50)c(70))> and m_minsup = 130. The sequence contains total monitory value = 100 + 50 + 70 = 220 $\geq$ 130, which satisfied monitory constraint.

Total Monitory: The Total Monitory (TM) constraint defines item in a sequence must be more than the defined threshold value. The Total Monitory constraint is formally represented in Equation 10.

$$C_{TM} \equiv \text{qty} * M\_pur(\alpha)\,\omega\,\Delta T \qquad (10)$$

Where, $\omega \in \{\geq\}$, ΔT integer value/ Profitable threshold. α is sequence.

A sequence $S_s = < (q_1(\text{qty}_1), t_1, M\_Sold_1, M\_Pur_1), (q_2(\text{qty}_2), M\_Sold_2, M\_Pur_2), \ldots, (q_m(\text{qty}_m), M\_Sold_m, M\_Pur_m) >$ is said to be a subsequence of S only if, (1) itemset S_s is a subsequence of S, $S_s \in S$ and (2) the number of items in S should satisfied Equation 11.

$$\left[\frac{\sum_{i=1}^{m}(\text{qty} * M\_Pur)i}{m} \right] \geq T_{TM} \qquad (11)$$

2.2.7. Length constraint

Length constraint is specified by giving minimum length support (l_minsup).Length of the discovered pattern must be greater than l_minsup. Suppose the pattern is <(a,b)(b,c)> and l_minsup = 2. The sequence is selected because length of the sequence = $2 \geq$ l_minsup(=2). (refer Equation 12) (Pei et al., 2007).

$$C_{Length} \equiv \text{len}(\alpha)\,\omega\,l \qquad (12)$$

Where, $\omega \in \{\geq\}$, l integer value/length threshold. α is sequence.

2.2.8. Item constraint

An *item constraint* specifies subset of items that should or should not be present in the patterns. Suppose the pattern is <(a), (bc)>. If the item constraint is b than it is satisfied by above pattern. It is in the form of Equation 13 (Pei et al., 2007).

$$C_{item}(\alpha) \equiv (\varphi\, i\colon 1 \leq i \leq \text{len}(\alpha), \quad \alpha[i]\theta V)$$
$$\text{OR}\quad C_{item}(\alpha) \equiv (\varphi i\colon 1 \leq i \leq \text{len}(\alpha), \quad \alpha[i] \cap V \neq \phi) \qquad (13)$$

Where V is a subset of items, $\phi \in \{\forall, \exists\}$ and $\theta \in \{\subseteq, \subseteq, \supseteq, \supseteq, \in, \in\}$. For the sake of brevity, we omit the strict operators (e.g., $\subset, \supset$) in our discussion here. However, the same principles can be applied to them.

2.2.9. Representation of data sequence

Data-sequence A is represented as <(a1, t1, m1), (a2, t2, m2), ..., (an, tn, mn)>, where (aj, tj, mj) means that item ajis purchased at time tj with total value mj, $1 \leq j \leq n$, and tj-1 $\leq$ tj for $2 \leq j \leq n$ In the data-sequence, if items occur at the same time, they are ordered alphabetically.

Dataset Format (Sequence Database.txt)

<1> 1 -1 <2> 1 2 3 -1 <3> 1 2 -1 -2

<1> 1 -1 <2> 1 2 -1 <3> 1 2 -1 <4> 1 3 -1 -2

<1> 1 2 -1 <2> 1 2 -1 -2

<1> 2 -1 <2> 1 3 -1 -2

<1>, <2> ..... – Time Stamp (day at which transaction occurred)

-1 - End of Transaction

-2 - End of Sequence

1, 2, 3 - Actual Items

3. Proposed system framework

3.1. Strength and working of proposed algorithm

(i) The proposed algorithm being FP-Growth based, *Constraint-based prefix span* reduces candidate generation and works on projected prefix database.

(ii) First the algorithm scans the database and identifies frequent items. It recursively finds the prefix not only on frequent items but also with consideration of gap constraint which takes care of two adjacent time stamps *(max_gap,min_gap)*, with first and last time stamp of prefix sequence having to satisfy compactness constraint.

(iii) The sequence which does not follow such constraints can be pruned at pseudo projection level. This process reduces the database projection cost and search space as compared to sole parameter support threshold thereby increasing efficiency of proposed algorithm.

(iv) Incorporation of Length constraint limits the generation of sequences by pruning the sequences having more length at projection level. Item and Recency act as post processing parameters. Incorporation of such constraints in conventional Prefix Span gives more effective results as per user's interest.

(v) Proposed Emerging Pattern mining algorithm is identifying those patterns which are not in limelight but have potential to become strong in near future. Such hidden patterns can be highlighted using slight reduction of boundary value of support threshold and inclusion of recency constraint.

3.2. Constraint-based sequential pattern generation

Figure 1 shows three stages of sequential pattern generation. Dotted line and straight line denoted backward flow and forward flow. Figure 2 shows detail of Pre-processing of input data. After generation of sequential input file in format, file is used for sequence generation. Figure 3 and Figure 4 shows flow to generate sequences which satisfied frequency, compactness and gap constraints (FCG—sequences).

Figure 5 shows complete set of FCGLIRM (Frequent, Compact, Gap, Length, Item, Recent, Monitory) —constraint-based sequential patterns. Subjective analysis can be done from different amalgamation of constraints. Knowledge can be extracted from constraint-based patterns. Following thing can be derived from knowledge:

- Loyal customer
- Profitable customer or Profitable purchase
- Simplicity of patterns
- Chain purchase or Influence purchase
- Life style-driven shopping
- Trend analysis

3.3. Proposed algorithm[4]

I. Proposed constraint-based prefix span for SPM

Input: Sequence Database SDB

Values of following Constraints:-

Support threshold : f_minsup

Recency support :   r_min

Compactness :   (min_compact, max_compact)

Gap :   (min_gap,max-gap)

Length :   l_min

Quantity :   q_min

Item :   i_constraint

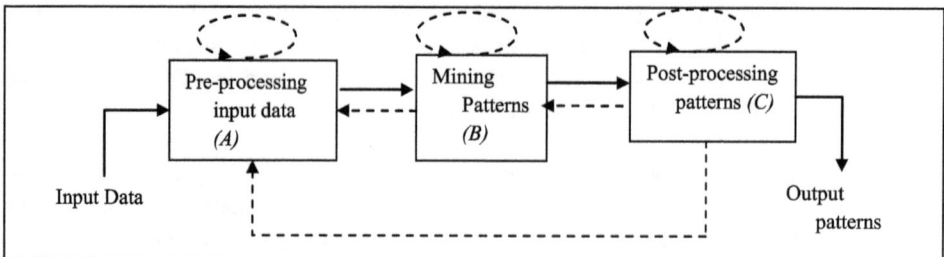

Figure 1. Generation of sequential pattern.

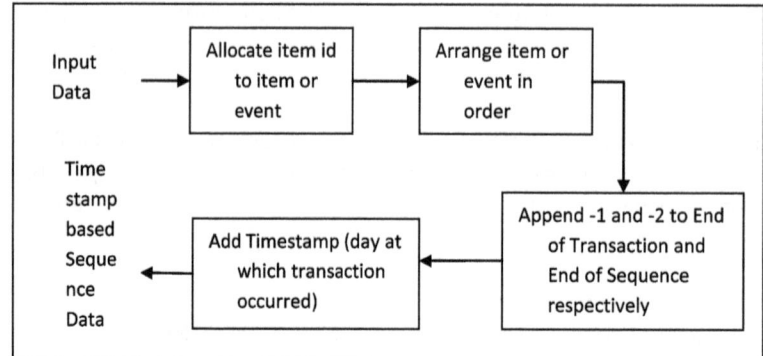

Figure 2. Pre-processing Input Data (A).

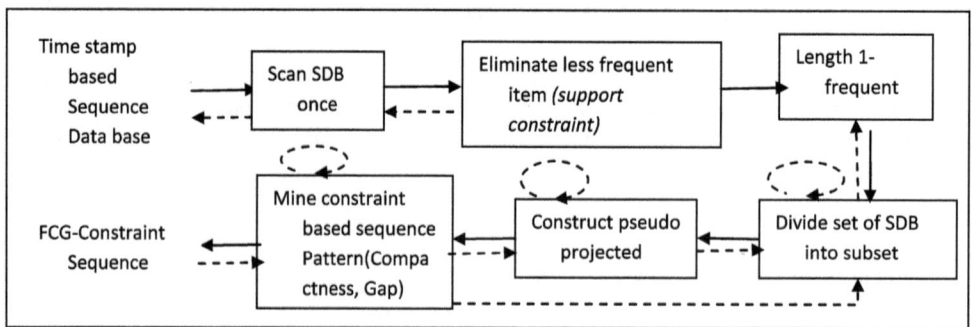

Figure 3. FCG-constraint sequence (B.1).

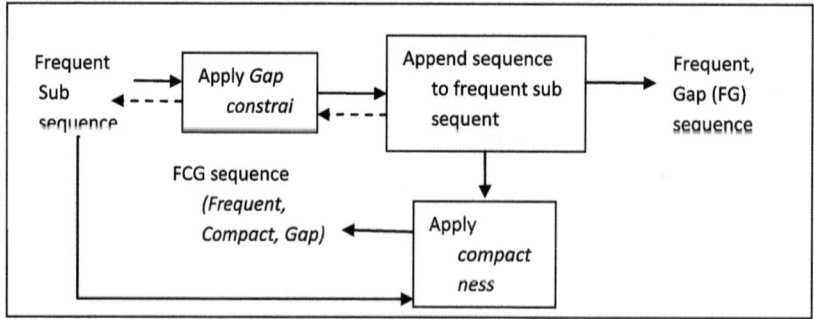

Figure 4. Mining constraint-based sequence (D - B.2).

Output:
(i) The complete set of constraint-based sequential patterns.

Procedure:
Step 1: Find length-1 patterns and remove irrelevant sequences.

  (i) Scan the sequence database SDB once to count f-support for each item set.

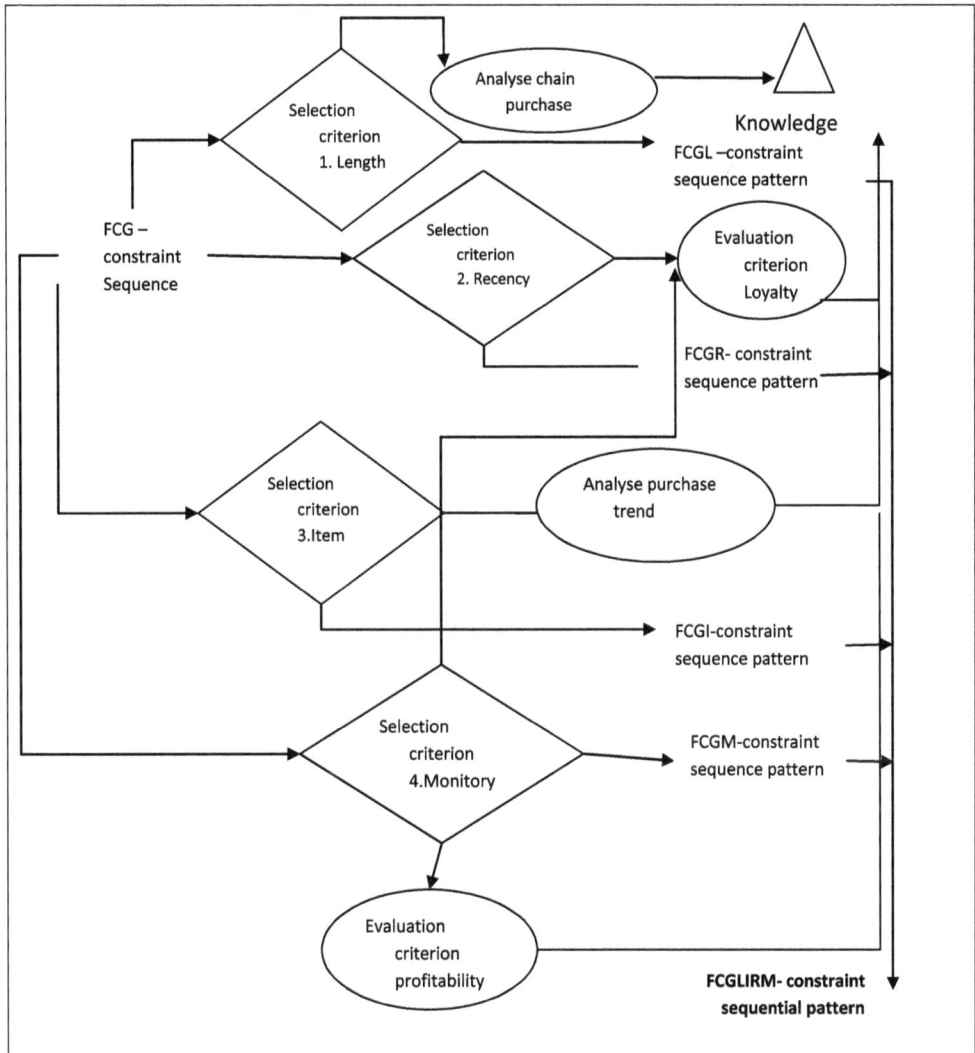

Figure 5. Generation of complete constraint-based sequential pattern (C).

  (ii) Identify patterns as length-1 patterns.

  (iii) Infrequent items are removed and generate pseudo-sequence database

Step 2: Divide the set of sequential patterns into subsets
Without considering constraint C, the complete set of sequential patterns should be divided into subsets without overlap according to the set of length-1 sequential patterns (prefix).

Step 3: Construct projected database and mine subsets recursively

(i) Construct projected database for each prefix.

(ii) Recursively generate projected database for each new prefix and mine it to find local frequent patterns.

Step 4: Mine constraint-based sequential Pattern from Projected database and mine subset recursively.

  (i) Apply gap and compactness constraint.
    (a) In each projected database, frequent adjacent item i and j, t_i and t_j are time stamped, respectively where, sequence $<(i, t_i), (j, t_j)>$.
    $|t_i - t_j| \le |\, min\_gap - max\_gap\,|$

(b) In each projected database, time stamp difference of first and last frequent items i and k,t_i and t_k are time stamped respectively, where sequence $<(i,t_i), (j,t_j), (k,t_k)>$.

$$|t_i - t_k| \geq |\text{min\_compact} - \text{max\_compact}|$$

(ii) For each frequent item i append it to prefix to generate new prefix in such a way that
  a) i can be assembled to the last element of prefix to form a sequential pattern
  or
  b) <i> can be appended to prefix to form a sequential pattern.

(iii) Recursively generate projected database for each new prefix which satisfies $C_{Compactness}$ and C_{Gap} constraints to find local frequent patterns.
Where, $C_{Compactness}$ and C_{Gap} are compactness and Gap constraint.

Repeat step 3 and step 4 recursively.

Step -5: Complete set of sequences SEQ $_{CFG}$ satisfied Frequency (f_min), Compactness (min_compact, max_compact) and Gap (min_gap, max_gap)

Step 6: Apply post mining constraints Recency, Length, Quantity and Item to local frequent Patterns.

i. Merge local frequent patterns which satisfy r_min,l_min, q_min to generate global frequent patterns.
  a) Time stamp of last frequent item k is t_k. Where, sequence $<(i, t_i), (j, t_j), (k, t_k)>$.
  $t_k \geq r\_min$
  b) Sequence SEQ $_{CFG}$ = $<(i, t_i), (j, t_j), (k, t_k)>$
  Length (SEQ $_{CFG}$) $\geq$ l_min
  c) Sequence SEQ $_{CFG}$ = $<(i, t_i, qty_i), (j, t_j, qty_j), (k, t_k, qty_k)>$ where, qty_i is quantity of item i is purchased. $\forall i \in$ SEQ, where i={1, 2 ... n}
  $(qty_1 + qty_2 + ... + qty_n) \geq c$

ii. Generate complete set of Constraint-based Sequences SEQ $_{CFGRLQ}$
  $SEQ_{CFGRLQ} = SEQ_{CFGR} \cap SEQ_{CFGL} \cap SEQ_{CFGQ}$
  where, SEQ_{CFGR}, SEQ_{CFGL}, SEQ_{CFGQ} satisfied r_min, l_min, q_min respectively.

iii. Apply item constraint to frequent patterns: Check item iis present in global frequent patterns.

Once frequent patterns are generated its check the prescribed item is present in the sequence or not, which should satisfied i_constraint.

Sequence SEQ_{CFGRLQ} = $<(i_1, t_1), (i_2, t_2), ... (i_n, t_n)>$, where items are $\{i_1, i_2 ... i_n\}$ and $\{t_1, t_2 ... t_n\}$ are respective timestamp. Suppose, i_constraint = i_k than,

$i_k \in SEQ_{CFGRLQ}$.item where SEQ_{CFGRLQ}.item = $\{i_1, i_2 ... i_n\}$

Step 7: Output the complete set of Constraint-based sequential patterns $SEQ_{CFGRLQI}$.

II. Proposed reduced boundary value and recency-based Emerging Patterns (EPs)

Input: Sequence Database SDB

Values of following Constraints:-

Support threshold : f_minsup

Recencysupport : r_min

Output:

(1) Emerging patterns (EPs)

Step 1 to 7

EPGen (SD, f_minsup, r_minsup) *//Emerging Pattern generation*
   Supply the sequence database SD
        //sequential database with timestamp
   SEQ_{f_minsup} = Call SequenceGen(<>, 0, S)
   boundary_sup = BoundaryCal (f_minsup)
   $SEQ_{boundary\_sup}$ = Call SequenceGen(<>, 0, S)   (Refer Section 2.1, Equation 1)
   $SEQ_{boundary}$ = **SEQ** $_{f\_minsup}$ **−SEQ**$_{boundary\_sup}$
   EP = SEQ $_{boundary}$ **.lasttimestamp ≥ r_minsup**
return **EP**// *Emerging patterns*
BoundaryCal (f_minsup) //   *Boundary value calculation*
   boundary_sup = f_minsup − (0.02 × f_minsup)   (Refer Section 2.1, Equation 2)
return **boundary_sup**

3.4. Challenges of proposed Algorithm

I. There is no scientific survey about boundary value reduction in proposed Emerging Patterns mining algorithm. Only domain experts can decide how much reduction is required for a particular
   application.

II. Reduction of support threshold boundary generates enormous numbers patterns.

4. Simulation study and data analysis

4.1. Justification for choosing the prefix span to modify

Following graph shows the execution time and memory usage of various SPM algorithms namely GSP
(Srikant & Agrawal, 1996), SPADE (Zaki, 2001), SPAM (Ayres et al., 2002), SPIRIT (Garofalakis et al., 1999)
and FP-Growth-based Freespan (Han, Dong et al., 2000), Prefixspan (Pei et al., 2001). Experiment conducted on four real-time datasets namely Breast cancer, Mushroom, Leviathan, MSNBC and six synthetic dataset generated by IBM generator.[5] IBM generated datasets are described in Table 1 and Table 2.
Statistical Description of Breast Cancer Dataset is described in Table 3. Figures 6, 7 and 8 describe performance of SPM algorithms on real-time Breast Cancer Dataset.

4.1.1. Working environment

Algorithms worked on Java environment and tested on an Intel Core Duo Processor with 2GB main memory under Windows operating system.

Following observations can be made from above experiments:

• Fifty-eight percent more time is taken by SPADE algorithm as compared to Prefix span, which is
  gradually reducing with respect to increasing support values. Approximately 18%–19% more
  execution time is taken by Prefix Span as compared to SPAM. Almost 68.6% more execution time
  is taken by GSP as compared by Prefix Span.

• Prefix Span and SPAM are generating same number of frequent sequences. Same way the same
  number of sequences are generated by SPADE and GSP. Ninety percent less sequences are generated by Prefix Span and SPAM as compare to SPADE and GSP.

• Memory consumption is less by Prefix Span as compare to other algorithms because of generation
  of pseudo database.

4.2. Comparative study of proposed algorithm with the traditional SPM algorithms

This section empirically compared the proposed Constraint-based Prefix Spanalgorithm with the traditional SPM algorithm Prefix Span (Zaki, 2001) and constraint-based SPM method RFM (Chen et al., 2009). Experimental study performed on synthetic datasets (describe in Table 4). Table 5, describes parameters of dataset. Time stamp is ignored for Prefix Span because it is design for SPM without timestamp. For ease of comparison, some parameters are kept fixed: *Confidence=30% Compactness = (1,5), Gap = (1,3), Recency =2, Length = 3*. Seven tests are performed to evaluate the proposed algorithm, which are described in Table 4.

The first test is designed for efficiency and effectiveness analysis in form of, execution time and number of pattern generation respectively. Test II emphasis of scalability analysis. Test III evaluates importance of individual constraint in form of pattern generation. Test IV tries to find out buying behaviour of customer using length constraint. Test V, VI and VII emphasis on Recency and Gap constraints, how number of pattern generation is changing for wider range to smaller range of Gap and for increment of Recency time stamp value.

Test I executed based on six synthetic datasets. Comparison made for run times and pattern generation of three algorithms: proposed constraint based Prefix Span (RFCGL) with RFM and algorithm Prefix Span. Here, result of C10S4T2.5N10 and C50S4T2.5N10 are shown. Rest of the results (for remaining four datasets) are same, (Refer Figure 9).

In Test II, six synthetic datasets were used to perform scalability analysis, which varied the value of |C| (from 10 K to 50 K) for support range (0.010%–0.025%) for 30% confidence value. (Refer Figure 10)

Test III explored how the recency, frequency, compactness, gap and length constraints influence the generation of sequential patterns. CFRGL patterns, CFRG* patterns, CFR** patterns,*FR** patterns and *F*** patterns, where *F*** patterns are the traditional sequential patterns. Table 5 lists the amounts of these five patterns and their corresponding percentages with respect to the traditional pattern (*F***). (Refer Figure 11)

Test VI shows, only one-fourth of patterns are recent and compact. Three-fourth patterns are traditional in C10S4T2.5N10 and C20S4T2.5N10 datasets, which is decreasing by more 5%–7% in remaining datasets. Inclusion of all the constraints reduced the patterns drastically. Only 3%–5% patterns are having length more than 3 means 95% times of purchase happen only ones or twice in sequence. Average 36% of time purchase happens only one time. People are not moving for further purchase. Average 45.25% of the purchase happen two times is moving for third or more time. (Refer Figure 12)

Test V shows, Numbers of sequential patterns are reducing gradually for older to later timestamp. But execution time remains same for confidence and support values. Execution time is getting reduced by reducing support count. Same way number of generated sequential patterns are also reduced. (Refer Figures 13, 14, 15)

Test VI, shows number of patterns generated and execution time for various supports and confidence. More no of patterns are generated for larger gap and it's reduced for smaller gap. Execution time remains same. Increases of confidence value also generate more number of patterns by 11% and 10% wrt. 20%–40%, 40%–60% confidence value. Decreasing rate of support also decrease execution time by 75%. (Refer Figure 16)

Table 1. Parameter description of synthetic data-set	
Parameter	**Description**
|C|	Number of Customers (1000's)
|S|	Average number of transactions per sequence
|T|	Average number of items per transaction
|N|	Number of distinct items (1000's)

Table 2. Parameter setting of synthetic data generation				
Dataset	|C|	|S|	|T|	|N|
C10S4T2.5N10	10,000	4	2.5	10,000
C20S4T2.5N10	20,000	4	2.5	10,000
C30S4T2.5N10	30,000	4	2.5	10,000
C40S4T2.5N10	40,000	4	2.5	10,000
C50S4T2.5N10	50,000	4	2.5	10,000
C10S6T2.5N10	10,000	6	2.5	10,000

Table 3. Statistical description of Breast Cancer dataset	
Number of distinct items	16
Largest item id	20
Average number of itemsets per sequence	9.977110157367669
Average number of distinct item per sequence	9.977110157367669
Average number of occurrences in a sequence for each item appearing in a sequence	1.0
Average number of items per itemset	1.0

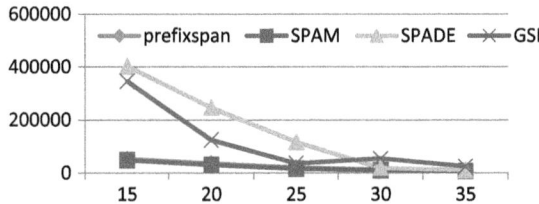

Figure 6. Execution time (ms) vs. Support for real-time dataset Breast Cancer.

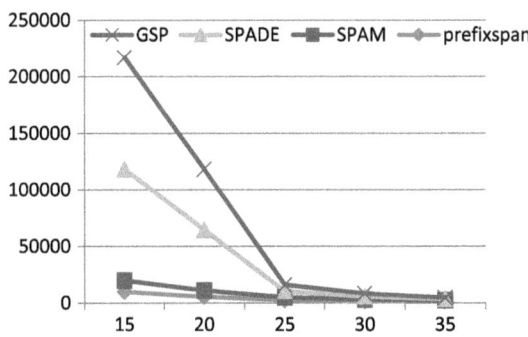

Figure 7. Number of frequent sequence vs. Support for real-time dataset Breast Cancer.

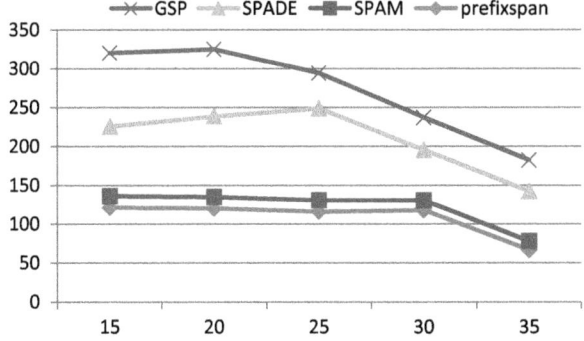

Figure 8. Memory (mb) vs. Support for real-time dataset Breast Cancer.

Table 4. Parameter setting for different test

Test	Dataset		Support	Confidence	Recency	Compactness	Gap	Length
I	C10S4T2.5N10C20S4T2.5N10C30S4T2.5N10C40S4T2.5N10C50S4T2.5N10C10S6T2.5N10		0.01%–0.025%	30%	2	*(min_comp, max_ comp) =(1, 5)*	*(min_gap, max_gap) =(2, 3)*	3
II	C10S4T2.5N10C20S4T2.5N10C30S4T2.5N10C40S4T2.5N10C50S4T2.5N10		0.01%–0.025%	30%	2	*(min_comp, max_ comp) =(1, 5)*	*(min_gap, max_gap) =(2, 3)*	—
III	C10S4T2.5N10C20S4T2.5N10C30S4T2.5N10C40S4T2.5N10C50S4T2.5N10C10S6T2.5N10		0.01%–0.025%	30%	2	*(min_comp, max_ comp) =(1, 5)*	*(min_gap, max_gap) =(2, 3)*	2, 3
IV	C10S4T2.5N10C20S4T2.5N10C30S4T2.5N10C40S4T2.5N10C50S4T2.5N10C10S6T2.5N10		0.01%–0.025%	30%	2	*(min_comp, max_ comp) =(1, 5)*	*(min_gap, max_gap) =(2, 3)*	0, 2, 3
V	C20S4T2.5N10		0.1%–0.5%	30%	1, 2, 3, 4, 5	—	*(min_gap, max_gap) =(2, 3)*	—
VI	C20S4T2.5N10		0.1% 0.25% 0.5% 1%	20%, 40%, 60% 20%, 40%, 60% 20%, 40%, 60% 20%, 40%, 60%	—	—	*(min_gap, max_gap) = (1, 4), (1, 3), (1, 2), (1, 1)*	—
VII	C20S4T2.5N10		0.1%	50%	—		*(min_gap, max_gap) =(1, 3)*	—

In Test VII, We have taken support, confidence as a fix value 0.001(0.1%) and 0.5(50%) respectively and gap = <1,3>.more number of patterns are generated for wider range. One percent more number of patterns are generated as compared to smaller range of timestamp e.g. <min,max>:<2,3>–<2,4>and <3,3>–<3,4>. (Refer Figure 17)

4.3. Experiment of emerging patterns (EPs)

Second experiment discovers such patterns which are lies on boundary but does not discover because of little low support value. Such patterns are not in lime light now but might be in high light for future. It's having potential to become strong in future known as Emerging Patterns (EPs). EPs based on customers' buying behaviour captured at various support values: 0.1%, 0.08% and 0.05%. Almost 10%–12% patterns are known as Emerging Patterns (EPs), are generated after reduction of boundary value for IBM generated synthetic dataset.

Table 5. Number of pattern generation (%)

Synthetic data-set	CFRGL		CFRG*		CFR**		*FR**		*F***	
Name	Number of patterns	%	Number of patterns	%	Number of patterns	%	Number of patterns	%	Number of patterns	%
C10S4T2.5N10	196	4.63	1078	25.49	1116	26.38	1174	27.76	4229	100
C20S4T2.5N10	123	3.64	761	22.54	786	23.28	804	23.82	3375	100
C30S4T2.5N10	103	2.84	594	16.41	623	17.21	661	18.26	3619	100
C40S4T2.5N10	85	2.43	547	15.52	547	15.52	557	15.95	3491	100
C50S4T2.5N10	84	2.41	541	15.57	541	15.57	549	15.8	3473	100
C10S6T2.5N10	499	8.06	1646	26.59	1796	29.01	1996	32.25	6189	100

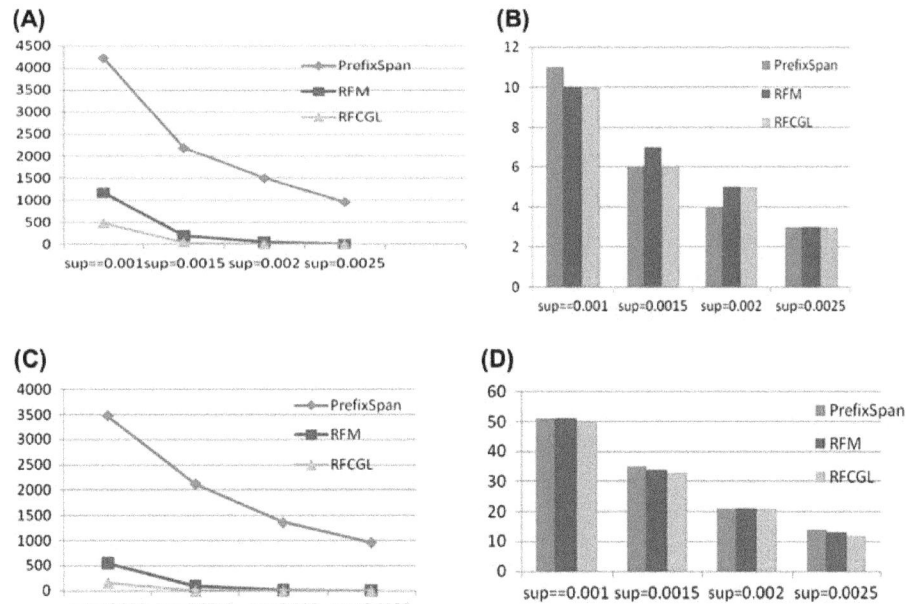

**Figure 9. (A) number of patterns vs. support (C10S4T2.5N10) (B) Execution time of patterns vs. support (C10S4T2.5N10) (C) number of patterns vs. support (C50S4T2.5N10) (D) Execution time of patterns vs. support
(C50S4T2.5N10).**

After reduction of boundary value more patterns are generated, out of them 36% (C10s4T2.5N10), 18% (C30s4T2.5N10) and 23% (C50s4T2.5N10) new patterns are generated which are known as forming stage patterns. Patterns which are already generated for normal support threshold are discovered at reduced boundary support with change support value. Sixty-four percent (C10s4T2.5N10), 82% (C30s4T2.5N10) and 77% (C50s4T2.5N10) patterns are older patterns. (Refer Figure 18).

5. Conclusion and future direction

Proposed *Constraint-based Prefix Span* algorithm is not restricted to conventional Sequential Pattern Mining (SPM) parameter frequency but incorporates six more important parameters like Gap, Recency, Compactness/Duration, Profitability, Item and Length. Incorporation of these constraints in FP-growth based—Prefix Span leads to more efficient and effective results by reduction of patterns. Concise patterns present relevant and precise results in terms of users' interest. Seven different experiments are performed on IBM generated six synthetic datasets. Comparison made for run times and pattern generation of three algorithms: proposed constraint-based Prefix Span with RFM and Prefix Span. Proposed constraint-based Prefix Span algorithm is more efficient and effective in terms of reduction of patterns generation of interesting patterns for user. Experiment studies also reveal that less number of patterns is generated by Duration/Compactness constraint with emphasis on patterns that are active for certain time span. Simulation study of Gap states that: *"less number of*

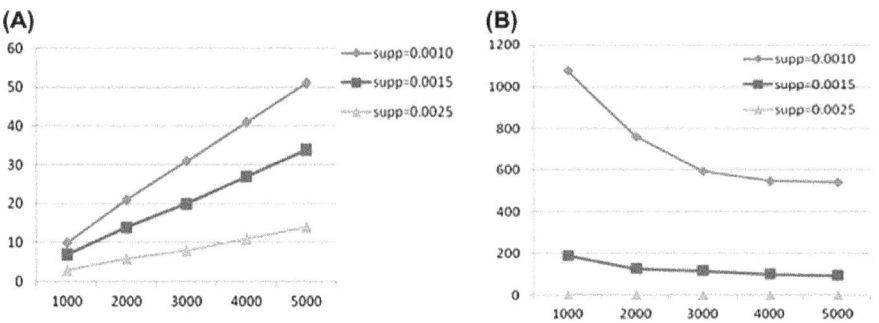

Figure 10. (A) Runtime Vs. |C| (B) number of pattern Vs. |C|.

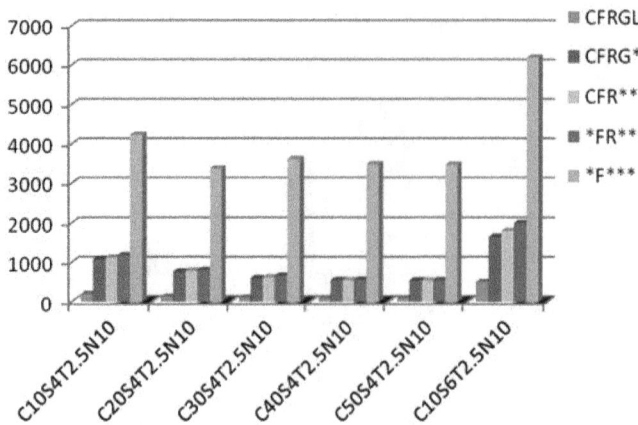

Figure 11. Number of patterns generated by different datasets

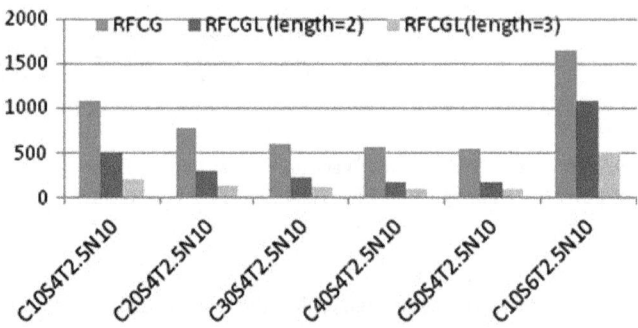

Figure 12. Number of patterns for length constraint.

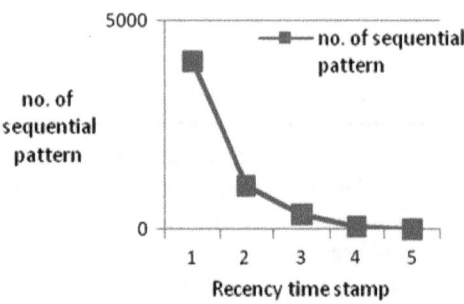

Figure 13. Number of sequential pattern wrt. recency constraint.

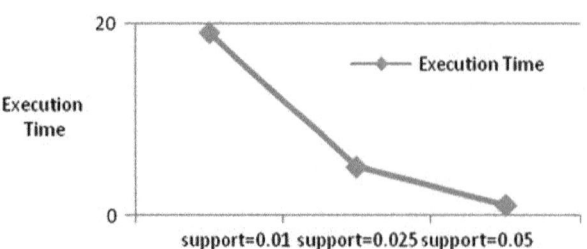

Figure 14. Execution time for various support count for wrt. recency time stamp = 1.

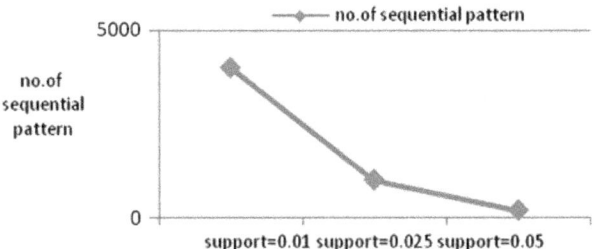

Figure 15. No. of sequential pattern for various support count w.r.t. recency time stamp = 1 (C20S4T2.5N10).

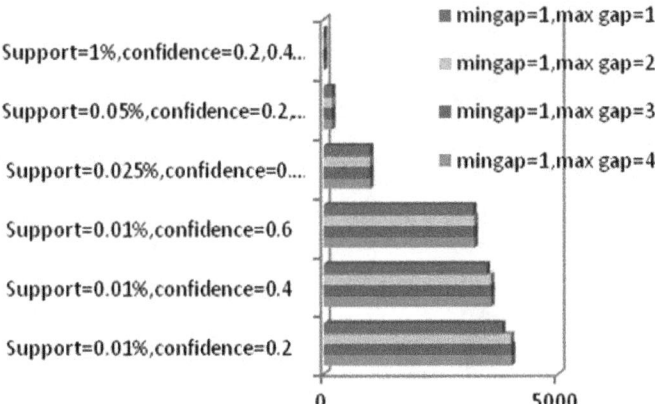

Figure 16. No of patterns for various confidence and confidence for gap constraints.

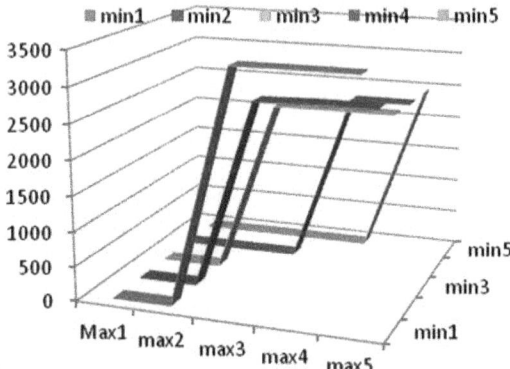

Figure 17. Number of pattern generated wrt. compactness constraint (C20S4T2.5N10).

people is moving towards another purchase within a short time period but increase in time gap will give more number of purchases." Recency and Profitability are important parameters to formulate marketing strategies and the proposed algorithm addresses both parameters. Proposed Constrained-based Prefix Span is scalable in terms of generation of patterns and execution time by varying range of customer from 10K to 50K. Simulation also captures Emerging Patterns (EPs) by reduction of support boundary and recency parameter. Algorithm is also able to identify pattern which are at formative stage. Sequential pattern-based clustering can be helpful for customer segmentation for enabling marketers to target loyal customer groups.

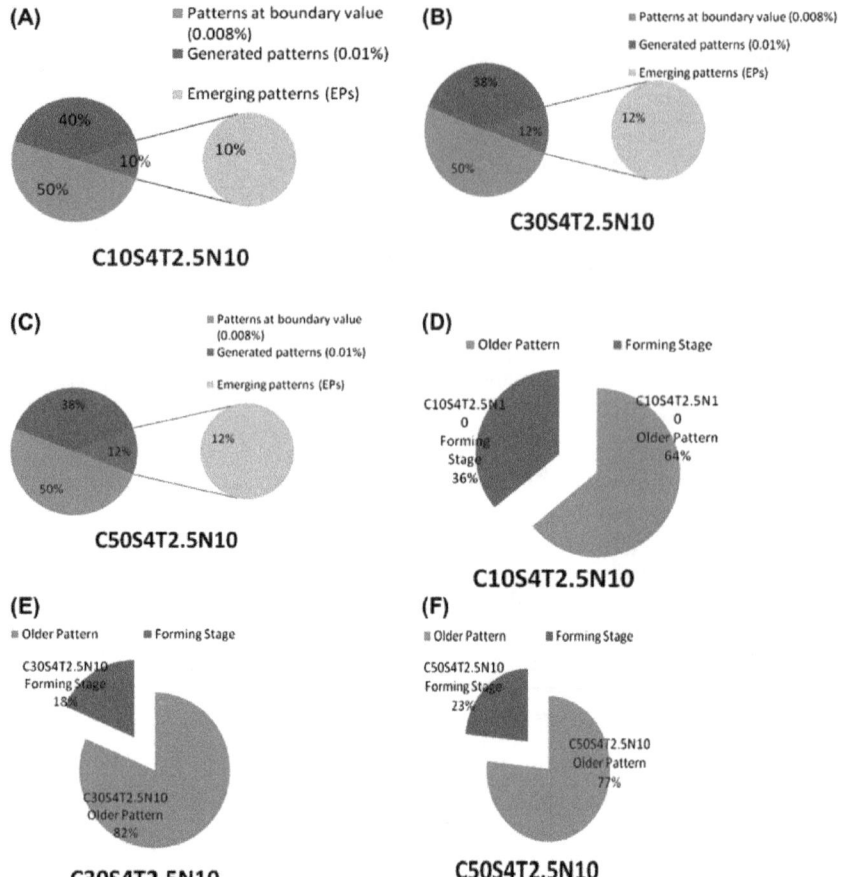

Figure 18. (A) EPs (C10s4T2.5N10) (B) EPs (C30s4T2.5N10) (C) EPs (C50s4T2.5N10) (D) EPs in detail (C10s4T2.5N10) (E) EPs in detail (C30s4T2.5N10) (F) EPs in detail (C50s4T2.5N10).

Funding

The authors received no direct funding for this research.

Author details

Niti Ashish Kumar Desai[1]

E-mail: nitiadesai@gmail.com

ORCID ID: http://orcid.org/0000-0001-7906-2236

Amit Ganatra[2]

E-mail: amitganatra.ce@ecchanga.ac.in

ORCID ID: http://orcid.org/0000-0001-7906-2236

[1] Department of Computer Engineering, Uka Tarsadia University, Bardoli, Surat, Gujarat, India.

[2] U and P U. Patel Department of Computer Engineering, Charotar University of Science and Technology, Changa, Anand, Gujarat 388421, India.

Notes

1. PhD Dissertation report on "The research of customer purchase behaviour using constraint-based SPM Approach," National Central University, Taiwan by Yen-Liang Chen Department of Information Management. (http://www.ncu.edu.tw)

2. Weinstein and Shane S., Game Plan: How can marketers face the challenge of managing customer value metrics. This article is adapted from Dr. Weinstein's new book (2012), *Superior Customer Value: Strategies for Winning and Retaining Customers* (3rd ed.). CRC Press.

3. Akshay Tritya – It also known as Akha Teej, Hindus considers Akshay Tritya to be a holy and supremely auspicious day. Starting a new activity or buying valu-ables on Akshay Tritya is considered to bring luck and success. So, many people buy new gold jewellery on Akshay Tritya.

   Lakshmi Pujan – Lakshmi Puja is third day of Diwali. Wor-ship of the goddess Lakshmi is the main event on Diwali in India. People buy gold and silver, precious gemstones, new utensils of copper, brass and bronze as a sign of good luck, prosperity, money and wealth.

   Pushya Nakshtra – Moon transiting in pushya nakshtra is considered as auspicious duration in India. It is believed to be the best time of the year for buying assets in India. Experts from the industry believe that there is a saying

that whoever buys gold on Pushya Nakshtra, survives for generations.
4. Originality in Algorithm I and II are written in bold.
5. IBM Quest Synthetic Data Generator is used to generate synthetic datasets.
  http://www.philippe-fournier-viger.com/spmf/datasets/IBM_Quest_data_generator.zip

References

Agrawal, R., & Srikant, R. (1994, September). Fast algorithms for mining association rules. In *Proceeding of International Conference of Very Large Data Bases* (pp. 487–499). Santiago.

Agrawal, R., & Srikant, R. (1995, March). Mining sequential patterns. In *Proceeding of the 11th International Conference on Data Engineering*. Taipei.

Ayres, J., Flannick, J., Gehrke, J., & Yiu, T. (2002). Sequential pattern mining using a bitmap representation. In *Proceedings of the 8th ACM SIGKDD International Conference on Knowledge Discovery and Data Mining*. Krakow.

Bhensdadia, C. K., & Kosta, Y. P. (2011). Discovering active and profitable patterns with RFM (recency, frequency and monetary) sequential pattern mining: A constraint based approach. *International Journal of Information Technology and Knowledge Management, 4*, 27–32.

Chen, M., Han, J., & Philip, S. Y. (1996, December). Data mining: An overview from a database perspective. *IEEE Transactions on Knowledge and Data Engineering, 8*, 866–883.

Chen, R.-S., Wu, R.-C., & Chen, J. Y. (2005). In *Proceedings of the 29th Annual International Computer Software and Applications Conference* (COMPSAC'05) 0730-3157/05 $20.00 © 2005 IEEE. Washington, DC.

Chen, Y.-L., Kuo, M.-H., Wu, S.-Y., & Tang, K. (2009). Discovering recency, frequency, and monetary (RFM) sequential patterns from customers' purchasing data. *Electronic Commerce Research and Applications, 8*, 241–251.

Garofalakis, M., Rastogi, R., & Shim K. (1999). SPIRIT: Sequential pattern mining with regular expression constraints. In *VLDB'99*. Edinburgh.

Goodman, J. (1992). Leveraging the customer database to your competitive advantage. *Journal of Direct Marketing, 55*, 26–27.

Han, J., Dong, G., Mortazavi-Asl, B., Chen, Q., Dayal, U., & Hsu, M.-C. (2000). Freespan: Frequent pattern-projected sequential pattern mining. In *Proceedings of International Conference of Knowledge Discovery and Data Mining* (pp. 355–359). New York, NY.

Han, J., Pei, J., & Yin, Y. (2000, May). Mining frequent patterns without candidate generation. In *Proceeding of ACM-SIGMOD. International Conference of Management of Data* (pp. 1–12). Dallas.

Hu, H. L. & Chen, Y. L. (2008). Mining typical patterns from databases. *Information Sciences, 19*, 3683–3696.

Hughes, A. M. (1994). *Strategic database marketing*. Chicago, IL: Probus Publishing.

Lawrence, R. D., Almasi, G. S., Kotlyar, V., Viveros, M. S., & Duri, S. S. (2001). Personalization of supermarket product recommendations. *Data Mining and Knowledge Discovery, 5*, 11–32.

Mahdavi, I., Cho, N., Shirazi, B., & Sahebjamnia, N. (2008). Designing evolving user profile in e-CRM with dynamic clustering of Web documents. *Data and Knowledge Engineering, 65*, 355–372.

Mallick, B., Garg, D., & Grover, B. (2012, July). CFM-prefixspan: A pattern growth Algorithm incorporating compactness and monitory. *International Journal of Innovative Computing, Information and Control, 8*, 1349–4198.

Mary, G., & Iyengar, S. N. (2010, April). A frame work for ontological privacy preserved mining. *International Journal of Network Security, 2*, 9–20.

Mohammad, S., Hosseini, S., Maleki, A., & Mohammad, R. (2009). Cluster analysis using data mining approach to develop CRM methodology to assess the customer loyalty. *Expert System with Applications, 37*, 5259–5264.

Pei, J., Han, J., Mortazavi, B., Pino, H. (2001). Prefix span: Mining sequential patterns efficiently by prefix- projected pattern growth. In *International Conference of Data and Engineering*. Heidelberg.

Pei, J., Han, J., & Wang, W. (2007). Constraint-based sequential pattern mining: The pattern growth methods. *Journal of Intelligent Information System, 28*, 133–160.

Qiasi, D., Minaei-Bidgoli, B., & Amooee, G. (2012). Developing a model for measuring customer's loyalty and value with RFM technique and clustering algorithms. *The Journal of Mathematics and Computer Science, 4*, 172–181.

Raza, K. (2010). Application of data mining in bioinformatics. *Indian Journal of Computer Science and Engineering, 1*, 114–118.

Shaw, M. J., Subramaniam, C., Tan, G.W., & Welge, M. E. (2001). Knowledge management and data mining for marketing. *Decision Support Systems, 31*, 127–137.

Shen, C., & Chuang, H. (2009). A study on the applications of data mining techniques to enhance customer lifetime value. *WSEAS Transactions on Information Science and Applications ISSN, 6*, 1790–1832.

Song, H. S., Kim, J. K., & Kim, S. H. (2001). Mining the change of customer behaviour in an Internet shopping mall. *Expert Systems with Applications, 21*, 157–168.

Srikant, R., & Agrawal, R. (1996). Mining sequential patterns: Generalizations and performance improvements. In *Proceedings of the 5th International Conference Extending Database Technology* (pp. 3–17). London.

Zaki, M. (2001). SPADE: An efficient algorithm for mining frequent sequences. *Machine Learning, 40*, 31–60.

11

A comparative study of the Bees Algorithm as a tool for function optimisation

Duc Truong Pham[1] and Marco Castellani[1]*

*Corresponding author: Marco Castellani, School of Mechanical Engineering, University of Birmingham, Birmingham B15 2TT, UK

E-mail: m.castellani@bham.ac.uk

Reviewing editor: Jenhui Chen, Chang Gung University, Taiwan

Abstract: The Bees Algorithm is a parameter optimisation method that mimics the foraging behaviour of honey bees. This paper presents an experimental study of the performance of the Bees Algorithm. Its strengths and weaknesses are analysed, and the most suitable parameterizations in relation to different optimisation tasks are revealed. The robustness of the optimisation results to reasonable modifications of the fitness landscape is studied for a large set of parameterizations. The Bees Algorithm is tested on 18 custom-made function minimisation benchmarks, and its performance compared to that of two state-of-the-art biologically inspired optimisation methods. Thanks to their two-dimensional nature, the proposed fitness landscapes are easy to visualise. Experimental evidence indicates also that they constitute a varied and challenging set of test cases, useful to reveal the specific abilities and biases of the search algorithms. In addition, the performance of the Bees Algorithm and the other two optimisation methods is tested on four real-world minimisation tasks from the literature. The results obtained on the benchmarks prove the effectiveness and robustness of the bees foraging metaphor, in particular on the most deceptive and high-dimensional fitness landscapes. They also confirm the ability of the Bees Algorithm to solve complex real-world optimisation tasks.

ABOUT THE AUTHORS

Duc Truong Pham has made wide-ranging contributions to the theory and practice of mechanical, manufacturing and systems engineering. His academic output includes over 500 technical papers and 15 books. He has supervised over 100 PhD theses to completion. He has won over of £30 M in research grants and contracts. He is the creator of the Bees Algorithm, a popular biologically inspired method for parameter optimisation. His is research interests include rapid manufacturing, micro manufacturing, automation, IT and intelligent systems.

Marco Castellani is lecturer at the School of Mechanical Engineering. He has done research for 20 years in a broad interdisciplinary area encompassing engineering, biology and computer science. He has worked on a wide range of application areas including motor control, remote sensing, pattern recognition, optimisation, systems modelling, natural language processing and ecological modelling. He has published over 40 research papers in scientific journals and international conferences.

PUBLIC INTEREST STATEMENT

This paper analyses the performance of the Bees Algorithm, a popular biologically inspired optimisation method. The Bees Algorithm is inspired by the foraging behaviour of honey bees, and can be used to solve a wide range of optimisation problems. The performance of the Bees Algorithm is based on a number of system parameters. This paper proves the effectiveness and efficiency of the Bees Algorithm, and its robustness to variations of the system parameters and optimisation landscape.

Subjects: Algorithms & Complexity; Artificial Intelligence; Evolutionary Computing

Keywords: optimisation; Bees Algorithm; swarm intelligence; evolutionary algorithms; optimisation benchmarks; variable neighbourhood search

1. Introduction

Technological and scientific advances, and the globalisation of social and economic networks, produced increasingly large and complex systems. Optimisation, modelling and control of these systems often involve the tuning of several system parameters, in order to maximise the quality of products, reduce manufacturing times, reduce manufacturing costs, improve the reliability and accuracy of processes, increase the efficiency of logistic and telecommunication networks, and so forth. Classical system optimisation methods are based on the identification of the relationship between the variables and the desired quality measure. Unfortunately, due to the intrinsic complexity and non-linearity of real-world systems, such relationship is difficult to obtain. The identification task is often complicated by discontinuities and constraints on both state and input variables.

Swarm Intelligence (SI) (Bonabeau, Dorigo, & Theraulaz, 1999) includes many model-free innovative metaheuristics based on nature-inspired decentralised search processes, such as Ant Colony Optimisation (ACO) (Dorigo, Maniezzo, & Colorni, 1996), Particle Swarm Optimisation (PSO) (Kennedy & Eberhart, 1995), the Bees Algorithm (Pham et al., 2006), the Firefly algorithm (Yang & He, 2013), etc.

Wolpert and Macready (1997) proved that, on the whole set of all possible problems, all optimisation algorithms perform equally (*No Free Lunch Theorem*). Yet, on arbitrary subsets of problems, distinct procedures perform differently. That is, the success of a search approach on a given task depends on how well its operators and parameters match the features of the search space. Unfortunately, the amount of knowledge about the nature of the fitness landscape is often scarce of null. As a consequence, the choice and design of optimisation methods entail time-consuming trial and error.

In the design of an optimisation procedure, a deep understanding of the specific capabilities of the various approaches is of great help. Any known feature of the fitness landscape may already point to suitable choices of procedures, operators and configurations. Conversely, by trying a few algorithms or configurations, the designer may get important clues on the nature of the search space. Finally, understanding of the role and robustness of different parameters and operators might narrow down the design task to a restricted set of crucial choices.

One of the priorities in SI research is currently to characterise precisely the merits and shortcomings of the different algorithms. Benchmarking of optimisation methods is usually performed on a number of test functions which are commonly held as good standards (Adorio, 2005; Bersini, Dorigo, Langerman, Seront, & Gambardella, 1996; Karaboga & Basturk, 2008; Molga & Smutnicki, 2005). Although often challenging, these functions were not created systematically, and sometimes replicate similar problems.

This paper reports an experimental study on the performance of the Bees Algorithm. The study aims to highlight the specific abilities and limitations of this procedure, and investigate the effects of different parameterizations.

Thirty-two different combinations of learning parameters are tested. To study methodically and in detail the behaviour, strengths and limitations of the Bees Algorithm, 18 continuous function minimisation tasks with different features and degrees of complexity are designed. Even though not fully exhaustive in terms of possible fitness landscapes, the proposed set of test functions aims to constitute a first step toward a more analytical procedure for benchmarking optimisation methods. Four samples of the proposed benchmarks are modified to test the robustness of the performance of the different parameterizations.

To put in context the performance of the Bees Algorithm and the challenges posed by the test functions, two popular nature-inspired optimisation methods are tested on the proposed benchmarks, and their performance is compared to that of the Bees Algorithm. In order to demonstrate the effectiveness of the proposed algorithm on a real-world optimisation task, the Bees Algorithm and the two other procedures are also tested on four popular protein-folding benchmark problems.

2. The Bees Algorithm

The Bees algorithm does not make assumptions such as the continuity of the search space, and requires limited problem domain knowledge beyond the desired solution performance. Different versions of the Bees Algorithm have been used to solve various engineering problems, such as pattern classifier training (Pham & Darwish, 2010), dynamic control problems (Castellani, Pham, & Pham, 2012), machine shop scheduling (Packianather et al., 2014), robotic swarm coordination (Jevtic, Gazi, Andina, & Jamshidi, 2010), non-linear model identification (Fahmy, Kalyoncu, & Castellani, 2012) and control system tuning (Pham, Darwish, & Eldukhri, 2009).

This section presents the standard Bees Algorithm (Pham & Castellani, 2009), describing its biological motivation and the computational procedures.

2.1. Bees foraging process in nature

In a bee colony, part of the population explores randomly the area surrounding the hive in search of new flower patches rich in nectar or pollen (Tereshko & Loengarov, 2005). When they return to the nest, those scouts that found a rich food source communicate their finding to resting bees through a procedure known as the "waggle dance" (Seeley, 1996). The waggle dance encodes information on the location of the flower patch, and its quality rating (Camazine et al., 2003). The rating of a food source depends on its net energy yield, which compounds factors like its proximity to the nest, abundance, and energy concentration (i.e. sugar content) (Seeley, 1996). Using the information communicated through the waggle dance, a number of unemployed bees proceed to harvest the advertised food sources. When a recruited bee comes back to the hive, it may in turn waggle dance to guide other nest mates to the food source. Since the length of the waggle dance is determined by the quality rating of the flower patch, the most profitable food sources are more extensively advertised, and thus are visited by the largest number of foragers (Tereshko & Loengarov, 2005). In this way, the bee colony maximises the efficiency (i.e. energy yield) of the food-harvesting process.

2.2. The Bees Algorithm

Without loss of generality, it will be hereafter assumed that the optimisation problem entails the minimisation of a specified cost measure. A candidate solution to the problem is defined by a given number of parameters, and its cost is measured via an objective function (*fitness function*) of these parameters.

In the Bees Algorithm, each point in the solution space is thought of as a food source. When a "bee" visits a food source, it rates its quality via the fitness function. "Scout bees" are employed to sample the fitness landscape randomly, looking for unexplored areas of high fitness. In other words, new solutions are randomly created and evaluated. The visited sites are ranked, and "forager bees" are recruited to harvest (i.e. search further) the neighbourhood of the highest ranking locations. That is, new solutions similar to the current best finds are created and evaluated. The neighbourhood of a candidate solution is termed a "flower patch". The Bees Algorithm explores the solution space, and samples the neighbourhood of the highest fitness points in search for the global fitness maximum (i.e. the solution that minimises the specified cost measure). Figure 1 shows the flowchart of the Bees Algorithm, whilst the main parameters of the algorithm are detailed in Table 1. The main steps of the algorithm are described below.

---------------------- Main procedure ---

BEES ALGORITHM {
for *i*=1,...,*ns*
  Initialise_flower_patch(*flower_patch*[*i*])
do until stopping_condition=TRUE
  Waggle_dance()
  for *i* =1,...,*nb*
    Local_search(*flower_patch*[*i*])
    Site_abandonment(*flower_patch*[*i*])
    Neighbourhood_shrinking(*flower_patch*[*i*])
  for *i* = *nb*,...,*ns*
    Global_search(*flower_patch*[*i*]) }

---------------------- Subroutines ---

Initialise_flower_patch(*flower_patch*[*i*]) {
Place random *scout*[*i*] in search space
Evaluate fitness of location visited by *scout*[*i*]
flower_patch[*i*] = {*scout[i]*, *foragers*=0, *neighbourhood*=a, *stgn*=TRUE, *stgn_counter*=0} }

Waggle_dance() {
Rank scouts in decreasing order of visited site fitness
for *i*=1,...,*ne*
  foragers∈patch[*i*] = *nre*
for *i*=ne,...,*nb*
  foragers∈patch[*i*] = *nrb* }

Local_search(*flower_patch*[*i*]) {
stgn∈patch[*i*] = TRUE
for *i*=1,...*foragers∈patch*[*i*]
Place *new_scout* inside *neighbourhood∈patch*[*i*]
Evaluate fitness of site visited by *new_scout*
if fitness of site visited by new_scout > fitness of site visited by *scout*[*i*]*∈patch*[*i*]
  scout[*i*]*∈patch*[*i*] = *new_scout*
  stgn∈patch[*i*] = FALSE }

Global_search(*flower_patch*[*i*]) {
  Initialise_flower_patch(*flower_patch*[*i*]) }

Neighbourhood_shrinking(*flower_patch*[*i*]) {
if *stgn∈patch*[*i*] = TRUE
  neighbourhood∈patch[*i*] = 0.8 · *neighbourhood patch*[*i*] }

Site_abandonment(*flower_patch*[*i*]) {
if *stgn∈patch*[*i*] = TRUE
  if *stgn_counter∈patch*[*i*] < *stlim*
    stgn_counter∈patch[*i*] = *stgn_counter∈patch*[*i*] + 1
  else
    Initialise_flower_patch(*flower_patch*[*i*]) }

Figure 1. Flowchart of the Bees Algorithm.

Notes: Variables are italicised, routines are in bold.

2.3. Solutions encoding

Given a minimisation problem defined over the *n*-dimensional continuous solution space $U = \{x \in R^n;$ $min_i < x_i < max_i, i = 1, ... , n\}$, each candidate solution is represented as an *n*-dimensional vector of decision variables $x = \{x_1, ... , x_n\}$. The goal of the optimisation task is to find the solution that minimises the set cost function $f(x):U \rightarrow R$.

Table 1. Bees Algorithm parameters	
ns	Number of scout bees
ne	Number of elite sites
nb	Number of best sites
nre	Recruited bees for elite sites
nrb	Recruited bees for remaining best sites
ngh	Initial size of neighbourhood
stlim	Limit of stagnation cycles for site abandonment

2.4. Random initialisation

The number of scout bees is a fixed system parameter, henceforth denoted as ns. The algorithm starts scattering at random the scout bees across the search space. Each scout rates the fitness of the visited location (i.e. candidate solution) through the cost function. The procedure then enters the main loop, which consists of four phases.

2.5. Waggle dance

The recruitment procedure is implemented via a deterministic cut-off method.

The ns sites (i.e. solutions) visited by the scout bees are ranked in descending order of fitness (i.e. ascending order of cost measure). The first nb < ns locations (the best locations) are picked for neighbourhood search. Amongst these nb selected sites, the first ne ≤ nb elite (top-rated) sites are allocated nre foragers for local exploration. The remaining (nb − ne) sites picked for neighbourhood search are allocated nrb (nrb ≤ nre) foragers for local exploration.

The above recruitment mechanism assigns a larger number of bees to search the neighbourhood of the ne elite sites, which are considered the most promising regions of the solution space.

2.6. Local search

The neighbourhood search phase mimics the harvesting process carried out by forager bees in nature. For each of the nb selected sites, the spatial extent of the local search is delimited by an n-dimensional hyper-box of sides $a_1, ... , a_n$ centred on the location marked by the scout bee. The recruited foragers are randomly spread with uniform probability inside this hyper-box (flower patch). If one of the forager bees lands in a position of higher fitness than the scout bee, that forager is retained as the new scout bee. This bee becomes the dancer once back at the hive.

Two procedures named *neighbourhood shrinking* and *site abandonment* (Pham & Castellani, 2009) are called when local search fails to yield any fitness improvement within a flower patch. These two procedures aim to improve the search accuracy of the Bees Algorithm and avoid unnecessary computations.

2.7. Neighbourhood shrinking

The size $a = \{a_1, ... , a_n\}$ of the local neighbourhood of a selected site is initially set to a large value. For each variable a_i, it is set as follows:

$$a_i(t) = ngh(t) * \left(\max_i - \min_i\right)$$
$$ngh(\tau) = 1.0 \tag{1}$$

where ngh(t) is a time-dependent variable, t is the tth cycle of the Bees Algorithm main loop, and τ is the cycle where the site is first selected for local search. If the local search yields higher points of fitness within a flower patch, the size of that patch is kept unchanged. Each time that local search does not bring any improvement in fitness, the extent of the flower patch is reduced according to the following empirical formula:

$$ngh(t + 1) = 0.8 * ngh(t). \qquad (2)$$

At the level of the individual flower patches, the neighbourhood shrinking method acts in a way that is similar to the simulated annealing procedure (Zäpfel, Braune, & Bögl, 2010). The flower patches are initialised over a large area to foster the exploration of the search space. The size of the patches is then progressively reduced to make the search increasingly exploitative around the local optimum.

2.8. Site abandonment
Site abandonment is operated when the local search routine is not able anymore to find solutions of higher fitness than the scout within a flower patch. In this case, it is assumed that the local fitness peak has been reached, and the site is abandoned.

After each cycle of the local search procedure, the neighbourhood of those flower patches where the fitness stagnated is shrunk. If the fitness in a flower patch has stagnated for more than a prede-fined number (*stlim*) of consecutive cycles, the site is considered exhausted. In this case, the patch is abandoned and the scout bee is re-initialised to a new random point in the solution space. If the abandoned site corresponds to the best-so-far fitness value, its position is recorded. If no other solu-tion of higher fitness is subsequently found, the recorded solution is taken as the final one.

2.9. Global search
In a bee colony, at any time a percentage of the population scouts the environment in search for new food sources. The Bees Algorithm mimics this exploration effort via random sampling of the solution space. That is, $ns - nb$ scout bees are randomly scattered across the search space.

2.10. Population update
In the final phase of the main loop, the population of the bee colony is updated. The new population is formed out of two groups that combine respectively the products of the local and global search efforts. The first group is formed of nb scouts, each related to the centre (the best solution) of one of the high-fitness flower patches. The second group comprises $ns - nb$ scouts, each consisting of a randomly generated solution.

2.11. Stopping criterion
The stopping criterion is set by the user. It can be either the location of a solution of fitness above a predefined threshold (e.g. in a minimisation problem, the cost $f(x)$ of solution x is equal to $f(x) \leq$ thresh-old or the completion of a predefined number of learning cycles, or the elapsing of a pre-set compu-tation time.

3. Related literature
The Bees Algorithm combines iterative neighbourhood search with random global search. The local search procedure in one flower patch is akin to the variable neighbourhood search (VNS) algorithm proposed by Mladenović and Hansen (1997). Each optimisation cycle is equivalent to a move to a new neighbourhood in VNS. Occasionally, the shrinking procedure reduces the size of the new neigh-bourhood. The main difference between the two algorithms is that the size of a flower patch is kept constant or reduced in the Bees Algorithm, whilst in the customary VNS routine is expanded. Moreover, flower patches are randomly sampled in the Bees Algorithm, whilst they are fully explored in VNS. The Bees Algorithm can be described as running nb VNS searches in parallel, and is thus akin to parallel VNS methods (Crainic, Gendreau, Hansen, & Mladenovic, 2004). The main difference be-tween parallel VNS methods and the Bees Algorithm is in the exchange of information between the local search procedures. In the former, the result of the individual VNS procedures is shared at fixed time intervals, or at the end of the search. In the latter, no candidate solutions are exchanged be-tween parallel searches. Instead, information on the progress of the local searches is shared through the waggle dance, and the amount of local exploitation is allocated accordingly. The differential recruitment method used in the Bees Algorithm represents the 'social' aspect of the procedure, akin

to the forager recruitment process in honey bees. Another difference in the two procedures concerns the way the local search is restarted once a neighbourhood has been explored. Whilst the Bees Algorithm uses the asynchronous site abandonment routine, parallel VNS methods synchronously restart the local searches once they have been all exhausted.

Amongst the various population-based metaheuristics, the Bees Algorithm shows some resemblance with $(\mu + \lambda)$-evolutionary strategies (ES) (Fogel, 2000). In common with these procedures, the Bees Algorithm employs a deterministic selection method, and samples a number of points (offspring in ES terminology) in the neighbourhood of the selected solutions (parents in ES terminology). Like some kinds of ESs, the Bees Algorithm employs only selection and mutation to evolve the population. In contrast to ESs, the local exploitation effort is not fixed but allocated proportionally to the fitness of the parents. Also, competition for survival in the Bees Algorithm is decentralised at a local level amongst the scout and its recruits. In ESs, the whole parent population is pooled with the offspring in the replacement procedure, or is fully replaced by the offspring.

Compared to many popular SI algorithms, the Bees Algorithm does not exchange information through an interaction medium like pheromone in ACO or attraction forces in PSO. That is, the exploitation of the candidate solutions in the Bees Algorithm is set directly through the waggle dance, and not indirectly through a medium. Strictly speaking, due to the centralised apportionment of the sampling effort, the Bees Algorithm is not a true SI procedure.

Differently from customary evolutionary and swarm algorithms, the Bees Algorithm features the site abandonment procedure which prevents foragers from being trapped at a local fitness peak. Site abandonment is also useful to reinstate population diversity if several scouts converge on the same neighbourhood. A similar procedure is featured in some PSO versions like the multiswarm PSO proposed by Blackwell and Branke (2004). A consequence of the site abandonment procedure is that there is no population convergence in the Bees Algorithm.

In the field of bees-inspired optimisation, there are similarities between the Bees Algorithm and the Artificial Bee Colony (ABC) algorithm (Karaboga & Basturk, 2007). The two optimisation procedures can be visualised using the same flowchart. However, in ABC the waggle dance is simulated through the stochastic roulette wheel selection method (Fogel, 2000), instead of the deterministic cut-off procedure used in the Bees Algorithm. The most substantial difference between the Bees Algorithm and ABC is in how neighbourhood search is implemented. That is, ABC does not use mutation which is the local search operator in the Bees Algorithm. Instead, ABC uses the extrapolation crossover operator (Fogel, 2000).

For a more in-depth analysis of the differences and similarities between the Bees Algorithm and SI methods, the reader is referred to Pham and Castellani (2009, 2013).

4. Experimental setup

As previously mentioned, the performance of the Bees Algorithm is tested on 18 custom-made and 4 real-world continuous function minimisation benchmarks. An evolutionary algorithm (EA) (Fogel, 2000) and a PSO are used as terms of reference for the performance of the Bees Algorithm. All the optimisation problems entail the minimisation of a cost function $F(x)$. Given a candidate solution $x = \{x_1, \ldots, x_n\}$, the associated cost is calculated as follows:

$$F(x) = f(x) - \bar{f} \tag{3}$$

where $f(x)$ is the value of the benchmark function f at x, and $\bar{f}$ is the global minimum of f. The fitness of solution x is inversely proportional to its cost.

4.1. 2D function minimisation benchmarks

Pham and Castellani (2009) tested the Bees Algorithm and 3 other procedures on 12 popular minimisation benchmarks: Easom, Goldstein and Price, Martin and Gaddy, Schaffer, Schwefel, Ackley, Griewank, Hypersphere, Langermann, Rastrigin, Rosenbrock and Shekel. These functions are amongst the most widely used in the literature (Adorio, 2005; Bersini et al., 1996; Molga & Smutnicki, 2005), and have become de facto standards for the benchmarking of optimisation algorithms (Macnish, 2007). They will be called henceforth the customary functions.

Although some of the customary functions can be regarded as challenging tasks, they often repeat similar cases. In many instances, it is possible to obtain easily an indication of the approximate location of the optimum. This is the case in the four unimodal functions (*Hypersphere, Martin and Gaddy, Easom* and *Rosenbrock*), the *Schaffer* function (a high-frequency-damped sinusoid) and three functions characterised by an overall unimodal behaviour and local pockets added via a cosinusoidal "noise" component (*Ackley, Griewank, Rastrigin*). Moreover, optimisation methods that use averaging operators to exchange information amongst individuals (e.g. PSO and some EAs) are known to be biased toward the origin of the solution space (Monson & Seppi, 2005). These algorithms are best suited to functions where the minimum lies at or near the centre of the search space. This is the case of many of the customary functions.

Several of the customary functions share also a number of other features that might bias the benchmarking of optimisation methods, such as axial alignment of the peaks (*Ackley, Griewank, Rastrigin, Schwefel*), regular spacing of the peaks (*Ackley, Griewank, Rastrigin, Schwefel*), rotational symmetry of the function (*Easom, Hypersphere, Schaffer*) and linear separability of the function into a sum of independent one-variable functions (*Hypersphere, Easom, Rastrigin, Ackley*) (Macnish, 2007). Whilst rigid transformations of the fitness landscape can remove the biases caused by the location of the optimum and linear separability of the variables (Tang et al., 2009), other sources of bias (e.g. regular spacing of the peaks, rotational symmetry) are inherently related to the analytical formulation of the functions.

In order to provide a fairer and more thorough comparison of the Bees Algorithm, 18 test functions have been created. For ease of analysis and visualisation, all the proposed benchmarks are two-dimensional. All functions are defined within the interval [−100, 100], and map a fitness landscape defined within the continuous interval [0, 1] where zero is the value of the global minimum. The equations and fitness landscapes of the 18 benchmarks are given in the online electronic supplementary material (Online Appendix).

Function *1* maps two "holes" on opposite sides of the search space. It is designed to challenge algorithms that employ averaging search operators, since they are likely to produce several solutions in between the two poles of attraction.

Functions *2–6* are multimodal functions devised to test different biases in the search procedures. In the first three cases, the secondary minima are aligned on a regular grid, in the remaining two cases they are randomly arranged. In function 4 and 6 the global optimum lies at the centre of the search space, whilst in the other functions lies near the top-right corner of the search space. Finally, the peak is aligned with the grid of secondary minima in function 4, and is not in functions *2* and *3*. Algorithms using procedures able to exploit regularities in the search space, such as the two-point crossover operator used in EAs (Fogel, 2000), are likely to be biased toward solutions aligned on grids. They should perform best on function 4, but also be more liable to get trapped in the secondary minima of functions *2* and *3*. Search procedures biased toward the origin of the search space are expected to perform best on functions 4 and 6.

In functions *7* and *8,* the global minimum lies in a hole characterised by a large flat step and a steep and narrow ending. The two functions are identical, with the exception that in the latter the minima are arranged on a grid. These two functions aim to test the ability of search algorithms to overcome flat surfaces. It should be noted that none of the customary functions includes this case.

Functions *9*, *10* and *11* test the ability of the search algorithms to negotiate valleys. Function *9* is similar to function *2*, it maps two valleys on opposite sides of the search space. Function *10* is characterised by two pairs of valleys of opposite slopes that create four narrow competing basins of attraction. The minimum is located near the borders of the search surface at the end of the narrowest valley. The four valleys join at the origin, where a further basin was placed to challenge origin-biased search algorithms. Function *11* is similar to the *Rosenbrock* function. However, in this case, the narrow parabolic valley is surrounded by a large flat surface. The valley is located in the half plane of positive x_1 values ($x_1 > 0$). The other half of the fitness landscape is covered by a sliding plane that makes the overall search surface extremely deceptive.

Function *12* combines two cosinusoidal functions. Each function depends on one of the two input variables, and its amplitude increases linearly with the associated variable. The global minimum is in a narrow hole that is added to one of the "pockets" of the search surface. Like many of the multi-pocketed customary functions, function *12* has an overall unimodal characteristic corresponding to a plane slanted toward the positive values of the two input variables. The optimum is located before the end of the plane, and therefore does not correspond to the minimum of the unimodal characteristic. Function *12* tests the capability of a search algorithm to explore and escape many local minima. Function *13* represents a more difficult optimisation task. In this case, the two sinusoidal oscillations that generate the mapping have constant amplitude and variable period. There is thus no regularity (i.e. fixed period) or general behaviour (i.e. slanted plane) that may help the search. Also in this case, the global minimum is in a narrow hole added to one of the pockets of the search surface.

Similarly to many of the customary functions, functions *14–18* are characterised by an overall unimodal fitness landscape and many local "potholes". The local pockets of fitness are generated by a cosinusoidal high-frequency term. The minimum lies at the bottom of one of the potholes in the middle of the first quadrant. Functions *14*, *15* and *16* differ for the magnitude of the cosinusoidal term, which is respectively 10, 25 and 40% of the magnitude of the unimodal term. Functions *17* and *18* differ from function *15* for the period of the oscillatory term, which is respectively 4 and ¼ times the period of the term of function *15*.

The functions can be divided into five main groups, characterised respectively by two- and multi-modal, flat, valley-like, wavelike and 'noisy' unimodal fitness surfaces. To distinguish them from noisy unimodal functions, the first four groups of multi-modal functions will be henceforth referred as 'true multi-modal'. For each class, a sample function is plotted in Figure 2. Table 2 summarises the main features of the 18 benchmarks.

4.2. Protein folding benchmarks
The protein folding problem consists of finding the minimal energy structure of a molecular cluster to find the configuration of a protein (Vavasis, 1994). The energy function of the molecular structure is defined by the following non-linear partially separable function:

$$f(x_1, \ldots, x_n) = \sum_{i=1}^{n-1} \sum_{j=i+1}^{n} r \left[\sqrt{\sum_{k=1}^{3} (x_{ik} - x_{jk})^2} \right] \tag{4}$$

where $r(s)$ is the Lennard–Jones potential.

$$r(s) = s^{-12} - 2 \cdot s^{-6} \tag{5}$$

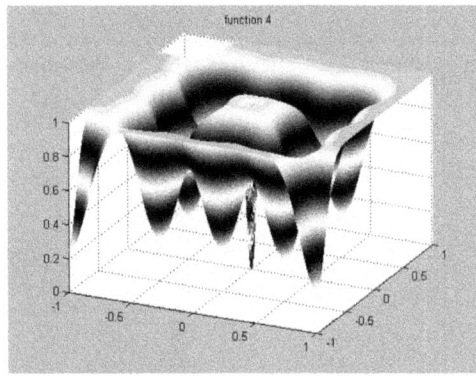

a) true multimodal

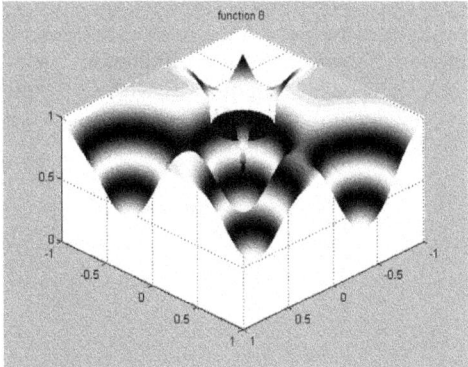

b) flat surfaces

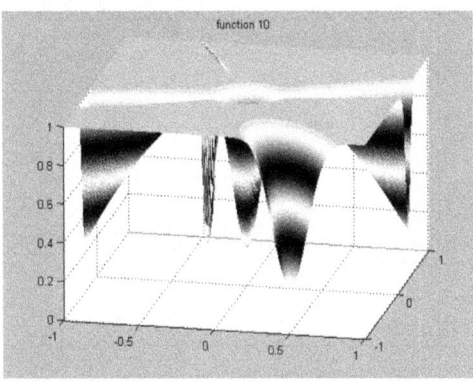

c) valleys

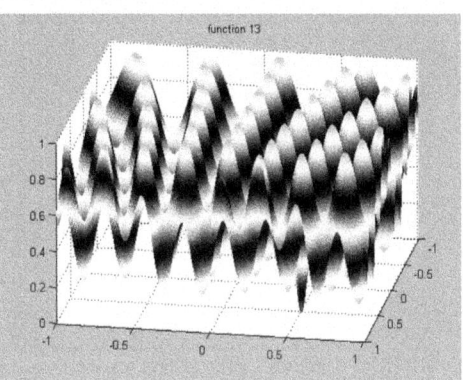

d) wavelike

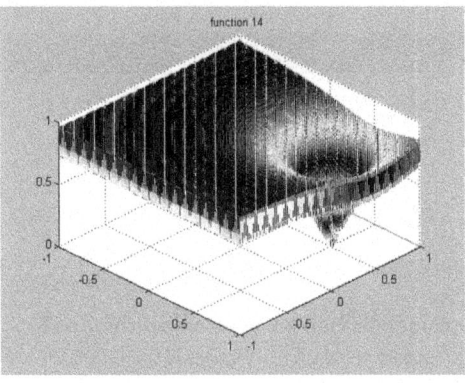

e) "noisy" unimodal

Figure 2. Examples of proposed benchmarks.

The vectors $x_l = \{x_{l1}, x_{l2}, x_{l3}\}, l \in [1, n], l \in I^+$ correspond to the positions of n atoms in the 3D space, and are constrained as follows: $x_{lk} \in [-1, 1], k \in \{1, 2, 3\}$. The overall function f is non-convex, and has an exponential number of local minima (Mongeau, Karsenty, Rouzé, & Hiriart-Urruty, 2000). The global minimum is known only for $n \leq 4$ (Mongeau et al., 2000; Vavasis, 1994).

In this study, the four cases $n = 3$–6 are considered. They will be henceforth called *pf3*, *pf4*, *pf5*, and *pf6*. The solutions are encoded using $3 \cdot n$ long strings of real numbers, which are built chaining the 3D vectors of atom position coordinates $x_1, \ldots, x_n$. The global minima for the four functions are given in Table 3, for $n > 4$, they are taken from the search results of Coleman, Shalloway, and Wu (1993).

Function	Two peaks	True multi-modal	Unimodal with potholes	Minima on a grid	Minimum at the origin	Valleys	Flat surface	Wavelike
1	X	X						
2		X		X				
3		X		X				
4		X		X	X			
5		X						
6		X			X			
7		X		X			X	
8		X					X	
9	X					X		
10		X				X		
11		X				X		
12		X						X
13		X						X
14			X					
15			X					
16			X					
17			X					
18			X					

Table 2. Main features of function benchmarks

Table 3. Global minima of protein folding problem	
pf3	−3.0
pf4	−6.0
pf5	−9.1038F
pf6	−12.7120F

4.3. Performance measures

Each algorithm is tested 50 times with different random initialisations on each benchmark. Each time, the optimisation procedure is run until either it locates a solution ξ of fitness $F(\xi) < 0.001$, or the maximum number of learning cycles is reached. The learning speed S is measured as the number of solutions evaluated throughout the optimisation procedure. Whenever the site abandonment procedure of the Bees Algorithm requires the random re-initialisation of a new solution, the extra solution is counted in the computation of the speed S. The location error E of the final solution x_f is computed as in the equation below.

$$E = \begin{cases} 0 & \text{if} \quad F(x_f) \le 0.001 \\ F\left(x_f\right) & \text{otherwise} \end{cases} \tag{6}$$

The average location error μ_E and optimisation speed μ_S over the 50 independent learning trials are calculated for each parameter setting on each benchmark problem.

5. Experimental tests—2d benchmarks

This set of experiments is designed to evaluate the performance of the Bees Algorithm on the eighteen two-dimensional benchmarks. For each function, 32 different parameterizations of the algorithm are tested. They are shown in Table 4. In 16 cases, the optimisation procedure performs 102

No.	Population size	Learning cycles	stlim	ne	nre	nb	nrb	Random scouts
								Table 4. Bees Algorithm parameterizations tested
1	51	10,000	5	1	10	9	5	1
2	51	10,000	5	1	15	8	5	1
3	51	10,000	5	1	20	4	10	1
4	51	10,000	5	1	20	7	5	1
5	51	10,000	5	1	25	6	5	1
6	51	10,000	5	1	30	3	10	1
7	51	10,000	5	2	20	3	10	1
8	51	10,000	5	2	20	4	5	1
9	51	10,000	10	1	10	9	5	1
10	51	10,000	10	1	15	8	5	1
11	51	10,000	10	1	20	4	10	1
12	51	10,000	10	1	20	7	5	1
13	51	10,000	10	1	25	6	5	1
14	51	10,000	10	1	30	3	10	1
15	51	10,000	10	2	20	3	10	1
16	51	10,000	10	2	20	4	5	1
17	102	5,000	5	1	10	19	5	2
18	102	5,000	5	1	20	9	10	2
19	102	5,000	5	1	20	17	5	2
20	102	5,000	5	1	30	8	10	2
21	102	5,000	5	1	30	15	5	2
22	102	5,000	5	1	40	4	20	2
23	102	5,000	5	1	40	7	10	2
24	102	5,000	5	2	20	8	10	2
25	102	5,000	5	2	30	6	10	2
26	102	5,000	10	1	10	19	5	2
27	102	5,000	10	1	20	9	10	2
28	102	5,000	10	1	30	8	10	2
29	102	5,000	10	1	30	15	5	2
30	102	5,000	10	1	40	4	20	2
31	102	5,000	10	2	20	8	10	2
32	102	5,000	10	2	30	6	10	2

function evaluations per learning cycle, and is run until the global minimum is located or 5,000 learning cycles have elapsed (see Section 4.3). In the remaining 16 cases, 51 function evaluations are performed per learning cycle, and the algorithm is run for a maximum of 10,000 learning cycles. These figures correspond to 100 (50) local search samples plus 2 (1) global search samples per evolution cycle, for a total of at most 510,000 fitness evaluations. The first strategy emphasises the role of the population size in the search process. It will be called henceforth "breadth-search" approach. The second strategy relies on the length of the evolution span, and will be called henceforth "depth-search" approach.

For each benchmark, the average location error and learning speed (Section 4.3), and the success rate (Section 4.3) achieved by the best performing Bees Algorithm configurations are reported in Table 5.

Function	Population	Generations	stlim	ne	nre	nb	nrb	Success	Accuracy	Speed
1	51	10,000	10	1	10	9	5	50	0.0000	2,300
2	51	10,000	10	1	10	9	5	50	0.0000	7,659
3	51	10,000	10	1	10	9	5	50	0.0000	10,218
4	51	10,000	10	1	10	9	5	50	0.0000	7,162
5	51	10,000	10	1	10	9	5	50	0.0000	21,781
6	51	10,000	10	1	10	9	5	50	0.0000	18,782
7	102	5,000	10	1	30	15	5	50	0.0000	7,118
8	51	10,000	10	1	10	9	5	50	0.0000	5,300
9	51	10,000	10	1	20	7	5	50	0.0000	1,364
10	51	5,000	10	1	20	7	5	50	0.0000	31,599
11	51	5,000	10	1	10	9	5	3	0.0143	464,068
12	51	10,000	10	1	30	3	10	50	0.0000	2,747
13	102	5,000	10	1	30	15	5	50	0.0000	5,814
14	51	10,000	10	2	20	4	5	50	0.0000	5,776
15	51	10,000	10	2	20	3	10	50	0.0000	19,807
16	51	10,000	10	1	30	3	10	50	0.0000	53,837
17	51	10,000	10	2	20	4	5	50	0.0000	3,010
18	51	10,000	10	2	20	4	5	50	0.0000	13,934

Table 5. Bees Algorithm—Minimisation results

5.1. Optimisation results

On the first eight true multimodal functions the best configurations of the Bees Algorithm correspond to fairly explorative strategies. They split the population amongst many selected nb sites without committing too many foragers on any location. The presence of a flat surface in functions 7 and 8 does not seem to affect much the optimisation speed, or require a substantially different search strategy.

In terms of optimisation speed, the Bees Algorithm appears to perform better on landscapes where the minima are aligned on a grid (3 and 4 vs. 5 and 6), and the global optimum is at the centre of the optimisation space (4 and 6 vs. 3 and 5). However, the differences in speed didn't appear to be significant following a Mann–Whitney test.

On benchmarks 9 and 10 (valleys), the best-performing settings are still mainly explorative, even though less markedly than in the previous eight cases. A clearly explorative configuration excels on the highly deceptive function 11. This is likely due to the misleading nature of the fitness landscape, which makes it risky to commit a high number of foragers on a (few) location(s).

In function 12 the overall characteristic of the fitness surface is inclined (Section 4.1). Even though the global minimum does not correspond exactly with the end of the underlying slope, it lies in the same quadrant. This may help the search process, and make function 12 easier to optimise than function 13. This hypothesis might explain why a more exploitative configuration excels on function 12 than on function 13, and the Bees Algorithm performs better on the first benchmark than the second. Highly exploitative search strategies emerge also on the noisy unimodal functions (14–18).

In all the eighteen cases, the best configuration uses the high value for the stagnation limit. This feature balances the explorative search strategies used for many benchmarks, ensuring adequate exploitation of the search results.

Regarding the trade-off between the population size and number of optimisation cycles, depth-search appears the most suitable strategy for the Bees Algorithm. This is always the case except for function 7 (flat surface), and function 13 (wavelike).

The Bees Algorithm attains 100% success rate on all benchmarks, with the only exception of function 11.

6. Experimental tests—Robustness of performance

This set of experiments is designed to test the robustness of the performance of the Bees Algorithm configurations to alterations of the fitness surface. Four functions (4, 8, 10, 13) sampled from different landscape groups (see Figure 2) are slightly modified. In the case of functions 4, 8, and 10, the

Table 6. Robustness of optimisation results

Parameterization	Function									
	4a	4b	8a	8b	10a	10b	13a	13b	14	16
1	0.250	0.266	0.004	0.009	0.442	0.145	0.063	0.967	0.000	0.005
2	0.612	0.357	0.871	0.003	0.948	0.454	0.200	0.127	0.000	0.005
3	0.506	0.266	0.931	0.068	0.021	0.654	0.934	0.136	0.000	0.000
4	0.398	0.450	0.011	0.000	1.000	0.059	0.108	0.556	0.000	0.000
5	0.241	0.027	0.000	0.264	0.677	0.471	0.022	0.839	0.000	0.000
6	0.959	0.085	0.888	0.361	0.605	0.213	0.915	0.278	0.000	0.000
7	0.099	0.329	0.014	0.396	0.203	0.182	0.266	0.402	0.000	0.001
8	0.145	0.165	0.828	0.374	0.136	0.091	0.031	0.764	0.000	0.000
9	0.008	0.347	0.003	0.725	0.764	0.994	0.804	0.432	0.000	0.000
10	0.598	0.506	0.359	0.869	0.669	0.480	0.446	0.002	0.000	0.000
11	0.574	0.920	0.749	0.863	0.574	0.408	0.012	0.015	0.000	0.000
12	0.551	0.161	0.664	0.001	0.099	0.524	0.379	0.890	0.000	0.000
13	0.546	0.281	0.063	0.245	0.010	0.572	0.617	0.009	0.000	0.000
14	0.817	0.013	0.311	0.456	0.986	0.738	0.967	0.381	0.000	0.147
15	0.049	0.506	0.634	0.000	0.657	0.959	0.836	0.153	0.000	0.000
16	0.151	0.275	0.374	0.622	0.809	0.772	0.785	0.004	0.000	0.000
17	0.184	0.702	0.177	0.393	0.159	0.615	0.248	0.166	0.000	0.011
18	0.586	0.085	0.001	0.510	0.336	0.817	0.078	0.416	0.000	0.004
19	0.040	0.087	0.537	0.014	0.484	0.446	0.622	0.037	0.000	0.000
20	0.940	0.090	0.028	0.956	0.196	0.642	0.301	0.896	0.000	0.000
21	0.953	0.476	0.517	0.008	0.975	0.150	0.199	0.068	0.000	0.000
22	0.385	0.008	0.486	0.041	0.833	0.203	0.546	0.264	0.000	0.001
23	0.208	0.920	0.000	0.208	0.989	0.780	0.469	0.336	0.000	0.000
24	0.667	0.054	0.067	0.012	0.161	0.823	0.270	0.973	0.000	0.006
25	0.501	0.956	0.343	0.372	0.450	0.370	0.682	0.422	0.000	0.000
26	0.233	0.023	0.057	0.521	0.025	0.637	0.348	0.117	0.000	0.001
27	0.488	0.298	0.570	0.123	0.004	0.095	0.164	0.027	0.000	0.000
28	0.588	0.287	0.556	0.016	0.608	0.270	0.644	0.465	0.000	0.000
29	0.839	0.005	0.820	0.191	0.754	0.929	0.603	0.404	0.000	0.000
30	0.200	0.815	0.245	0.057	0.245	0.677	0.480	0.190	0.000	0.018
31	0.442	0.418	0.002	0.131	0.556	0.210	0.410	0.081	0.000	0.000
32	0.136	0.493	0.697	0.001	0.177	0.588	0.937	0.034	0.000	0.000
Different	3	5	9	11	4	0	3	7	32	31

parameter k defining the value of the secondary minima (see electronic supplementary material) is changed from 0.25 to 0.3 (functions *4a*, *8a*, and *10a*), and 0.2 (functions *4b*, *8b*, and *10b*). This corresponds to raising (lowering) the depth of the local minima from 0.25 to 0.3 (0.2), whilst the value of the global minimum is kept fixed to 0. Similarly, functions *13a* and *13b* are created respectively increasing and decreasing the width k_1 (see electronic supplementary material) of the wavelike oscillations. Finally, functions *14* and *16* can be seen as variants of function *15* where the noise component is slightly modified.

For each of the eight modified fitness surfaces, 50 independent runs of the Bees Algorithm are executed. The significance of the differences between the distribution of the optimisation speeds obtained on the original and modified functions is analysed using Mann–Whitney U tests. The tests are run for a 0.05 (5%) level of significance. Table 6 reports, for each modified function, the *p*-value of the significance tests for each configuration. The total number of cases where the optimisation speeds obtained on the original functions differed in a statistically significant way from the optimisation speeds obtained on the modified functions is given at the bottom of the table. The shaded cells correspond to configurations that performed optimally on the original functions (i.e. their performance is not statistically distinguishable from the best reported in Table 5). The *p*-values in bold indicate configurations that performed optimally on the modified fitness landscapes.

In most of the cases, the significance tests indicate that the optimisation speeds obtained by the 32 configurations on the modified functions are statistically indistinguishable from those obtained on the original functions. The only exceptions are functions *14* and *16*. The set of configurations that perform optimally on the original and modified functions are also largely overlapping.

7. Experimental tests—Comparison with similar nature-inspired search methods
This set of experiments serves two purposes: to give terms of comparison to evaluate the performance of the Bees Algorithm, and test how challenging the proposed benchmarks are for different algorithms. It is important to emphasise that the results of the comparison cannot be used to support any claim regarding the absolute superiority of one optimisation procedure over any other (cf. the *No Free Lunch Theorem*). This study also does not intend compare the Bees Algorithm with the whole state-of-the-art in the literature. A comparison with every other continuous optimisation method would be impractical.

An EA and a PSO are chosen as control procedures. These two algorithms are amongst the best known and understood population-based metaheuristics. Hence, they are ideal terms of comparison to characterise the abilities of the Bees Algorithm, and evaluate the challenges that the test functions pose.

7.1. General settings
In order to test the algorithms on the same fitness landscape, the two control methods use the same representation scheme outlined in Section 2.3, and the fitness function described in Equation (3). The EA and PSO are also allocated the same sampling opportunities as the Bees Algorithm. Like in the case of the Bees Algorithm, the performance of the EA and PSO are optimised using 32 different combinations of system parameters and operators. The settings are divided into 16 depth-search (51 fitness evaluations repeated for a maximum of 10,000 learning cycles) and 16 breadth-search configurations (102 fitness evaluations repeated for a maximum of 5,000 learning cycles). Like the Bees Algorithm, the EA and PSO use general purpose operators and routines, and their configuration is optimised via a comparable number of trials (32 configurations each). This should ensure a fairly unbiased comparison of the three procedures.

7.2. Control algorithm I—EA
Two kinds of selection routines are tested: *fitness ranking* (Fogel, 2000) and an adaptive procedure recently introduced by Pham and Castellani (2010). *Generational replacement* (Fogel, 2000) is employed to update the population at the end of every evolution cycle.

Elitism (Fogel, 2000) is used to ensure that a copy of the fittest solution survives into the next generation. The population update strategy of the Bees Algorithm could be viewed as a form of local elitism, which preserves the best solution of every neighbourhood searched. However, elitism in EAs is usually applied at a global level, and thus is more likely to lead to loss of population diversity. For this reason, elitism is restricted only to the best fit solution.

The mutation operator picks at random a solution and slightly modifies the value of all its variables. The modification is sampled with uniform probability within an interval of width $[-a, a]$. The parameter a is encoded into the representation of the solutions $x = \{x_1, \dots, x_n, a\}$, and is adaptively tuned by the evolution process. The effect of mutation corresponds to the creation of a recruited bee in a flower patch of size ^{a} and centred on the mutant solution.

Four kinds of recombination (Fogel, 2000) operators are evaluated. In the first instance, genetic recombination is not used; mutation is the only genetic operator. In the second instance, the customary two-point recombination operator (hereafter called *binary* crossover) is used (Monson & Seppi, 2005). In the other two instances, the offspring are created from a weighted average of the parameters of the parent solutions. Given two solutions $x = \{x_1, \dots, x_n, a_x\}$ and $y = \{y_1, \dots, y_n, a_y\}$, *interpolation* and *extrapolation* crossover create a new solution $z = \{z_1, \dots, z_n, a_z\}$ as:

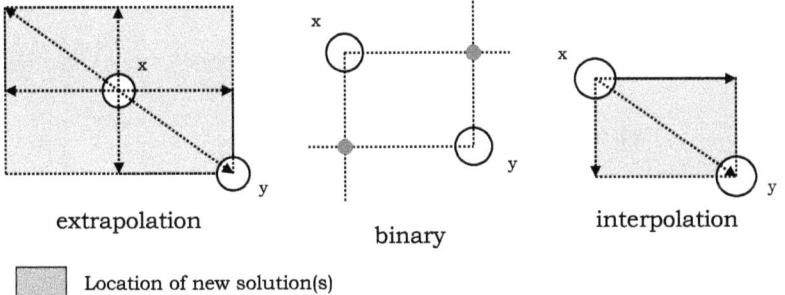

extrapolation

binary

interpolation

| | Location of new solution(s) |

Figure 3. Action of the 3 EA crossover operators tested.

Note: The x and y circles represent the locations of the parent solutions.

Function	Population	Generations	Selection procedure	Crossover type	Crossover rate	Mutation rate	Mutation width
1	102	5,000	Adaptive	Extra	1	0.05	0.1
2	102	5,000	Adaptive	Extra	1	0.05	0.1
3	102	5,000	Adaptive	Extra	1	0.05	0.1
4	51	10,000	Adaptive	Inter	1	0.05	0.1
5	102	5,000	Adaptive	Extra	1	0.05	0.1
6	102	5,000	Adaptive	Extra	1	0.05	0.1
7	102	5,000	Adaptive	Extra	1	0.05	0.1
8	102	5,000	Adaptive	Extra	1	0.05	0.1
9	102	5,000	Adaptive	Extra	1	0.05	0.1
10	102	5,000	Adaptive	Extra	1	0.05	0.1
11	102	5,000	Adaptive	Binary	1	0.05	0.1
12	102	5,000	Adaptive	Binary	1	0.05	0.1
13	51	10,000	Adaptive	Extra	1	0.05	0.1
14	51	10,000	Adaptive	Inter	1	0.05	0.1
15	51	10,000	Adaptive	Inter	1	0.05	0.1
16	51	10,000	Adaptive	Inter	1	0.05	0.1
17	51	10,000	Ranking	Inter	0.75	0.25	0.05
18	51	10,000	Adaptive	Inter	1	0.05	0.1

Table 7. EA learning parameters

$$z_i = x_i \cdot (1 - random) + y_i \cdot random \quad \text{(interpolation crossover)} \tag{7}$$

$$z_i = x_i + random \cdot (x_i - y_i) \quad \text{(extrapolation crossover)} \tag{8}$$

where $i = 1, \ldots, n + 1$, and $random \in [0, 1]$ is a random number. The children generated using interpolation crossover lie inside a hyperbox delimited by the two parents (see Figure 3). The action of three crossover operators is shown in Figure 3. For each test function, the best-performing EA configuration is given in Table 7.

7.3. Control algorithm II—PSO

PSO regards candidate solutions as particles that move across the fitness landscape. The procedure used in this study follows the PSO algorithm formulated by Kennedy and Eberhart (1995).

Each particle moves onto the solution space according to its velocity vector v. This vector is made up of three components modelling respectively the particle's persistence (momentum), past experience (attraction toward the fittest location visited), and social interaction with its neighbours (attraction toward the fittest neighbour). The velocity and position of a particle are updated according to the equations proposed by Kennedy and Eberhart (1995).

$$x_i(t + 1) = x_i(t) + v_i(t + 1)$$
$$i = 1, \ldots, n \tag{9}$$

$$p_i(t) = random_1 \cdot \left[pbest(t)_i - x(t)_i \right]$$
$$s_i(t) = random_2 \cdot \left[gbest(t)_i - x(t)_i \right]$$
$$v_i(t + 1) = w(t) \cdot v(t)_i + c_1 \cdot p_i(t) + c_2 \cdot s_i(t) \tag{10}$$
$$i = 1, \ldots, n$$

where t is the tth PSO cycle, $v = \{v_1, \ldots, v_n\}$ is the velocity vector of particle x, c_1 and c_2 are pre-defined parameters, $random_1$ and $random_2$ are randomly sampled with uniform probability in the interval [0, 1], $pbest(t)$ (personal best) is the vector of coordinates of the site of highest fitness found so far by the particle, and $gbest(t)$ (global best) is the vector of coordinates of the site of highest fitness found so far by the social neighbours of the particle.

The weight $w(t)$ is decayed as follows:

$$w(t) = w_{max} - \frac{w_{max} - w_{min}}{T} \cdot t \tag{11}$$

where w_{max} and w_{min} are predefined parameters, and T is the maximum allowed number of optimisation cycles.

All the components of the velocity vector are constrained within the interval $[-v_i^{max}, v_i^{max}]$

$$v_i^{max} = u \cdot \frac{max_i - min_i}{2} \tag{12}$$

where max_i and min_i are the upper and lower boundaries of variable i, and u is a system parameter. The learning parameters are set as recommended by Shi and Eberhart (1998).

The search efficiency of a PSO optimiser is by and large defined by the connectivity of the population (i.e. the number of social neighbours for each particle) and the maximum speed (v^{max}) of the particles. In this study, 16 combinations of v^{max} (obtained through u) and connectivity types are considered. Each combination is evaluated using the breadth-search and depth-search approach, for a total of 32 overall tests. For each test function, the best-performing PSO configuration is given in Table 8a. Table 8b refers to standard parameters that are not changed in the 32 PSO optimisation tests. A 102– (51–) neighbour connectivity corresponds to a fully connected population.

Table 8a. PSO learning parameters				
Function	Population	Generations	Connectivity	Speed
1	102	5,000	10	0.01
2	102	5,000	102	0.01
3	102	5,000	20	0.005
4	51	10,000	20	0.01
5	102	5,000	2	0.01
6	102	5,000	20	0.01
7	102	5,000	2	0.1
8	102	5,000	2	0.1
9	102	5,000	2	0.1
10	102	5,000	2	0.005
11	102	5,000	20	0.01
12	102	5,000	20	0.1
13	102	5,000	2	0.05
14	51	10,000	20	0.01
15	51	10,000	102	0.01
16	51	10,000	102	0.01
17	51	10,000	102	0.05
18	51	10,000	20	0.01

Table 8b. Fixed PSO learning parameters	
Parameter	Value
c_1 (Shi & Eberhart, 1998)	2.0
c_2 (Shi & Eberhart, 1998)	2.0
w_{max} (Shi & Eberhart, 1998)	0.9
w_{min} (Shi & Eberhart, 1998)	0.4

7.4. Results of comparison

For each function, Table 9 shows the median of the optimisation results attained by the three algorithms. The significance of the differences between the results obtained by the Bees Algorithm, and those achieved by the EA and PSO, was analysed via Mann–Whitney U-tests. The p-values are given in Table 9, highlighting in bold differences above the 5% level of significance.

The benchmarks prove challenging for the PSO, which fails to reach full success rates in several cases. In five cases, the success rate obtained by the PSO was inferior to two-thirds. The origin-bias (Section 4.1) of the PSO's velocity composition operator is clearly revealed by the large difference between the optimisation speeds attained on functions 4 and 6 (origin-centred) and the equivalent 3 and 5.

The EA achieves optimisation results comparable to those achieved by the Bees Algorithm. The origin bias of interpolation crossover is likely the reason for the very high optimisation speed on functions 4 and 6. Nearly all the best-performing EA configurations include the adaptive selection procedure. Extrapolation crossover excels in the majority of the cases. The success of extrapolation crossover is probably due to its large reach (Figure 2), which fosters the exploration of the search space. Interpolation crossover is instead more suitable to exploitative searches (Pham & Castellani, 2009), and for this reason excels on the noisy unimodal functions. The good performance of binary crossover on function 12 is likely due to the grid-like arrangement of the minima.

Table 9. Comparison of optimisation procedures on proposed benchmarks

Function	Bees Algorithm			PSO					EA				
	Success	Accuracy	Speed	Success	Accuracy	p (Accuracy)	Speed	p (Speed)	Success	Accuracy	p (Accuracy)	Speed	p (Speed)
1	50	0.0000	2,300	50	0.0000	–	3,111	0.0000	50	0.0000	–	4,029	0.0000
2	50	0.0000	7,659	23	0.2500	0.0000	510,000	0.1779	50	0.0000	–	1,9074	0.0000
3	50	0.0000	10,218	17	0.2442	0.0000	510,000	0.0001	50	0.0000	–	23,715	0.0001
4	50	0.0000	7,162	49	0.0007	0.0358	5,406	0.0027	46	0.0005	0.5556	765	0.0000
5	50	0.0000	2,178	10	0.1580	0.0000	510,000	0.0000	50	0.0000	–	29,274	0.0231
6	50	0.0000	18,782	49	0.0005	0.9368	7,242	0.0005	50	0.0000	–	12,750	0.0445
7	50	0.0000	7,118	39	0.0006	0.0189	8,568	0.0745	50	0.0000	–	3,876	0.0000
8	50	0.0000	5,300	37	0.0006	0.0218	8,976	0.0003	50	0.0000	–	5,457	0.3683
9	50	0.0000	1,364	45	0.0002	0.9423	11,985	0.0000	50	0.0000	–	1,785	0.0486
10	50	0.0000	31,559	13	0.1927	0.0000	510,000	0.0000	49	0.0007	0.0013	4,1973	0.5327
11	3	0.0143	464,058	0	0.2000	0.0000	510,000	0.0000	1	0.2000	0.0000	510,000	0.0000
12	50	0.0000	2,747	50	0.0000	–	6,885	0.0000	50	0.0000	–	8,466	0.0000
13	50	0.0000	5,814	48	0.0005	0.6466	15,402	0.0000	50	0.0000	–	3,723	0.0016
14	50	0.0000	5,775	50	0.0000	–	5,636	0.8388	50	0.0000	–	3,749	0.0000
15	50	0.0000	19,807	50	0.0000	–	9,690	0.0055	50	0.0000	–	4,998	0.0000
16	50	0.0000	53,837	50	0.0000	–	18,437	0.0000	50	0.0000	–	12,291	0.0000
17	50	0.0000	3,010	50	0.0000	–	4,641	0.0603	50	0.0000	–	2,168	0.0000
18	50	0.0000	13,934	50	0.0000	–	10,710	0.1546	50	0.0000	–	5,916	0.0000

Table 10. Summary of comparative tests on proposed benchmarks

Function	Two peaks	True multi-modal	Unimodal with potholes	Minima on a grid	Minimum at the origin	Valleys	Flat surface	Wavelike	Winner
1	x	x							BA
2		x		x					BA
3		x		x					BA
4		x		x	x				BA
5		x							BA
6		x			x				EA
7		x		x			x		EA
8		x					x		BA – EA
9	x					x			BA
10		x				x			BA
11		x				x			BA
12		x						x	BA
13		x						x	EA
14			x						EA
15			x						EA
16			x						EA
17			x						EA
18			x						EA

For each function, Table 10 reports the best-performing algorithm(s) versus the benchmarks features. The evaluation of the performance takes into consideration first the success rate, and successively accuracy and speed to break ties. If two or more algorithms attain the same success rate, and the differences in accuracy and speed are not statistically significant (Mann–Whitney U-test), they are considered to perform equally. Overall, the Bees Algorithm excels on true multi-modal functions, except for those characterised by flat surfaces where the EA performs best. The EA dominates the noisy unimodal functions.

8. Experimental tests—Protein folding benchmarks

This set of experiments is designed to test the performance of the Bees Algorithm on a popular set of real-world test functions. The best-performing configurations for the Bees Algorithm, PSO and EA are given in Table 11.

The optimisation results are compared in Table 12. For each benchmark, the results obtained by the best-performing configurations are compared using same criteria (success rate, accuracy and speed) utilised in Table 10. The results of the best-performing algorithm are shaded in grey.

Figures 4–7 plot the evolution of the top fitness in the population during a sample run of the three optimisation procedures.

On this set of benchmarks, the Bees Algorithm benefits from mainly exploitative approaches, where all the foragers congregate on only four sites at a time. Also in this case, all the best parameterizations feature the highest value for the stagnation limit. Except for the highest dimensional *pf6* benchmark, an exploitative search approach works best for the PSO. In this case, the use of full population connectivity (51) speeds up the convergence towards the fittest particle, and a low maximum speed reduces the exploration capability of the agents. The results confirm the importance of

Table 11. Protein folding benchmark problem—Parameter settings

(a) Bees Algorithm

Function	Population	Generations	*stlim*	*ne*	*nre*	*nb*	*nrb*
pf3	51	10,000	10	2	20	4	5
pf4	51	10,000	10	2	20	4	5
pf5	51	10,000	10	2	20	4	5
pf6	102	5,000	10	1	40	4	20

(b) PSO

Function	Population	Generations	Connec-tivity	Speed			
pf3	51	10,000	51	0.01			
pf4	51	10,000	51	0.01			
pf5	51	10,000	51	0.005			
pf6	102	5,000	2	0.1			

(c) EA

Function	Population	Generations	Selection proce-dure	Crossover type	Cross-over rate	Muta-tion rate	Muta-tion width
pf3	51	10,000	Ranking	Inter	0.75	0.25	0.05
pf4	51	10,000	Adaptive	2-point	1	0.05	0.1
pf5	51	10,000	Ranking	Inter	0.75	0.05	0.05
pf6	102	5,000	Ranking	Inter	0.75	0.05	0.05

a high crossover rate for the performance of the EA, whilst fitness ranking and interpolation crossover work best in three cases out of four.

For all three algorithms, depth-search configurations excel on the first three functions, and breadth search on the last. The use of a large population probably helps the exploration of the large 18D *pf6* space.

In terms of optimisation results, the Bees Algorithm excels on the two test functions of highest dimensionality, and obtains very competitive results in the other two. In particular, the Bees Algorithm is the only procedure that obtains nearly full success rate on the high-dimensional *pf6* benchmark. Figure 7 shows that on this benchmark the performance of the EA stagnates after a certain number of generations, whilst the PSO maintains a slower but steady progress. The steepness of the optimisation curves (Figures 4–7) proves the ability of the Bees Algorithm to achieve fast progress on the protein folding benchmarks.

In general, the results obtained by the three algorithms compare well with the literature. For a reference, the reader may compare the results plotted in Figures 4–7 with those obtained by other six public domain optimisation methods plotted by Mongeau et al. (2000).

Table 12. Comparison of optimisation procedures on protein folding benchmarks

Fun-ction	Bees Algorithm			PSO					EA				
	Suc-cess	Accu-racy	Speed	Suc-cess	Accu-racy	*p* (Accuracy)	Speed	*p* (Speed)	Suc-cess	Accu-racy	*p* (Accuracy)	Speed	*p* (Speed)
pf3	50	0.0000	1,454	50	0.0000	–	4,845	**0.0000**	50	0.0000	–	1,275	**0.0059**
pf4	49	0.0007	2,346	47	0.0008	**0.0015**	17,876	**0.0000**	50	0.0000	–	71,961	**0.0000**
pf5	50	0.0000	3,188	50	0.0000	–	29,631	**0.0000**	50	0.0000	–	25,985	**0.0000**
pf6	48	0.0008	14,8642	18	0.4092	**0.0000**	510,000	**0.0000**	0	0.7158	**0.0000**	510,000	**0.0000**

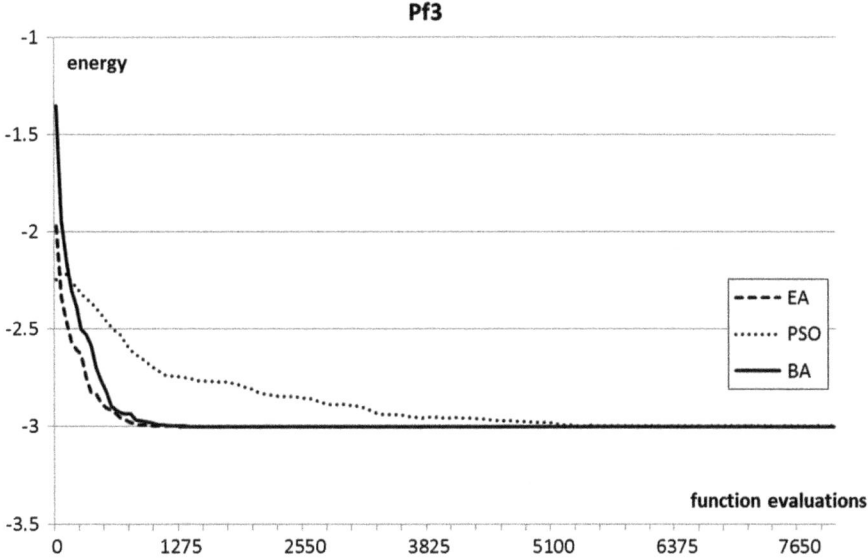

Figure 4. Optimisation plots for *pf3* folding benchmarks.

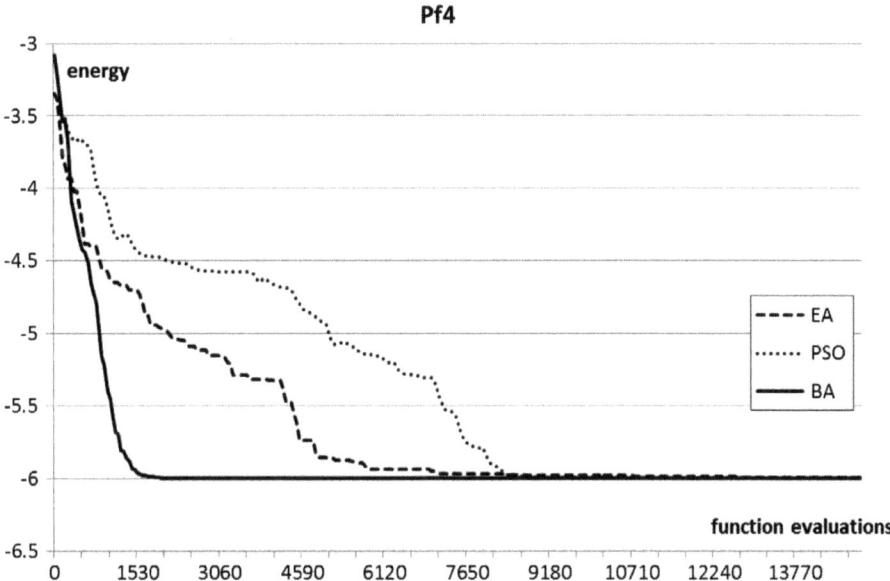

Figure 5. Optimisation plots for *pf4* folding benchmarks.

9. Discussion of results

The results of the tests on the two-dimensional benchmarks show that when the fitness landscape gives some information on the location of the optimum, the Bees Algorithm benefits most from exploitative search approaches. Otherwise, the winning strategy is to split the foragers and perform many parallel local searches. Overall, the Bees Algorithm benefitted most from a high stagnation limit and the use of the depth-search strategy.

Pham and Castellani (2009) reported the good performance of exploitative strategies characterised by a high stagnation limit, and focusing the search effort on a few selected sites. As mentioned in Section 4.1, the tests were performed on 12 popular benchmarks. Given that many of these functions are unimodal or give some indication on the location of the peak, the observations of Pham and Castellani (2009) are in good agreement with the results obtained on functions 12 and 14–18.

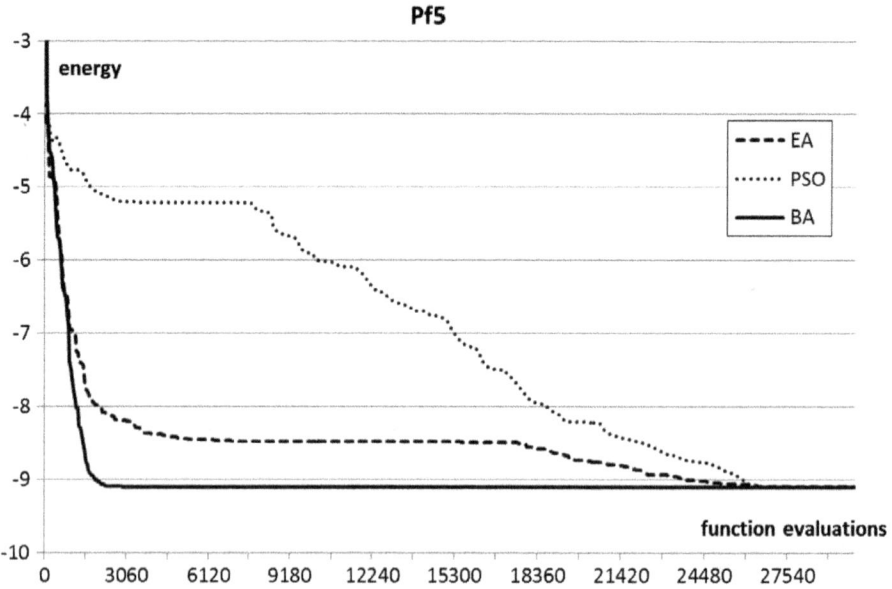

Figure 6. Optimisation plots for *pf5* folding benchmarks.

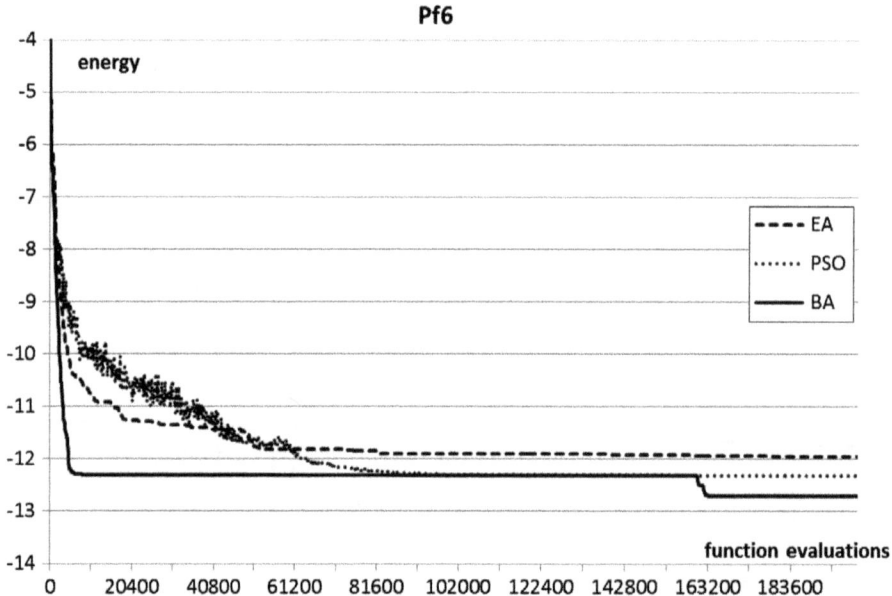

Figure 7. Optimisation plots for *pf6* folding benchmarks.

Functions *3–18* were used by Pham and Castellani (2013) to investigate specific abilities and biases of the Bees Algorithm, PSO, EA and ABC. Functions *1, 2, 4a, 4b, 8a, 8b, 10a,*and *10b* were purpose built for the specific tests described in this paper. The results of the comparison performed in Section 7 corroborate and complement the findings of the previous study (Pham & Castellani, 2013). In their earlier work, the authors (Pham & Castellani, 2013) focused on robust performance across the various groups of benchmarks (two- and multi-modal, flat, valley-like, etc.). In the present study (Section 7), they focused on top performance, and considered the best performing configuration for each algorithm on each individual benchmark. Other specific contributions of the present work are the study of the robustness of the Bees Algorithm to changes of parameterization (Section 6), and the comparison of the performance of the Bees Algorithm, PSO and EA on real-world test cases of varying dimensionality (Section 8).

The results confirm also that the proposed benchmarks constitute a set of varied and challenging functions for the study of optimisation algorithms. Fairly different configurations of the Bees Algorithm, PSO and EA are needed to solve optimally the test problems. The difference in the configurations can be often explained in term of the trade-off between exploration and exploitation needs, or known biases of the algorithms. Several benchmarks proved also difficult for the PSO. Even though the proposed study is limited to the particular implementations of the procedures used, and the restricted number of configurations tested, the results may point out some specific abilities of the Bees Algorithm.

It is important to emphasise that the features of the proposed benchmarks (arrangement of the peaks, position of the optimum, flat surfaces, unimodal with potholes, etc.) are independent of the dimensionality of the functions. That is, the experimental results presented in this paper are of general validity for any number of optimisation parameters. Thus, the proposed benchmarks allow the user to test the performance of different optimisation algorithms using simple and easy to visualise low-dimensional functions.

The comparison with the EA and PSO confirms the weaker performance of the Bees Algorithm (Karaboga & Basturk, 2008; Pham & Castellani, 2009) on noisy unimodal search surfaces (functions 14–18). On all the other benchmarks, the Bees Algorithm performs comparatively well.

The results highlight the advantages of the adaptive EA selection procedure used in this study. Thanks to its adoption, the performance of the EA compared much more favourably than in other studies to the performance of the PSO and Bees Algorithm (Karaboga & Basturk, 2008; Pham & Castellani, 2009).

Out of the three algorithms tested, the PSO is the only algorithm that does not use any feedback to adjust its behaviour according to the progress of the search, like the site abandonment procedure (Bees Algorithm) and the adaptive selection routine (EA). This might explain the inferior results obtained by the PSO on the benchmarks used in this study. Future work should include more complex PSO implementations such as multiswarm PSO (Blackwell & Branke, 2004), where a mechanism equivalent to site abandonment is used.

Even though it is not guaranteed that the EA and PSO are the most competitive algorithms on the proposed benchmarks, it is reasonable to assume that the best-performing configurations were fairly adapted to the test problems. Indeed, for every benchmark the best-performing algorithm was chosen out of 32 configurations including different operators and parameterizations. It is also important to point out that the proposed study did not aim to find the best-performing algorithm on the various test problems. The study compared the relative performances of the Bees Algorithm and two others in order to understand which algorithm and why works best. To make the study easily accessible to the widest audience, well-known and well-understood procedures such as EAs and PSO were chosen for the comparison.

Overall, the main factors affecting the performance of the algorithms and configurations tested were the complexity and deceptiveness of the search space. The effect of search biases resulting from the arrangement of the minima (e.g. on a grid) or the position of the global optimum were not statistically significant. In terms of location error and success rate the Bees Algorithm and EA performed comparably. The Bees Algorithm attained top accuracy (i.e. zero location error) in all 18 cases (Table 9) and the EA 15 times. The Bees Algorithm achieved 100% success rate on 17 benchmarks out of 18, the EA obtained full or close to 100% success rate on 17 benchmarks. These results suggest that, if speed is not paramount, the two algorithms can be considered to perform equivalently on this kind of functions.

The tests on the protein folding benchmarks confirm the competitiveness of the Bees Algorithm also on benchmarks of higher dimensionality. In particular, the Bees Algorithm outperforms the other two search procedures on the two highest dimensional functions, in terms of optimisation speed (*pf5*) and success rate (*pf6*). The results obtained by the Bees Algorithm on the protein folding functions are competitive also with those obtained by other algorithms in the literature.

10. Conclusions
Given a search problem, which optimisation algorithm should be chosen? How should the algorithm be configured? The optimisation literature offers a wide choice of procedures and operators, which are often tried on a common set of popular test functions. Unfortunately, the representativeness of this set of benchmarks is limited, allowing only a partial evaluation of the merits and drawbacks of the different methods.

This paper made two main contributions to the understanding of the behaviour of the Bees Algorithm: the first in the general field of benchmarking of population-based optimisation systems, and the second in the characterisation of the Bees Algorithm.

The first contribution consists of the eighteen new function minimisation benchmarks presented in Section 4. Although not exhaustive, the proposed set of functions offers a wide and varied choice of test cases. To the best of our knowledge, this is one of the few attempts in the literature to build a systematic collection of fitness landscapes.

All the 18 test functions are two-dimensional, and many of them present relatively straightforward fitness landscapes. This allows the user easily to visualise and understand the nature and the difficulty of the optimisation problem.

The 18 benchmarks were used to test the performance of the Bees Algorithm (Section 5), and compare it with that of an EA and a PSO (Section 7). Different algorithms excelled on different benchmarks, and each algorithm required different parameterizations to achieve top performance on the different benchmarks. Some of the benchmarks proved difficult to solve, particularly for the PSO. These results prove that, in spite of their simplicity, the proposed benchmarks represent a varied and challenging set of test problems.

As discussed in Section 9, the optimisation trials on the eighteen benchmarks highlighted the strengths and weaknesses of the Bees Algorithms in comparison to the EA and PSO. They also revealed the effects of different choices of parameterization on the search performance of the algorithms. These results represent the second contribution made by the present paper.

On the true multidimensional benchmarks, the main configuration issue for the Bees Algorithm concerns the allocation of foragers. A high stagnation limit, a moderate population size, and a long evolution time give optimal results across several kinds of fitness landscapes. The experimental results show also a substantial equivalence of the Bees Algorithm and EA in terms of success rate, search accuracy, and optimisation speed. However, the two algorithms excelled In complementary optimisation landscapes. Overall, the Bees Algorithm seems to work best when the search requires the exploration of large spaces, and landscapes composed of several basins of attraction. When the search problem requires overcoming many local potholes on a more regular fitness surface, the EA excelled.

The optimisation trials on the protein folding benchmarks added further evidence that the Bees Algorithm is able to achieve performances competitive with those of the EA, PSO and other state-of-the-art optimisers.

The experimental tests described in Section 6 proved that, given a fixed parameterization, the performance of the Bees Algorithm is robust to reasonable variations of the fitness surface. To the best of our knowledge, this is the first study of the tolerance of the Bees Algorithm to moderate variations of the fitness landscape.

Despite the great care taken in designing the benchmark functions, the results of this paper should not be taken as an indication of the absolute effectiveness of the optimisation methods tested (*No Free Lunch Theorem* (Wolpert & Macready, 1997)). The validity of the results is limited to the kind of benchmarks tested, the versions of the algorithms examined in the tests, and the kind of operators used.

The range of applicability of the Bees Algorithm to the field of engineering encompasses a large number of optimisation tasks. It comprises any problem amenable to being encoded via a fitness evaluation function, and allowing some sort of parametric representation of the solutions. Fields of application include mechanical components design (Pham, Ghanbarzadeh, Otri, & Koç, 2009), pattern classifier optimisation (Pham & Darwish, 2010), time-series modelling and prediction, control and identification of dynamic (Castellani et al., 2012) and nonlinear processes (Fahmy et al., 2012), optimisation of controllers (Pham et al., 2009), robotic swarm coordination (Jevtic et al., 2010), protein structure prediction (Jana, Sil, & Das, 2015), thermal engineering design (Zarea, Moradi Kashkooli, Mansuri Mehryan, Saffarian, & Namvar Beherghani, 2014), multimodal function optimisation (Zhou, Xie, Pham, Kamsani, & Castellani, 2015), chaos control in a rod-type plasma torch system (Gholipour, Khosravi, & Mojallali, 2015), feature selection (Packianather & Kapoor, 2015) and combinatorial optimisation problems such as PCB assembly optimisation (Pham, Otri, & Darwish, 2007), gene regulatory networks learning (Ruz & Goles, 2013) and machine job scheduling (Packianather et al., 2014).

In this study, we analysed only benchmarks constrained within convex continuous solution spaces. Further benchmarking work should include combinatorial optimisation problems, continuous problems including discontinuous or concave solution sets and problems characterised by mixed variables.

Notation

ABC   artificial bee colony

ACO   ant colony optimisation

EA   evolutionary algorithm

ES   evolutionary strategies

PSO   particle swarm optimisation

SI   swarm intelligence

VNS   variable neighbourhood search

Funding
The authors received no direct funding for this research.

Author details
Duc Truong Pham[1]
E-mail: d.t.pham@bham.ac.uk
Marco Castellani[1]
E-mail: m.castellani@bham.ac.uk
[1] School of Mechanical Engineering, University of Birmingham, Birmingham B15 2TT, UK.

References
Adorio, E. P. (2005). *MVF - Multivariate test functions library in C for unconstrained global optimization*. Retrieved from http://geocities.com/eadorio/mvf.pdf

Bersini, H., Dorigo, M., Langerman, S., Seront, G., & Gambardella, L. (1996). Results of the first international contest on evolutionary optimisation. In *Proceedings of IEEE International Conference on Evolutionary Computation* (1st ICEO, pp. 611–615). Nagoya. http://dx.doi.org/10.1109/ICEC.1996.542670

Blackwell, T., & Branke, J. (2004). Multi-swarm optimization in dynamic environments. In G. R. Raidl (Ed.), *Applications of evolutionary computing*, Lecture notes in computer science (Vol. 3005, pp. 489–500). Berlin: Springer-Verlag.

Bonabeau, E., Dorigo, M., & Theraulaz, G. (1999). *Swarm intelligence: From natural to artificial systems*. New York, NY: Oxford University Press.

Camazine, S., Deneubourg, J.-L., Franks, N. R., Sneyd, J., Theraulaz, G., & Bonabeau, E. (2003). *Self-organization in biological systems*. Princeton, NJ: Princeton University Press.

Castellani, M., Pham, Q. T., & Pham, D. T. (2012). Dynamic optimisation by a modified Bees Algorithm. *Proceedings of the Institution of Mechanical Engineers, Part I: Journal of Systems and Control Engineering, 226*, 956–971.

Coleman, T., Shalloway, D., & Wu, Z. (1993). Isotropic effective energy simulated annealing searches for low energy molecular cluster states. *Computational Optimization and Applications, 2*, 145–170. http://dx.doi.org/10.1007/BF01299154

Crainic, T. G., Gendreau, M., Hansen, P., & Mladenovic, N. (2004). Cooperative parallel variable neighborhood search for the p-median. *Journal of Heuristics, 10*, 293–314. http://dx.doi.org/10.1023/B:HEUR.0000026897.40171.1a

Dorigo, M., Maniezzo, V., & Colorni, A. (1996). Ant system: Optimization by a colony of cooperating agents. *IEEE Transactions on Systems, Man, and Cybernetics, Part B, 26*, 29–41.

Fahmy, A. A., Kalyoncu, M., & Castellani, M. (2012). Automatic design of control systems for robot manipulators using the Bees Algorithm. *Proceedings of the Institution of Mechanical Engineers, Part I: Journal of Systems and Control Engineering, 226*, 497–508.

Fogel, D. B. (2000). *Evolutionary computation: Toward a new philosophy of machine intelligence* (2nd ed.). New York, NY: IEEE Press.

Gholipour, R., Khosravi, A., & Mojallali, H. (2015). Multi-objective optimal backstepping controller design for chaos control in a rod-type plasma torch system using Bees Algorithm. *Applied Mathematical Modelling, 39*, 4432–4444. http://dx.doi.org/10.1016/j.apm.2014.12.049

Jana, N. D., Sil, J., & Das S. (2015). Improved Bees Algorithm for protein structure prediction using AB off-lattice model. In *Mendel 2015* (pp. 39–52). Springer International.

Jevtic, A., Gazi, P., Andina, D., & Jamshidi, M. (2010). Building a swarm of robotic bees. In *Proceedings 2010 World Automation Congress, WAC 2010*. Kobe.

Karaboga, D., & Basturk, B. (2007). A powerful and efficient algorithm for numerical function optimization: Artificial bee colony (ABC) algorithm. *Journal of Global Optimization, 39*, 459–471. http://dx.doi.org/10.1007/s10898-007-9149-x

Karaboga, D., & Basturk, B. (2008). On the performance of artificial bee colony (ABC) algorithm. *Applied Soft Computing, 8*, 687–697. http://dx.doi.org/10.1016/j.asoc.2007.05.007

Kennedy, J., & Eberhart, R. (1995). Particle swarm optimization. In *Proceedings of 1995 IEEE International Conference on Neural Networks* (Vol. 4, pp. 1942–1948). Perth: IEEE Press.

Macnish, C. (2007). Towards unbiased benchmarking of evolutionary and hybrid algorithms for real-valued optimisation. *Connection Science, 19*, 361–385. http://dx.doi.org/10.1080/09540090701725581

Mladenović N., & Hansen, P. (1997). Variable neighborhood search. *Computers and Operations Research, 24*, 1097–1100.

Molga, M., & Smutnicki, C. (2005). *Test functions for optimization needs*. Retrieved from http://www.zsd.ict.pwr.wroc.pl/˜les/docs/functions.pdf

Mongeau, M., Karsenty, H., Rouzé, V., & Hiriart-Urruty, J. B. (2000). Comparison of public-domain software for black box global optimization. *Optimization Methods and Software, 13*, 203–226. http://dx.doi.org/10.1080/10556780008805783

Monson, C. K., & Seppi, K. D. (2005, June 25–29). Exposing origin-seeking bias in PSO. In *The 7th Genetic and Evolutionary Computation Conference. Washington, DC*.

Packianather, M. S., & Kapoor, B. (2015). A wrapper-based feature selection approach using Bees Algorithm for a wood defect classification system. In *Proceedings 10th System of Systems Engineering Conference (SoSE) 2015* (pp. 498–503). San Antonio, TX: IEEE Press.

Packianather, M. S., Yuce, B., Mastrocinque, E., Fruggiero, F., Pham, D. T., & Lambiase, A. (2014). Novel genetic Bees Algorithm applied to single machine scheduling problem. In *Proceedings World Automation Congress (WAC)* (pp. 906–911). Kona, HI: IEEE Press.

Pham, D. T., & Castellani, M. (2009). The Bees Algorithm—Modelling foraging behaviour to solve continuous optimisation problems. *Proceedings of the Institution of Mechanical Engineers, Part C, 223*, 2919–2938.

Pham, D. T., & Castellani, M. (2010). Adaptive selection routine for evolutionary algorithms. *Journal of Systems and Control Engineering, 224*, 623–633.

Pham, D. T., & Castellani, M. (2013). Benchmarking and comparison of nature-inspired population-based continuous optimisation algorithms. *Soft Computing, 18*, 871–903.

Pham, D. T., & Darwish, A. H. (2010). Using the Bees Algorithm with Kalman filtering to train an artificial neural network for pattern classification. *Journal of Systems and Control Engineering, 224*, 885–892.

Pham, D. T., Darwish, A. H., & Eldukhri, E. E. (2009). Optimisation of a fuzzy logic controller using the Bees Algorithm. *International Journal of Computer Aided Engineering and Technology, 1*, 250–264.

Pham, D. T., Ghanbarzadeh, A., Koç, E., Otri, S., Rahim, S., & Zaidi, M. (2006). The Bees Algorithm, a novel tool for complex optimisation problems. In *Proceedings of the Second International Virtual Conference on Intelligent Production Machines and Systems (IPROMS 2006)* (pp. 454–459). Oxford: Elsevier.

Pham, D. T., Ghanbarzadeh, A., Otri, S., & Koç, E. (2009). Optimal design of mechanical components using the Bees Algorithm. *Proceedings of the Institution of Mechanical Engineers, Part C: Journal of Mechanical Engineering Science, 223*, 1051–1056.

Pham, D. T., Otri, S., & Darwish, A. (2007). Application of the Bees Algorithm to PCB assembly optimisation. In *Proceedings 3rd International Virtual Conference on Intelligent Production Machines and Systems (IPROMS 2007)* (pp. 511–516). Dunbeath: Whittles.

Ruz, G. A., & Goles, E. (2013). Learning gene regulatory networks using the Bees Algorithm. *Neural Computing and Applications, 22*, 63–70. http://dx.doi.org/10.1007/s00521-011-0750-z

Seeley, T. D. (1996). *The wisdom of the hive: The social physiology of honey bee colonies*. Cambridge, MA: Harvard University Press.

Shi, Y., & Eberhart, R. (1998). Parameter selection in particle swarm optimization. In *Proceedings of the Seventh Annual Conference on Evolutionary Programming, San Diego, CA, Lecture notes in computer science* (Vol. 1447, pp. 591–600). Berlin, Heidelberg: Springer-Verlag.

Tang, K., Li, X., Suganthan, P.N., Yang, Z., & Weise, T. (2009). *Benchmark functions for the CEC'2010 special session and competition on large scale global optimization* (Technical Report). Hefei Nature Inspired Computation and Applications Laboratory, USTC. Retrieved from http://nical.ustc.edu.cn/cec10ss.php

Tereshko, V., & Loengarov, A. (2005). Collective decision-making in honey bee foraging dynamics. *Journal of Computing and Information Systems, 9*, 1–7.

Vavasis, S. A. (1994). Open problems. *Journal of Global Optimization, 4*, 343–344.

Wolpert, D. H., & Macready, W. G. (1997). No free lunch theorems for optimization. *IEEE Transactions on Evolutionary Computation, 1*, 67–82. http://dx.doi.org/10.1109/4235.585893

Yang, X. S., & He, X. (2013). Firefly algorithm: Recent advances and applications. *International Journal of Swarm Intelligence, 1*, 36–50. http://dx.doi.org/10.1504/IJSI.2013.055801

Zäpfel, G., Braune, R., & Bögl, M. (2010). *Metaheuristic search concepts*. Berlin, Heidelberg: Springer-Verlag. http://dx.doi.org/10.1007/978-3-642-11343-7

Zarea, H., Moradi Kashkooli, F. M., Mansuri Mehryan, A. M., Saffarian, M. R., & Namvar Beherghani, E. N. (2014). Optimal design of plate-fin heat exchangers by a Bees Algorithm. *Applied Thermal Engineering, 69*, 267–277. http://dx.doi.org/10.1016/j.applthermaleng.2013.11.042

Zhou, Z. D., Xie, Y. Q., Pham, D. T., Kamsani, S., & Castellani, M. (2015). Bees Algorithm for multimodal function optimisation. *Proceedings of the Institution of Mechanical Engineers, Part C: Journal of Mechanical Engineering Science*. doi:10.1177/0954406215576063

Permissions

List of Contributors

Cheng-Ching Chang
Department of Library and Information Science, National Taiwan University, Taipei, Taiwan

Ssu-Han Chen
Department of Industrial Engineering and Management, Ming Chi University of Technology, New Taipei City, Taiwan

Shaukat Ali and Shah Khusro
Department of Computer Science, University of Peshawar, Peshawar 25120, Pakistan

Youness Aliyari Ghassabeh
Toronto Rehabilitation Institute (UHN), 550 University Avenue, Toronto, Canada M5G 2A2

Ruhul Sarker and Saber Elsayed
School of Engineering and Information Technology, University of New South Wales at Canberra, Northcott Drive, Canberra, 2600 Australia

Stavros I. Souravlas and Manos Roumeliotis
Department of Applied Informatics, University of Macedonia, Thessaloniki, Greece

Mhand Hifi, Sagvan Saleh and Lei Wu
Université de Picardie Jules Verne, EPROAD-EA 4669, 7 rue du Moulin Neuf, 80000 Amiens, France

Virender Ranga and Mayank Dave
Department of Computer Engineering, National Institute of Technology, Kurukshetra, Haryana, India

Anil Kumar Verma
Department of Computer Science and Engineering, Thapar University, Patiala, Punjab, India

Saeb M. Besarati and Philip D. Myers
Department of Chemical and Biomedical Engineering, University of South Florida, 4202 E Fowler Ave, ENB118, Tampa, FL, USA

David C. Covey
Department of Mechanical Engineering, University of South Florida, 4202 E Fowler Ave, ENB118, Tampa, FL, USA

Ali Jamali
Department of Mechanical Engineering, Engineering Faculty, The University of Guilan, P.O. Box 3756, Rasht, Iran

Dhiya Al-Jumeily and Abir J. Hussain
Faculty of Engineering and Technology, Applied Computing Research Group, Liverpool John Moores University, Byrom Street, Liverpool L3 3AF, UK

Niti Ashish Kumar Desai
Department of Computer Engineering, Uka Tarsadia University, Bardoli, Surat, Gujarat, India

Amit Ganatra
U and P U. Patel Department of Computer Engineering, Charotar University of Science and Technology, Changa, Anand, Gujarat 388421, India

Duc Truong Pham and Marco Castellani
School of Mechanical Engineering, University of Birmingham, Birmingham B15 2TT, UK

Index

Printed in the USA
CPSIA information can be obtained
at www.ICGtesting.com
JSHW051415221024
72173JS00006B/1363